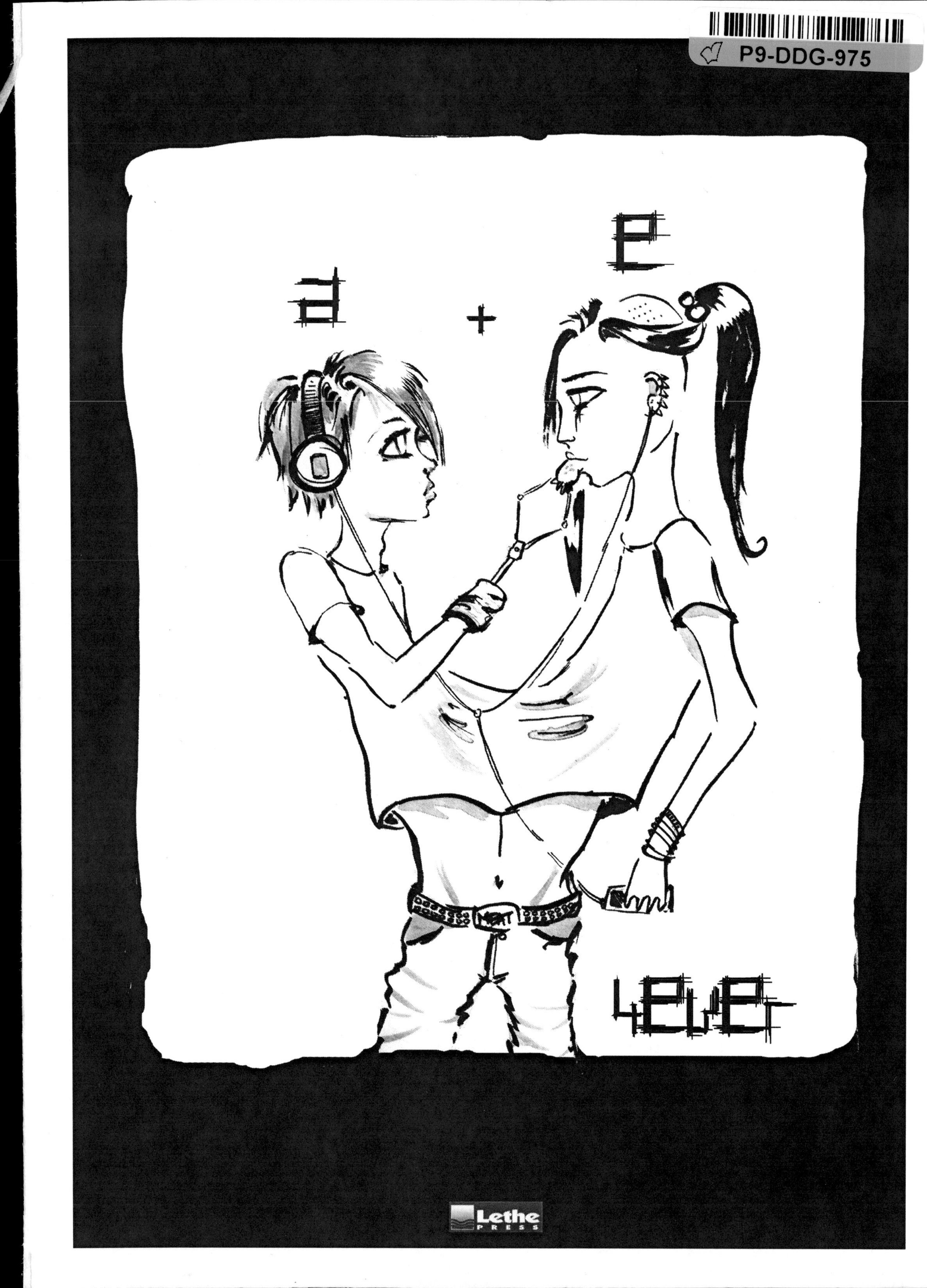
d + e
4ever

Lethe Press

a + e

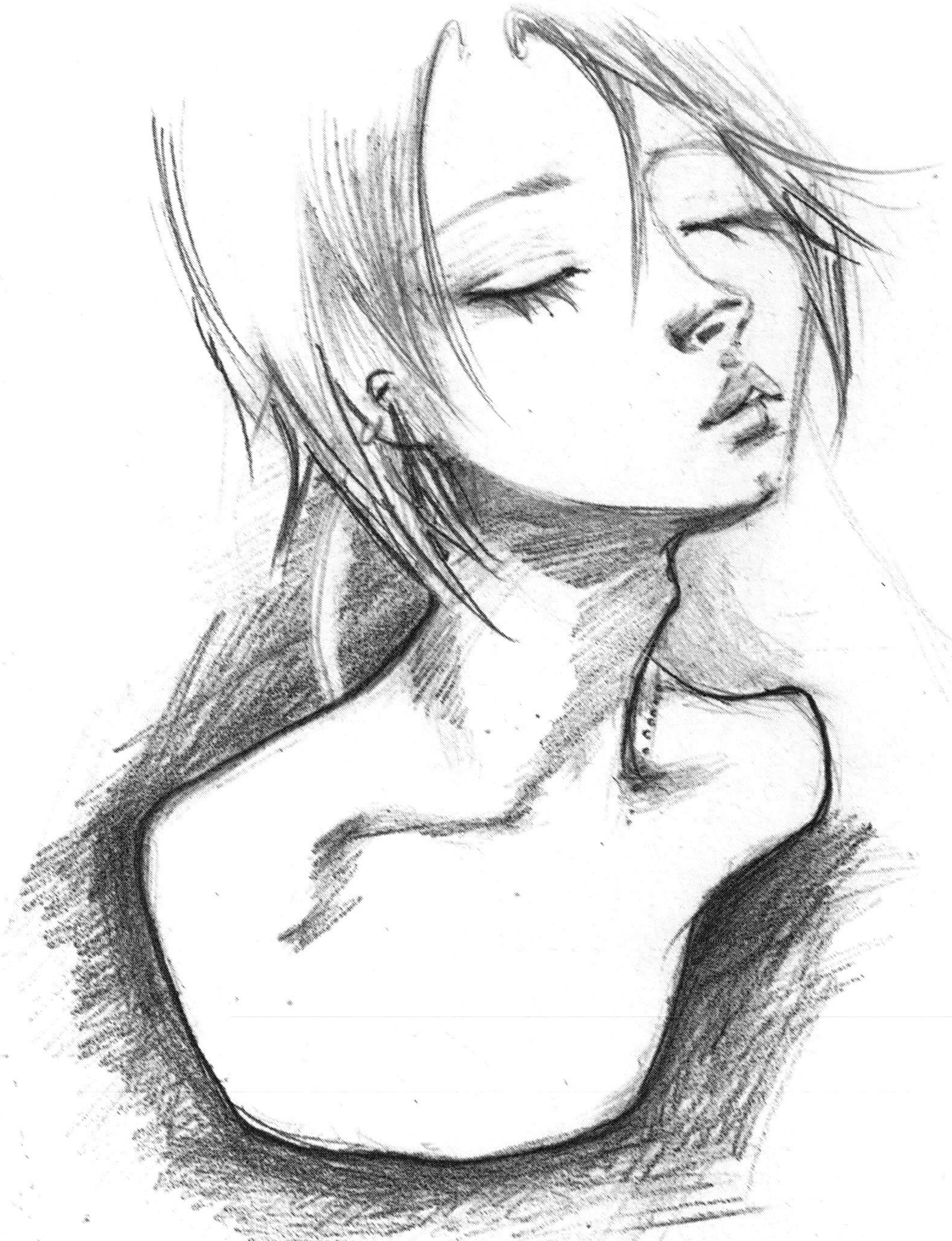

a Graphic novel

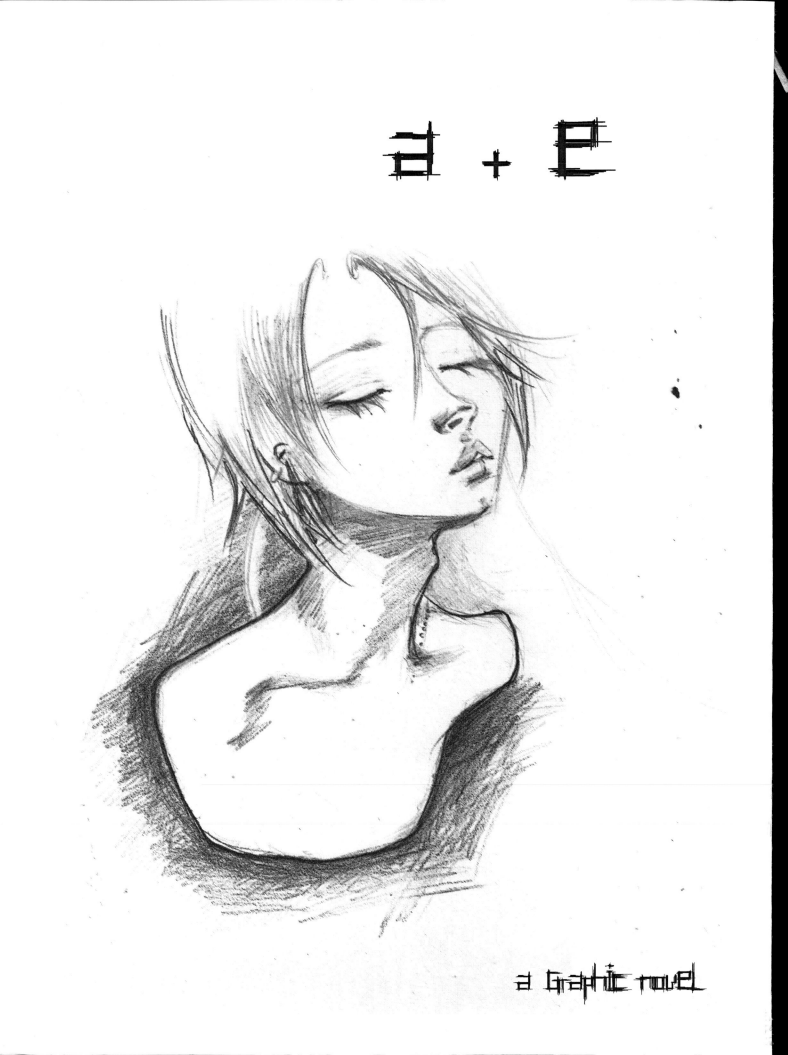

4EVER

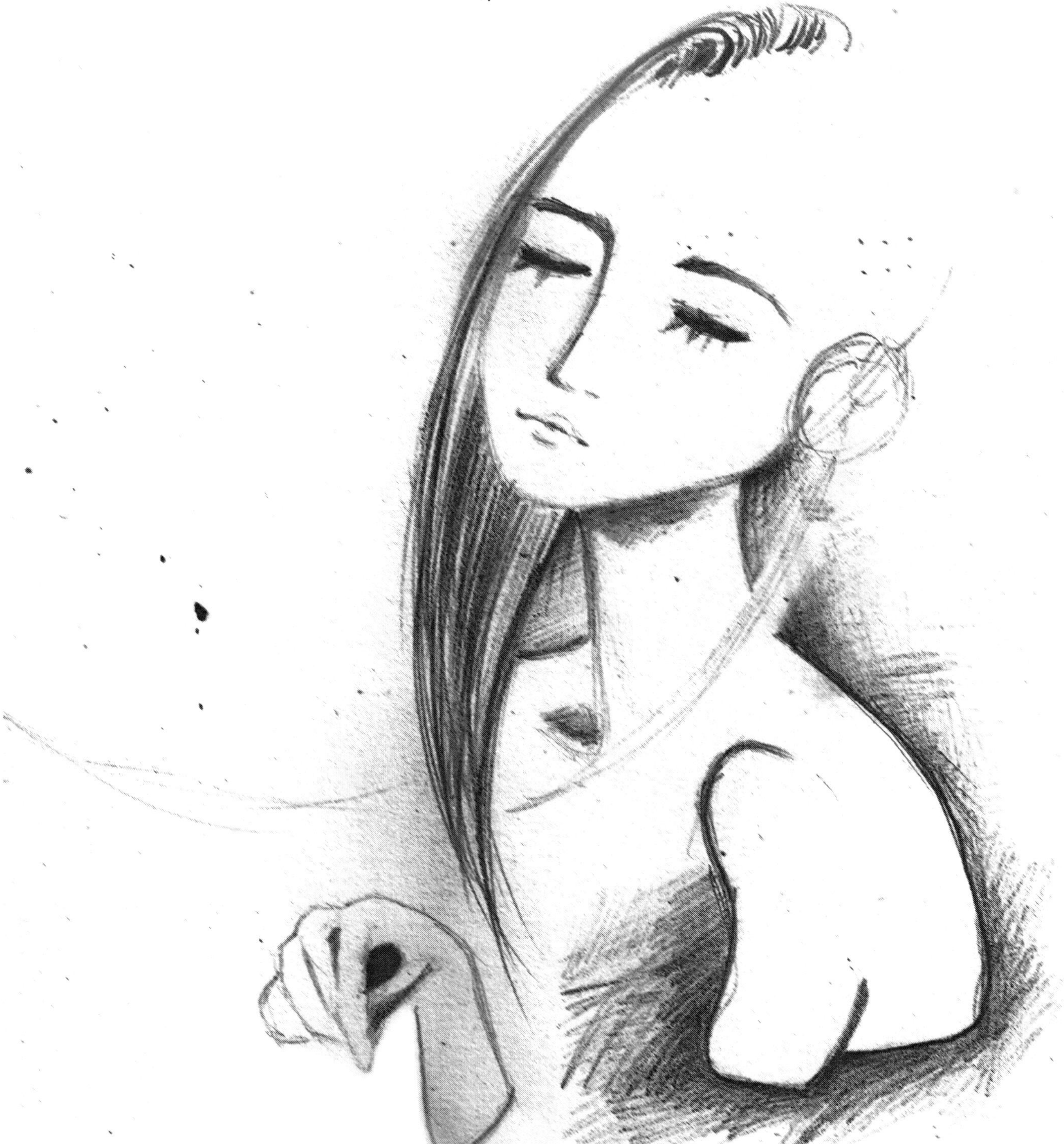

drawn and written by I. Merey

A + E 4EVER

PUBLISHED IN 2011 BY LETHE PRESS, INC.
118 HERITAGE AVENUE MAPLE SHADE, NJ 08052-3018
WWW.LETHEPRESSBOOKS.COM
LETHEPRESS@AOL.COM

ISBN - 1-59021-390-4
ISBN - 13: 978-1-59021-390-2

APHENPHOSMPHOBIA. ALSO KNOWN AS HAPHEPHOBIA, IS AN EXTREME AVERSION TO BEING TOUCHED OR TOUCHING OTHER PEOPLE.

RATHER RARE, THIS PHOBIA CAN FORM IN INDIVIDUALS WHO HAVE HAD A HISTORY OF PHYSICAL OR SEXUAL ABUSE, THOSE WHO HAVE SUFFERED FROM CHRONIC EMOTIONAL NEGLECT FROM AN EARLY AGE...

OR THOSE WHO HAVE COME TO ASSOCIATE THE TOUCH OF ANOTHER PERSON ONLY WITH SOMETHING NEGATIVE.

YEAR: JUNIOR
DAY OF SCHOOL: THIRD
HAIR: LIGHT BROWN
PANTS: SKIN-TIGHT
ORIENTATION: SHY
DIRECTION: PENDING
SEX: STILL WAITING
RELIGION: JEWISH

soy un perdedor

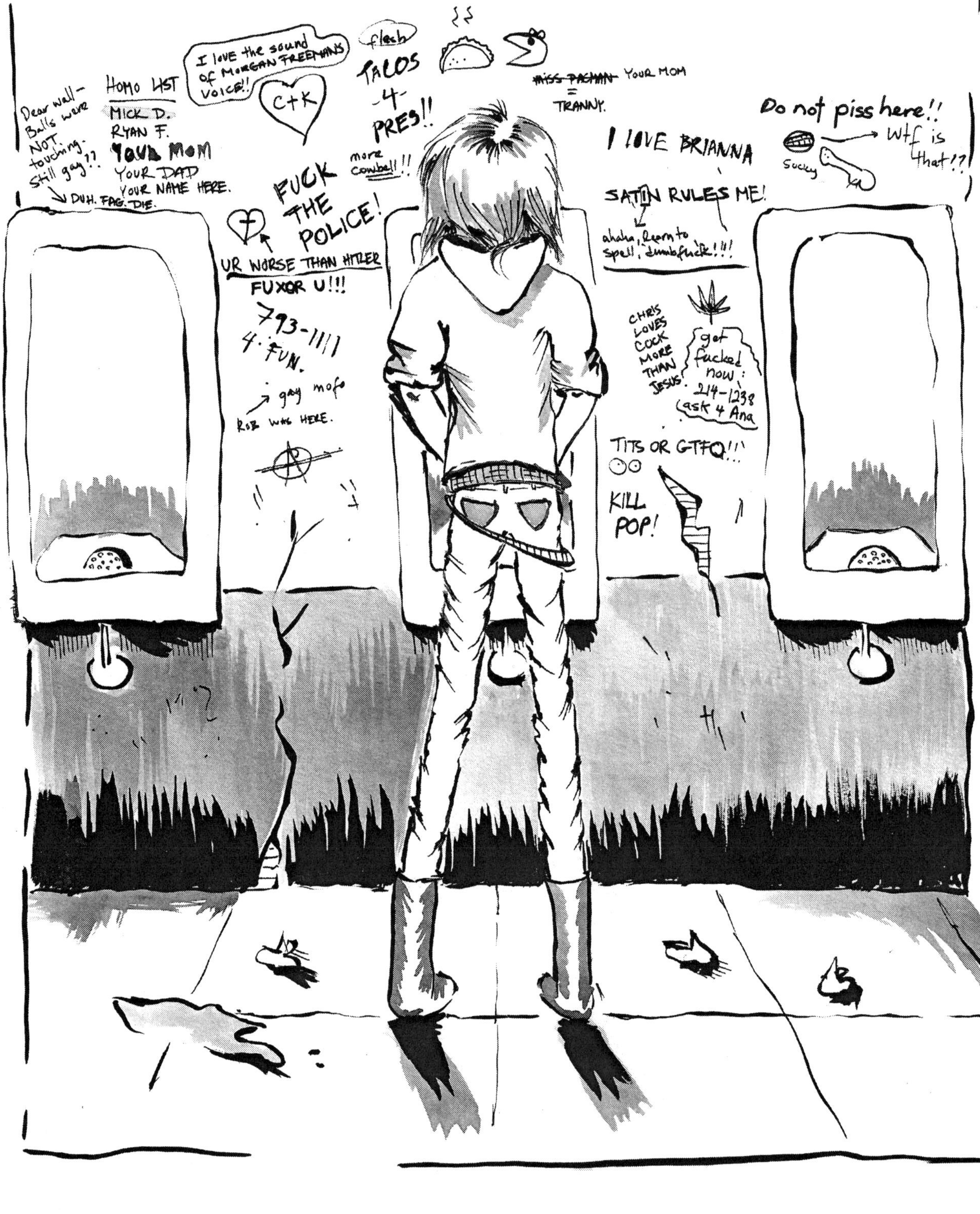

Dear wall— Balls were NOT touching. Still gay??
DUH. FAG. DIE.
HOMO LIST
MICK D.
RYAN F.
YOUR MOM
YOUR DAD
YOUR NAME HERE.
I love the sound of MORGAN FREEMAN'S VOICE!!
C+K
flesh
TACOS -4- PRES!!
more cowbell!!
FUCK THE POLICE!
UR WORSE THAN HITLER
FUXOR U!!!
793-1111 4 FUN.
gay mofo
ROB WAS HERE.
MISS PACMAN = TRANNY.
YOUR MOM
Do not piss here!!
wtf is that!?
I LOVE BRIANNA
SATIN RULES ME!
ahaha, learn to spell, dumbfuck!!!
CHRIS LOVES COCK MORE THAN JESUS!
got fucked now: 214-1238 ask 4 Ana
TITS OR GTFO!!!
KILL POP!

im a loser

-OK. SO, WHAT ARE YOU?

-....

-HEY, WE'RE TALKING TO YOU.
 ARE YOU A GUY
 OR ARE YOU A GIRL?
 ...ARE YOU A FAGGOT?

-HEH HEH, WHY DON'T WE check?

-I DUNNO. I'M KIND OF scared TO FIND OUT WHAT'S DOWN THERE.
 BUT ALL RIGHT. ....LET'S GET HER IN THE STALL. IT. WHATEVER.
 I DON'T WANT SOMEONE COMING IN...

THEY'RE GOING TO TOUCH ME, THEY'RE GOING TO TOUCH ME,
THEY'RE GOING TO TOUCH ME, THEY'RE GOING TO TOUCH ME,
THEY'RE GOING TO TOUCH ME, THEY'RE GOING TO...

-GET... OFF... OF.... ME!

-OWW, THE LITTLE DICKHEAD JUST BIT ME!
 I TOLD YOU TO HOLD HIM DOWN!

-HEY, IT'S NOT EASY WHEN HE'S FLIPPING OUT.

-I'M GOING TO PUKE! STOP!

-HEY, YOU KNOW... MAYBE WE SHOULD.
 HE'S SWEATING LIKE CRAZY. I DON'T WANT HIM TO UPCHUCK
 ALL OVER..

-LOOK, IT'S NOT LIKE I'M GONNA HURT HIM.
 YOU HEAR THAT? I'M NOT GONNA HURT YOU,
 SO JUST CALM DOWN.

CALM DOWN. BREATHE DEEP. I CAN'T. YES YOU CAN. DON'T CRY.
BREATHE, BREATHE. BREATHE. DEEP. DON'T CRY. SWALLOW.
AND THEY'LL LEAVE YOU ALONE. IT'LL BE OVER IF YOU JUST...

-THAT'S GOOD. THAT'S GOOD.
 SEE? YOU'RE OK. NOBODY'S HURTING YOU.

WE JUST WANT TO HAVE...

...A LOOK.

LET'S SEE YOUR FACE....

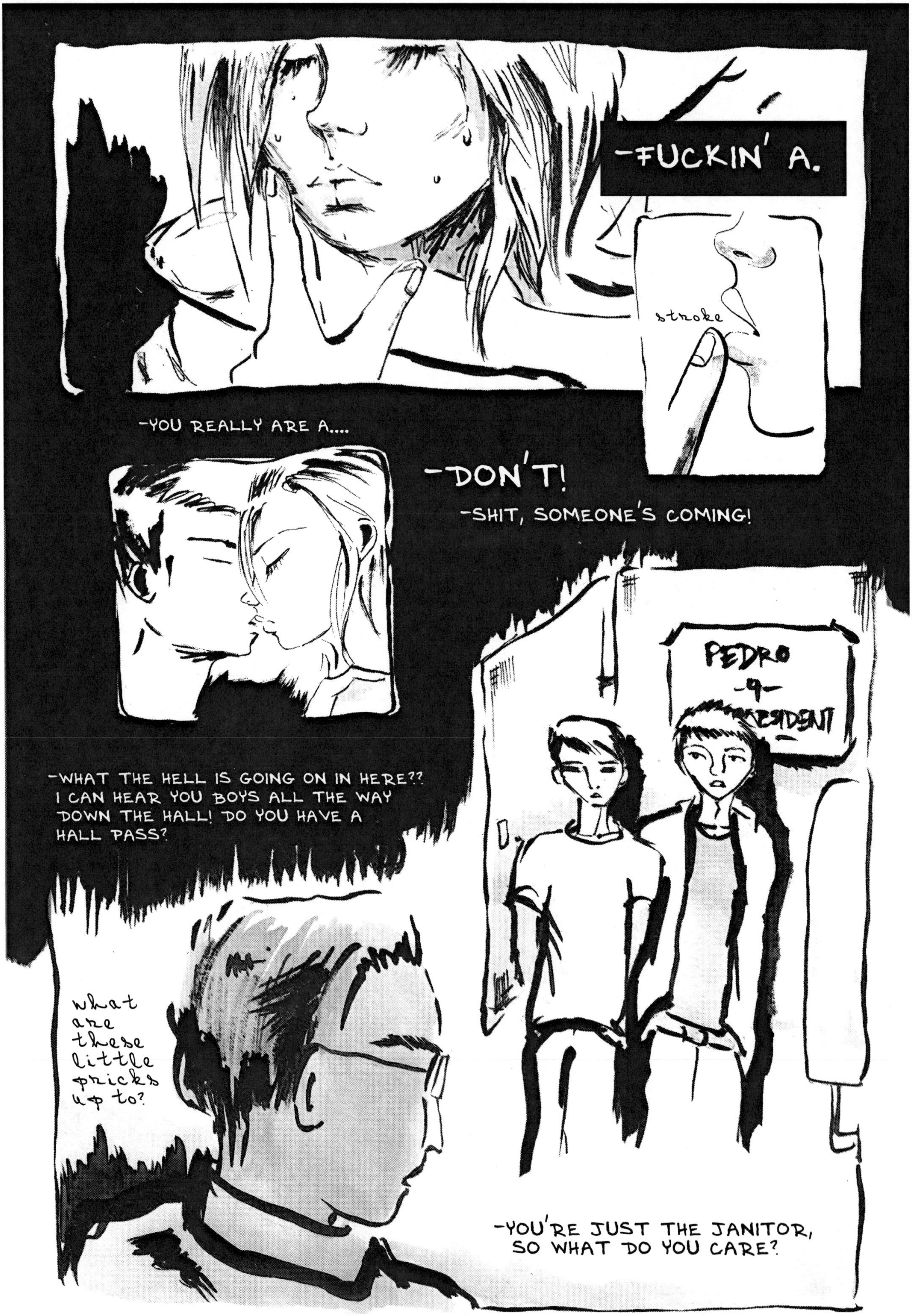

-FUCKIN' A.
stroke
-YOU REALLY ARE A....
-DON'T!
-SHIT, SOMEONE'S COMING!
PEDRO
-4-
-WHAT THE HELL IS GOING ON IN HERE?? I CAN HEAR YOU BOYS ALL THE WAY DOWN THE HALL! DO YOU HAVE A HALL PASS?
what are these little pricks up to?
-YOU'RE JUST THE JANITOR, SO WHAT DO YOU CARE?

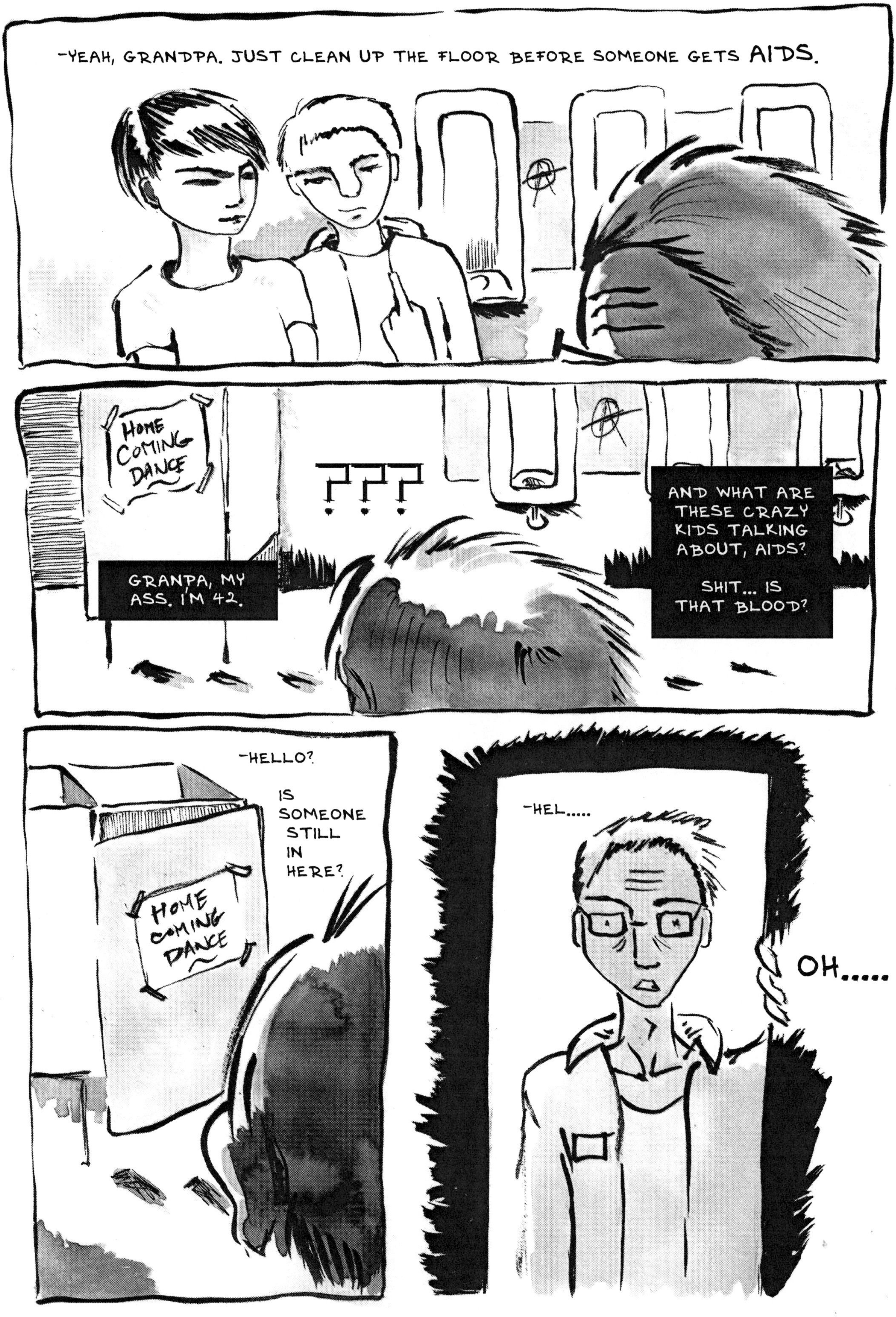

-YEAH, GRANDPA. JUST CLEAN UP THE FLOOR BEFORE SOMEONE GETS AIDS.
???
GRANPA, MY ASS. I'M 42.
AND WHAT ARE THESE CRAZY KIDS TALKING ABOUT, AIDS?
SHIT... IS THAT BLOOD?
HOME COMING DANCE
-HELLO?
IS SOMEONE STILL IN HERE?
HOME COMING DANCE
-HEL.....
OH.....

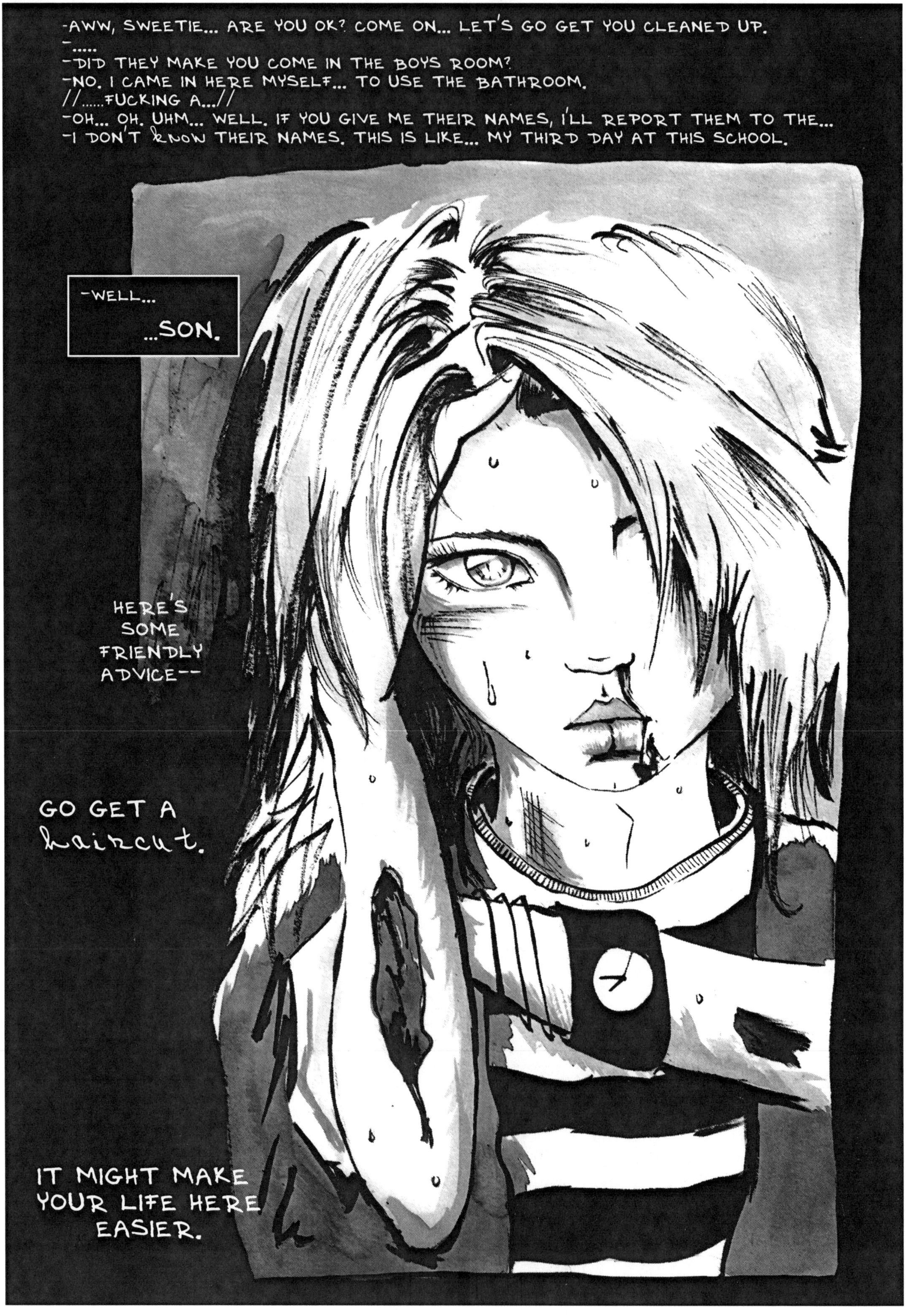
-AWW, SWEETIE... ARE YOU OK? COME ON... LET'S GO GET YOU CLEANED UP.
-.....
-DID THEY MAKE YOU COME IN THE BOYS ROOM?
-NO. I CAME IN HERE MYSELF... TO USE THE BATHROOM.
//......FUCKING A...//
-OH... OH. UHM... WELL. IF YOU GIVE ME THEIR NAMES, I'LL REPORT THEM TO THE...
-I DON'T KNOW THEIR NAMES. THIS IS LIKE... MY THIRD DAY AT THIS SCHOOL.
-WELL... ...SON.
HERE'S SOME FRIENDLY ADVICE--
GO GET A haircut.
IT MIGHT MAKE YOUR LIFE HERE EASIER.

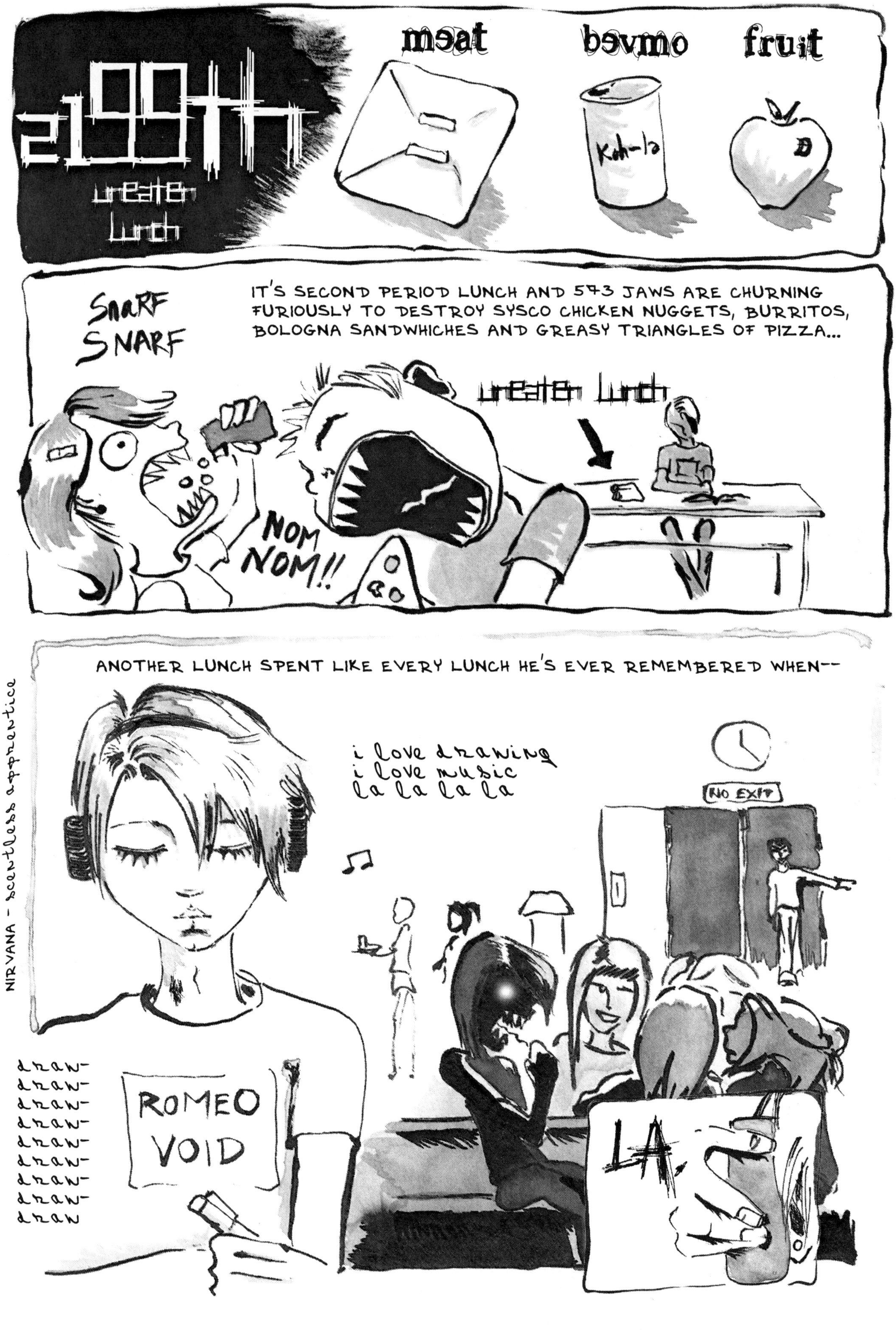
uneaten Lunch
meat
bevmo
fruit
Koh-la
Snarf
Snarf
IT'S SECOND PERIOD LUNCH AND 573 JAWS ARE CHURNING FURIOUSLY TO DESTROY SYSCO CHICKEN NUGGETS, BURRITOS, BOLOGNA SANDWHICHES AND GREASY TRIANGLES OF PIZZA...
uneaten Lunch
NOM NOM!!
ANOTHER LUNCH SPENT LIKE EVERY LUNCH HE'S EVER REMEMBERED WHEN--
NIRVANA - scentless apprentice
i love drawing
i love music
la la la la
NO EXIT
ROMEO VOID
draw-
draw-
draw-
draw-
draw-
draw-
draw-
draw-
draw
LA

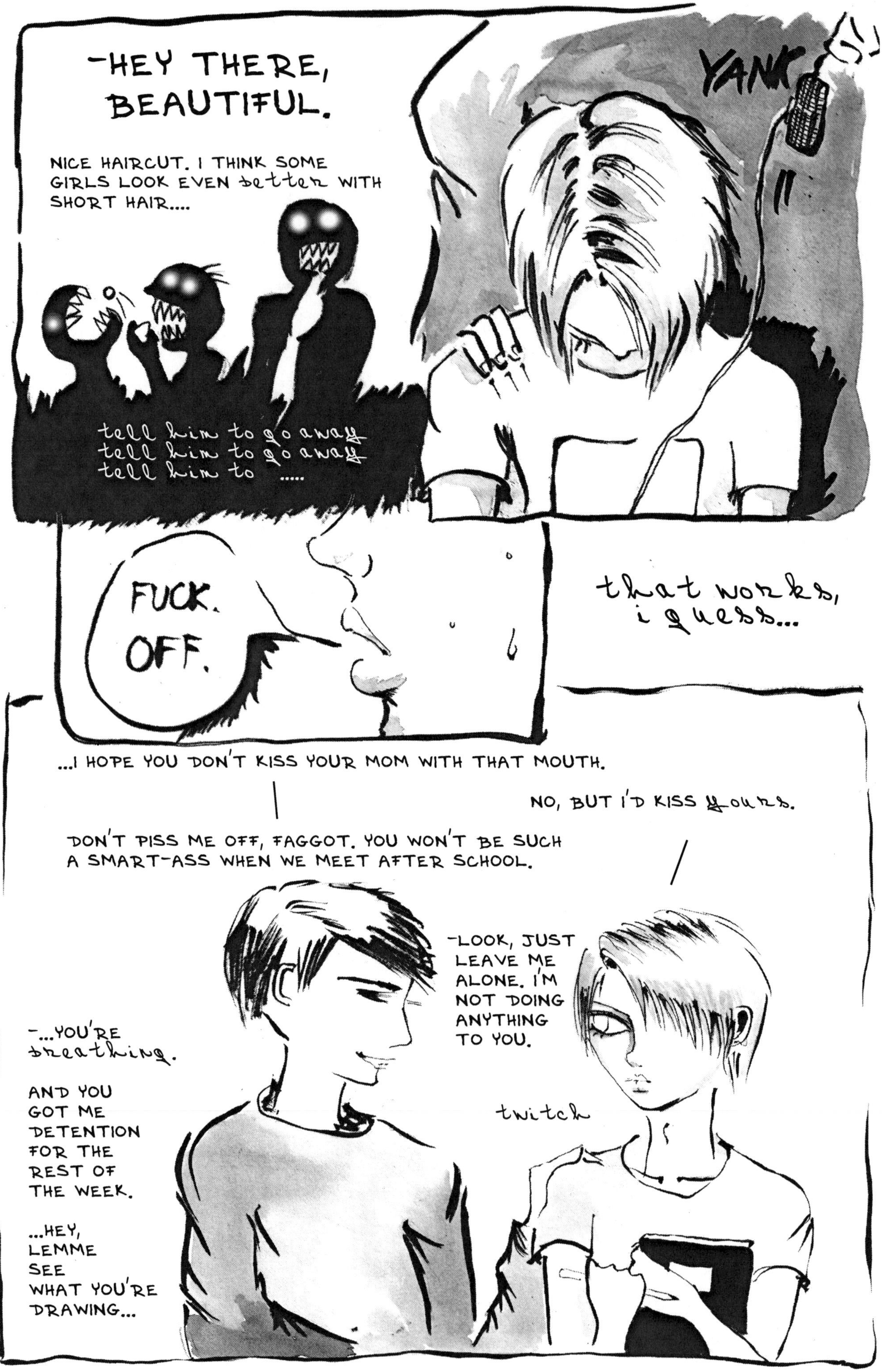
-HEY THERE, BEAUTIFUL.
NICE HAIRCUT. I THINK SOME GIRLS LOOK EVEN better WITH SHORT HAIR....
YANK
tell him to go away
tell him to go away
tell him to .....
FUCK. OFF.
that works, i guess...
...I HOPE YOU DON'T KISS YOUR MOM WITH THAT MOUTH.
NO, BUT I'D KISS yours.
DON'T PISS ME OFF, FAGGOT. YOU WON'T BE SUCH A SMART-ASS WHEN WE MEET AFTER SCHOOL.
-LOOK, JUST LEAVE ME ALONE. I'M NOT DOING ANYTHING TO YOU.
-...YOU'RE breathing.
AND YOU GOT ME DETENTION FOR THE REST OF THE WEEK.
...HEY, LEMME SEE WHAT YOU'RE DRAWING...
twitch

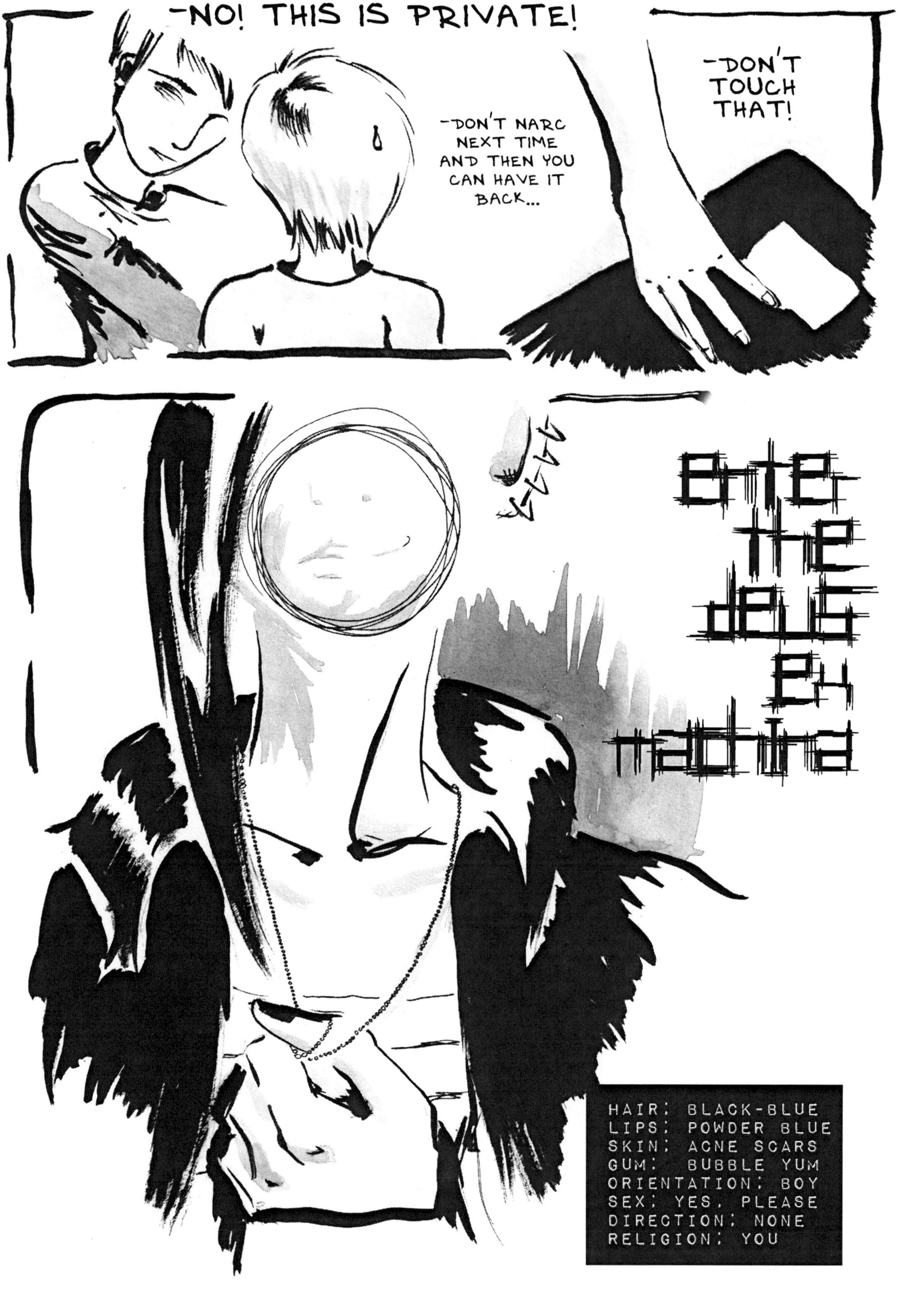
-NO! THIS IS PRIVATE!
-DON'T NARC NEXT TIME AND THEN YOU CAN HAVE IT BACK...
-DON'T TOUCH THAT!
enter the deus ex machina
HAIR: BLACK-BLUE
LIPS: POWDER BLUE
SKIN: ACNE SCARS
GUM: BUBBLE YUM
ORIENTATION: BOY
SEX: YES, PLEASE
DIRECTION: NONE
RELIGION: YOU

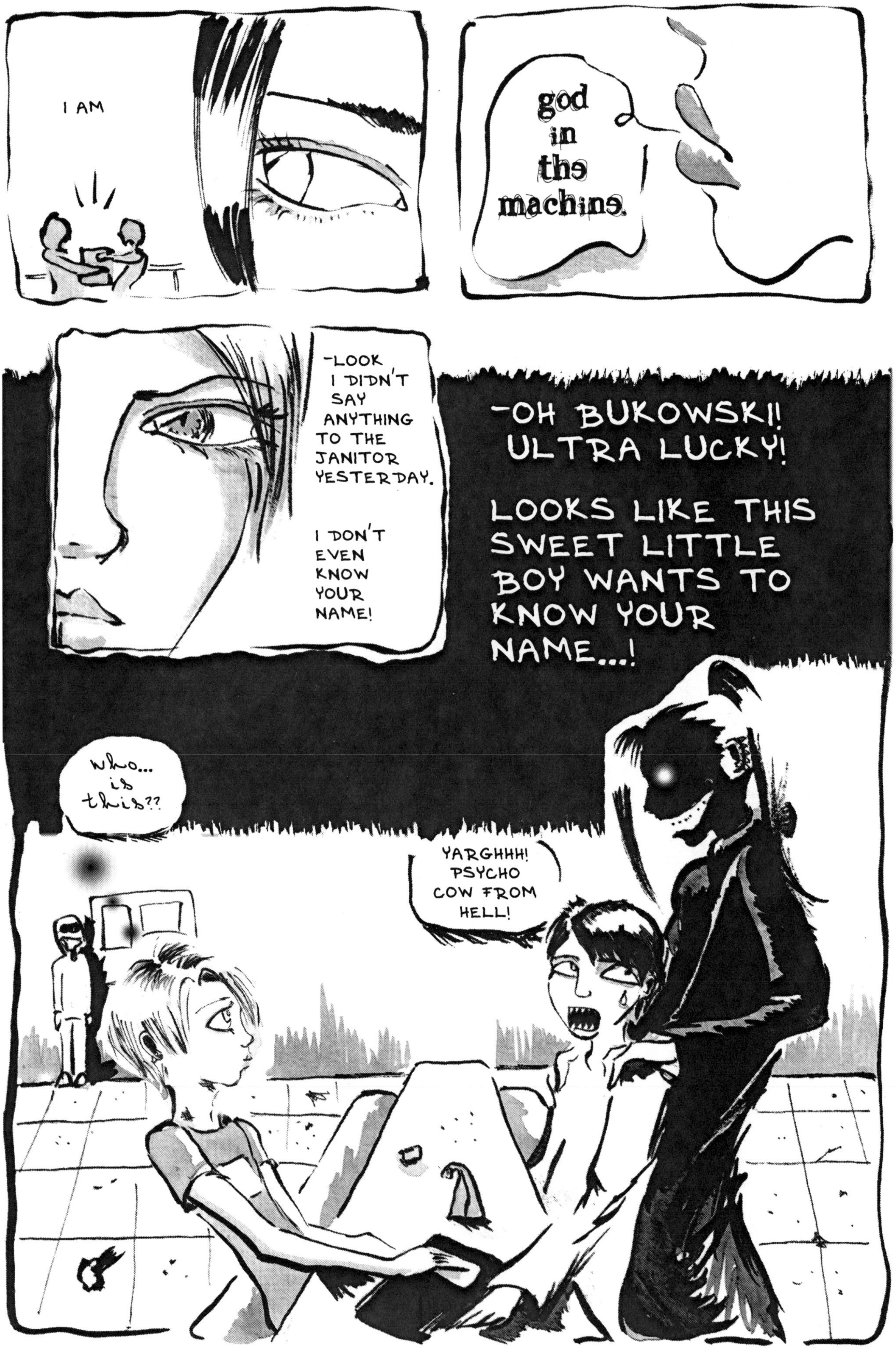
I AM
god in the machine.
-LOOK I DIDN'T SAY ANYTHING TO THE JANITOR YESTERDAY.
I DON'T EVEN KNOW YOUR NAME!
-OH BUKOWSKI! ULTRA LUCKY!
LOOKS LIKE THIS SWEET LITTLE BOY WANTS TO KNOW YOUR NAME...!
who... is this??
YARGHHH! PSYCHO COW FROM HELL!

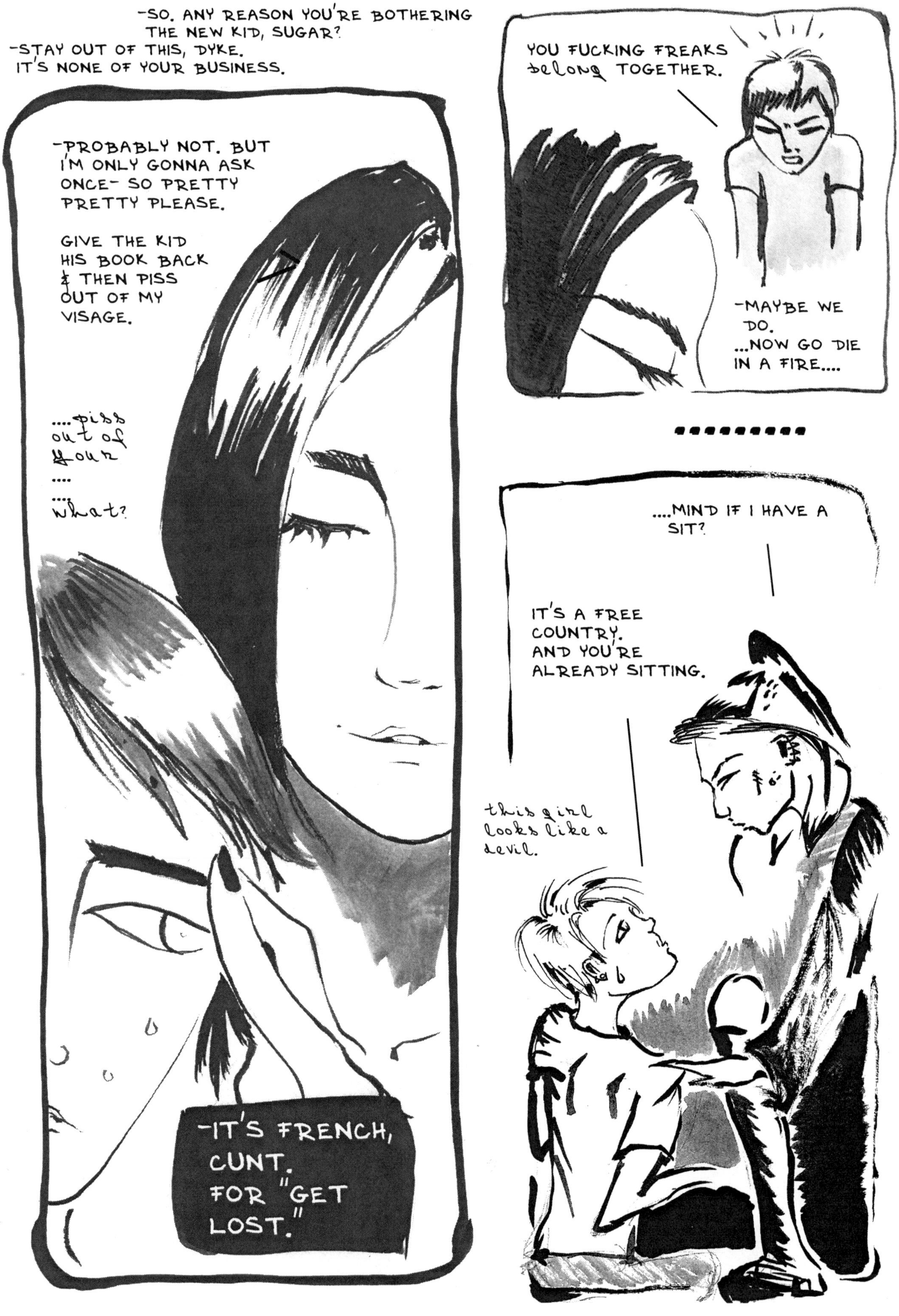
-SO. ANY REASON YOU'RE BOTHERING THE NEW KID, SUGAR?
-STAY OUT OF THIS, DYKE. IT'S NONE OF YOUR BUSINESS.
-PROBABLY NOT. BUT I'M ONLY GONNA ASK ONCE- SO PRETTY PRETTY PLEASE.
GIVE THE KID HIS BOOK BACK & THEN PISS OUT OF MY VISAGE.
....piss out of your .... what?
-IT'S FRENCH, CUNT. FOR "GET LOST."
YOU FUCKING FREAKS belong TOGETHER.
-MAYBE WE DO. ...NOW GO DIE IN A FIRE....
....MIND IF I HAVE A SIT?
IT'S A FREE COUNTRY. AND YOU'RE ALREADY SITTING.
this girl looks like a devil.

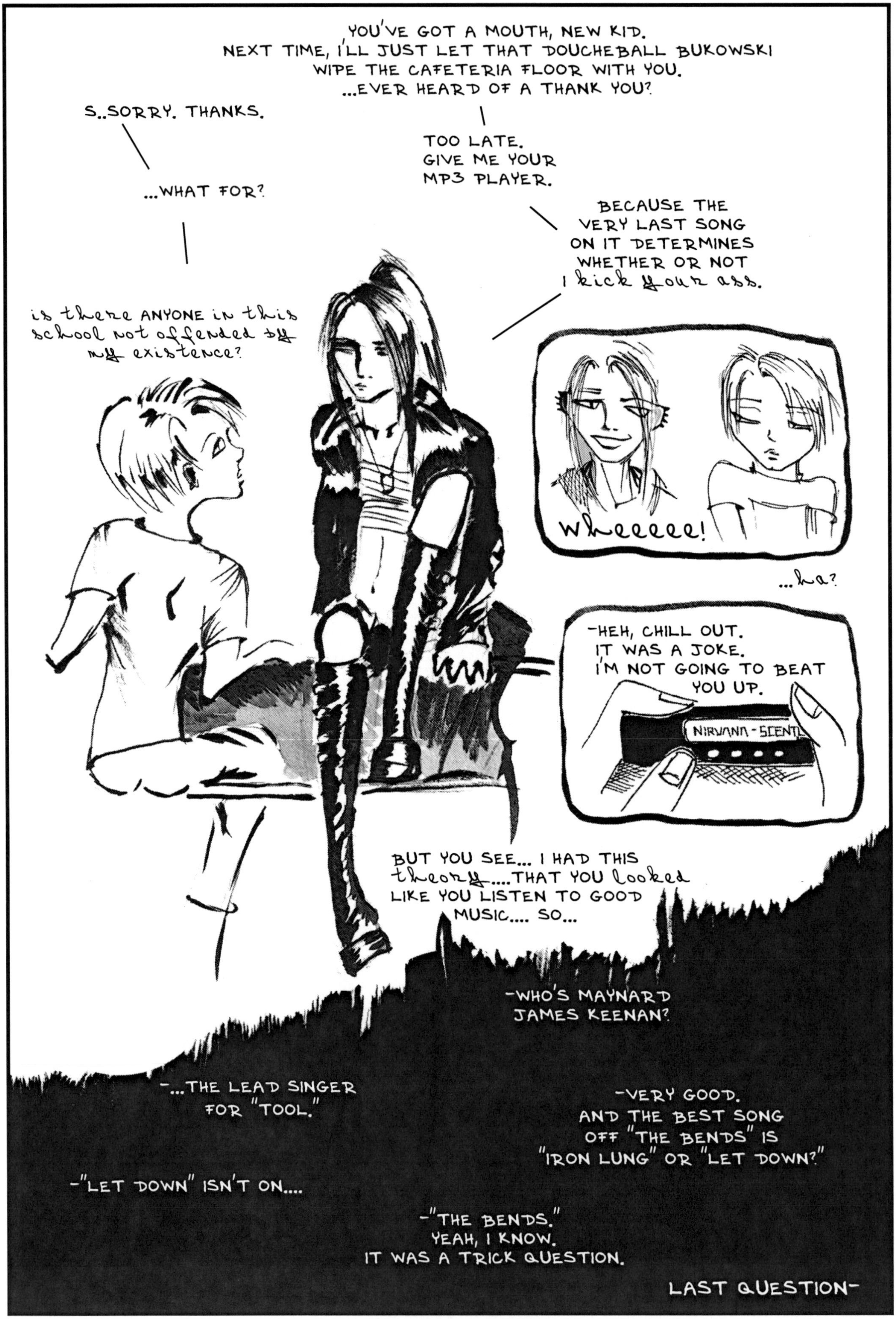

YOU'VE GOT A MOUTH, NEW KID. NEXT TIME, I'LL JUST LET THAT DOUCHEBALL BUKOWSKI WIPE THE CAFETERIA FLOOR WITH YOU. ...EVER HEARD OF A THANK YOU?
S..SORRY. THANKS.
TOO LATE. GIVE ME YOUR MP3 PLAYER.
...WHAT FOR?
BECAUSE THE VERY LAST SONG ON IT DETERMINES WHETHER OR NOT I kick your ass.
is there ANYONE in this school not offended by my existence?
Wheeeee!
...ha?
-HEH, CHILL OUT. IT WAS A JOKE. I'M NOT GOING TO BEAT YOU UP.
NIRVANA - SCENT
BUT YOU SEE... I HAD THIS theory....THAT YOU looked LIKE YOU LISTEN TO GOOD MUSIC.... SO...
-WHO'S MAYNARD JAMES KEENAN?
-...THE LEAD SINGER FOR "TOOL."
-VERY GOOD. AND THE BEST SONG OFF "THE BENDS" IS "IRON LUNG" OR "LET DOWN?"
-"LET DOWN" ISN'T ON....
-"THE BENDS." YEAH, I KNOW. IT WAS A TRICK QUESTION.
LAST QUESTION-

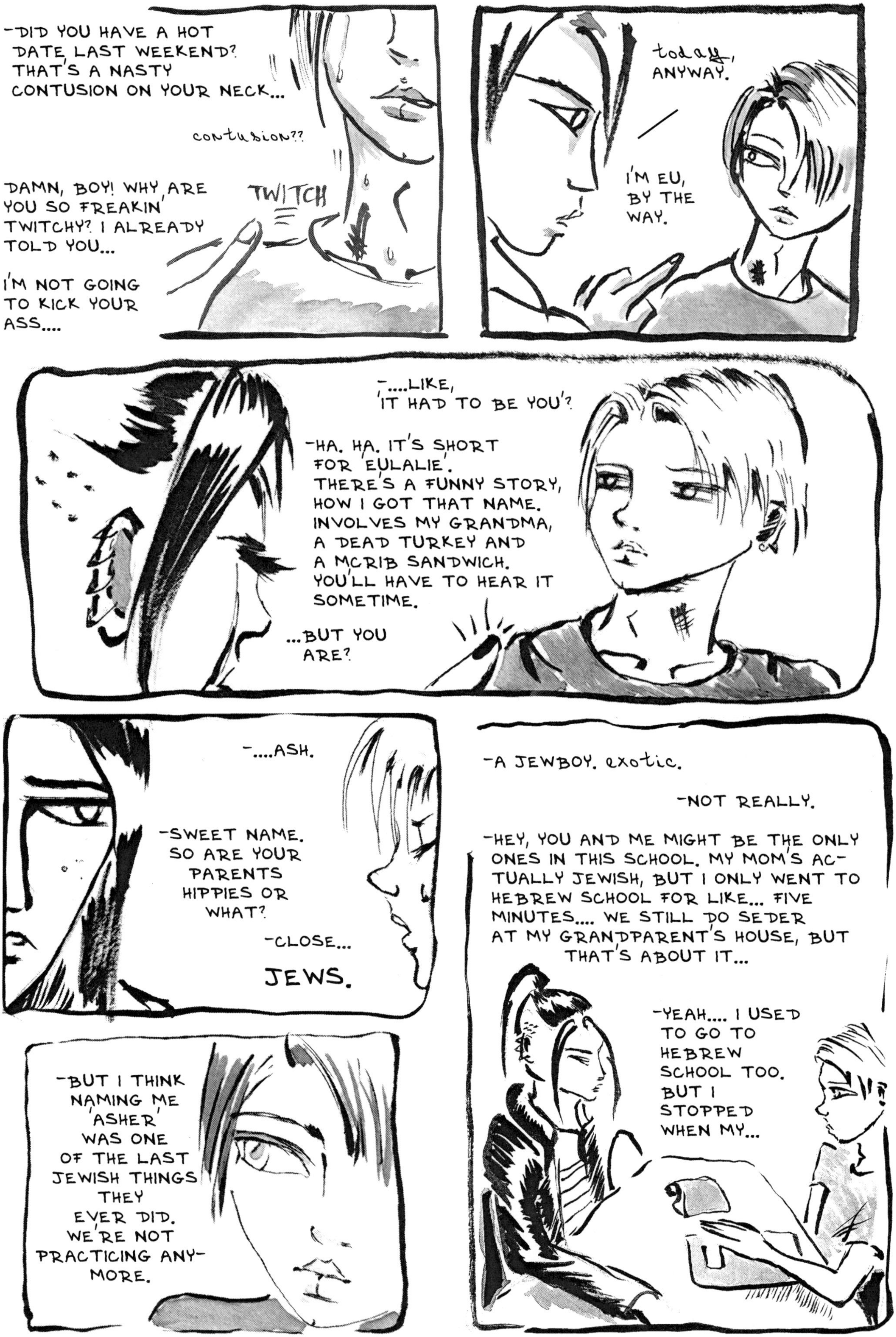
-DID YOU HAVE A HOT DATE LAST WEEKEND? THAT'S A NASTY CONTUSION ON YOUR NECK...
contusion??
TWITCH
DAMN, BOY! WHY ARE YOU SO FREAKIN' TWITCHY? I ALREADY TOLD YOU...
I'M NOT GOING TO KICK YOUR ASS....
today, ANYWAY.
I'M EU, BY THE WAY.
-....LIKE, 'IT HAD TO BE YOU'?
-HA. HA. IT'S SHORT FOR 'EULALIE'. THERE'S A FUNNY STORY, HOW I GOT THAT NAME. INVOLVES MY GRANDMA, A DEAD TURKEY AND A MCRIB SANDWICH. YOU'LL HAVE TO HEAR IT SOMETIME.
...BUT YOU ARE?
-....ASH.
-SWEET NAME. SO ARE YOUR PARENTS HIPPIES OR WHAT?
-CLOSE...
JEWS.
-BUT I THINK NAMING ME 'ASHER' WAS ONE OF THE LAST JEWISH THINGS THEY EVER DID. WE'RE NOT PRACTICING ANY-MORE.
-A JEWBOY. exotic.
-NOT REALLY.
-HEY, YOU AND ME MIGHT BE THE ONLY ONES IN THIS SCHOOL. MY MOM'S AC-TUALLY JEWISH, BUT I ONLY WENT TO HEBREW SCHOOL FOR LIKE... FIVE MINUTES.... WE STILL DO SEDER AT MY GRANDPARENT'S HOUSE, BUT THAT'S ABOUT IT...
-YEAH.... I USED TO GO TO HEBREW SCHOOL TOO. BUT I STOPPED WHEN MY...

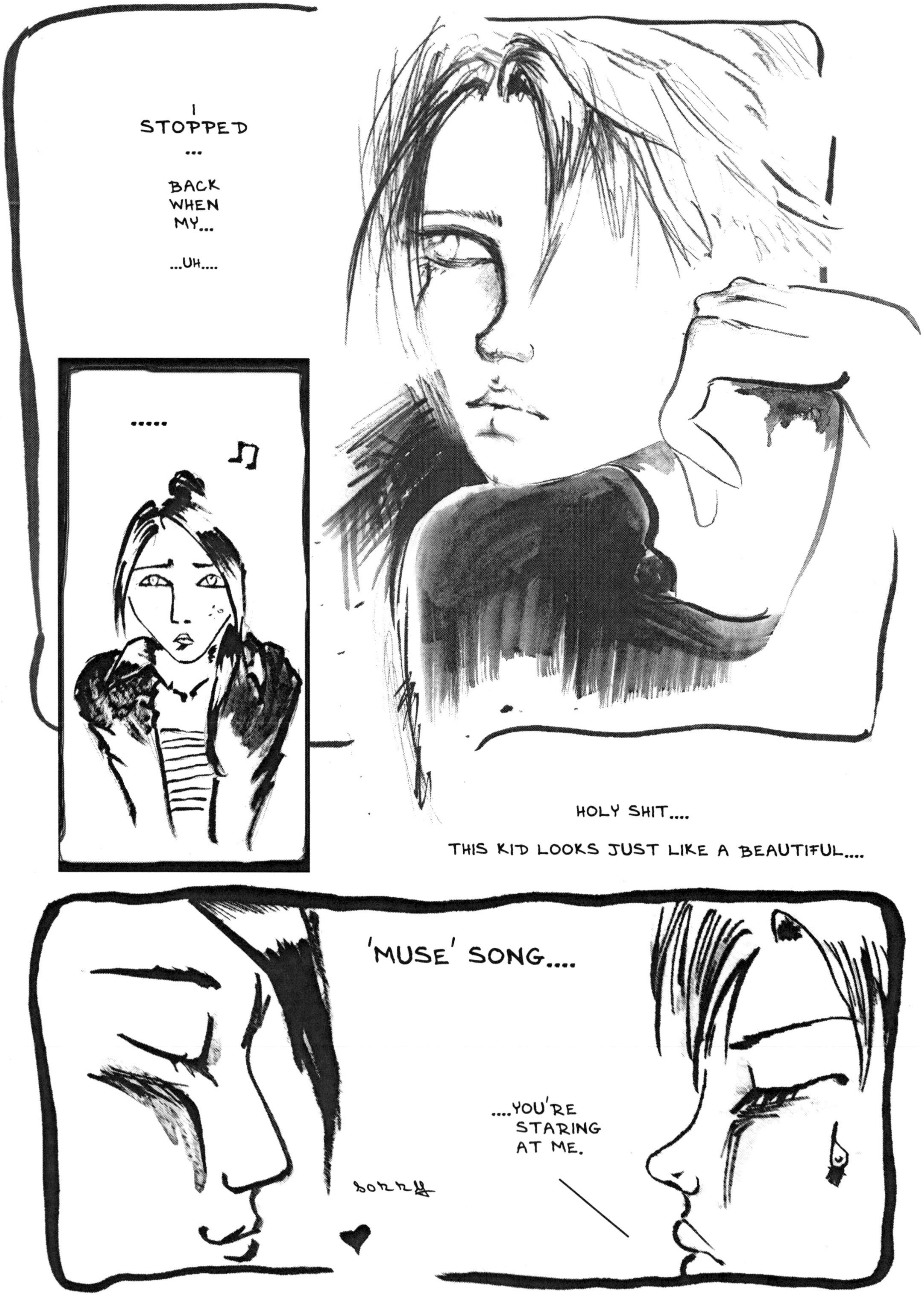
I STOPPED
...
BACK WHEN MY...
...UH....
.....
HOLY SHIT....
THIS KID LOOKS JUST LIKE A BEAUTIFUL....
'MUSE' SONG....
....YOU'RE STARING AT ME.
sorry

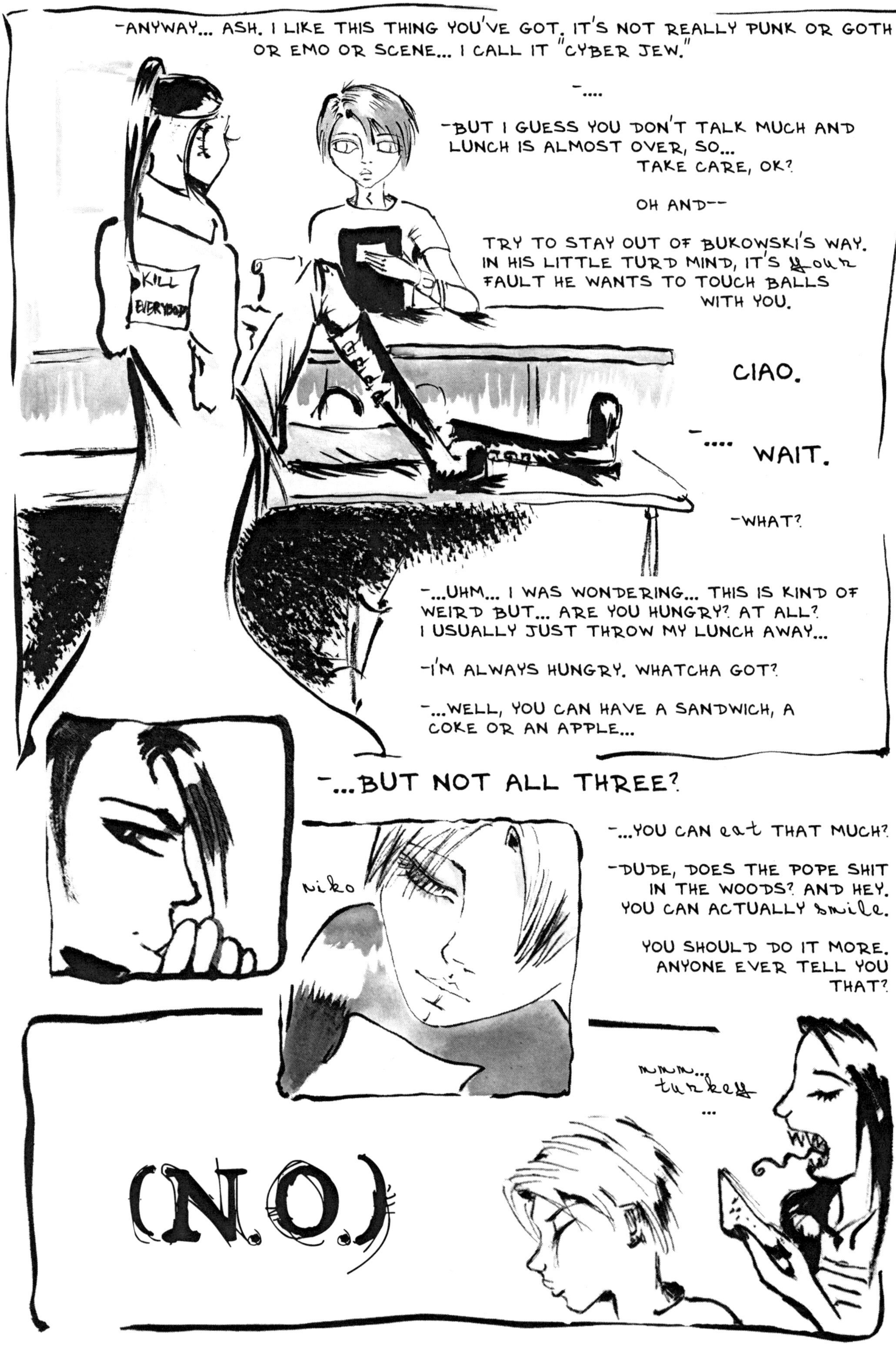
-ANYWAY... ASH. I LIKE THIS THING YOU'VE GOT. IT'S NOT REALLY PUNK OR GOTH OR EMO OR SCENE... I CALL IT "CYBER JEW."
KILL EVERYBODY
-....
-BUT I GUESS YOU DON'T TALK MUCH AND LUNCH IS ALMOST OVER, SO... TAKE CARE, OK?
OH AND--
TRY TO STAY OUT OF BUKOWSKI'S WAY. IN HIS LITTLE TURD MIND, IT'S your FAULT HE WANTS TO TOUCH BALLS WITH YOU.
CIAO.
-.... WAIT.
-WHAT?
-...UHM... I WAS WONDERING... THIS IS KIND OF WEIRD BUT... ARE YOU HUNGRY? AT ALL? I USUALLY JUST THROW MY LUNCH AWAY...
-I'M ALWAYS HUNGRY. WHATCHA GOT?
-...WELL, YOU CAN HAVE A SANDWICH, A COKE OR AN APPLE...
-...BUT NOT ALL THREE?
niko
-...YOU CAN eat THAT MUCH?
-DUDE, DOES THE POPE SHIT IN THE WOODS? AND HEY. YOU CAN ACTUALLY smile.
YOU SHOULD DO IT MORE. ANYONE EVER TELL YOU THAT?
mmm... turkey...
(N.O.)

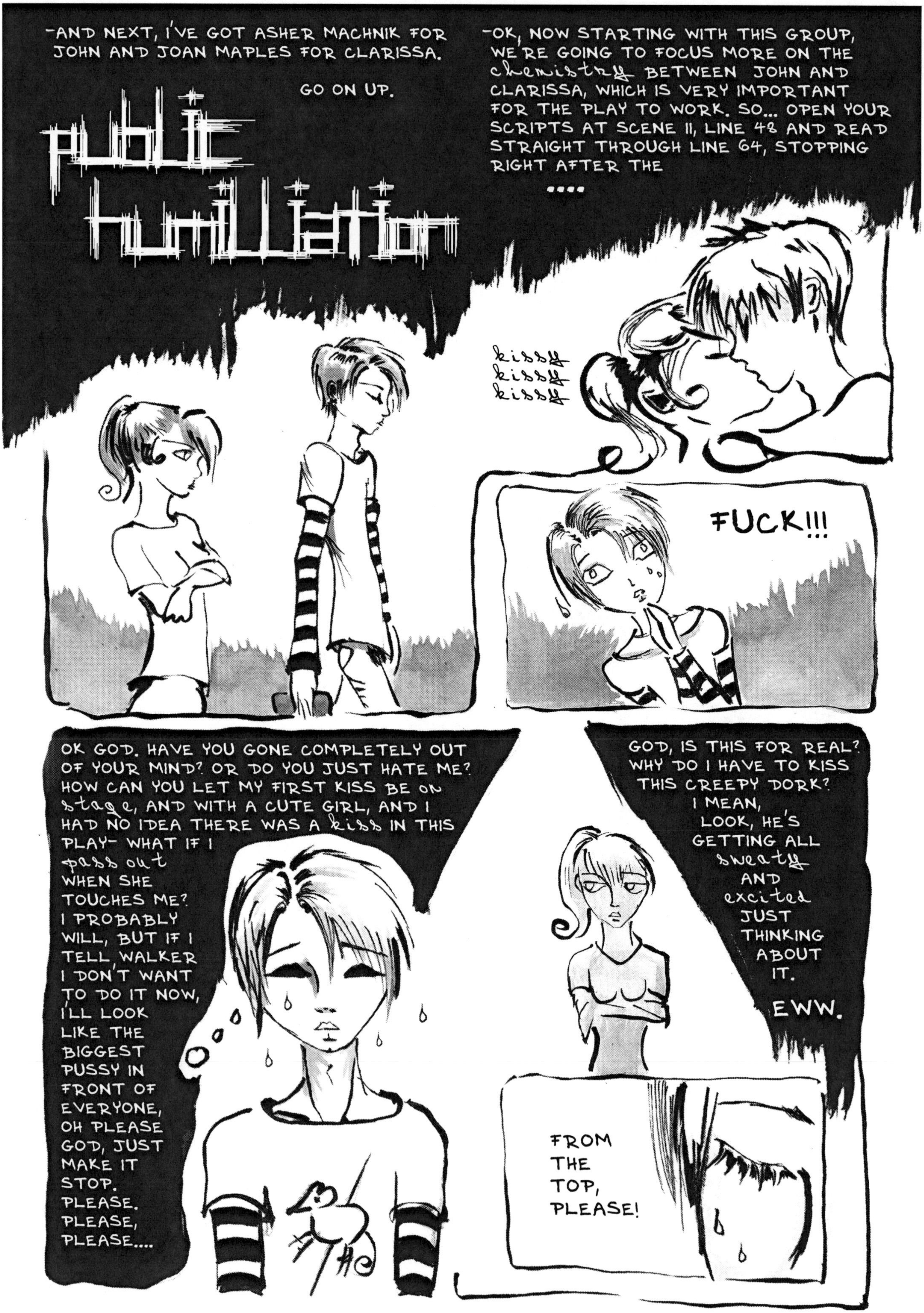
-AND NEXT, I'VE GOT ASHER MACHNIK FOR JOHN AND JOAN MAPLES FOR CLARISSA.
GO ON UP.
public humiliation
-OK, NOW STARTING WITH THIS GROUP, WE'RE GOING TO FOCUS MORE ON THE chemistry BETWEEN JOHN AND CLARISSA, WHICH IS VERY IMPORTANT FOR THE PLAY TO WORK. SO... OPEN YOUR SCRIPTS AT SCENE 11, LINE 48 AND READ STRAIGHT THROUGH LINE 64, STOPPING RIGHT AFTER THE
....
kissy kissy kissy
FUCK!!!
OK GOD. HAVE YOU GONE COMPLETELY OUT OF YOUR MIND? OR DO YOU JUST HATE ME? HOW CAN YOU LET MY FIRST KISS BE ON stage, AND WITH A CUTE GIRL, AND I HAD NO IDEA THERE WAS A kiss IN THIS PLAY- WHAT IF I pass out WHEN SHE TOUCHES ME? I PROBABLY WILL, BUT IF I TELL WALKER I DON'T WANT TO DO IT NOW, I'LL LOOK LIKE THE BIGGEST PUSSY IN FRONT OF EVERYONE, OH PLEASE GOD, JUST MAKE IT STOP. PLEASE. PLEASE, PLEASE....
GOD, IS THIS FOR REAL? WHY DO I HAVE TO KISS THIS CREEPY DORK? I MEAN, LOOK, HE'S GETTING ALL sweaty AND excited JUST THINKING ABOUT IT.
EWW.
FROM THE TOP, PLEASE!

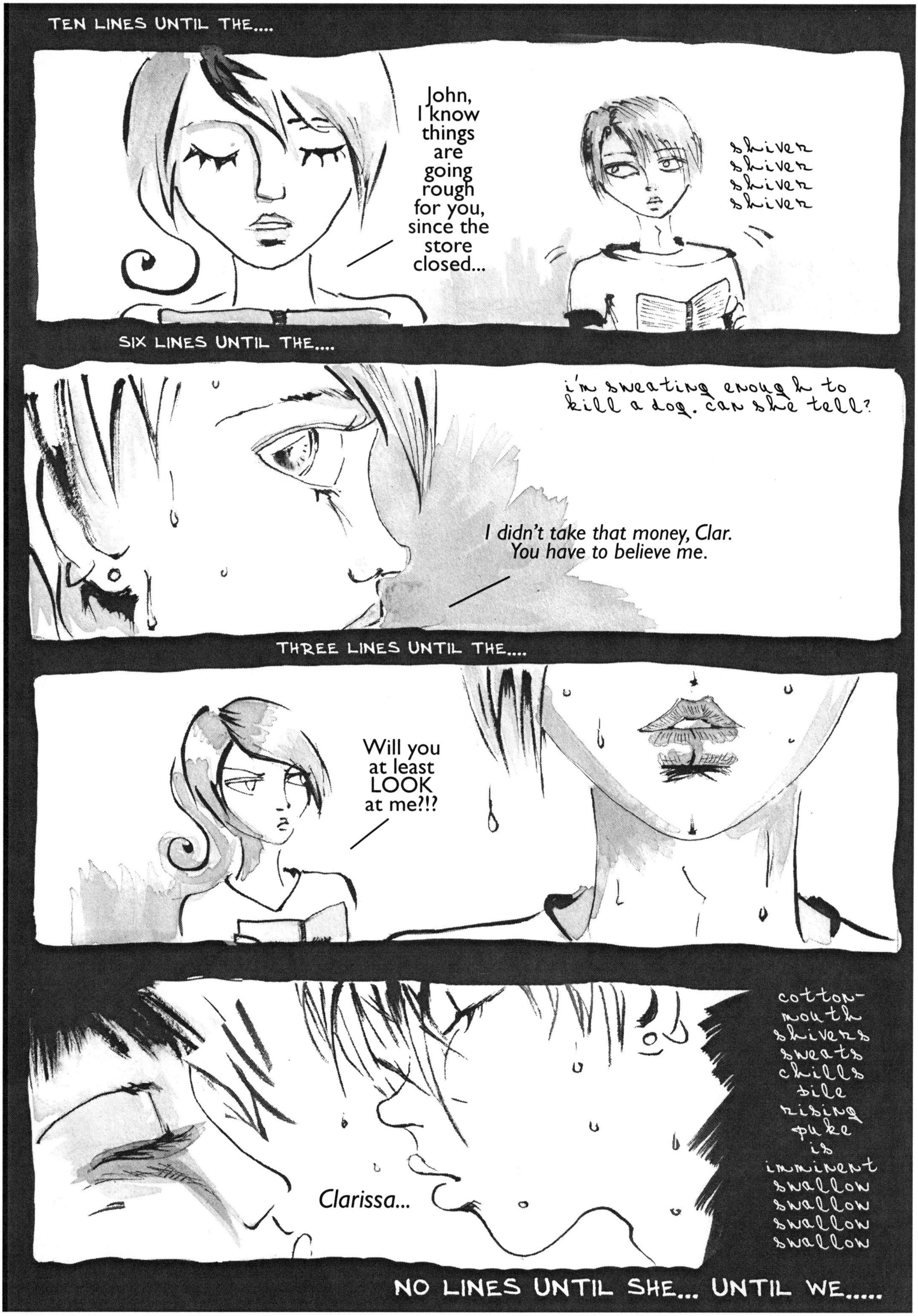
TEN LINES UNTIL THE....
John, I know things are going rough for you, since the store closed...
shiver shiver shiver shiver
SIX LINES UNTIL THE....
i'm sweating enough to kill a dog. can she tell?
I didn't take that money, Clar. You have to believe me.
THREE LINES UNTIL THE....
Will you at least LOOK at me?!?
cotton-mouth shivers sweats chills bile rising puke is imminent swallow swallow swallow swallow
Clarissa...
NO LINES UNTIL SHE... UNTIL WE.....

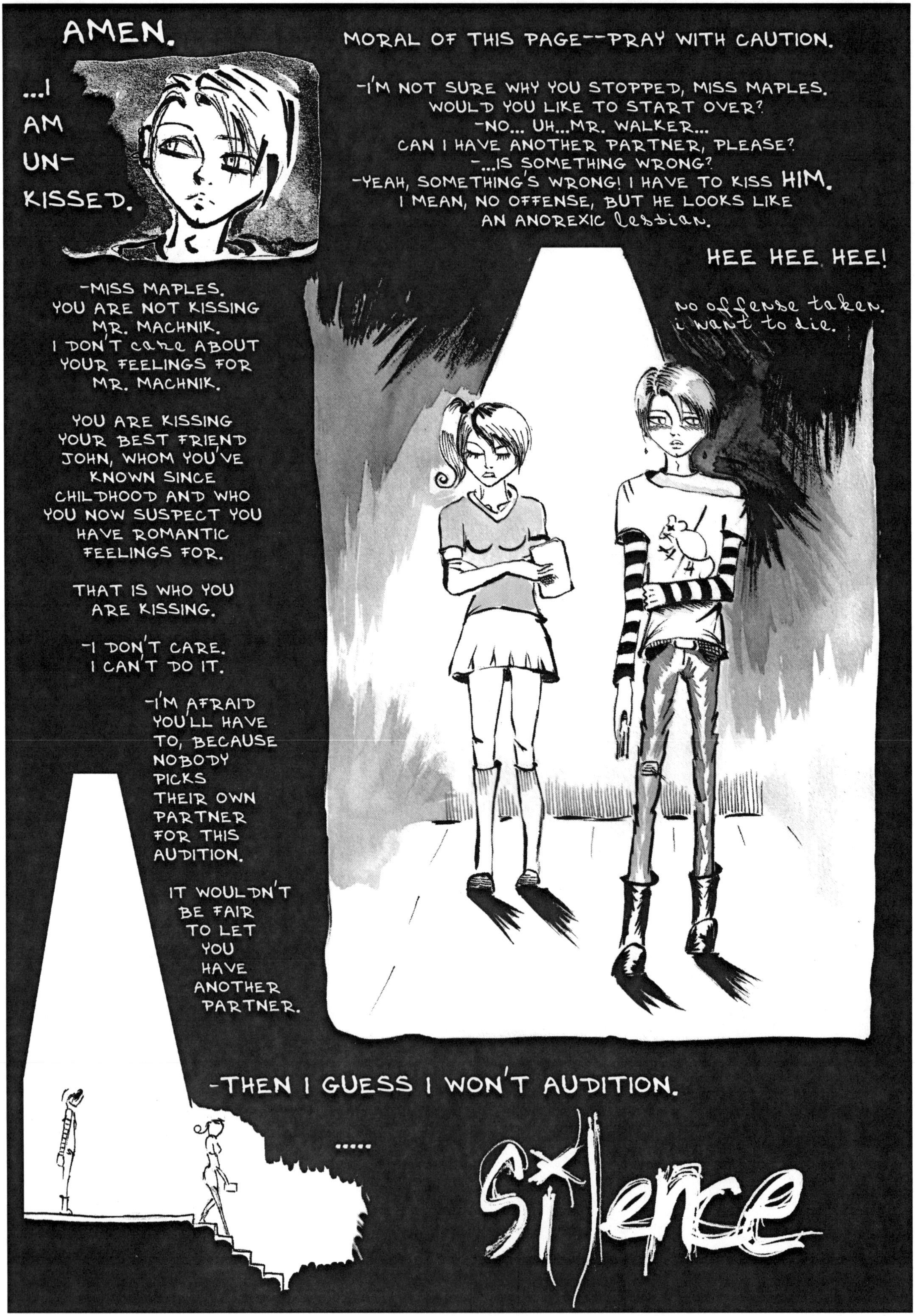
AMEN.
...I AM UN-KISSED.
MORAL OF THIS PAGE--PRAY WITH CAUTION.
-I'M NOT SURE WHY YOU STOPPED, MISS MAPLES. WOULD YOU LIKE TO START OVER?
-NO... UH...MR. WALKER... CAN I HAVE ANOTHER PARTNER, PLEASE?
-...IS SOMETHING WRONG?
-YEAH, SOMETHING'S WRONG! I HAVE TO KISS HIM. I MEAN, NO OFFENSE, BUT HE LOOKS LIKE AN ANOREXIC lesbian.
HEE HEE HEE!
no offense taken. i want to die.
-MISS MAPLES. YOU ARE NOT KISSING MR. MACHNIK. I DON'T care ABOUT YOUR FEELINGS FOR MR. MACHNIK.
YOU ARE KISSING YOUR BEST FRIEND JOHN, WHOM YOU'VE KNOWN SINCE CHILDHOOD AND WHO YOU NOW SUSPECT YOU HAVE ROMANTIC FEELINGS FOR.
THAT IS WHO YOU ARE KISSING.
-I DON'T CARE. I CAN'T DO IT.
-I'M AFRAID YOU'LL HAVE TO, BECAUSE NOBODY PICKS THEIR OWN PARTNER FOR THIS AUDITION.
IT WOULDN'T BE FAIR TO LET YOU HAVE ANOTHER PARTNER.
-THEN I GUESS I WON'T AUDITION.
......
silence

-....ALL RIGHT. I NEED SOMEONE TO READ WITH MACHNIK, AND THEN
AGAIN WITH THEIR ASSIGNED PARTNER. ANY VOLUNTEERS?
-MR. WALKER, IT'S OK. ...I DON'T WANT TO AUDITION
ANYMORE. CAN I GO SIT DOWN?
-NO ASHER, STAY RIGHT THERE! YOU WERE DOING great.
PLEASE, IS THERE ANYBODY? ANYBODY AT all?

HE STANDS IN UTTER HUMILLIATION. AND THEN--
A LONE VOICE.

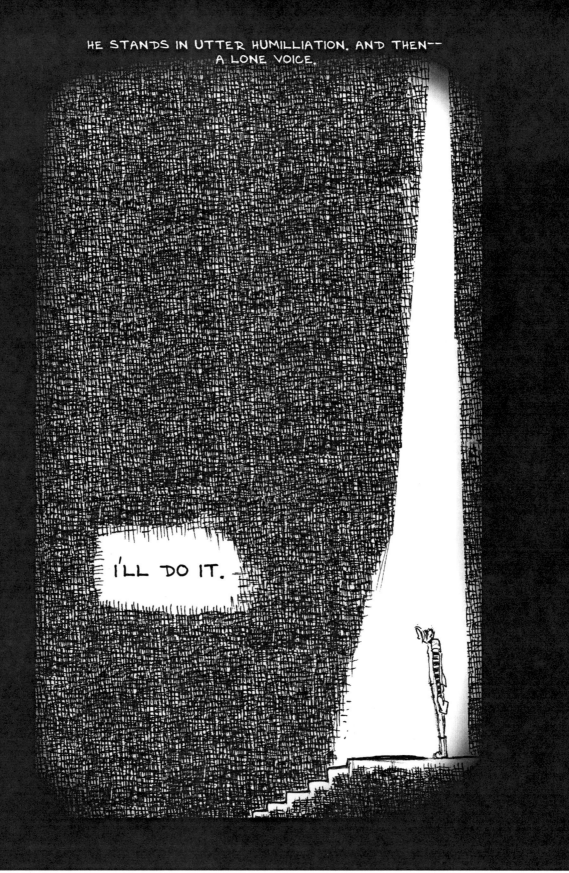

I'LL DO IT.

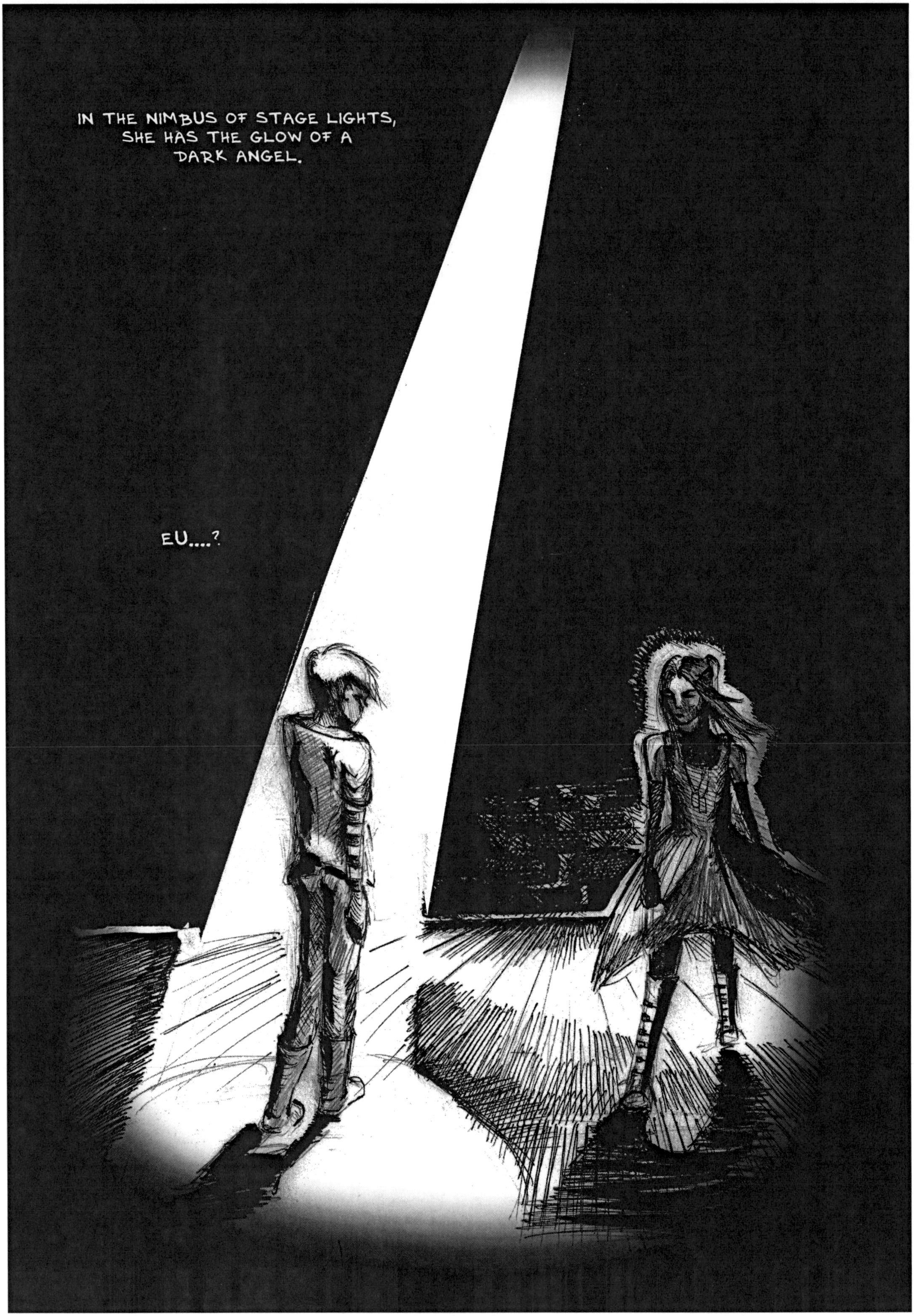
IN THE NIMBUS OF STAGE LIGHTS, SHE HAS THE GLOW OF A DARK ANGEL.
EU....?

HEH.

THOUGHT I OWED YOU ONE, AFTER YOU SO KINDLY GAVE ME YOUR LUNCH THE OTHER DAY.

-THANK YOU, MISS MASON. WILL YOU TWO TAKE IT FROM THE TOP, PLEASE?

THEY TAKE IT FROM THE TOP. ASH CAN ONLY IMAGINE HOW RIDICULOUSLY MISMATCHED THEY LOOK PHYSICALLY-- HE IS NOT SHORT, BUT EULALIE IS A GOOD HALF A HEAD TALLER THAN HIS FIVE ELEVEN SELF.

HE THINKS THERE'S NO HOPE EITHER OF THEM WILL GET THE PART. MAYBE SHE THINKS THAT TOO AND IT'S THE *fatalism* THAT ALLOWS HER TO LET GO.

IN THE SCRIPT, CLARISSA GRABS JOHN WHEN HE HESITATES...

EU GRABS HIM.

HE CLOSES HIS EYES, WAITING FOR HIS STOMACH TO TURN--BUT-- IS IT THE STAGE?

SOMEHOW, THIS ONCE-

IT'S ALL RIGHT.

THEN COMES THE KISS.

HE FEELS HER LIPS ON HIS-- THEY'RE SOFT.

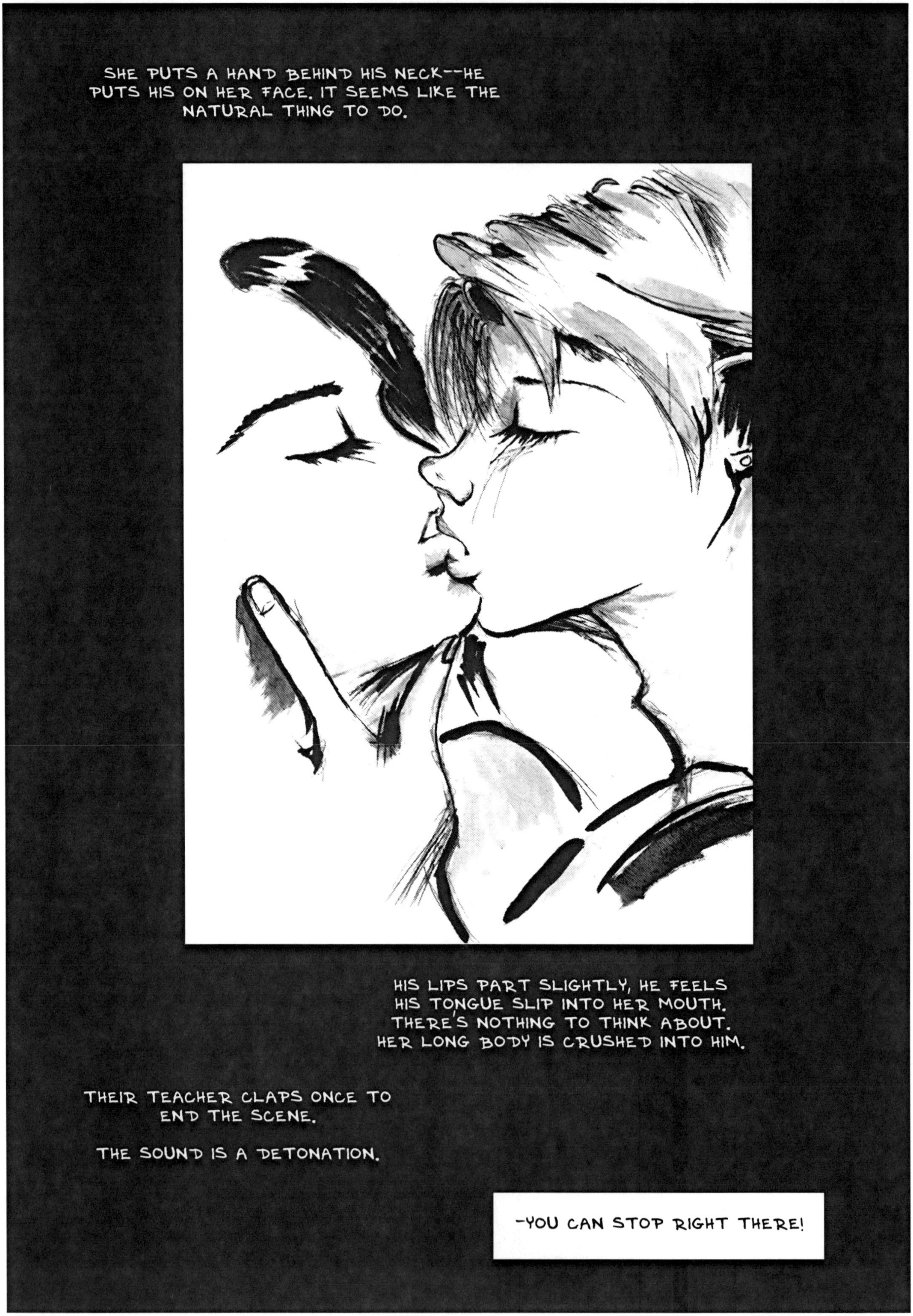
SHE PUTS A HAND BEHIND HIS NECK--HE PUTS HIS ON HER FACE. IT SEEMS LIKE THE NATURAL THING TO DO.
HIS LIPS PART SLIGHTLY, HE FEELS HIS TONGUE SLIP INTO HER MOUTH. THERE'S NOTHING TO THINK ABOUT. HER LONG BODY IS CRUSHED INTO HIM.
THEIR TEACHER CLAPS ONCE TO END THE SCENE.
THE SOUND IS A DETONATION.
-YOU CAN STOP RIGHT THERE!

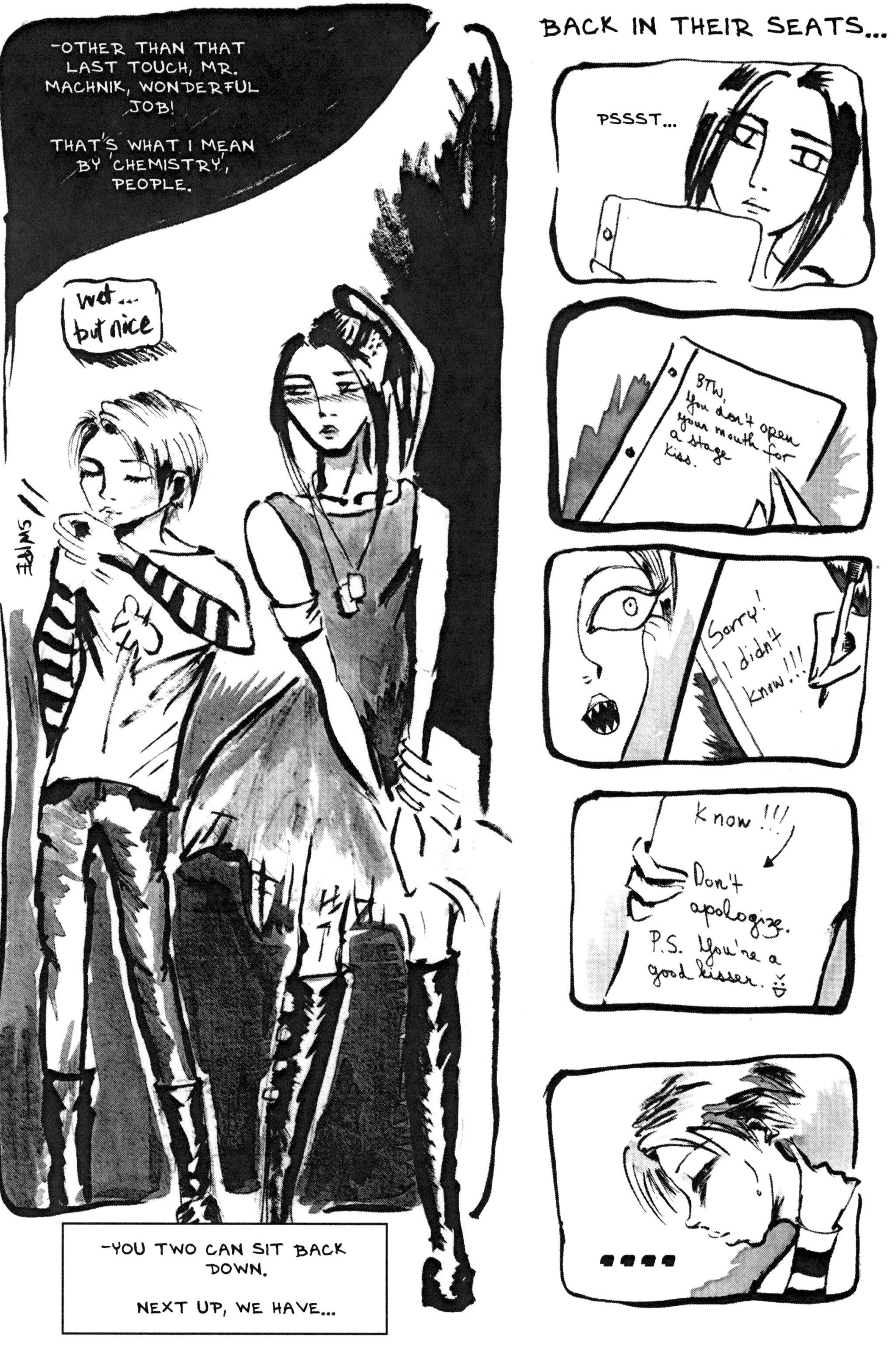
-OTHER THAN THAT LAST TOUCH, MR. MACHNIK, WONDERFUL JOB!
THAT'S WHAT I MEAN BY 'CHEMISTRY', PEOPLE.
wet... but nice
SWIPE
-YOU TWO CAN SIT BACK DOWN.
NEXT UP, WE HAVE...
BACK IN THEIR SEATS...
PSSST...
BTW, You don't open your mouth for a stage kiss.
Sorry! I didn't know!!!
Know!!!
Don't apologize.
P.S. You're a good kisser.
....

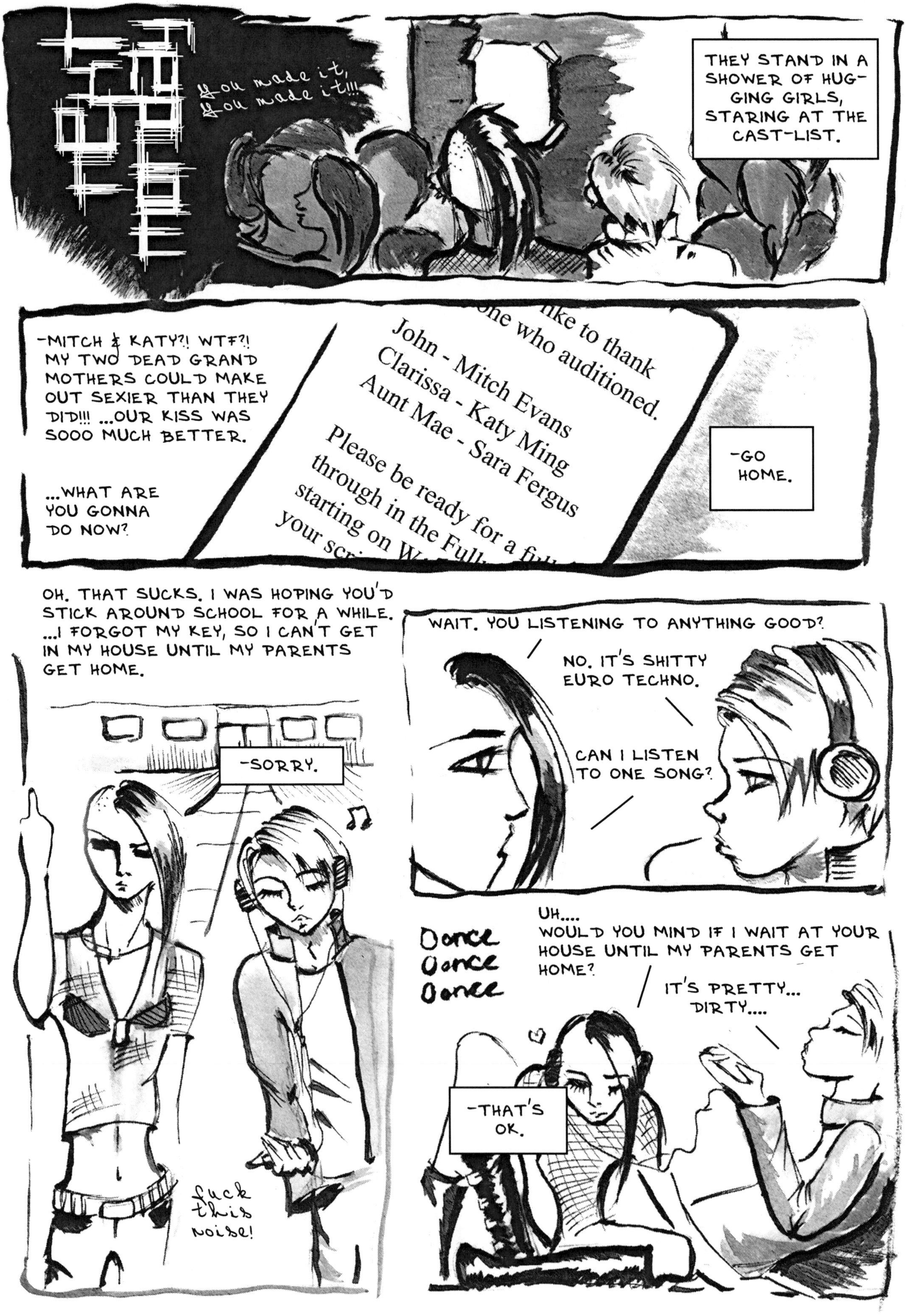
You made it, You made it!!!
THEY STAND IN A SHOWER OF HUGGING GIRLS, STARING AT THE CAST-LIST.
-MITCH & KATY?! WTF?! MY TWO DEAD GRAND MOTHERS COULD MAKE OUT SEXIER THAN THEY DID!!! ...OUR KISS WAS SOOO MUCH BETTER.
...WHAT ARE YOU GONNA DO NOW?
like to thank
one who auditioned.
John - Mitch Evans
Clarissa - Katy Ming
Aunt Mae - Sara Fergus
Please be ready for a full
through in the Full
starting on W
your scri
-GO HOME.
OH. THAT SUCKS. I WAS HOPING YOU'D STICK AROUND SCHOOL FOR A WHILE. ...I FORGOT MY KEY, SO I CAN'T GET IN MY HOUSE UNTIL MY PARENTS GET HOME.
-SORRY.
fuck this noise!
WAIT. YOU LISTENING TO ANYTHING GOOD?
NO. IT'S SHITTY EURO TECHNO.
CAN I LISTEN TO ONE SONG?
Oonce Oonce Oonce
UH.... WOULD YOU MIND IF I WAIT AT YOUR HOUSE UNTIL MY PARENTS GET HOME?
IT'S PRETTY... DIRTY....
-THAT'S OK.

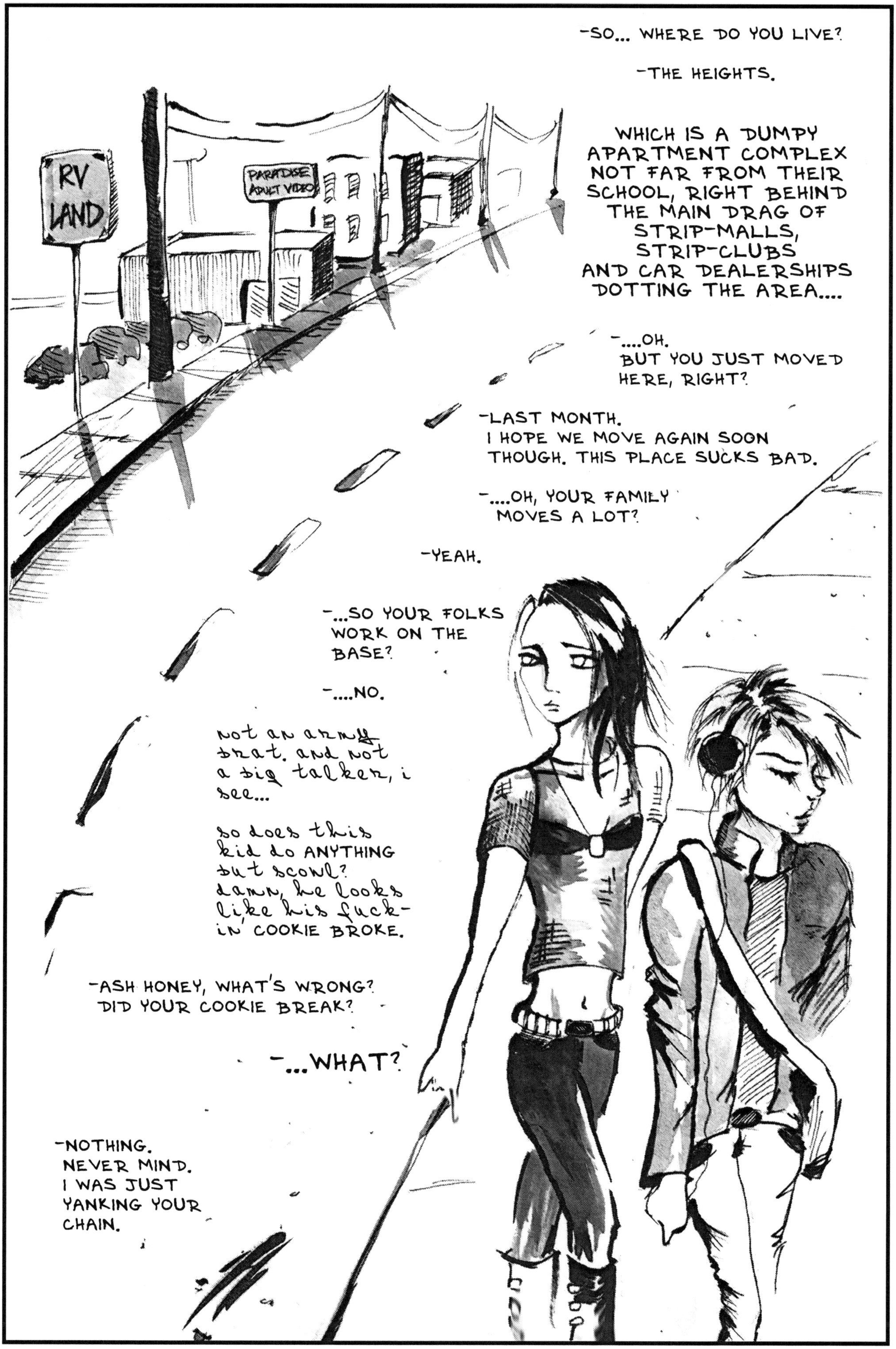

-SO... WHERE DO YOU LIVE?
-THE HEIGHTS.
WHICH IS A DUMPY APARTMENT COMPLEX NOT FAR FROM THEIR SCHOOL, RIGHT BEHIND THE MAIN DRAG OF STRIP-MALLS, STRIP-CLUBS AND CAR DEALERSHIPS DOTTING THE AREA....
RV LAND
PARADISE ADULT VIDEO
-....OH. BUT YOU JUST MOVED HERE, RIGHT?
-LAST MONTH. I HOPE WE MOVE AGAIN SOON THOUGH. THIS PLACE SUCKS BAD.
-....OH, YOUR FAMILY MOVES A LOT?
-YEAH.
-...SO YOUR FOLKS WORK ON THE BASE?
-....NO.
not an army brat. and not a big talker, i see...
so does this kid do ANYTHING but scowl? damn, he looks like his fuck-in' COOKIE BROKE.
-ASH HONEY, WHAT'S WRONG? DID YOUR COOKIE BREAK?
-...WHAT?
-NOTHING. NEVER MIND. I WAS JUST YANKING YOUR CHAIN.

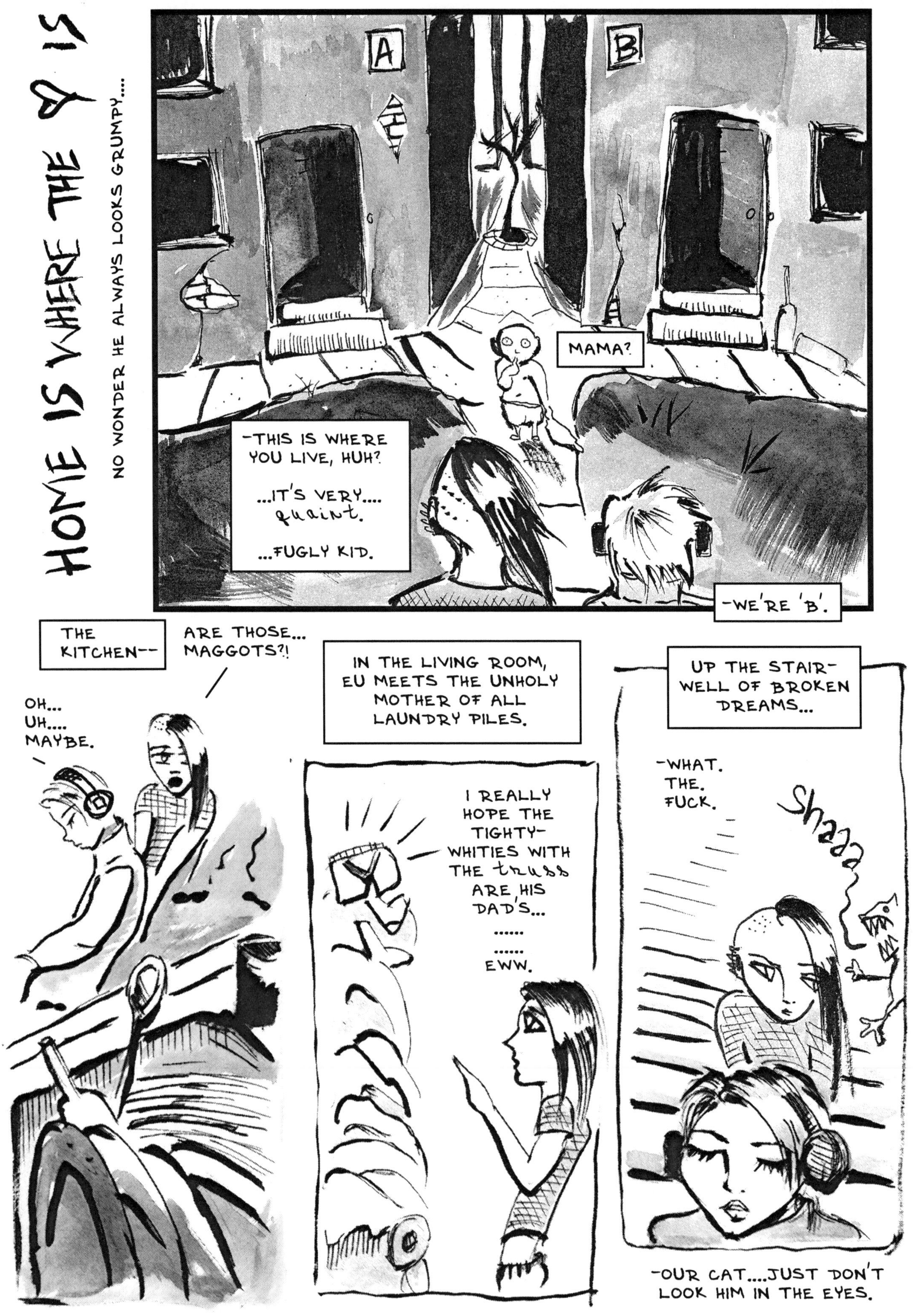
HOME IS WHERE THE ♥ IS
NO WONDER HE ALWAYS LOOKS GRUMPY....
A
B
MAMA?
-THIS IS WHERE YOU LIVE, HUH? ...IT'S VERY.... quaint. ...FUGLY KID.
-WE'RE 'B'.
THE KITCHEN--
ARE THOSE... MAGGOTS?!
OH... UH.... MAYBE.
IN THE LIVING ROOM, EU MEETS THE UNHOLY MOTHER OF ALL LAUNDRY PILES.
I REALLY HOPE THE TIGHTY-WHITIES WITH THE truss ARE HIS DAD'S... .... EWW.
UP THE STAIR-WELL OF BROKEN DREAMS...
-WHAT. THE. FUCK.
Shaaa
-OUR CAT....JUST DON'T LOOK HIM IN THE EYES.

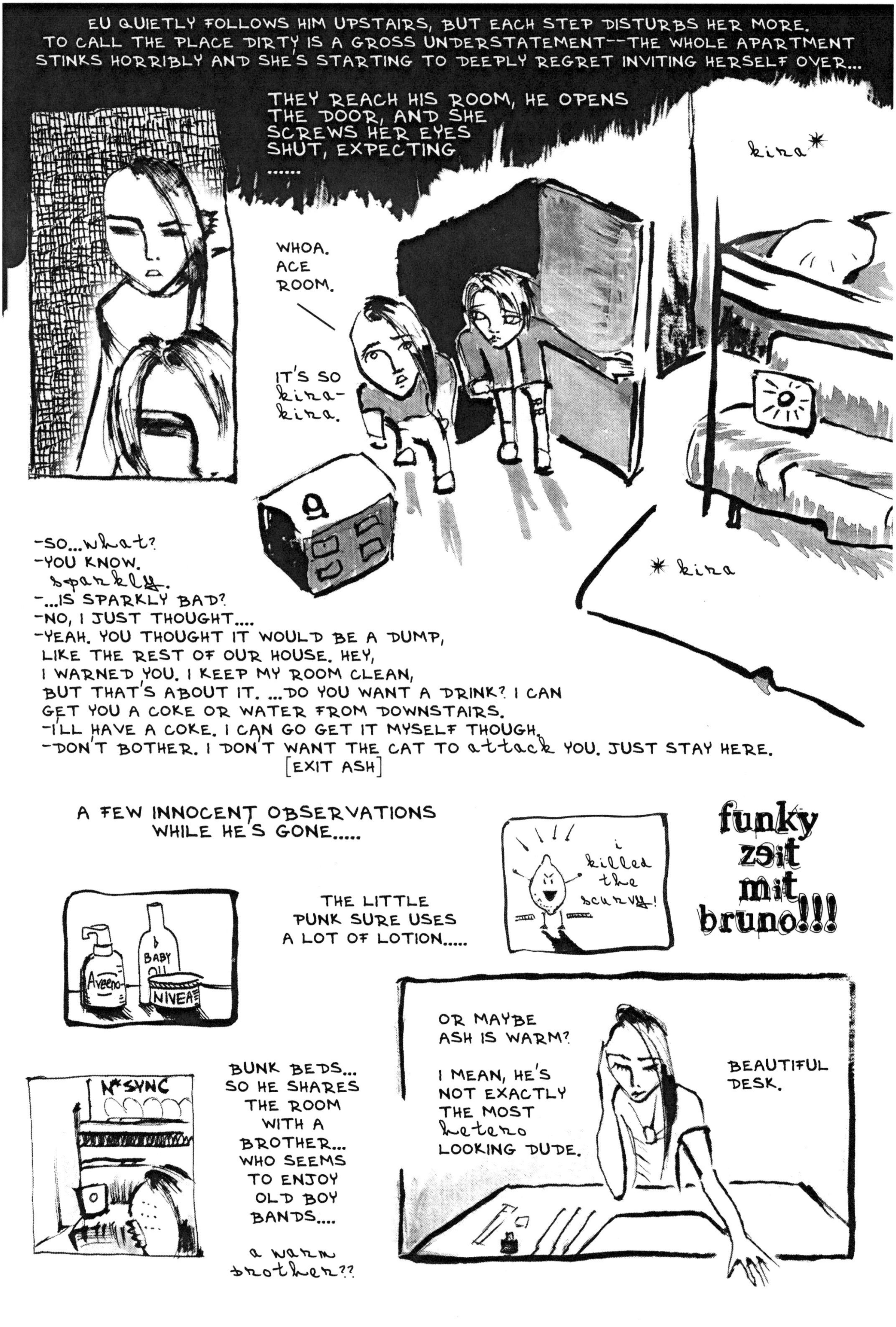

EU QUIETLY FOLLOWS HIM UPSTAIRS, BUT EACH STEP DISTURBS HER MORE. TO CALL THE PLACE DIRTY IS A GROSS UNDERSTATEMENT--THE WHOLE APARTMENT STINKS HORRIBLY AND SHE'S STARTING TO DEEPLY REGRET INVITING HERSELF OVER...
THEY REACH HIS ROOM, HE OPENS THE DOOR, AND SHE SCREWS HER EYES SHUT, EXPECTING ......
kira*
WHOA. ACE ROOM.
IT'S SO kira-kira.
*kira
-SO...what?
-YOU KNOW. sparkly.
-...IS SPARKLY BAD?
-NO, I JUST THOUGHT....
-YEAH. YOU THOUGHT IT WOULD BE A DUMP, LIKE THE REST OF OUR HOUSE. HEY, I WARNED YOU. I KEEP MY ROOM CLEAN, BUT THAT'S ABOUT IT. ...DO YOU WANT A DRINK? I CAN GET YOU A COKE OR WATER FROM DOWNSTAIRS.
-I'LL HAVE A COKE. I CAN GO GET IT MYSELF THOUGH.
-DON'T BOTHER. I DON'T WANT THE CAT TO attack YOU. JUST STAY HERE.
[EXIT ASH]
A FEW INNOCENT OBSERVATIONS WHILE HE'S GONE.....
i killed the scurvy!
funky zeit mit bruno!!!
Aveeno
BABY OIL
NIVEA
THE LITTLE PUNK SURE USES A LOT OF LOTION.....
N*SYNC
BUNK BEDS... SO HE SHARES THE ROOM WITH A BROTHER... WHO SEEMS TO ENJOY OLD BOY BANDS....
a warm brother??
OR MAYBE ASH IS WARM?
I MEAN, HE'S NOT EXACTLY THE MOST hetero LOOKING DUDE.
BEAUTIFUL DESK.

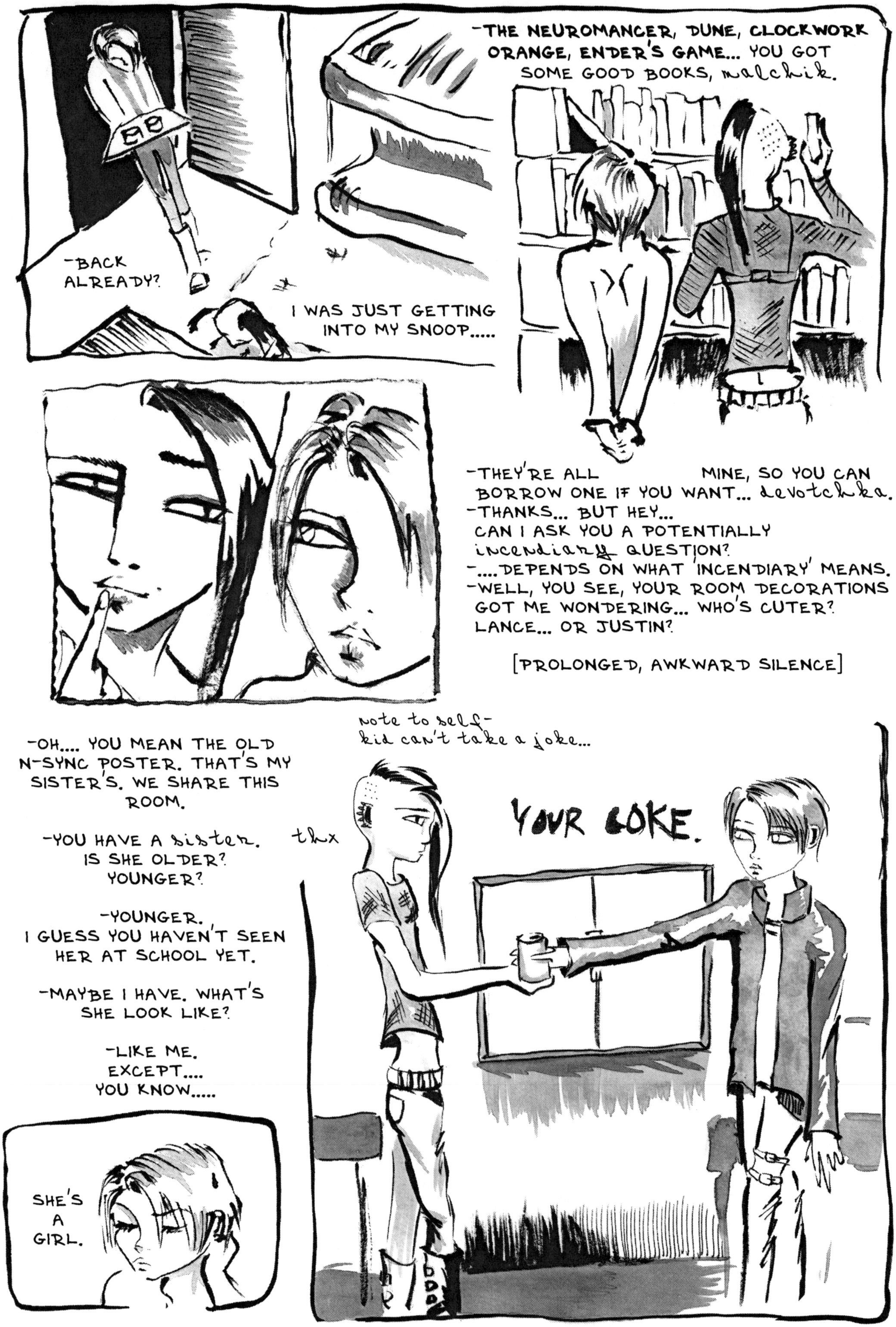
-BACK ALREADY?
I WAS JUST GETTING INTO MY SNOOP.....
-THE NEUROMANCER, DUNE, CLOCKWORK ORANGE, ENDER'S GAME... YOU GOT SOME GOOD BOOKS, malchik.
-THEY'RE ALL MINE, SO YOU CAN BORROW ONE IF YOU WANT... devotchka.
-THANKS... BUT HEY... CAN I ASK YOU A POTENTIALLY incendiary QUESTION?
-....DEPENDS ON WHAT 'INCENDIARY' MEANS.
-WELL, YOU SEE, YOUR ROOM DECORATIONS GOT ME WONDERING... WHO'S CUTER? LANCE... OR JUSTIN?
[PROLONGED, AWKWARD SILENCE]
note to self- kid can't take a joke...
-OH.... YOU MEAN THE OLD N-SYNC POSTER. THAT'S MY SISTER'S. WE SHARE THIS ROOM.
-YOU HAVE A sister. IS SHE OLDER? YOUNGER?
-YOUNGER. I GUESS YOU HAVEN'T SEEN HER AT SCHOOL YET.
-MAYBE I HAVE. WHAT'S SHE LOOK LIKE?
-LIKE ME. EXCEPT.... YOU KNOW.....
SHE'S A GIRL.
YOUR COKE.
thx

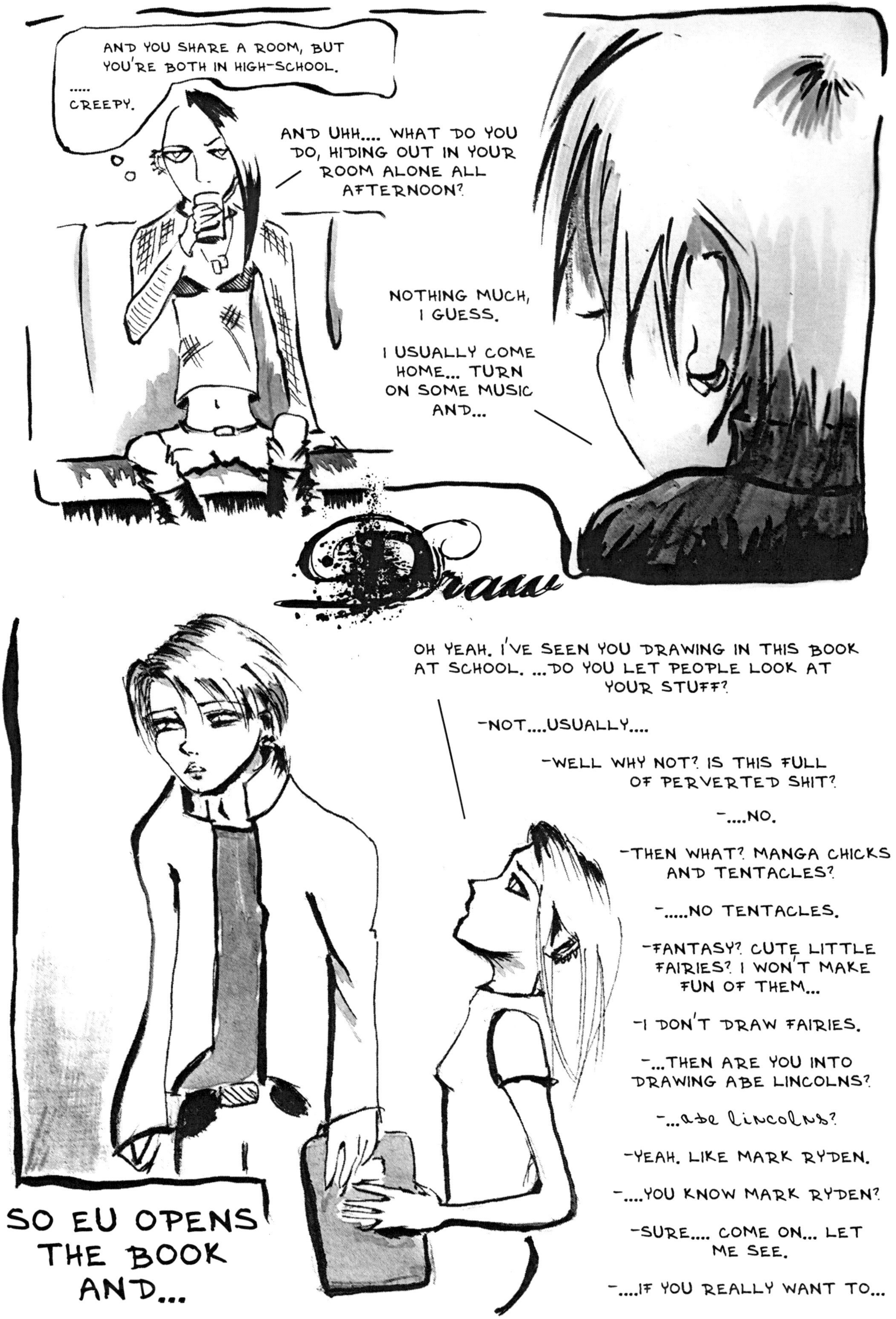
AND YOU SHARE A ROOM, BUT YOU'RE BOTH IN HIGH-SCHOOL.
..... CREEPY.
AND UHH.... WHAT DO YOU DO, HIDING OUT IN YOUR ROOM ALONE ALL AFTERNOON?
NOTHING MUCH, I GUESS.
I USUALLY COME HOME... TURN ON SOME MUSIC AND...
Draw
OH YEAH. I'VE SEEN YOU DRAWING IN THIS BOOK AT SCHOOL. ...DO YOU LET PEOPLE LOOK AT YOUR STUFF?
-NOT....USUALLY....
-WELL WHY NOT? IS THIS FULL OF PERVERTED SHIT?
-....NO.
-THEN WHAT? MANGA CHICKS AND TENTACLES?
-.....NO TENTACLES.
-FANTASY? CUTE LITTLE FAIRIES? I WON'T MAKE FUN OF THEM...
-I DON'T DRAW FAIRIES.
-...THEN ARE YOU INTO DRAWING ABE LINCOLNS?
-...abe lincolns?
-YEAH. LIKE MARK RYDEN.
-....YOU KNOW MARK RYDEN?
-SURE.... COME ON... LET ME SEE.
-....IF YOU REALLY WANT TO...
SO EU OPENS THE BOOK AND...

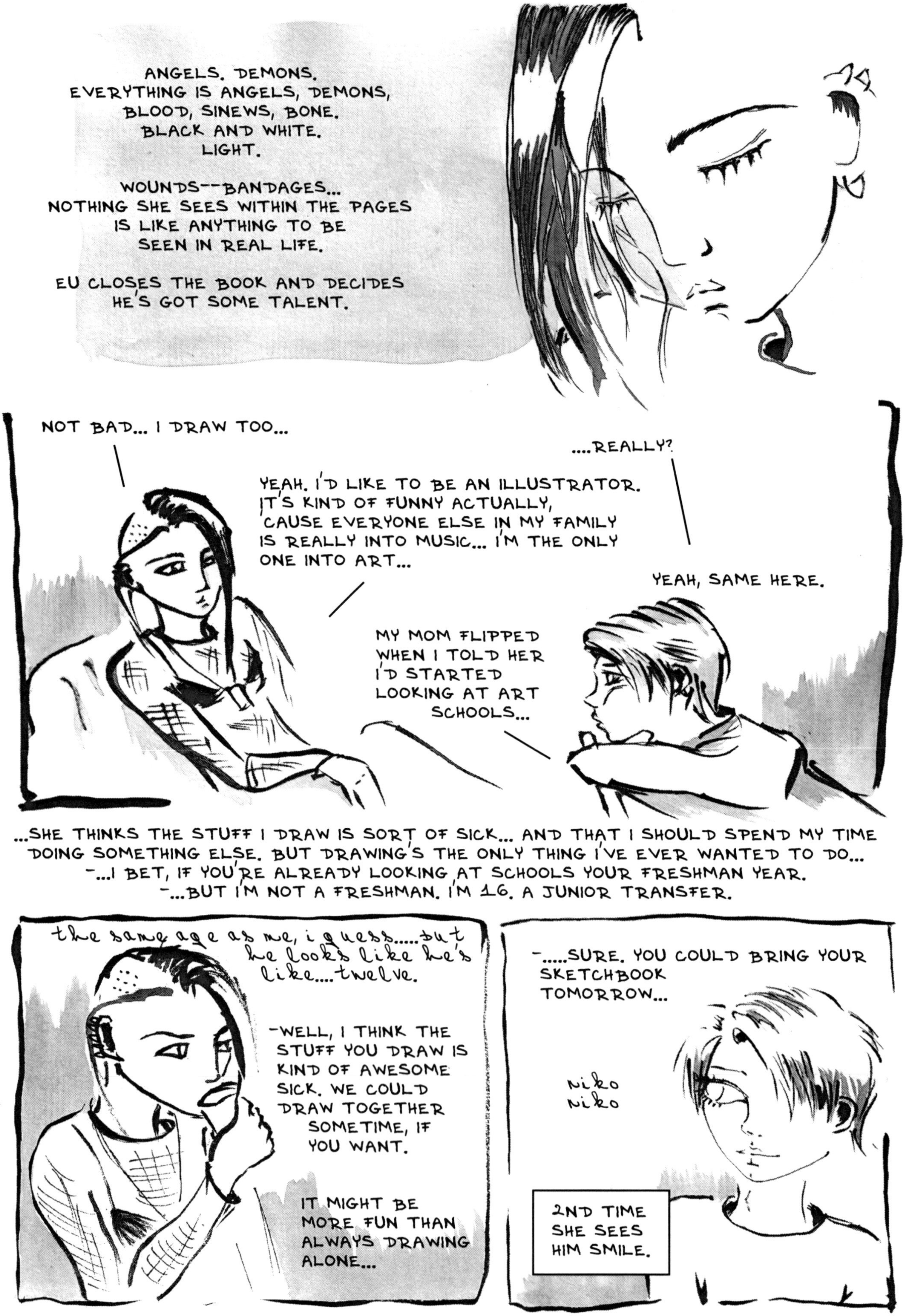
ANGELS. DEMONS.
EVERYTHING IS ANGELS, DEMONS, BLOOD, SINEWS, BONE. BLACK AND WHITE. LIGHT.
WOUNDS--BANDAGES... NOTHING SHE SEES WITHIN THE PAGES IS LIKE ANYTHING TO BE SEEN IN REAL LIFE.
EU CLOSES THE BOOK AND DECIDES HE'S GOT SOME TALENT.
NOT BAD... I DRAW TOO...
....REALLY?
YEAH. I'D LIKE TO BE AN ILLUSTRATOR. IT'S KIND OF FUNNY ACTUALLY, 'CAUSE EVERYONE ELSE IN MY FAMILY IS REALLY INTO MUSIC... I'M THE ONLY ONE INTO ART...
YEAH, SAME HERE.
MY MOM FLIPPED WHEN I TOLD HER I'D STARTED LOOKING AT ART SCHOOLS...
...SHE THINKS THE STUFF I DRAW IS SORT OF SICK... AND THAT I SHOULD SPEND MY TIME DOING SOMETHING ELSE. BUT DRAWING'S THE ONLY THING I'VE EVER WANTED TO DO...
-...I BET, IF YOU'RE ALREADY LOOKING AT SCHOOLS YOUR FRESHMAN YEAR.
-...BUT I'M NOT A FRESHMAN. I'M 16. A JUNIOR TRANSFER.
the same age as me, i guess..... but he looks like he's like....twelve.
-WELL, I THINK THE STUFF YOU DRAW IS KIND OF AWESOME SICK. WE COULD DRAW TOGETHER SOMETIME, IF YOU WANT.
IT MIGHT BE MORE FUN THAN ALWAYS DRAWING ALONE...
-.....SURE. YOU COULD BRING YOUR SKETCHBOOK TOMORROW...
niko niko
2ND TIME SHE SEES HIM SMILE.

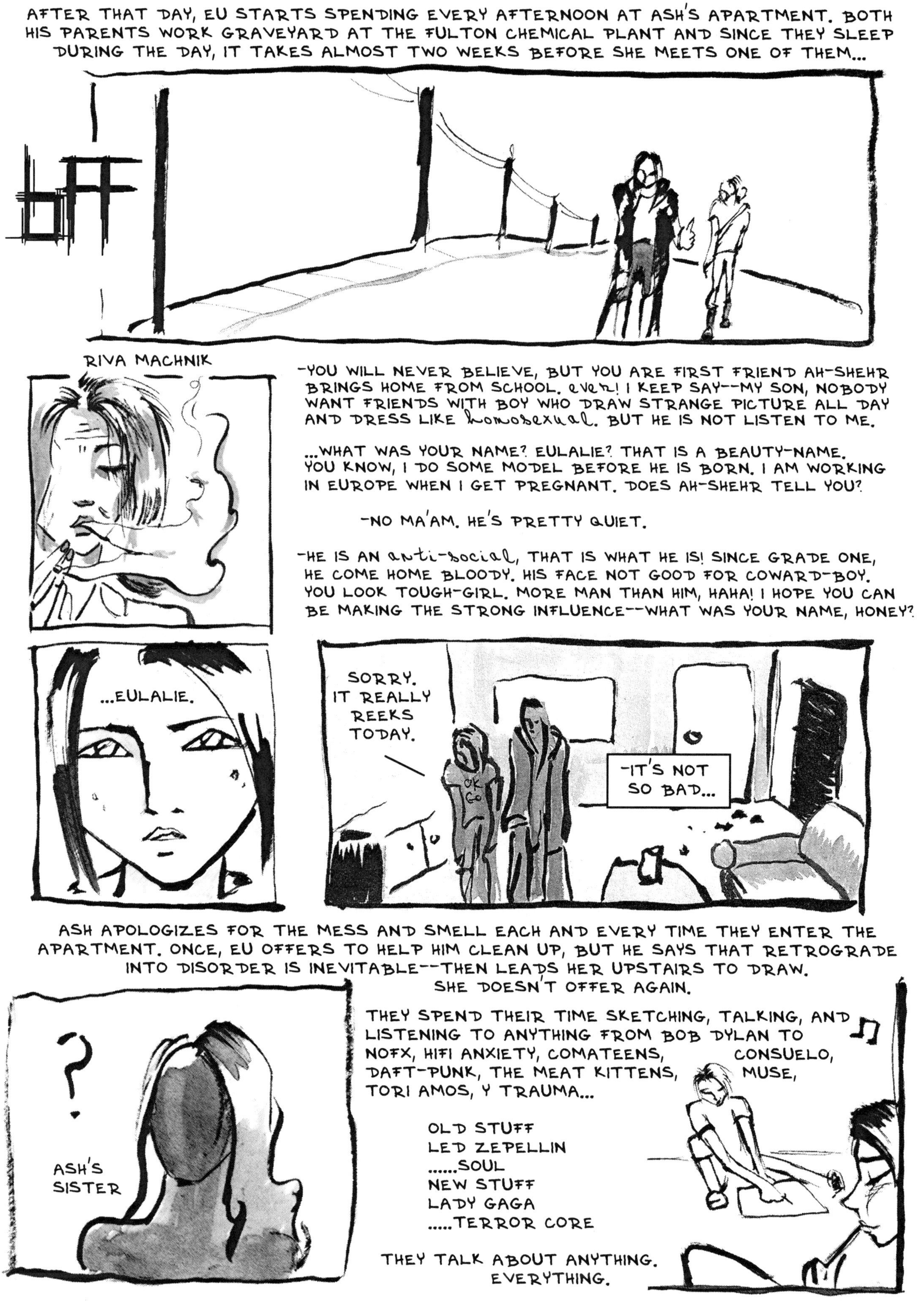
AFTER THAT DAY, EU STARTS SPENDING EVERY AFTERNOON AT ASH'S APARTMENT. BOTH HIS PARENTS WORK GRAVEYARD AT THE FULTON CHEMICAL PLANT AND SINCE THEY SLEEP DURING THE DAY, IT TAKES ALMOST TWO WEEKS BEFORE SHE MEETS ONE OF THEM...
bFF
RIVA MACHNIK
-YOU WILL NEVER BELIEVE, BUT YOU ARE FIRST FRIEND AH-SHEHR BRINGS HOME FROM SCHOOL. ever! I KEEP SAY--MY SON, NOBODY WANT FRIENDS WITH BOY WHO DRAW STRANGE PICTURE ALL DAY AND DRESS LIKE homosexual. BUT HE IS NOT LISTEN TO ME.
...WHAT WAS YOUR NAME? EULALIE? THAT IS A BEAUTY-NAME. YOU KNOW, I DO SOME MODEL BEFORE HE IS BORN. I AM WORKING IN EUROPE WHEN I GET PREGNANT. DOES AH-SHEHR TELL YOU?
-NO MA'AM. HE'S PRETTY QUIET.
-HE IS AN anti-social, THAT IS WHAT HE IS! SINCE GRADE ONE, HE COME HOME BLOODY. HIS FACE NOT GOOD FOR COWARD-BOY. YOU LOOK TOUGH-GIRL. MORE MAN THAN HIM, HAHA! I HOPE YOU CAN BE MAKING THE STRONG INFLUENCE--WHAT WAS YOUR NAME, HONEY?
...EULALIE.
SORRY. IT REALLY REEKS TODAY.
OK GO
-IT'S NOT SO BAD...
ASH APOLOGIZES FOR THE MESS AND SMELL EACH AND EVERY TIME THEY ENTER THE APARTMENT. ONCE, EU OFFERS TO HELP HIM CLEAN UP, BUT HE SAYS THAT RETROGRADE INTO DISORDER IS INEVITABLE--THEN LEADS HER UPSTAIRS TO DRAW. SHE DOESN'T OFFER AGAIN.
?
ASH'S SISTER
THEY SPEND THEIR TIME SKETCHING, TALKING, AND LISTENING TO ANYTHING FROM BOB DYLAN TO NOFX, HIFI ANXIETY, COMATEENS, CONSUELO, DAFT-PUNK, THE MEAT KITTENS, MUSE, TORI AMOS, Y TRAUMA...
OLD STUFF
LED ZEPELLIN
......SOUL
NEW STUFF
LADY GAGA
.....TERROR CORE
THEY TALK ABOUT ANYTHING. EVERYTHING.

HE FINDS OUT THAT HER MOTHER IS FROM IRAN AND THAT HER FATHER OWNS A GUITAR REPAIR SHOP DOWNTOWN. SHE FINDS OUT THAT HE SURVIVES ENTIRELY OFF OF ORANGE SODA, CANDY AND TICTACS, AND THAT HE HATES BEING TOUCHED BY ANYONE. IN ANY WAY.

EU FIGURES SHE CAN RESPECT THAT. ONLY ONCE DOES SHE FORGET AND TRY TO HUG HIM... HE PUSHES HER AWAY, SWEATING AND EMBARASSED AND BOTH OF THEM PRETEND A SECOND LATER THAT NOTHING HAPPENED...

WHEN THEY WALK HOME FROM SCHOOL, BOYS YELL AT THEM OUT THEIR CAR WINDOWS--

-HEY DYKE, IS THAT YOUR NEW GIRLFRIEND?

-MASON, ASK YOUR GIRL IF THERE ARE FAGGOTS ON MARS...

-ASK HIM YOURSELF. FUCKFACE.

EU'S SKETCHBOOK
THE MASONS DO HAWAII, TWO SUMMERS AGO.

EU WON'T BACK DOWN FROM ANY CONFRONTATION--HE JUST SHOE-GAZES...

-C'MON ASH. THEY'LL NEVER LEAVE YOU ALONE IF YOU JUST TAKE IT.

BUT HIS DEFENSE STRATEGY REMAINS TRYING TO STAY INVISIBLE.

EU'S SKETCHBOOK- MOUNTAIN SKETCH FROM FAMILY SKI TRIP LAST WINTER

THE ONLY TIME HE LOOKS HAPPY IS WHEN THEY'RE IN HIS ROOM SKETCHING. EU DRAWS FROM A STILL LIFE SHE SETS UP IN FRONT OF HER OR FROM PHOTOGRAPHS.

ASH DRAWS STRICTLY FROM HIS HEAD. HE GETS A LOOK WHEN HE DRAWS THAT SHE TRIES TO SECRETLY SKETCH. IT'S AN EXPRES-SION THAT MAKES HER ASK HIM ONCE...

-HEY. WHAT DOES DRAWING MEAN TO YOU?

HE STARES OUT THE WINDOW AND SHE'S SURE HE WON'T ANSWER, BUT THEN HE MUTTERS ONE WORD--

-escape.

THAT'S ALL HE SAYS. EU WONDERS THEN IF HE'LL ALWAYS BE LIKE THIS. OR IF....

EU'S SKETCHBOOK
ASH SMUDGING A DRAWING

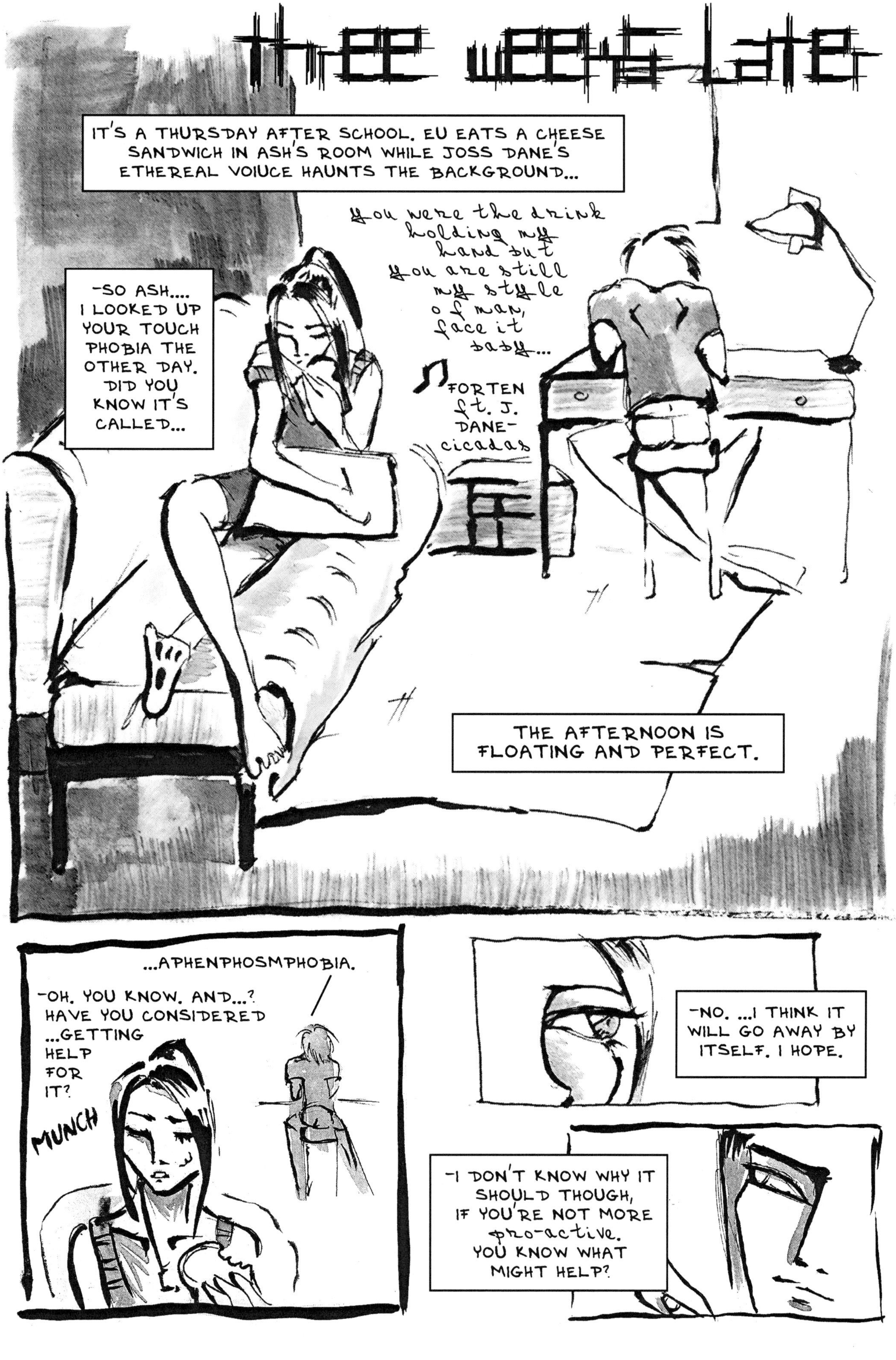
THREE WEEKS LATER
IT'S A THURSDAY AFTER SCHOOL. EU EATS A CHEESE SANDWICH IN ASH'S ROOM WHILE JOSS DANE'S ETHEREAL VOIUCE HAUNTS THE BACKGROUND...
-SO ASH.... I LOOKED UP YOUR TOUCH PHOBIA THE OTHER DAY. DID YOU KNOW IT'S CALLED...
You were the drink holding my hand but you are still my style of man, face it baby...
FORTEN ft. J. DANE- cicadas
THE AFTERNOON IS FLOATING AND PERFECT.
...APHENPHOSMPHOBIA.
-OH. YOU KNOW. AND...? HAVE YOU CONSIDERED ...GETTING HELP FOR IT?
MUNCH
-NO. ...I THINK IT WILL GO AWAY BY ITSELF. I HOPE.
-I DON'T KNOW WHY IT SHOULD THOUGH, IF YOU'RE NOT MORE pro-active. YOU KNOW WHAT MIGHT HELP?

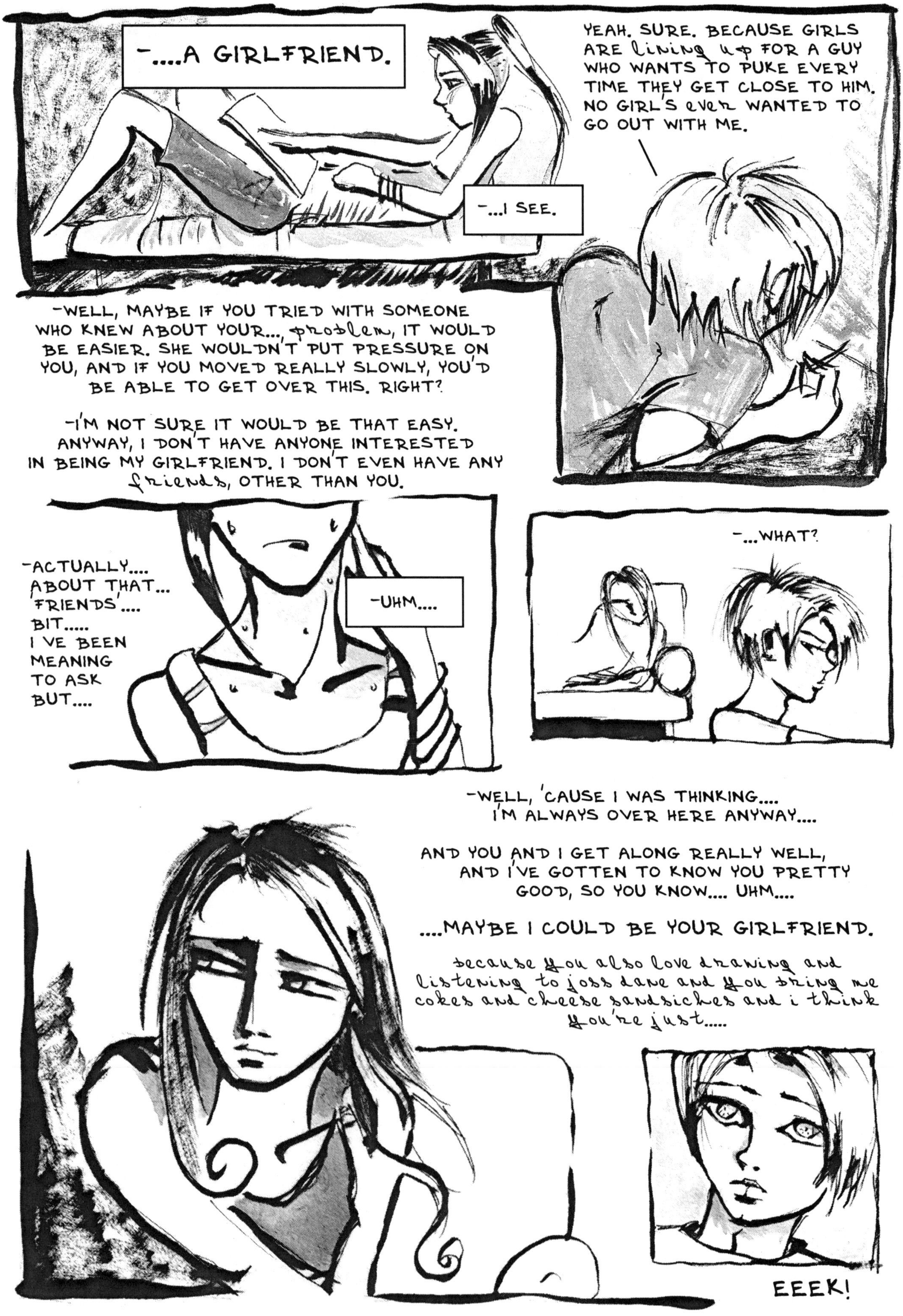
-....A GIRLFRIEND.
YEAH. SURE. BECAUSE GIRLS ARE lining up FOR A GUY WHO WANTS TO PUKE EVERY TIME THEY GET CLOSE TO HIM. NO GIRL'S ever WANTED TO GO OUT WITH ME.
-...I SEE.
-WELL, MAYBE IF YOU TRIED WITH SOMEONE WHO KNEW ABOUT YOUR..., problem, IT WOULD BE EASIER. SHE WOULDN'T PUT PRESSURE ON YOU, AND IF YOU MOVED REALLY SLOWLY, YOU'D BE ABLE TO GET OVER THIS. RIGHT?
-I'M NOT SURE IT WOULD BE THAT EASY. ANYWAY, I DON'T HAVE ANYONE INTERESTED IN BEING MY GIRLFRIEND. I DON'T EVEN HAVE ANY friends, OTHER THAN YOU.
-ACTUALLY.... ABOUT THAT... 'FRIENDS'.... BIT..... I'VE BEEN MEANING TO ASK BUT....
-UHM....
-...WHAT?
-WELL, 'CAUSE I WAS THINKING.... I'M ALWAYS OVER HERE ANYWAY....
AND YOU AND I GET ALONG REALLY WELL, AND I'VE GOTTEN TO KNOW YOU PRETTY GOOD, SO YOU KNOW.... UHM....
....MAYBE I COULD BE YOUR GIRLFRIEND.
because you also love drawing and listening to joss dane and you bring me cokes and cheese sandwiches and i think you're just.....
EEEK!

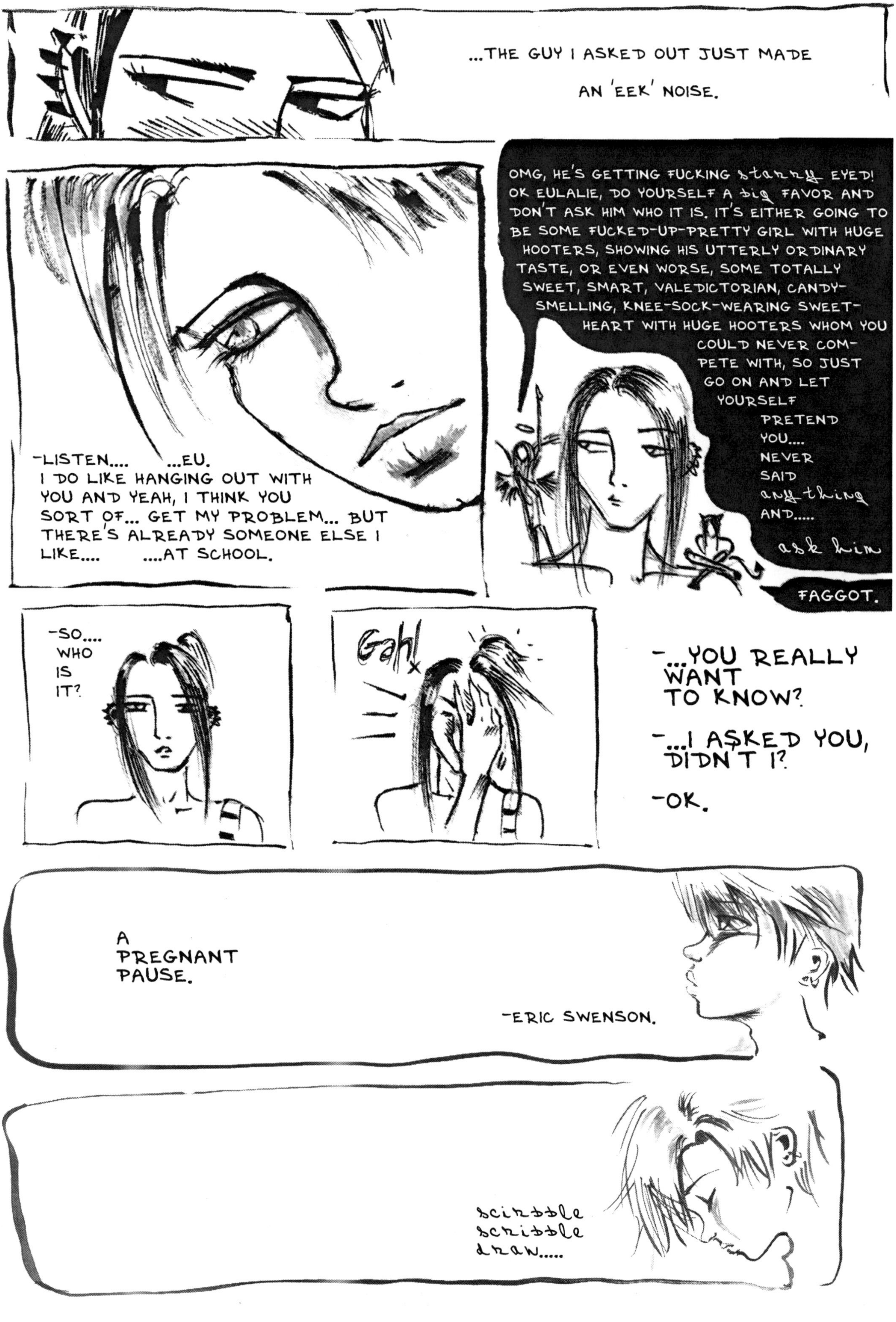
...THE GUY I ASKED OUT JUST MADE AN 'EEK' NOISE.
OMG, HE'S GETTING FUCKING starry EYED! OK EULALIE, DO YOURSELF A big FAVOR AND DON'T ASK HIM WHO IT IS. IT'S EITHER GOING TO BE SOME FUCKED-UP-PRETTY GIRL WITH HUGE HOOTERS, SHOWING HIS UTTERLY ORDINARY TASTE, OR EVEN WORSE, SOME TOTALLY SWEET, SMART, VALEDICTORIAN, CANDY-SMELLING, KNEE-SOCK-WEARING SWEET-HEART WITH HUGE HOOTERS WHOM YOU COULD NEVER COM-PETE WITH, SO JUST GO ON AND LET YOURSELF PRETEND YOU.... NEVER SAID anything AND..... ask him
-LISTEN.... ...EU. I DO LIKE HANGING OUT WITH YOU AND YEAH, I THINK YOU SORT OF... GET MY PROBLEM... BUT THERE'S ALREADY SOMEONE ELSE I LIKE.... ....AT SCHOOL.
FAGGOT.
-SO.... WHO IS IT?
Gah!
-...YOU REALLY WANT TO KNOW?
-...I ASKED YOU, DIDN'T I?
-OK.
A PREGNANT PAUSE.
-ERIC SWENSON.
scribble scribble draw.....

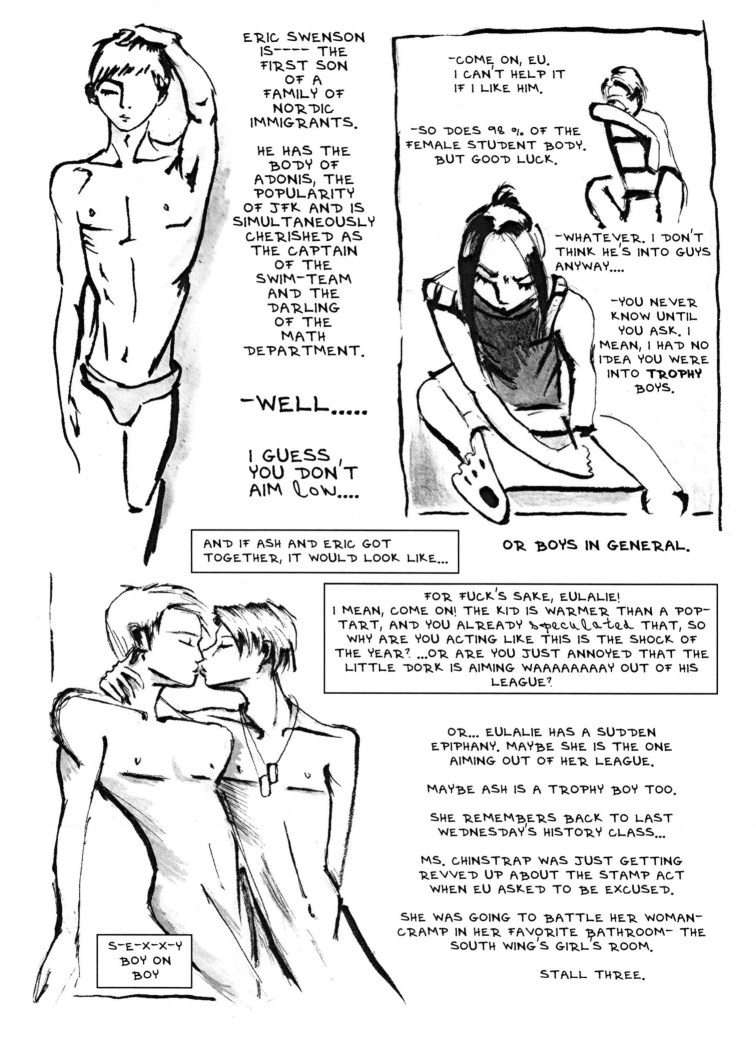

ERIC SWENSON IS---- THE FIRST SON OF A FAMILY OF NORDIC IMMIGRANTS.

HE HAS THE BODY OF ADONIS, THE POPULARITY OF JFK AND IS SIMULTANEOUSLY CHERISHED AS THE CAPTAIN OF THE SWIM-TEAM AND THE DARLING OF THE MATH DEPARTMENT.

-WELL.....

I GUESS, YOU DON'T AIM Low....

-COME ON, EU. I CAN'T HELP IT IF I LIKE HIM.

-SO DOES 98% OF THE FEMALE STUDENT BODY. BUT GOOD LUCK.

-WHATEVER. I DON'T THINK HE'S INTO GUYS ANYWAY....

-YOU NEVER KNOW UNTIL YOU ASK. I MEAN, I HAD NO IDEA YOU WERE INTO TROPHY BOYS.

AND IF ASH AND ERIC GOT TOGETHER, IT WOULD LOOK LIKE...

OR BOYS IN GENERAL.

FOR FUCK'S SAKE, EULALIE! I MEAN, COME ON! THE KID IS WARMER THAN A POP-TART, AND YOU ALREADY speculated THAT, SO WHY ARE YOU ACTING LIKE THIS IS THE SHOCK OF THE YEAR? ...OR ARE YOU JUST ANNOYED THAT THE LITTLE DORK IS AIMING WAAAAAAAAY OUT OF HIS LEAGUE?

OR... EULALIE HAS A SUDDEN EPIPHANY. MAYBE SHE IS THE ONE AIMING OUT OF HER LEAGUE.

MAYBE ASH IS A TROPHY BOY TOO.

SHE REMEMBERS BACK TO LAST WEDNESDAY'S HISTORY CLASS...

MS. CHINSTRAP WAS JUST GETTING REVVED UP ABOUT THE STAMP ACT WHEN EU ASKED TO BE EXCUSED.

SHE WAS GOING TO BATTLE HER WOMAN-CRAMP IN HER FAVORITE BATHROOM- THE SOUTH WING'S GIRL'S ROOM.

STALL THREE.

S-E-X-X-Y BOY ON BOY

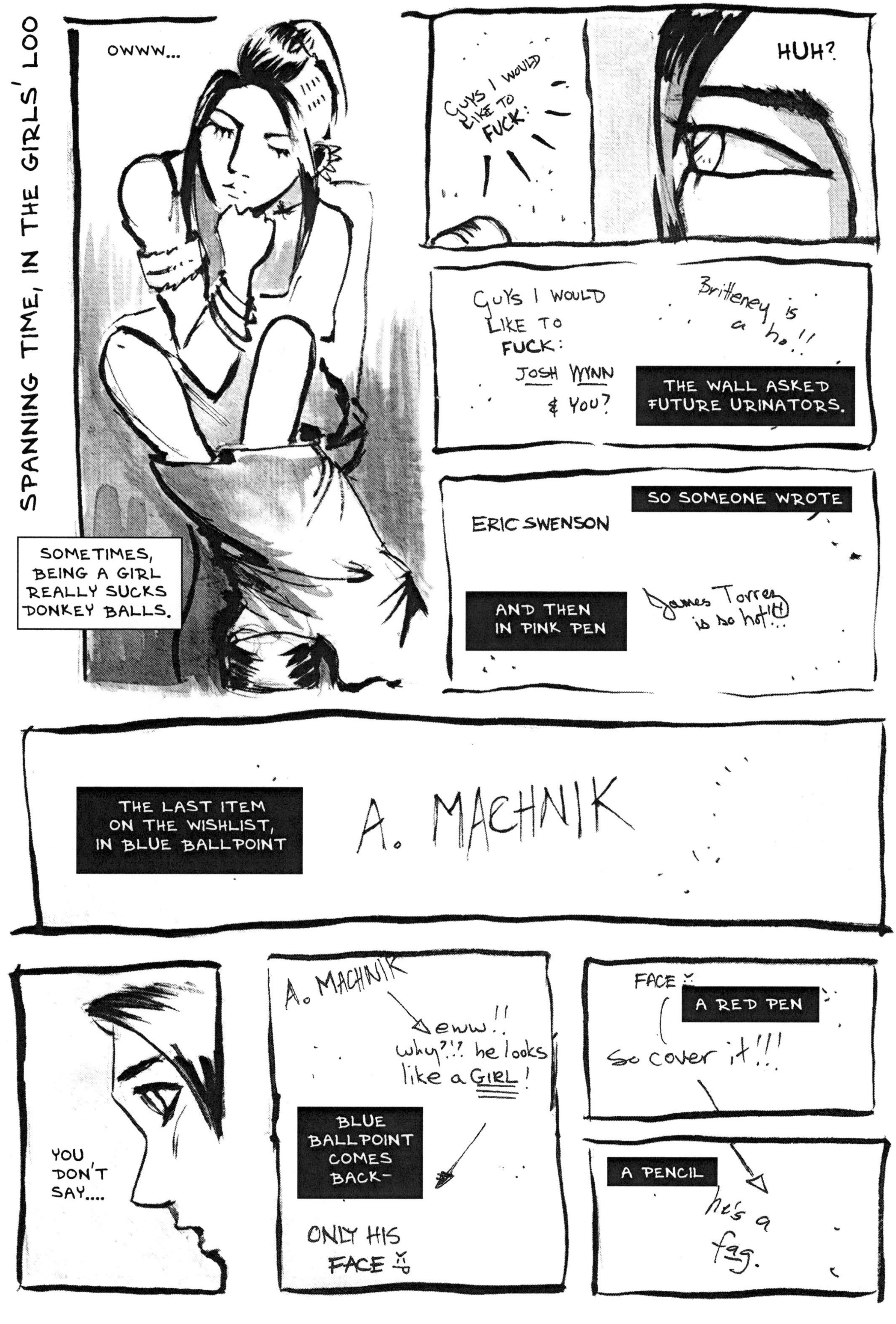
SPANNING TIME, IN THE GIRLS' LOO
OWWW...
SOMETIMES, BEING A GIRL REALLY SUCKS DONKEY BALLS.
GUYS I WOULD LIKE TO FUCK:
HUH?
GUYS I WOULD LIKE TO FUCK:
JOSH WYNN
& YOU?
Britteney is a ho!!
THE WALL ASKED FUTURE URINATORS.
SO SOMEONE WROTE
ERIC SWENSON
AND THEN IN PINK PEN
James Torres is so hot!!...
THE LAST ITEM ON THE WISHLIST, IN BLUE BALLPOINT
A. MACHNIK
YOU DON'T SAY....
A. MACHNIK
eww!! why?!? he looks like a GIRL!
BLUE BALLPOINT COMES BACK-
ONLY HIS FACE
FACE
A RED PEN
So cover it!!!
A PENCIL
he's a fag.

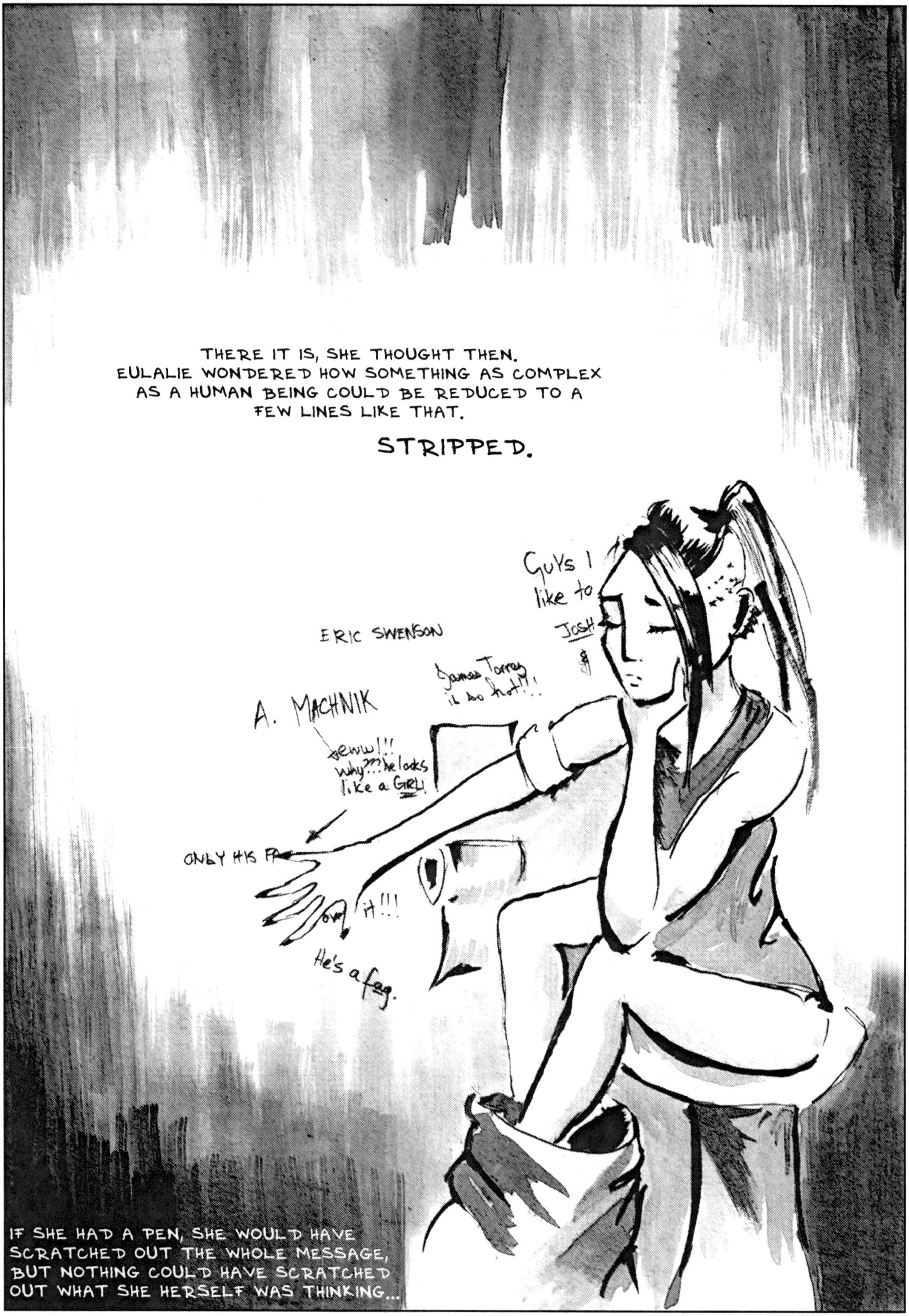
THERE IT IS, SHE THOUGHT THEN.
EULALIE WONDERED HOW SOMETHING AS COMPLEX AS A HUMAN BEING COULD BE REDUCED TO A FEW LINES LIKE THAT.
STRIPPED.
Guys I like to
JOSH
&
ERIC SWENSON
James Torrey is so hot!!!
A. MACHNIK
eww!!! why??? he looks like a GIRL!
ONLY HIS FA
it!!!
He's a fag.
IF SHE HAD A PEN, SHE WOULD HAVE SCRATCHED OUT THE WHOLE MESSAGE, BUT NOTHING COULD HAVE SCRATCHED OUT WHAT SHE HERSELF WAS THINKING...

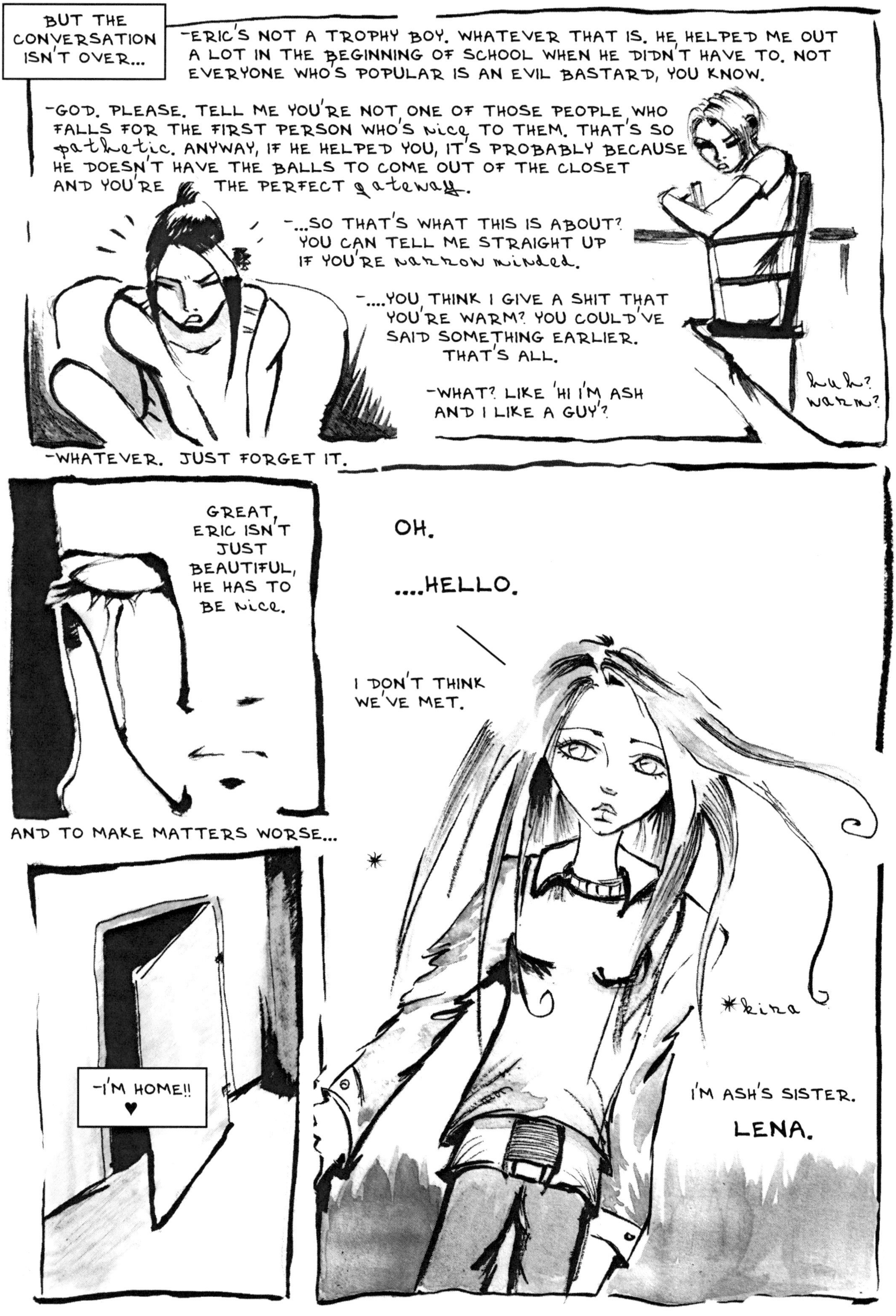

BUT THE CONVERSATION ISN'T OVER...
-ERIC'S NOT A TROPHY BOY. WHATEVER THAT IS. HE HELPED ME OUT A LOT IN THE BEGINNING OF SCHOOL WHEN HE DIDN'T HAVE TO. NOT EVERYONE WHO'S POPULAR IS AN EVIL BASTARD, YOU KNOW.
-GOD. PLEASE. TELL ME YOU'RE NOT ONE OF THOSE PEOPLE WHO FALLS FOR THE FIRST PERSON WHO'S nice TO THEM. THAT'S SO pathetic. ANYWAY, IF HE HELPED YOU, IT'S PROBABLY BECAUSE HE DOESN'T HAVE THE BALLS TO COME OUT OF THE CLOSET AND YOU'RE THE PERFECT gateway.
-...SO THAT'S WHAT THIS IS ABOUT? YOU CAN TELL ME STRAIGHT UP IF YOU'RE narrow minded.
-....YOU THINK I GIVE A SHIT THAT YOU'RE WARM? YOU COULD'VE SAID SOMETHING EARLIER. THAT'S ALL.
-WHAT? LIKE 'HI I'M ASH AND I LIKE A GUY'?
huh? warm?
-WHATEVER. JUST FORGET IT.
GREAT, ERIC ISN'T JUST BEAUTIFUL, HE HAS TO BE nice.
AND TO MAKE MATTERS WORSE...
-I'M HOME!! ♥
OH.
....HELLO.
I DON'T THINK WE'VE MET.
I'M ASH'S SISTER.
LENA.
*kira

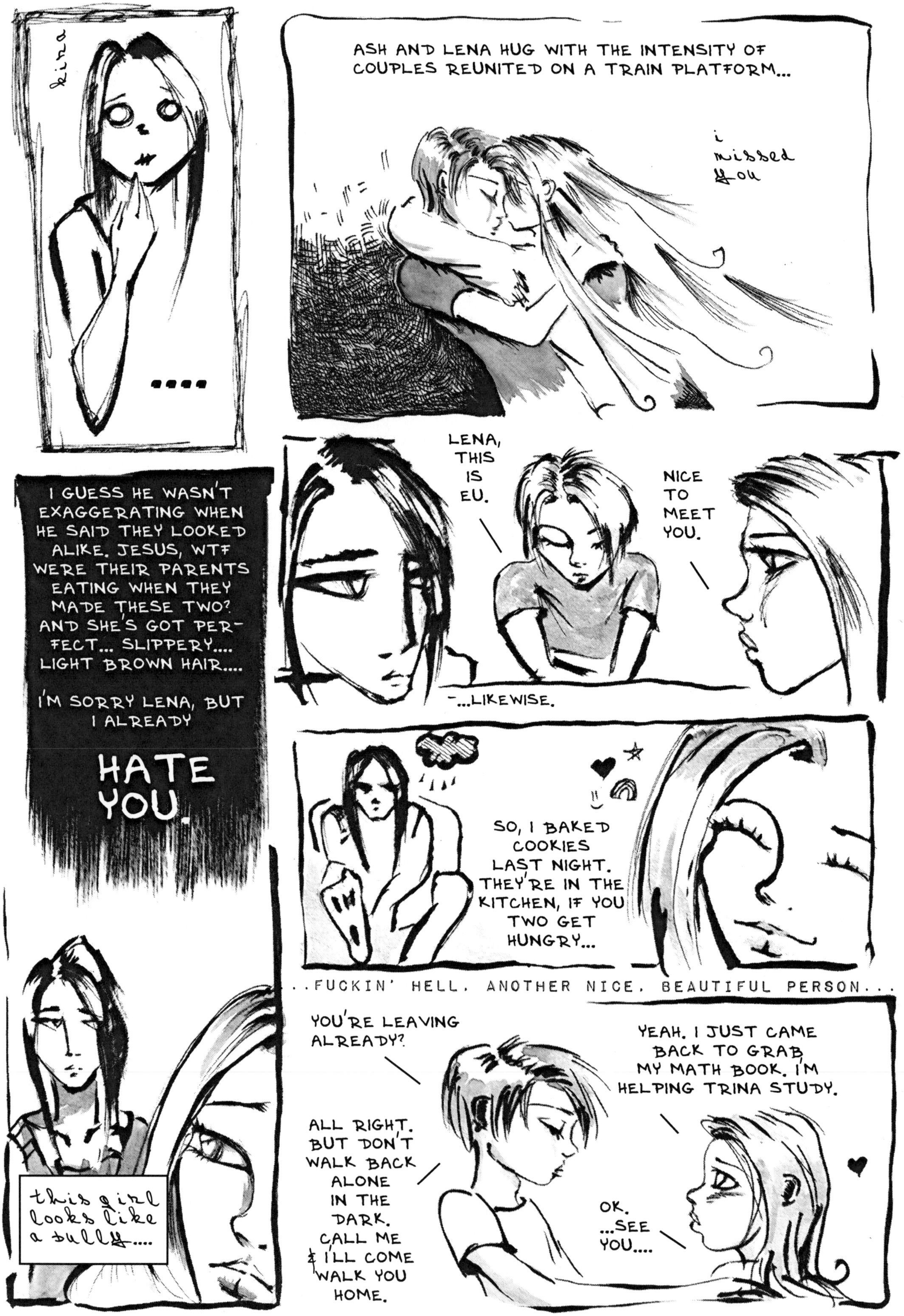
kina
....
ASH AND LENA HUG WITH THE INTENSITY OF COUPLES REUNITED ON A TRAIN PLATFORM...
i missed you
I GUESS HE WASN'T EXAGGERATING WHEN HE SAID THEY LOOKED ALIKE. JESUS, WTF WERE THEIR PARENTS EATING WHEN THEY MADE THESE TWO? AND SHE'S GOT PER-FECT... SLIPPERY.... LIGHT BROWN HAIR....
I'M SORRY LENA, BUT I ALREADY
HATE YOU.
LENA, THIS IS EU.
NICE TO MEET YOU.
-...LIKEWISE.
SO, I BAKED COOKIES LAST NIGHT. THEY'RE IN THE KITCHEN, IF YOU TWO GET HUNGRY...
this girl looks like a bully....
..FUCKIN' HELL. ANOTHER NICE, BEAUTIFUL PERSON...
YOU'RE LEAVING ALREADY?
YEAH. I JUST CAME BACK TO GRAB MY MATH BOOK. I'M HELPING TRINA STUDY.
ALL RIGHT. BUT DON'T WALK BACK ALONE IN THE DARK. CALL ME & I'LL COME WALK YOU HOME.
OK. ...SEE YOU....

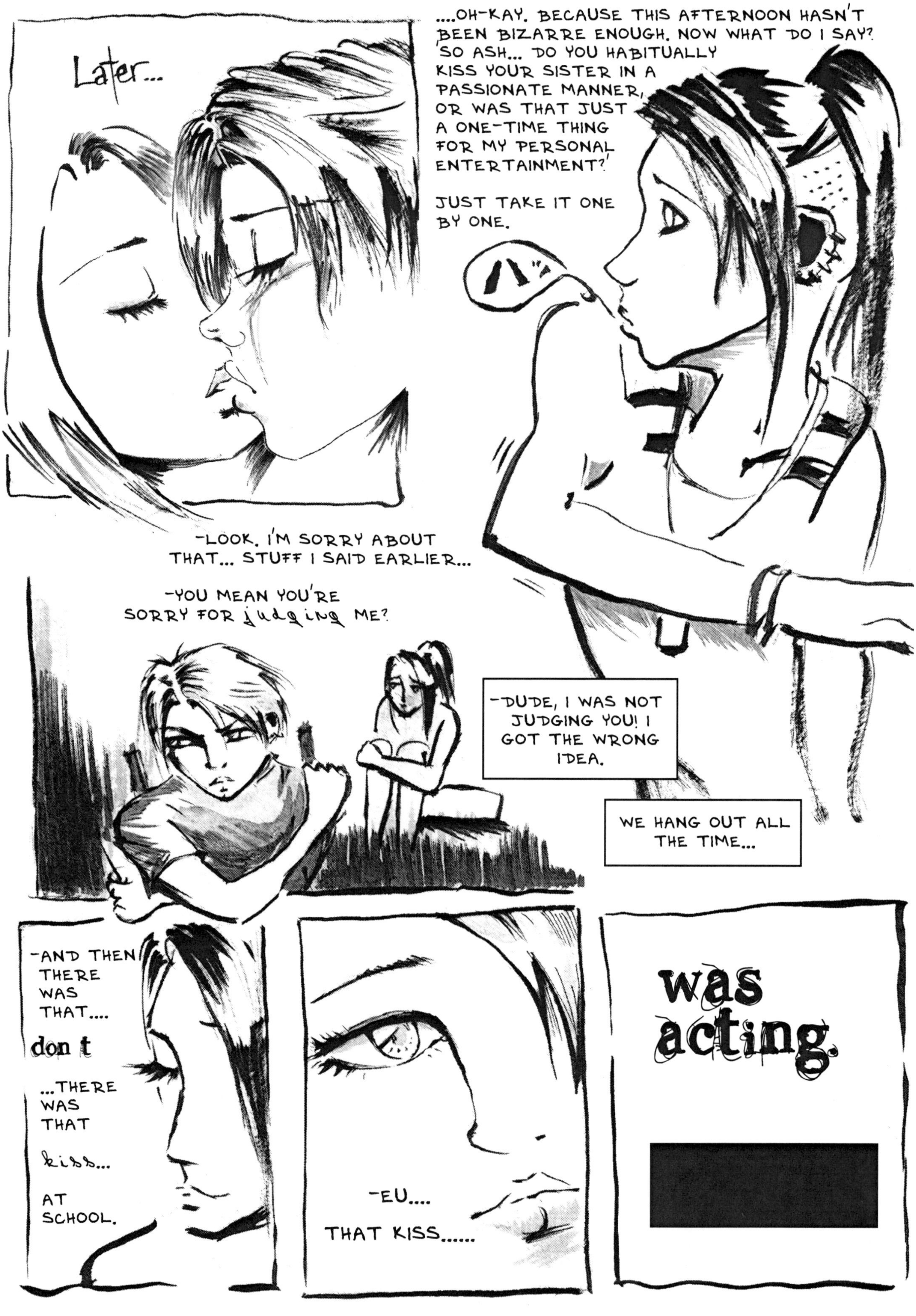

Later...
....OH-KAY. BECAUSE THIS AFTERNOON HASN'T BEEN BIZARRE ENOUGH. NOW WHAT DO I SAY? 'SO ASH... DO YOU HABITUALLY KISS YOUR SISTER IN A PASSIONATE MANNER, OR WAS THAT JUST A ONE-TIME THING FOR MY PERSONAL ENTERTAINMENT?'
JUST TAKE IT ONE BY ONE.
-LOOK. I'M SORRY ABOUT THAT... STUFF I SAID EARLIER...
-YOU MEAN YOU'RE SORRY FOR judging ME?
-DUDE, I WAS NOT JUDGING YOU! I GOT THE WRONG IDEA.
WE HANG OUT ALL THE TIME...
-AND THEN THERE WAS THAT....
don t
...THERE WAS THAT
kiss...
AT SCHOOL.
-EU....
THAT KISS......
was acting.
[redacted]

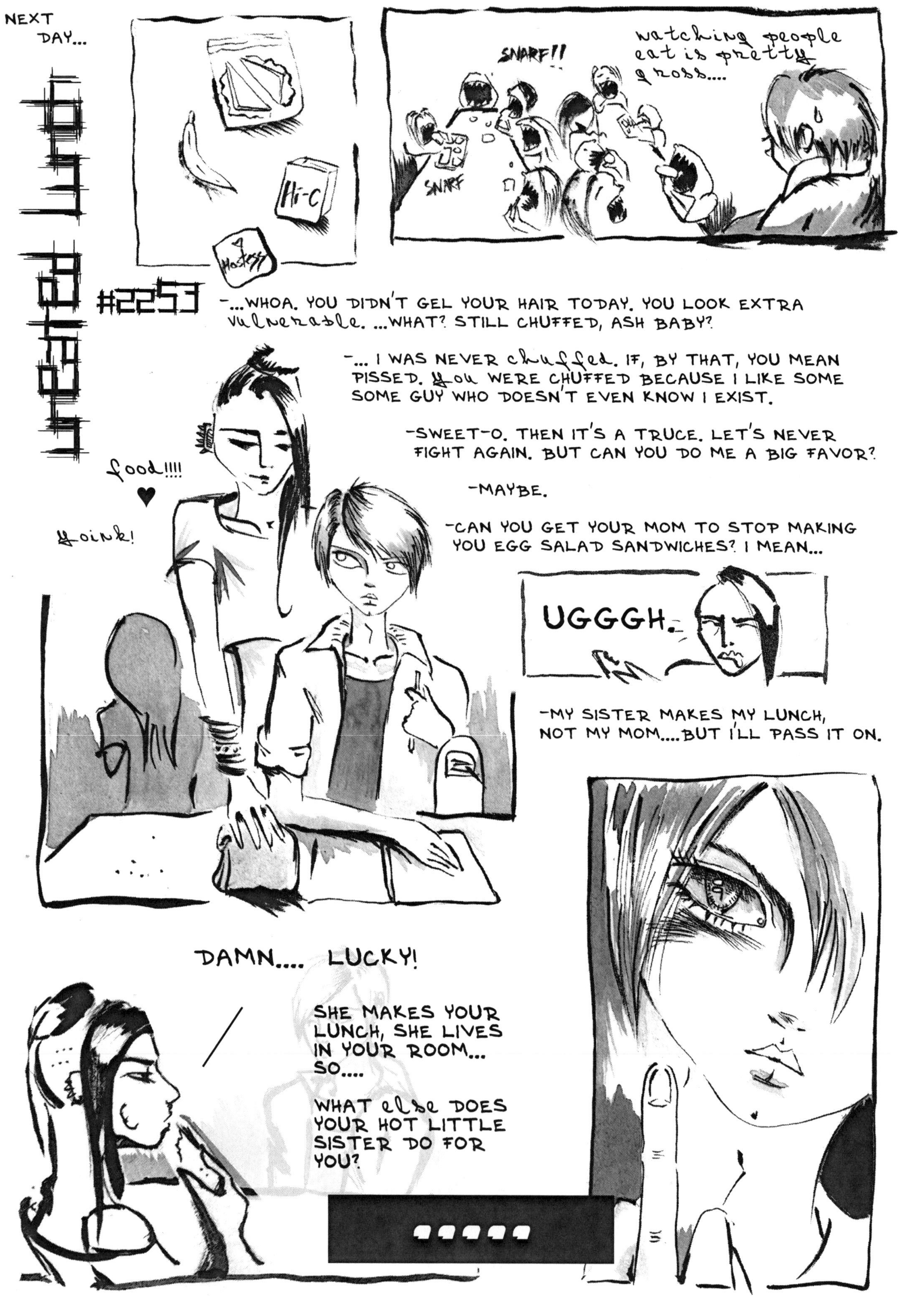
NEXT DAY...
Hi-C
Hostess
SNARF!!
SNARF
watching people eat is pretty gross....
#2253
-...WHOA. YOU DIDN'T GEL YOUR HAIR TODAY. YOU LOOK EXTRA vulnerable. ...WHAT? STILL CHUFFED, ASH BABY?
-... I WAS NEVER chuffed. IF, BY THAT, YOU MEAN PISSED. You WERE CHUFFED BECAUSE I LIKE SOME SOME GUY WHO DOESN'T EVEN KNOW I EXIST.
-SWEET-O. THEN IT'S A TRUCE. LET'S NEVER FIGHT AGAIN. BUT CAN YOU DO ME A BIG FAVOR?
-MAYBE.
-CAN YOU GET YOUR MOM TO STOP MAKING YOU EGG SALAD SANDWICHES? I MEAN...
food!!!!
Yoink!
UGGGH.
-MY SISTER MAKES MY LUNCH, NOT MY MOM....BUT I'LL PASS IT ON.
DAMN.... LUCKY!
SHE MAKES YOUR LUNCH, SHE LIVES IN YOUR ROOM... SO....
WHAT else DOES YOUR HOT LITTLE SISTER DO FOR YOU?
.....

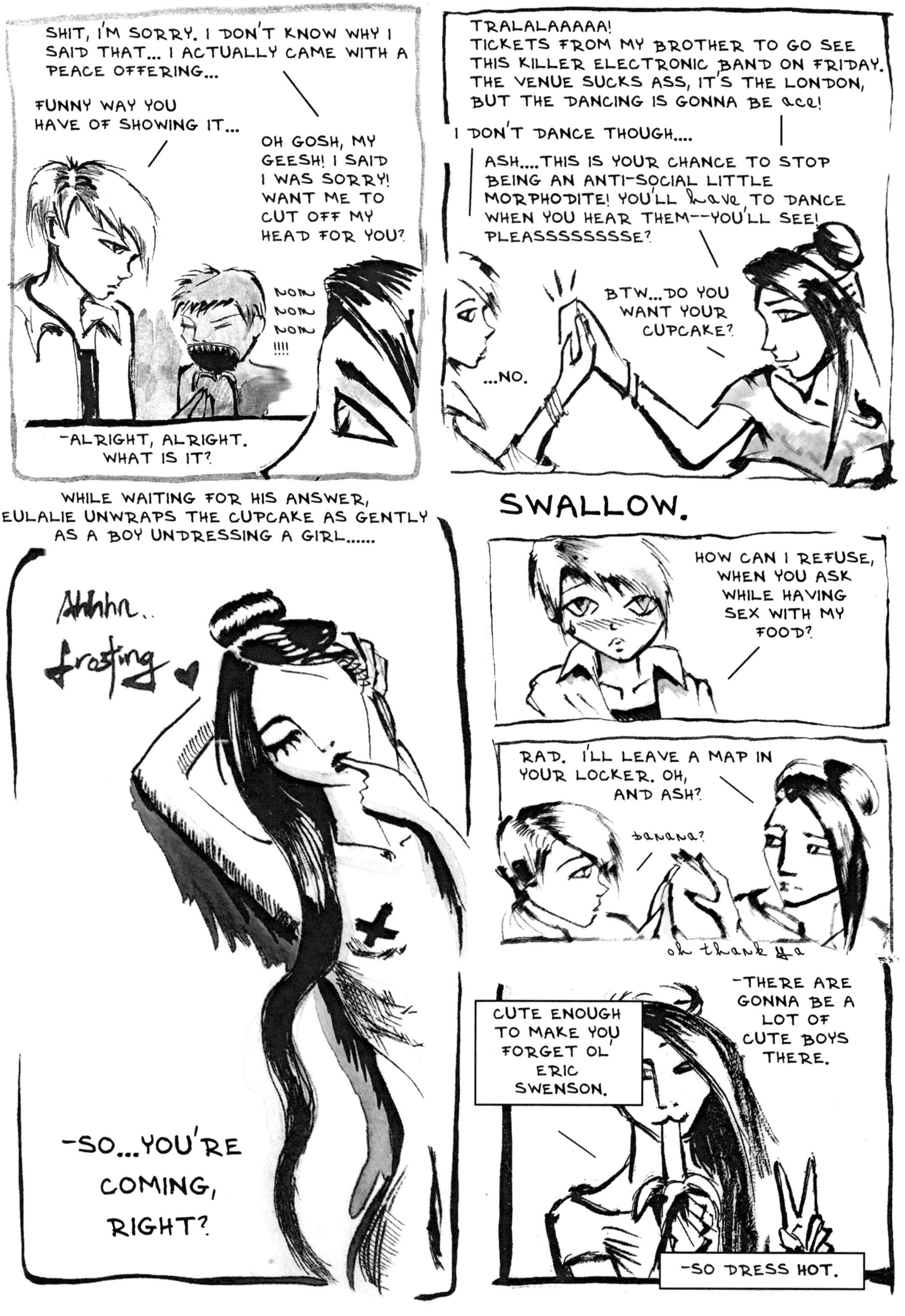
SHIT, I'M SORRY. I DON'T KNOW WHY I SAID THAT... I ACTUALLY CAME WITH A PEACE OFFERING...
FUNNY WAY YOU HAVE OF SHOWING IT...
OH GOSH, MY GEESH! I SAID I WAS SORRY! WANT ME TO CUT OFF MY HEAD FOR YOU?
NOM NOM NOM !!!!
-ALRIGHT, ALRIGHT. WHAT IS IT?
TRALALAAAAA! TICKETS FROM MY BROTHER TO GO SEE THIS KILLER ELECTRONIC BAND ON FRIDAY. THE VENUE SUCKS ASS, IT'S THE LONDON, BUT THE DANCING IS GONNA BE ace!
I DON'T DANCE THOUGH....
ASH....THIS IS YOUR CHANCE TO STOP BEING AN ANTI-SOCIAL LITTLE MORPHODITE! YOU'LL have TO DANCE WHEN YOU HEAR THEM--YOU'LL SEE! PLEASSSSSSSSE?
BTW...DO YOU WANT YOUR CUPCAKE?
...NO.
WHILE WAITING FOR HIS ANSWER, EULALIE UNWRAPS THE CUPCAKE AS GENTLY AS A BOY UNDRESSING A GIRL......
Ahhhn.. frosting ♥
-SO...YOU'RE COMING, RIGHT?
SWALLOW.
HOW CAN I REFUSE, WHEN YOU ASK WHILE HAVING SEX WITH MY FOOD?
RAD. I'LL LEAVE A MAP IN YOUR LOCKER. OH, AND ASH?
banana?
oh thank ya
-THERE ARE GONNA BE A LOT OF CUTE BOYS THERE.
CUTE ENOUGH TO MAKE YOU FORGET OL' ERIC SWENSON.
-SO DRESS HOT.

Take Me Out 1.

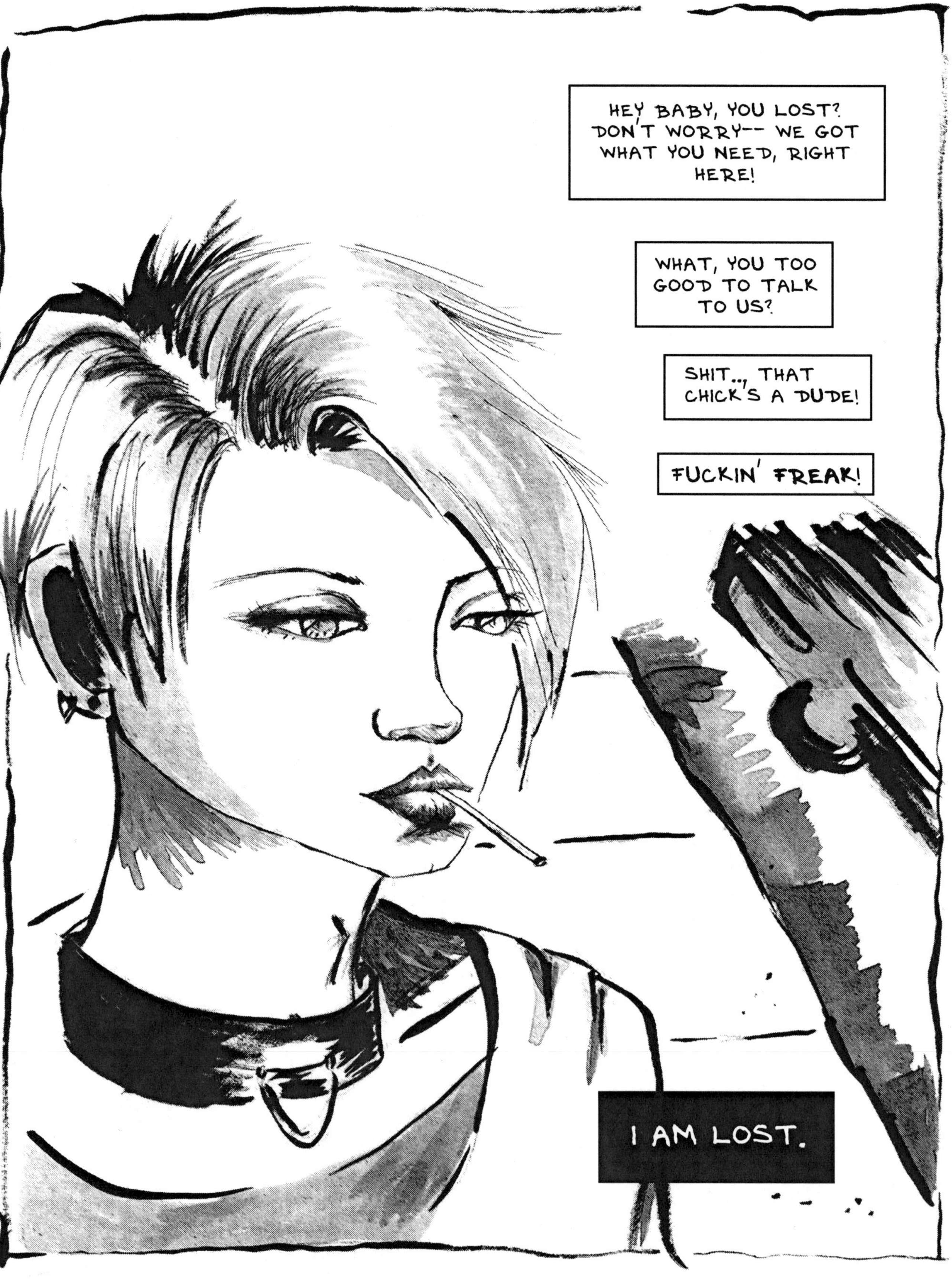
HEY BABY, YOU LOST? DON'T WORRY-- WE GOT WHAT YOU NEED, RIGHT HERE!
WHAT, YOU TOO GOOD TO TALK TO US?
SHIT.., THAT CHICK'S A DUDE!
FUCKIN' FREAK!
I AM LOST.

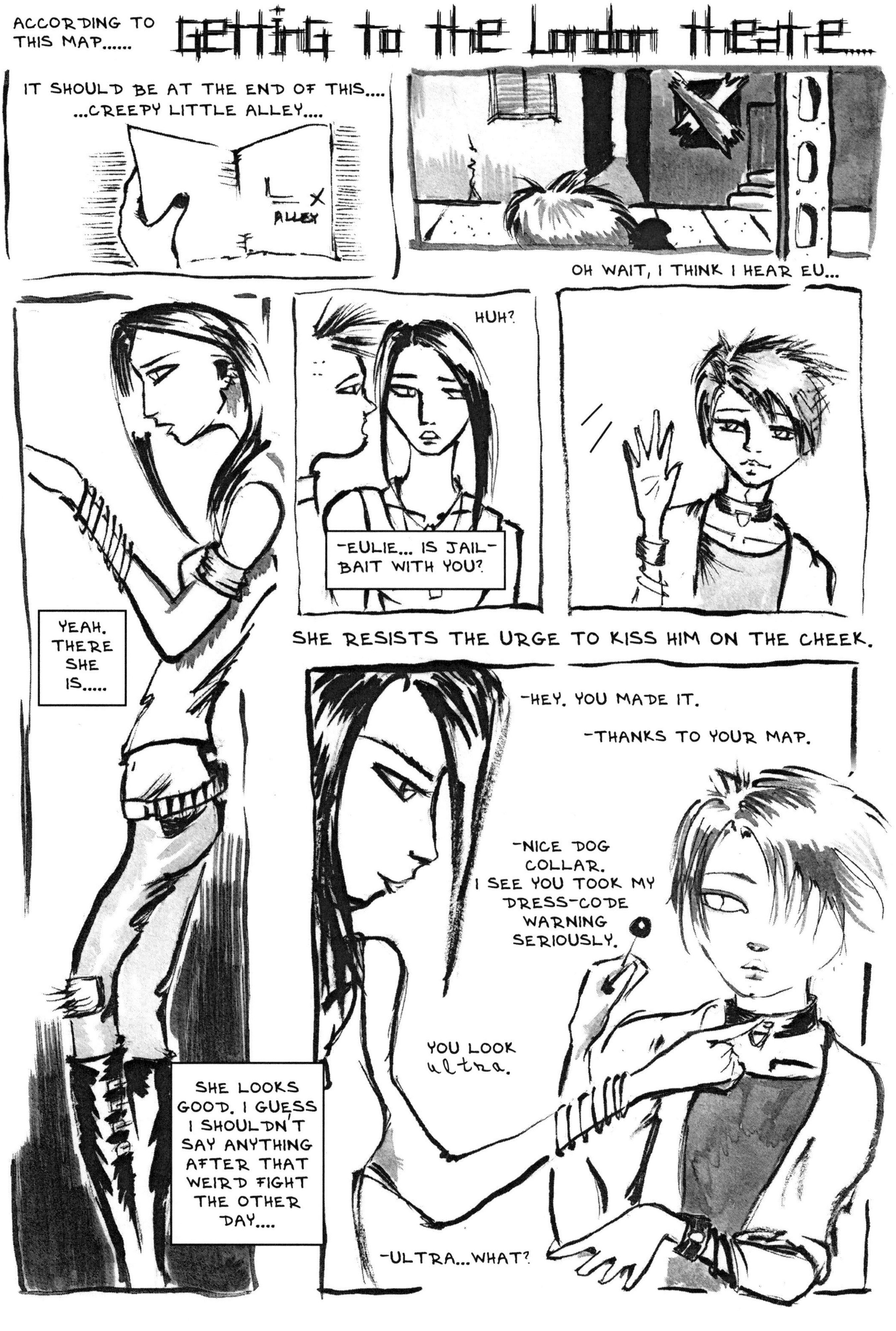
ACCORDING TO THIS MAP......
GETTING TO THE LONDON THEATRE....
IT SHOULD BE AT THE END OF THIS.... ...CREEPY LITTLE ALLEY....
ALLEY
OH WAIT, I THINK I HEAR EU...
YEAH. THERE SHE IS.....
HUH?
-EULIE... IS JAIL-BAIT WITH YOU?
SHE RESISTS THE URGE TO KISS HIM ON THE CHEEK.
-HEY. YOU MADE IT.
-THANKS TO YOUR MAP.
-NICE DOG COLLAR. I SEE YOU TOOK MY DRESS-CODE WARNING SERIOUSLY.
YOU LOOK ultra.
SHE LOOKS GOOD. I GUESS I SHOULDN'T SAY ANYTHING AFTER THAT WEIRD FIGHT THE OTHER DAY....
-ULTRA...WHAT?

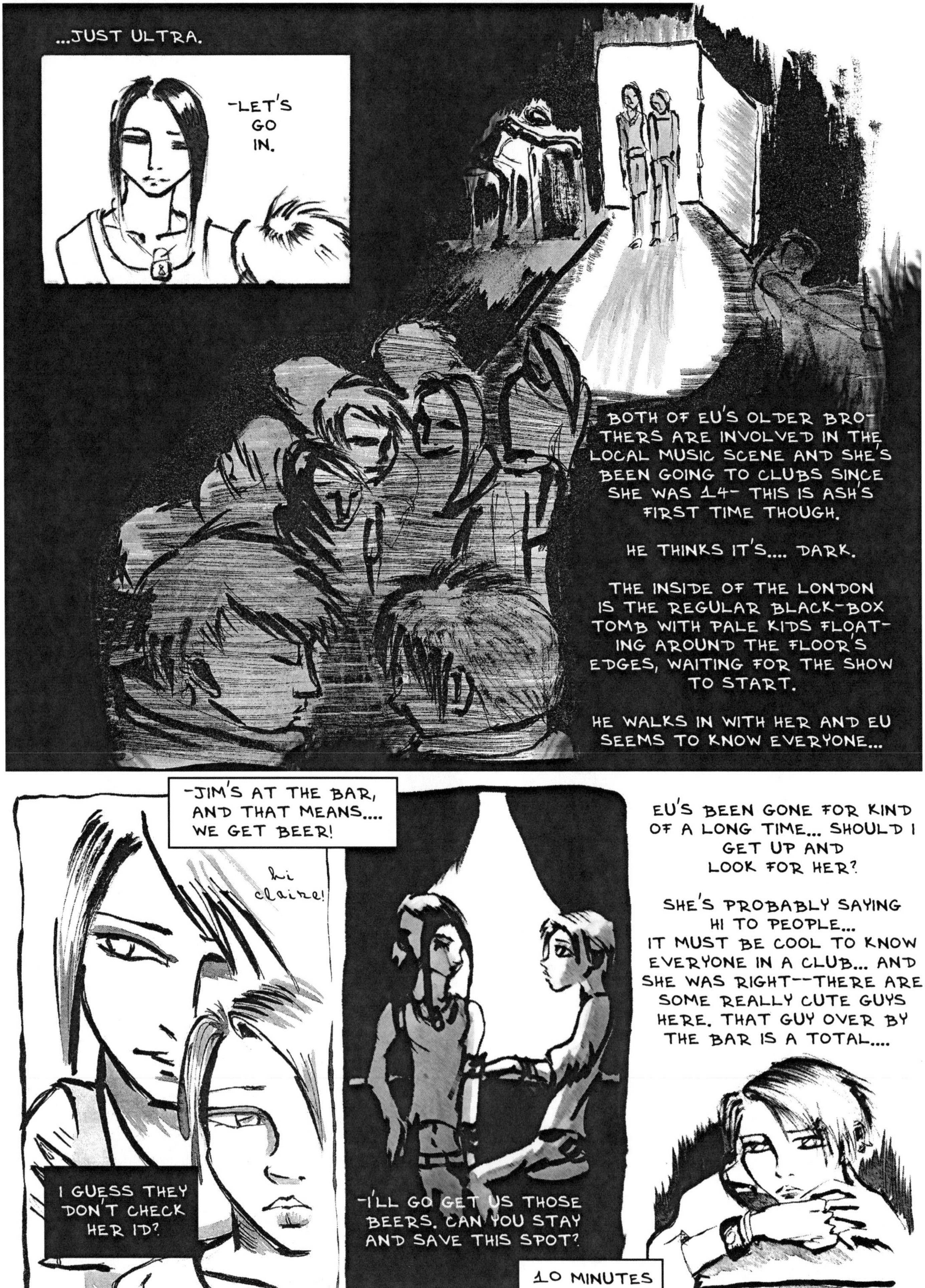
...JUST ULTRA.
-LET'S GO IN.
BOTH OF EU'S OLDER BROTHERS ARE INVOLVED IN THE LOCAL MUSIC SCENE AND SHE'S BEEN GOING TO CLUBS SINCE SHE WAS 14- THIS IS ASH'S FIRST TIME THOUGH.
HE THINKS IT'S.... DARK.
THE INSIDE OF THE LONDON IS THE REGULAR BLACK-BOX TOMB WITH PALE KIDS FLOATING AROUND THE FLOOR'S EDGES, WAITING FOR THE SHOW TO START.
HE WALKS IN WITH HER AND EU SEEMS TO KNOW EVERYONE...
-JIM'S AT THE BAR, AND THAT MEANS.... WE GET BEER!
hi claire!
I GUESS THEY DON'T CHECK HER ID?
-I'LL GO GET US THOSE BEERS. CAN YOU STAY AND SAVE THIS SPOT?
-SURE.
10 MINUTES LATER
EU'S BEEN GONE FOR KIND OF A LONG TIME... SHOULD I GET UP AND LOOK FOR HER?
SHE'S PROBABLY SAYING HI TO PEOPLE... IT MUST BE COOL TO KNOW EVERYONE IN A CLUB... AND SHE WAS RIGHT--THERE ARE SOME REALLY CUTE GUYS HERE. THAT GUY OVER BY THE BAR IS A TOTAL....

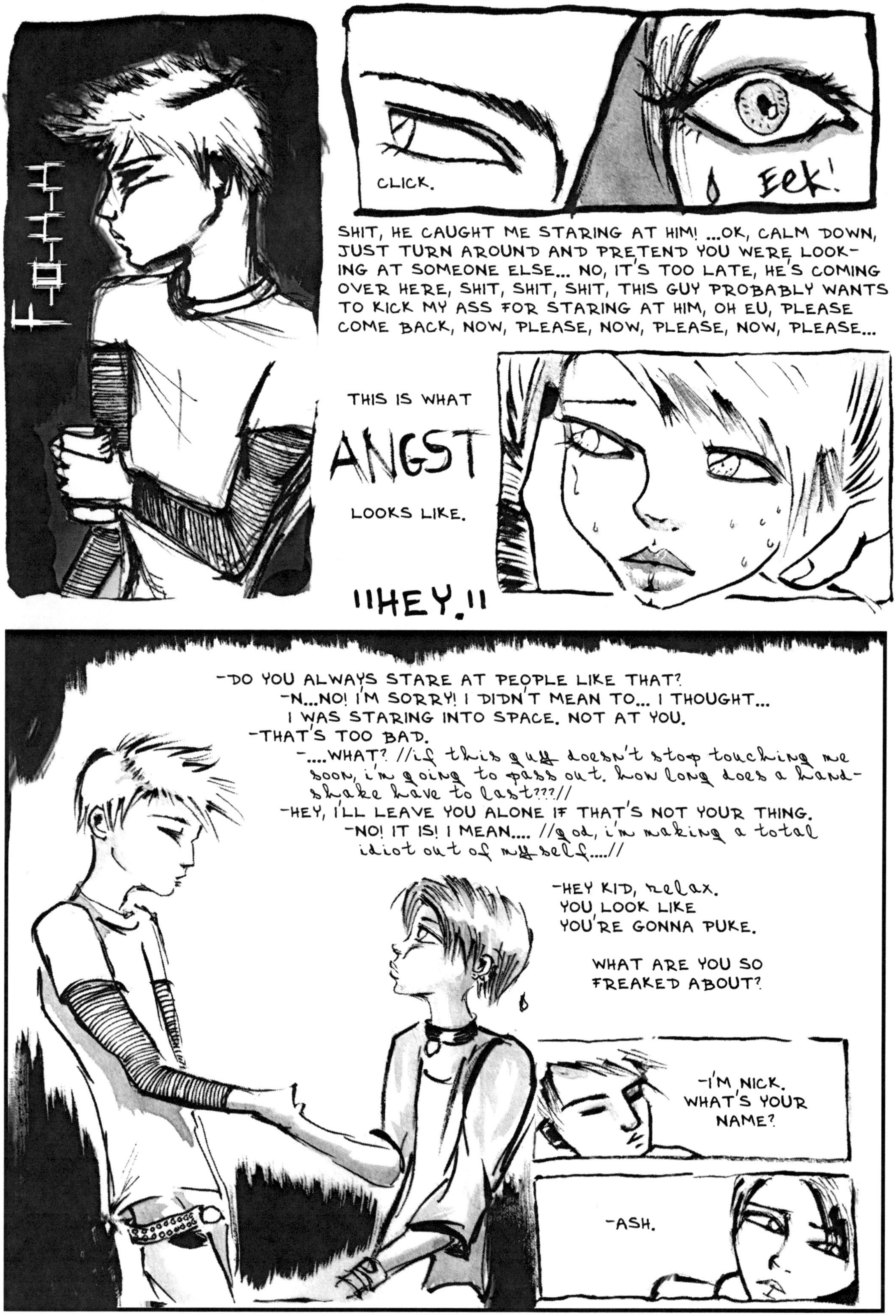
CLICK.
EEK!
SHIT, HE CAUGHT ME STARING AT HIM! ...OK, CALM DOWN, JUST TURN AROUND AND PRETEND YOU WERE LOOKING AT SOMEONE ELSE... NO, IT'S TOO LATE, HE'S COMING OVER HERE, SHIT, SHIT, SHIT, THIS GUY PROBABLY WANTS TO KICK MY ASS FOR STARING AT HIM, OH EU, PLEASE COME BACK, NOW, PLEASE, NOW, PLEASE, NOW, PLEASE...
THIS IS WHAT
ANGST
LOOKS LIKE.
¡¡HEY!!
-DO YOU ALWAYS STARE AT PEOPLE LIKE THAT?
-N...NO! I'M SORRY! I DIDN'T MEAN TO... I THOUGHT... I WAS STARING INTO SPACE. NOT AT YOU.
-THAT'S TOO BAD.
-....WHAT? //if this guy doesn't stop touching me soon, i'm going to pass out. how long does a handshake have to last???//
-HEY, I'LL LEAVE YOU ALONE IF THAT'S NOT YOUR THING.
-NO! IT IS! I MEAN.... //god, i'm making a total idiot out of myself....//
-HEY KID, relax. YOU LOOK LIKE YOU'RE GONNA PUKE.
WHAT ARE YOU SO FREAKED ABOUT?
-I'M NICK. WHAT'S YOUR NAME?
-ASH.

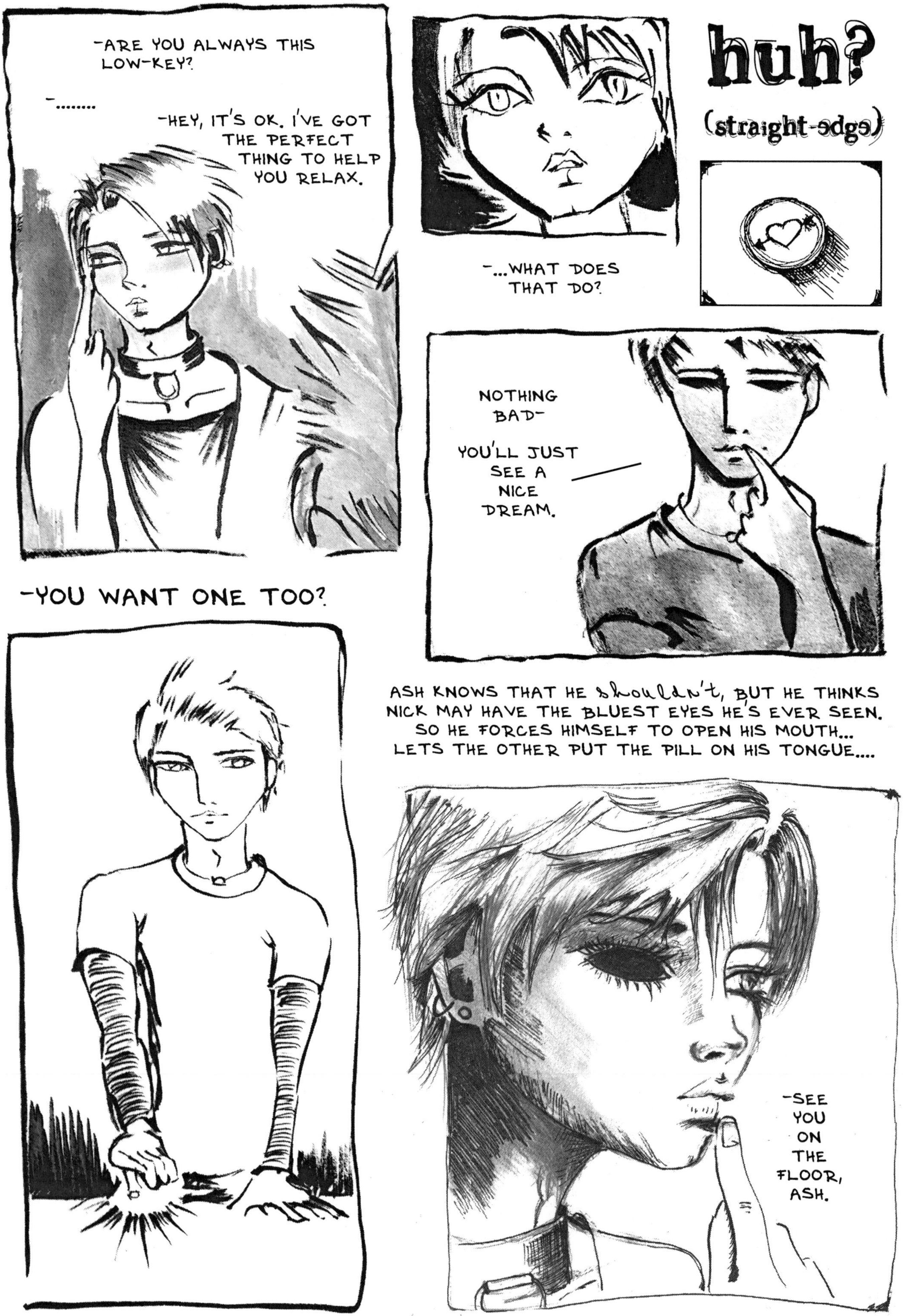
huh?
(straight-edge)
-ARE YOU ALWAYS THIS LOW-KEY?
-........
-HEY, IT'S OK. I'VE GOT THE PERFECT THING TO HELP YOU RELAX.
-...WHAT DOES THAT DO?
NOTHING BAD-
YOU'LL JUST SEE A NICE DREAM.
-YOU WANT ONE TOO?
ASH KNOWS THAT HE shouldn't, BUT HE THINKS NICK MAY HAVE THE BLUEST EYES HE'S EVER SEEN. SO HE FORCES HIMSELF TO OPEN HIS MOUTH... LETS THE OTHER PUT THE PILL ON HIS TONGUE....
-SEE YOU ON THE FLOOR, ASH.

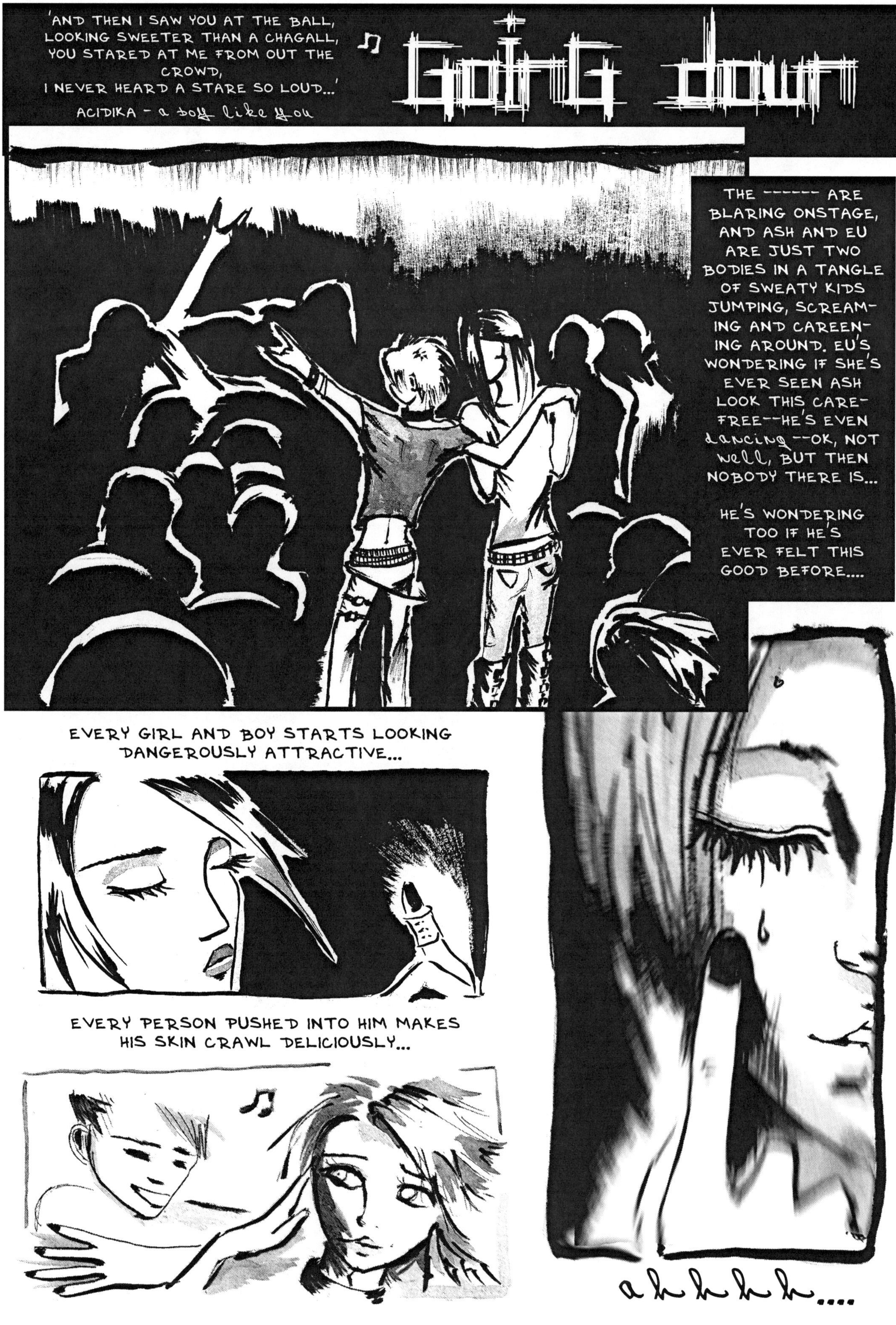
'AND THEN I SAW YOU AT THE BALL,
LOOKING SWEETER THAN A CHAGALL,
YOU STARED AT ME FROM OUT THE CROWD,
I NEVER HEARD A STARE SO LOUD...'
ACIDIKA - a boy like you
Going down
THE ------ ARE BLARING ONSTAGE, AND ASH AND EU ARE JUST TWO BODIES IN A TANGLE OF SWEATY KIDS JUMPING, SCREAMING AND CAREENING AROUND. EU'S WONDERING IF SHE'S EVER SEEN ASH LOOK THIS CAREFREE--HE'S EVEN dancing--OK, NOT well, BUT THEN NOBODY THERE IS...
HE'S WONDERING TOO IF HE'S EVER FELT THIS GOOD BEFORE....
EVERY GIRL AND BOY STARTS LOOKING DANGEROUSLY ATTRACTIVE...
EVERY PERSON PUSHED INTO HIM MAKES HIS SKIN CRAWL DELICIOUSLY...
ahhhhh....

//AHHHH.... I FEEL SO GOOD, IT'S SO hot IN HERE, THIS IS SUCH A GOOD SHOW, EU IS SO pretty, I JUST WANNA touch HER ALL OVER AND HAVE HER TOUCH ME--WHY NOT? AHH, HER SKIN IS soft, LIKE A fluffy bath towel, I SHOULD TELL HER, THESE LIGHTS ARE SO hot.//

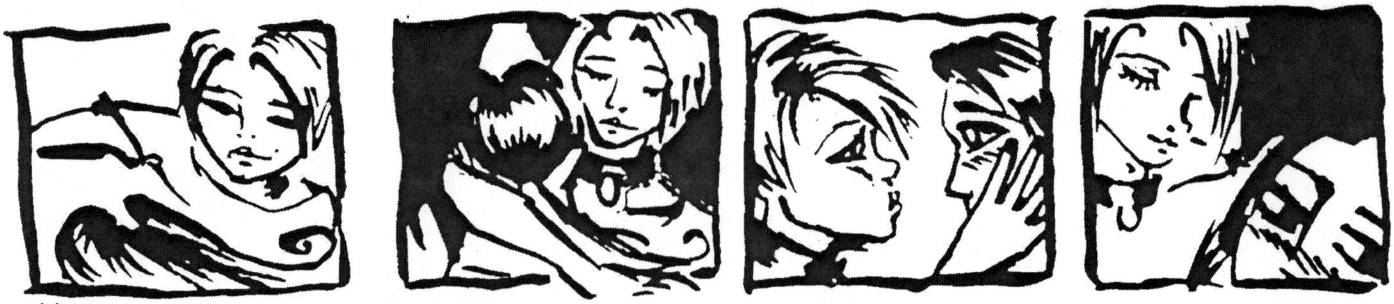

//OK, SO WHAT THE HELL IS GOING ON? WHY IS HE ACTING ALL CUTE AND TOUCHY? HE CANNOT BE THIS DRUNK AFTER...WAIT, I DRANK HIS BEER!!!!//

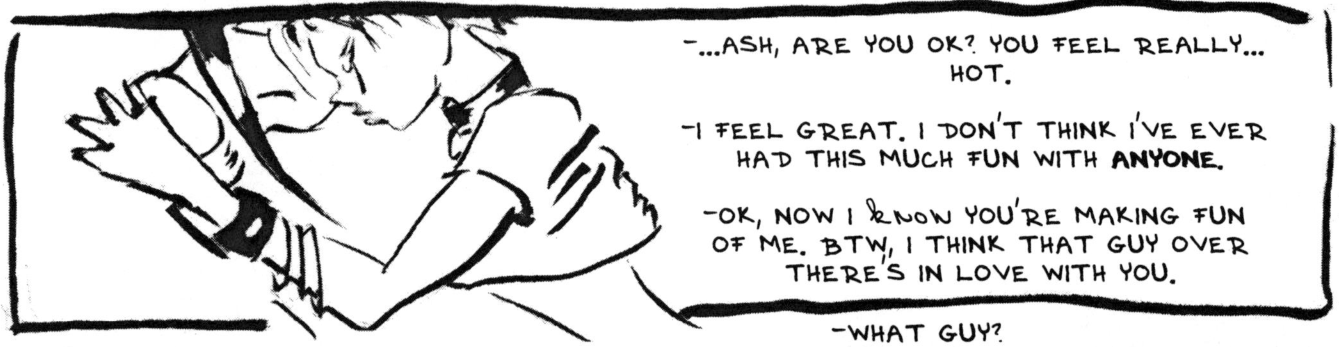
-...ASH, ARE YOU OK? YOU FEEL REALLY... HOT.
-I FEEL GREAT. I DON'T THINK I'VE EVER HAD THIS MUCH FUN WITH **ANYONE**.
-OK, NOW I know YOU'RE MAKING FUN OF ME. BTW, I THINK THAT GUY OVER THERE'S IN LOVE WITH YOU.

-WHAT GUY?

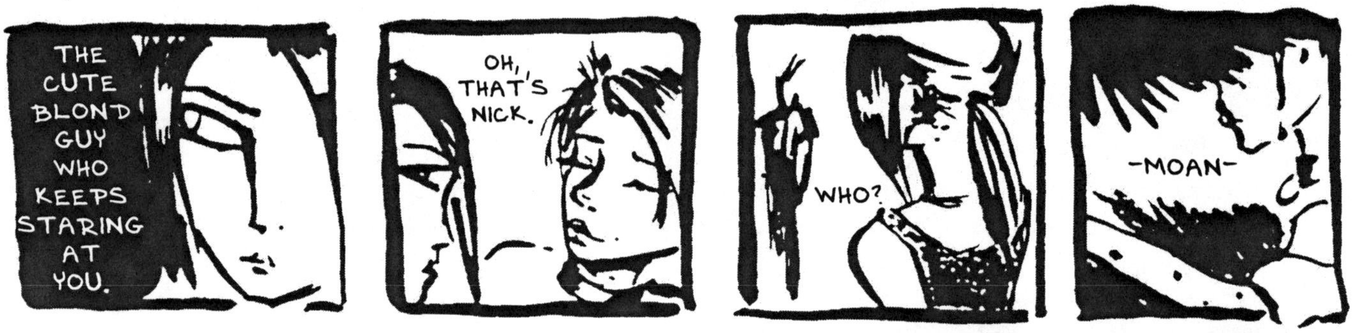
THE CUTE BLOND GUY WHO KEEPS STARING AT YOU.
OH, THAT'S NICK.
WHO?
-MOAN-

-DUDE, ARE YOU SURE YOU'RE OK? YOUR FACE IS REALLY RED.

ASH STARTS FEELING HIS OWN FACE, STRANGELY, AS IF HE'S NEVER FELT IT BEFORE.

-I GUESS SO. I GUESS YOU'RE RIGHT. MAYBE I SHOULD GO WASH IT IN THE BATHROOM.

-YEAH, THAT MIGHT BE A GOOD IDEA.

HE HEADS OFF TOWARDS THE BATHROOMS, THEN SUDDENLY TURNS. GRABS HER HAND AND GENTLY KISSES THE BACK OF IT....

EU TENSES.

RIGHT THEN, SHE FEELS LIKE SHE COULD GET HIM TO DO MORE THAN THAT--

SHE COULD HUG HIM OR EVEN KISS HIM LIKE THEY DID ON STAGE THAT ONE TIME, BUT SOMETHING ABOUT HIS STATE MAKES HER NOT WANT TO.

HE ASKS, WILL YOU BE OUT HERE WHEN I GET BACK?

AND SHE SAYS, SURE.

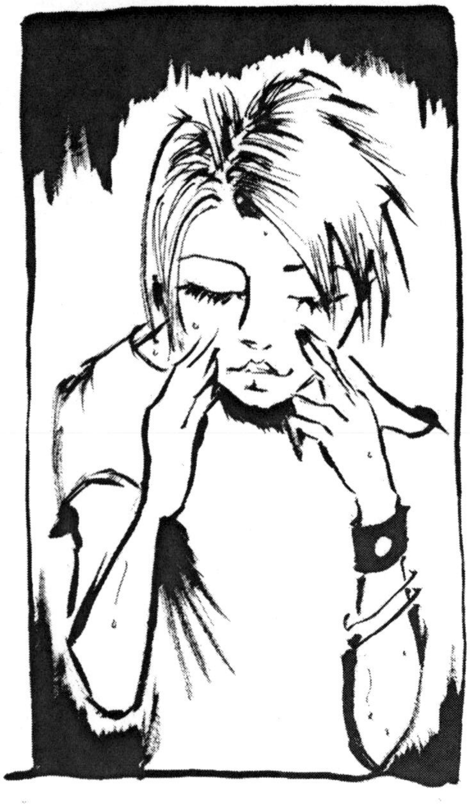

where else would i be?

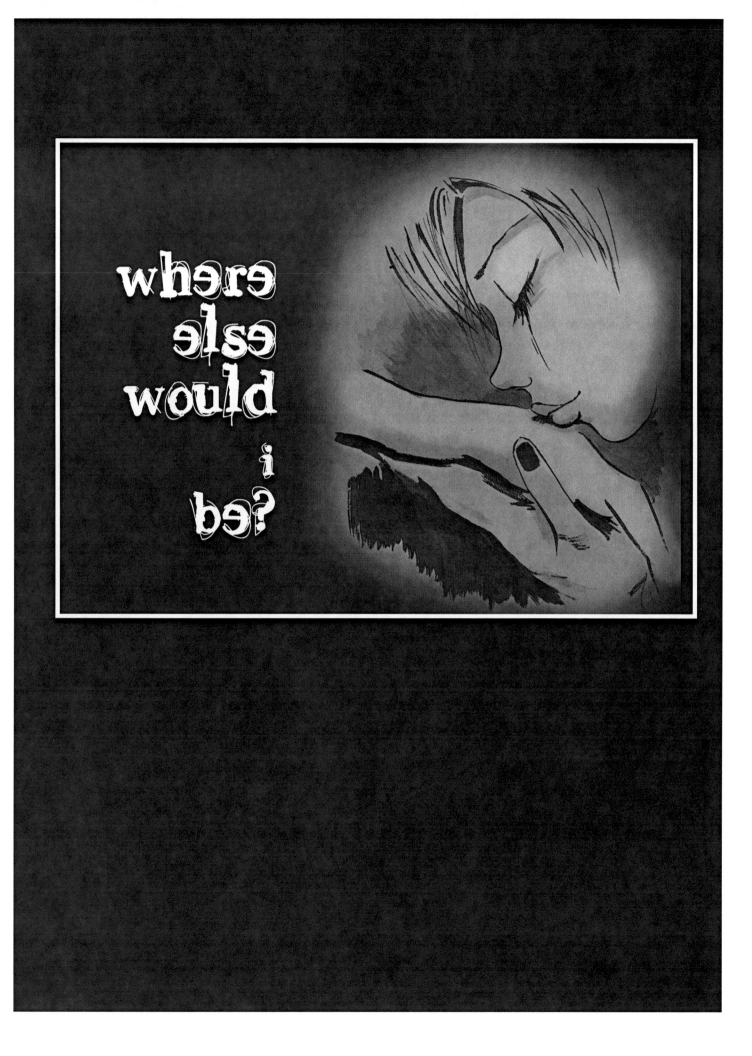

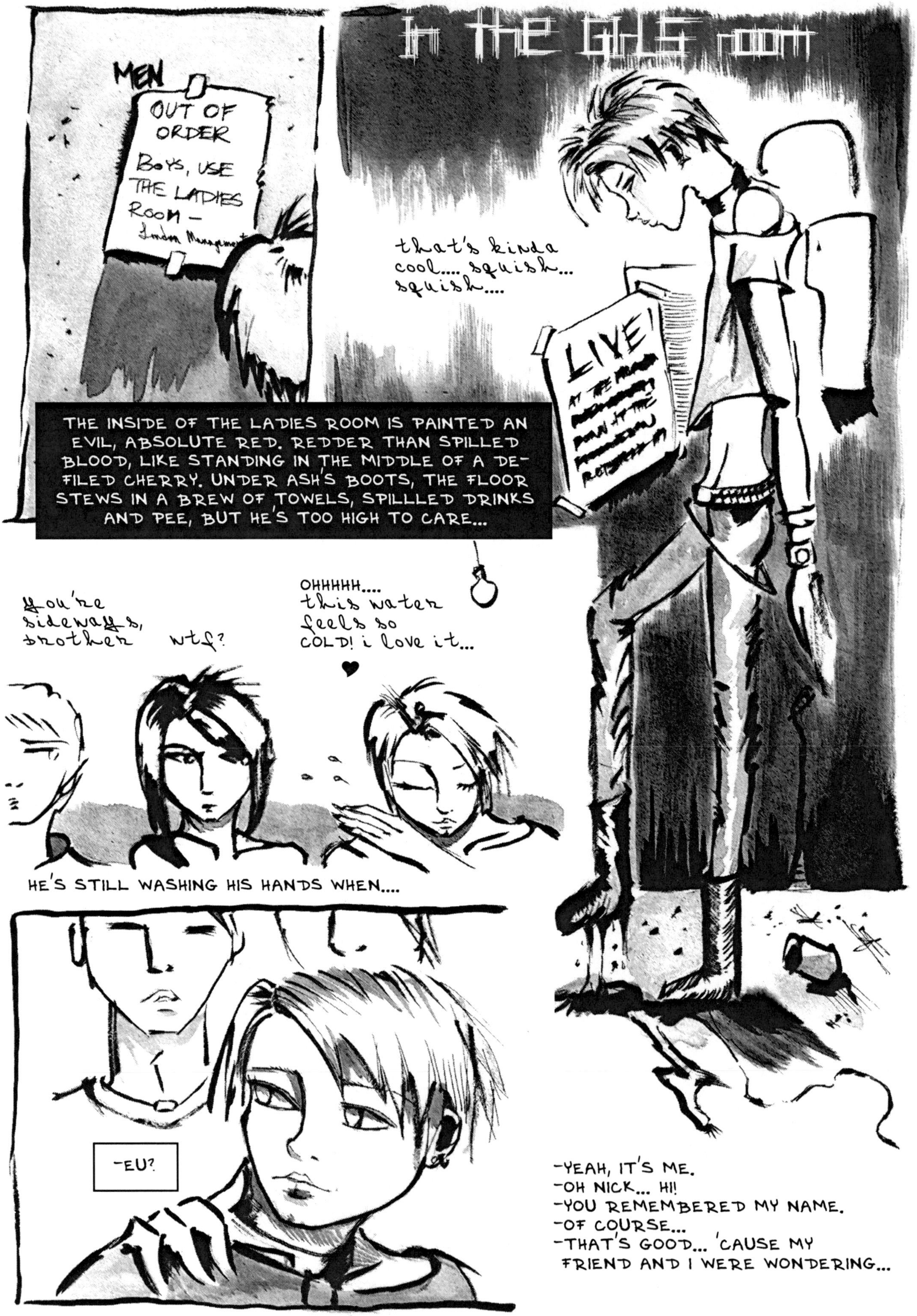
In the Girls room
MEN
OUT OF ORDER
Boys, USE THE LADIES Room –
that's kinda cool.... squish... squish....
LIVE
THE INSIDE OF THE LADIES ROOM IS PAINTED AN EVIL, ABSOLUTE RED. REDDER THAN SPILLED BLOOD, LIKE STANDING IN THE MIDDLE OF A DEFILED CHERRY. UNDER ASH'S BOOTS, THE FLOOR STEWS IN A BREW OF TOWELS, SPILLLED DRINKS AND PEE, BUT HE'S TOO HIGH TO CARE...
you're sideways, brother
wtf?
OHHHHH.... this water feels so COLD! i love it...
HE'S STILL WASHING HIS HANDS WHEN....
-EU?
-YEAH, IT'S ME.
-OH NICK... HI!
-YOU REMEMBERED MY NAME.
-OF COURSE...
-THAT'S GOOD... 'CAUSE MY FRIEND AND I WERE WONDERING...

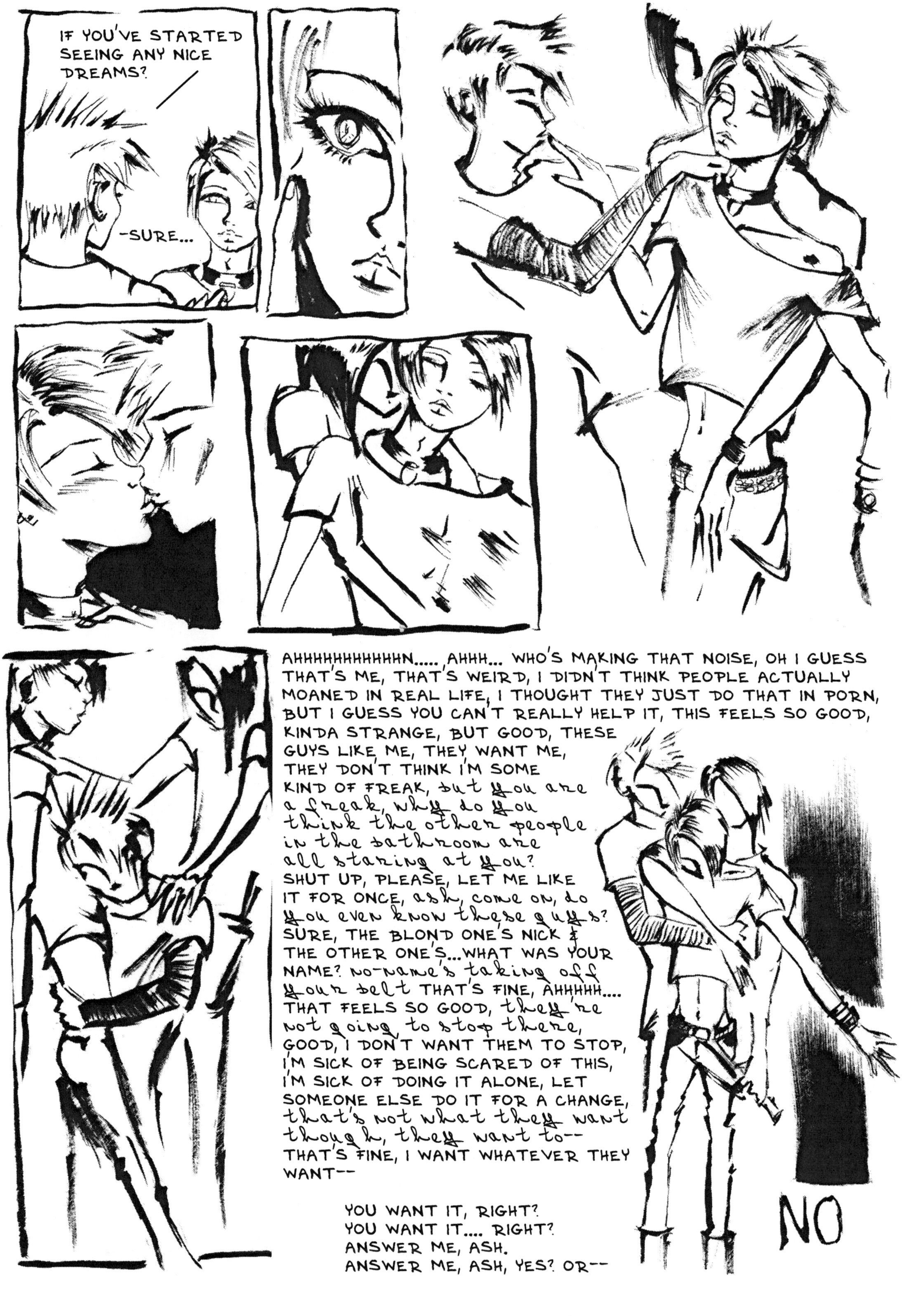
IF YOU'VE STARTED SEEING ANY NICE DREAMS?
-SURE...
AHHHHHHHHHHHHN..... AHHH... WHO'S MAKING THAT NOISE, OH I GUESS THAT'S ME, THAT'S WEIRD, I DIDN'T THINK PEOPLE ACTUALLY MOANED IN REAL LIFE, I THOUGHT THEY JUST DO THAT IN PORN, BUT I GUESS YOU CAN'T REALLY HELP IT, THIS FEELS SO GOOD, KINDA STRANGE, BUT GOOD, THESE GUYS LIKE ME, THEY WANT ME, THEY DON'T THINK I'M SOME KIND OF FREAK, but you are a freak, why do you think the other people in the bathroom are all staring at you? SHUT UP, PLEASE, LET ME LIKE IT FOR ONCE, ash, come on, do you even know these guys? SURE, THE BLOND ONE'S NICK & THE OTHER ONE'S...WHAT WAS YOUR NAME? no-name's taking off your belt THAT'S FINE, AHHHHH.... THAT FEELS SO GOOD, they're not going to stop there, GOOD, I DON'T WANT THEM TO STOP, I'M SICK OF BEING SCARED OF THIS, I'M SICK OF DOING IT ALONE, LET SOMEONE ELSE DO IT FOR A CHANGE, that's not what they want though, they want to-- THAT'S FINE, I WANT WHATEVER THEY WANT--
YOU WANT IT, RIGHT?
YOU WANT IT.... RIGHT?
ANSWER ME, ASH.
ANSWER ME, ASH, YES? OR--
NO

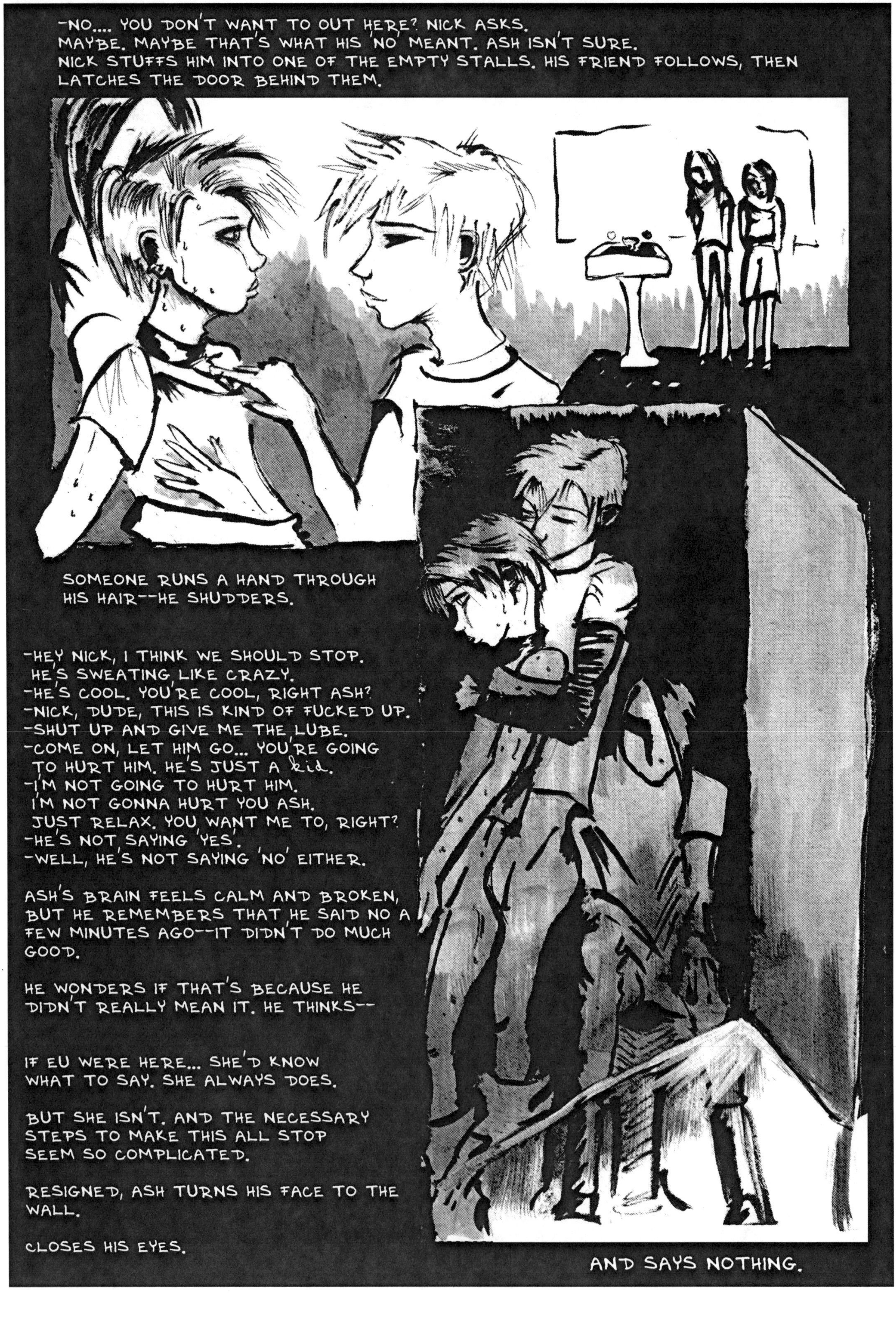
-NO.... YOU DON'T WANT TO OUT HERE? NICK ASKS.
MAYBE. MAYBE THAT'S WHAT HIS 'NO' MEANT. ASH ISN'T SURE.
NICK STUFFS HIM INTO ONE OF THE EMPTY STALLS. HIS FRIEND FOLLOWS, THEN LATCHES THE DOOR BEHIND THEM.
SOMEONE RUNS A HAND THROUGH HIS HAIR--HE SHUDDERS.
-HEY NICK, I THINK WE SHOULD STOP. HE'S SWEATING LIKE CRAZY.
-HE'S COOL. YOU'RE COOL, RIGHT ASH?
-NICK, DUDE, THIS IS KIND OF FUCKED UP.
-SHUT UP AND GIVE ME THE LUBE.
-COME ON, LET HIM GO... YOU'RE GOING TO HURT HIM. HE'S JUST A kid.
-I'M NOT GOING TO HURT HIM. I'M NOT GONNA HURT YOU ASH. JUST RELAX. YOU WANT ME TO, RIGHT?
-HE'S NOT SAYING 'YES'.
-WELL, HE'S NOT SAYING 'NO' EITHER.
ASH'S BRAIN FEELS CALM AND BROKEN, BUT HE REMEMBERS THAT HE SAID NO A FEW MINUTES AGO--IT DIDN'T DO MUCH GOOD.
HE WONDERS IF THAT'S BECAUSE HE DIDN'T REALLY MEAN IT. HE THINKS--
IF EU WERE HERE... SHE'D KNOW WHAT TO SAY. SHE ALWAYS DOES.
BUT SHE ISN'T. AND THE NECESSARY STEPS TO MAKE THIS ALL STOP SEEM SO COMPLICATED.
RESIGNED, ASH TURNS HIS FACE TO THE WALL.
CLOSES HIS EYES.
AND SAYS NOTHING.

WHEN IT HAPPENS, HE WONDERS IF
HE'S EVER FELT SUCH PAIN IN HIS LIFE.

so... this is what sex feels like...
NO... this cannot be it....

—RELAX, KID. IT DOESN'T HURT IF YOU
RELAX.

SOMEONE IN THE STALL TO THE RIGHT
FLUSHES AND LEAVES. SOMEONE IN THE
STALL TO THE LEFT IS TAKING A DUMP.

NICK GROANS AND TUGS THE RING OF HIS
DOG COLLAR HARD--ASH COUGHS, AND THE
OTHER GUY SEEMS TO PITY HIM, SO HE TURNS
HIS BODY SLIGHTLY TOWARDS HIM
AND STARTS TO...

—SO FOR OUR NEXT SONG, WE'RE GONNA DO
A COVER OF 'MAD WORLD'...

HE TRIES TO FOCUS ON THE MUSIC AND
IT'S WHEN HIS MIND TURNS COMPLETELY
OFF THAT HIS BODY TURNS
AGAINST HIM...

ASH GRIPS THE TOILET PAPER DISPENSER
HARDER. ALL HE CAN DO IS PRETEND IT'S
NOT HAPPENING.

—FUCK, KID, YOU COULD'VE WARNED ME!
DAMN, THAT IS A lot....!!
—HAHA, I TOLD YOU HE WANTED IT.

—NICK, CAN YOU HURRY UP? I WANT TO
CATCH AT LEAST THE END OF THIS SONG.
—ALL RIGHT!...
I'M ALMOST.... AHHH.....

THE EXTRACTION HURTS ABOUT AS MUCH
AS THE INSERTION--

—HEY. DON'T LOOK SO DOWN.
YOU WERE GREAT.

SEE
YA.

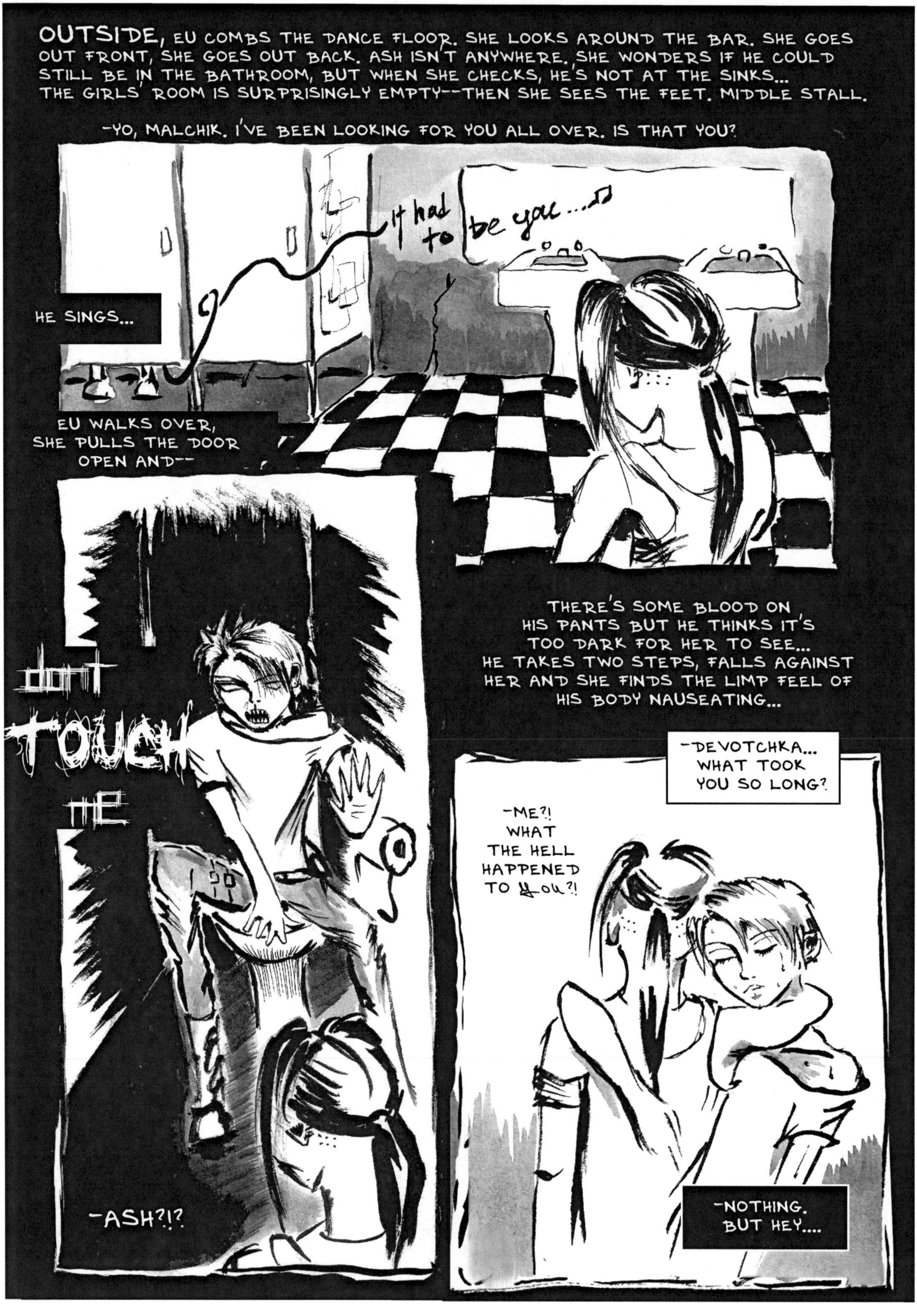
OUTSIDE, EU COMBS THE DANCE FLOOR. SHE LOOKS AROUND THE BAR. SHE GOES OUT FRONT, SHE GOES OUT BACK. ASH ISN'T ANYWHERE. SHE WONDERS IF HE COULD STILL BE IN THE BATHROOM, BUT WHEN SHE CHECKS, HE'S NOT AT THE SINKS... THE GIRLS' ROOM IS SURPRISINGLY EMPTY--THEN SHE SEES THE FEET. MIDDLE STALL.
-YO, MALCHIK. I'VE BEEN LOOKING FOR YOU ALL OVER. IS THAT YOU?
HE SINGS...
it had to be you...
EU WALKS OVER, SHE PULLS THE DOOR OPEN AND--
don't TOUCH me
-ASH?!?
THERE'S SOME BLOOD ON HIS PANTS BUT HE THINKS IT'S TOO DARK FOR HER TO SEE... HE TAKES TWO STEPS, FALLS AGAINST HER AND SHE FINDS THE LIMP FEEL OF HIS BODY NAUSEATING...
-DEVOTCHKA... WHAT TOOK YOU SO LONG?
-ME?! WHAT THE HELL HAPPENED TO YOU?!
-NOTHING. BUT HEY....

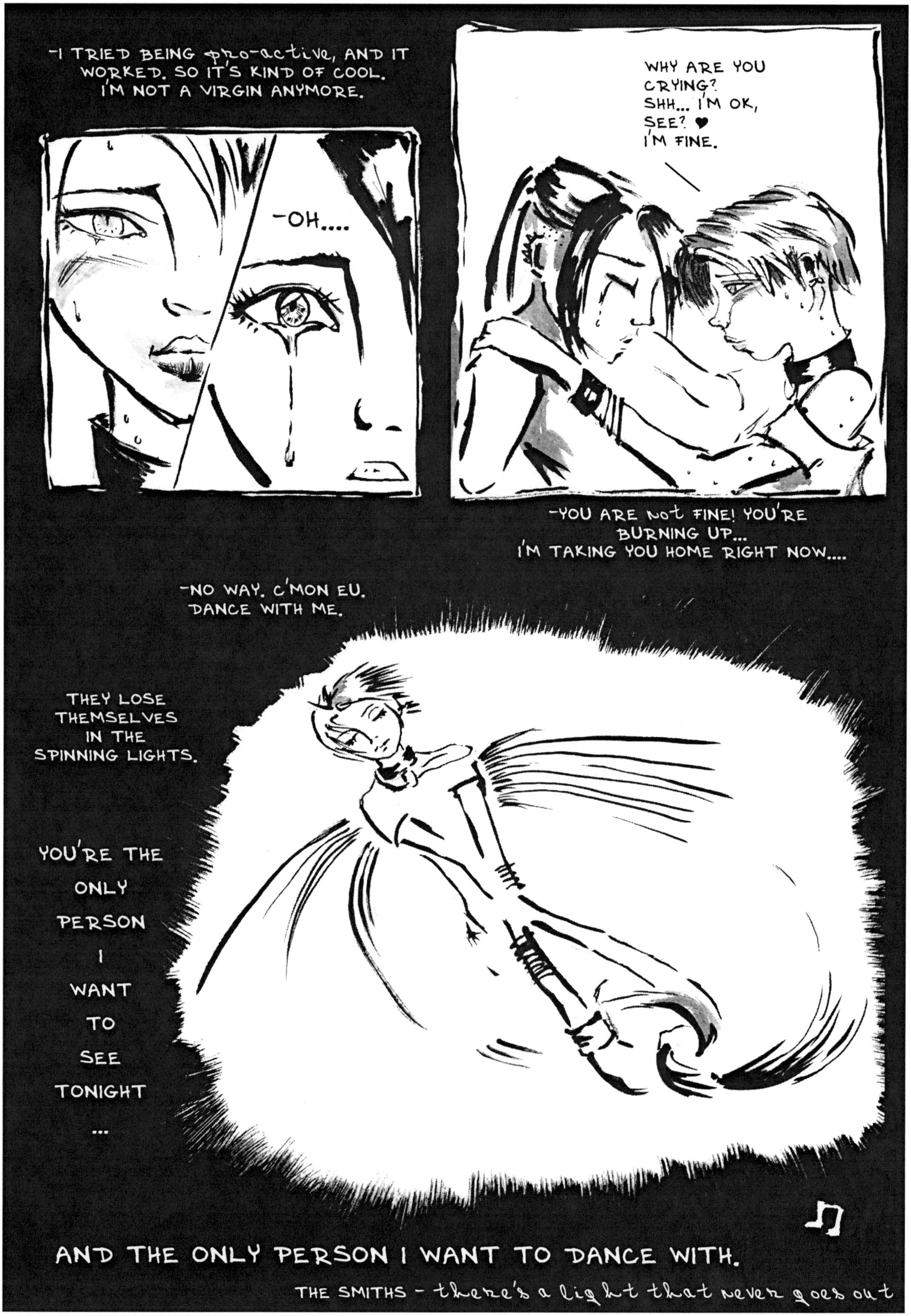
-I TRIED BEING pro-active, AND IT WORKED. SO IT'S KIND OF COOL. I'M NOT A VIRGIN ANYMORE.
-OH....
WHY ARE YOU CRYING? SHH... I'M OK, SEE? ♥ I'M FINE.
-YOU ARE not FINE! YOU'RE BURNING UP... I'M TAKING YOU HOME RIGHT NOW....
-NO WAY. C'MON EU. DANCE WITH ME.
THEY LOSE THEMSELVES IN THE SPINNING LIGHTS.
YOU'RE THE ONLY PERSON I WANT TO SEE TONIGHT ...
AND THE ONLY PERSON I WANT TO DANCE WITH.
THE SMITHS - there's a light that never goes out

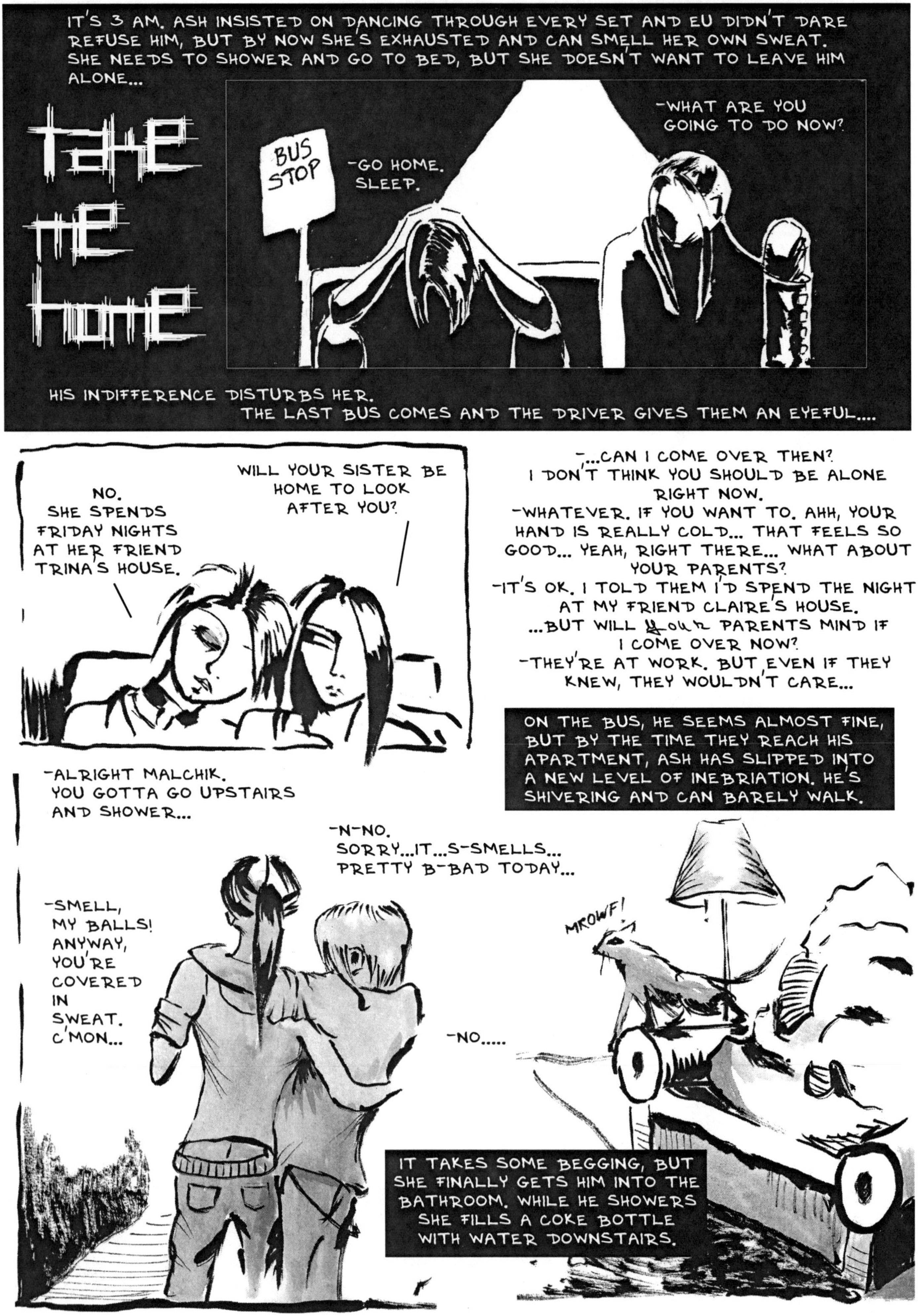
IT'S 3 AM. ASH INSISTED ON DANCING THROUGH EVERY SET AND EU DIDN'T DARE REFUSE HIM, BUT BY NOW SHE'S EXHAUSTED AND CAN SMELL HER OWN SWEAT. SHE NEEDS TO SHOWER AND GO TO BED, BUT SHE DOESN'T WANT TO LEAVE HIM ALONE...
TAKE ME HOME
BUS STOP
-WHAT ARE YOU GOING TO DO NOW?
-GO HOME. SLEEP.
HIS INDIFFERENCE DISTURBS HER.
THE LAST BUS COMES AND THE DRIVER GIVES THEM AN EYEFUL....
WILL YOUR SISTER BE HOME TO LOOK AFTER YOU?
NO. SHE SPENDS FRIDAY NIGHTS AT HER FRIEND TRINA'S HOUSE.
-...CAN I COME OVER THEN? I DON'T THINK YOU SHOULD BE ALONE RIGHT NOW.
-WHATEVER. IF YOU WANT TO. AHH, YOUR HAND IS REALLY COLD... THAT FEELS SO GOOD... YEAH, RIGHT THERE... WHAT ABOUT YOUR PARENTS?
-IT'S OK. I TOLD THEM I'D SPEND THE NIGHT AT MY FRIEND CLAIRE'S HOUSE. ...BUT WILL YOUR PARENTS MIND IF I COME OVER NOW?
-THEY'RE AT WORK. BUT EVEN IF THEY KNEW, THEY WOULDN'T CARE...
ON THE BUS, HE SEEMS ALMOST FINE, BUT BY THE TIME THEY REACH HIS APARTMENT, ASH HAS SLIPPED INTO A NEW LEVEL OF INEBRIATION. HE'S SHIVERING AND CAN BARELY WALK.
-ALRIGHT MALCHIK. YOU GOTTA GO UPSTAIRS AND SHOWER...
-N-NO. SORRY...IT...S-SMELLS... PRETTY B-BAD TODAY...
-SMELL, MY BALLS! ANYWAY, YOU'RE COVERED IN SWEAT. C'MON...
-NO.....
MROWF!
IT TAKES SOME BEGGING, BUT SHE FINALLY GETS HIM INTO THE BATHROOM. WHILE HE SHOWERS SHE FILLS A COKE BOTTLE WITH WATER DOWNSTAIRS.

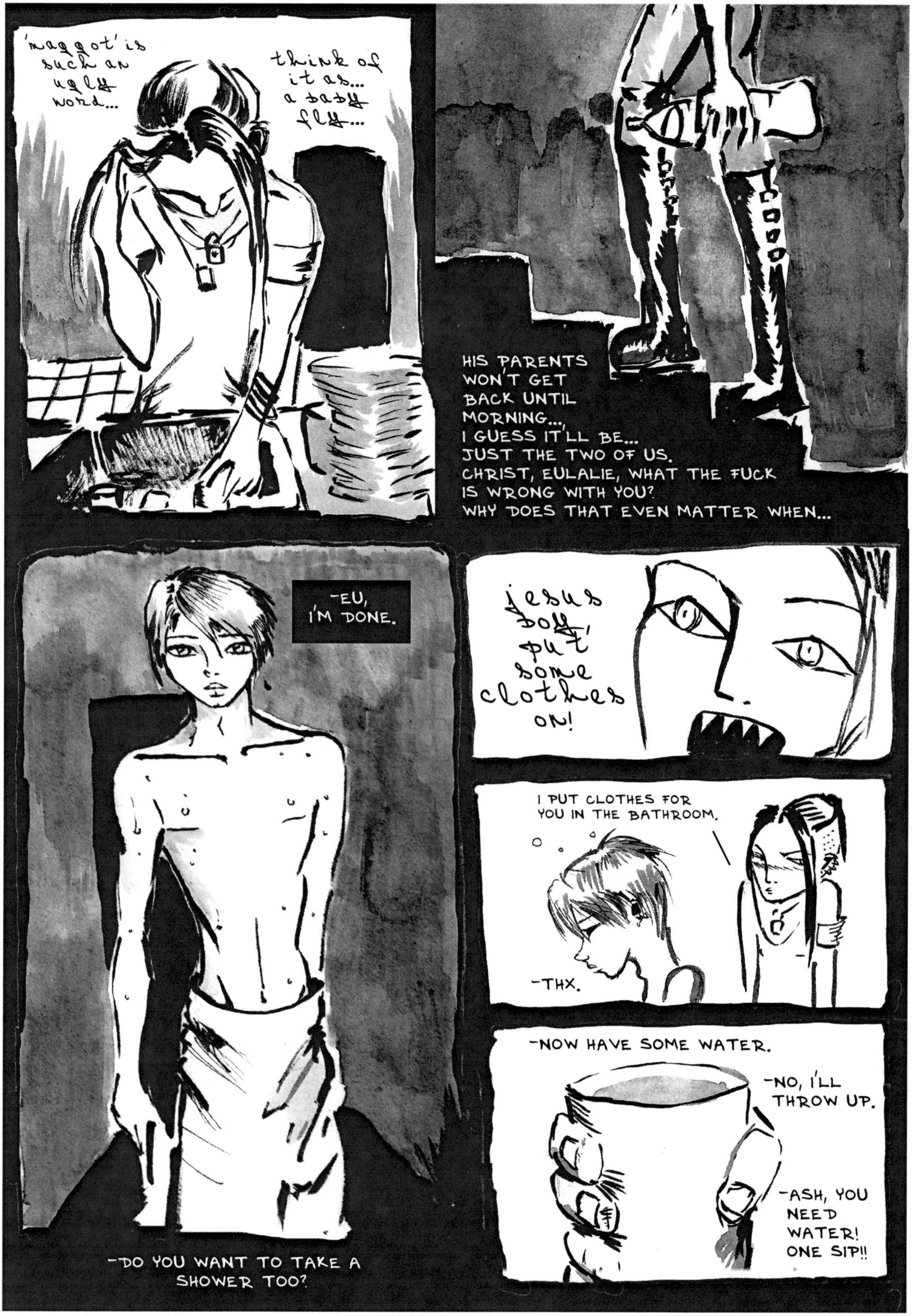
'maggot' is such an ugly word...
think of it as... a baby fly...
HIS PARENTS WON'T GET BACK UNTIL MORNING...,
I GUESS IT'LL BE... JUST THE TWO OF US.
CHRIST, EULALIE, WHAT THE FUCK IS WRONG WITH YOU?
WHY DOES THAT EVEN MATTER WHEN...
-EU, I'M DONE.
-DO YOU WANT TO TAKE A SHOWER TOO?
jesus boy, put some clothes on!
I PUT CLOTHES FOR YOU IN THE BATHROOM.
-THX.
-NOW HAVE SOME WATER.
-NO, I'LL THROW UP.
-ASH, YOU NEED WATER! ONE SIP!!

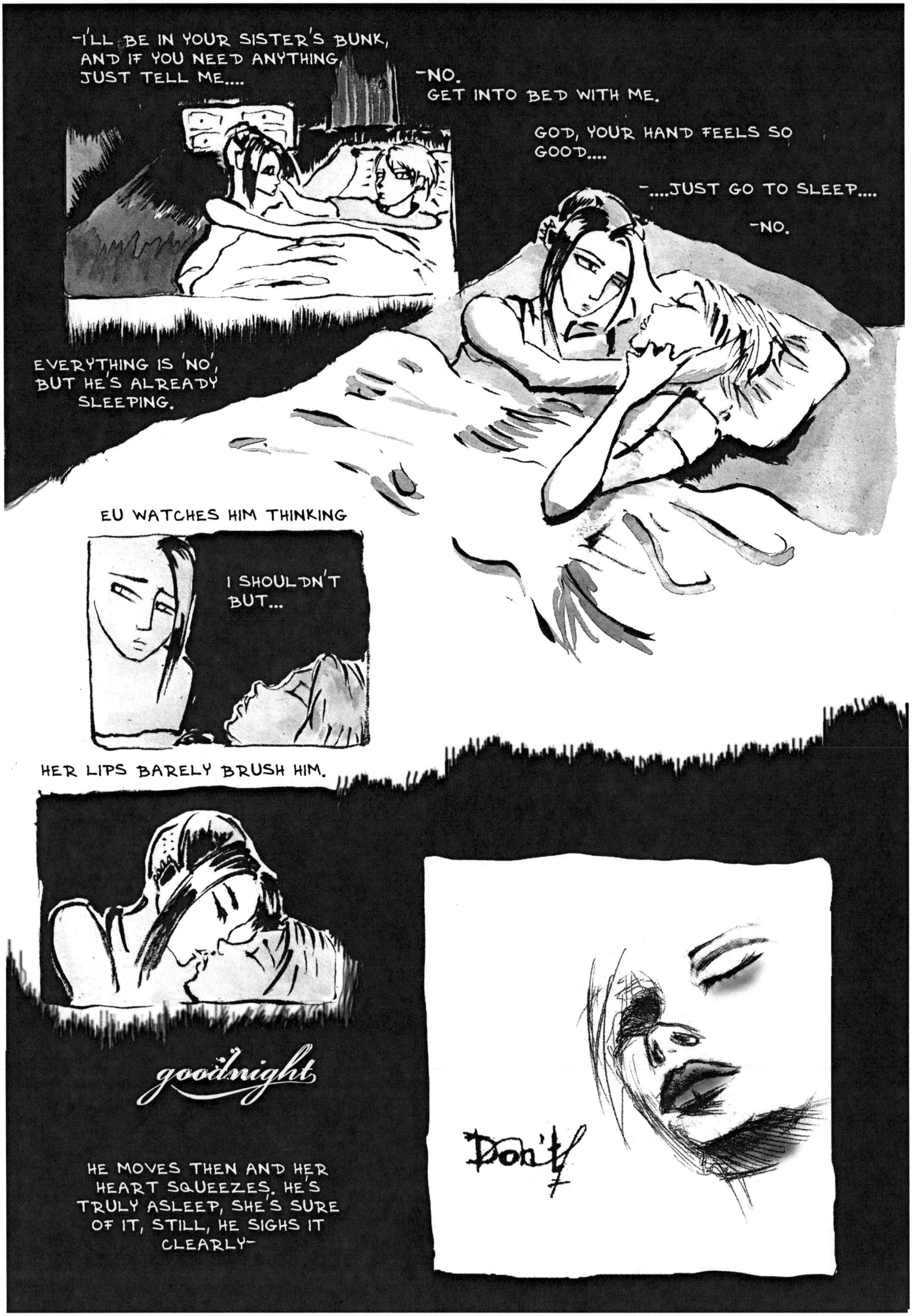
-I'LL BE IN YOUR SISTER'S BUNK, AND IF YOU NEED ANYTHING, JUST TELL ME....
-NO. GET INTO BED WITH ME.
GOD, YOUR HAND FEELS SO GOOD....
-....JUST GO TO SLEEP....
-NO.
EVERYTHING IS 'NO', BUT HE'S ALREADY SLEEPING.
EU WATCHES HIM THINKING
I SHOULDN'T BUT...
HER LIPS BARELY BRUSH HIM.
goodnight
HE MOVES THEN AND HER HEART SQUEEZES. HE'S TRULY ASLEEP, SHE'S SURE OF IT, STILL, HE SIGHS IT CLEARLY-
Don't

DOOO-DOOOOOO......
DOOO-DOOOOOO........

dreamtime #1

Asher...
You're eating!
Shh...
Don't tell anyone...

ANOTHER DREAM THAT SOUNDS JUST LIKE THAT PIXIES TRACK
ABOUT NOT FINDING YOUR MIND....

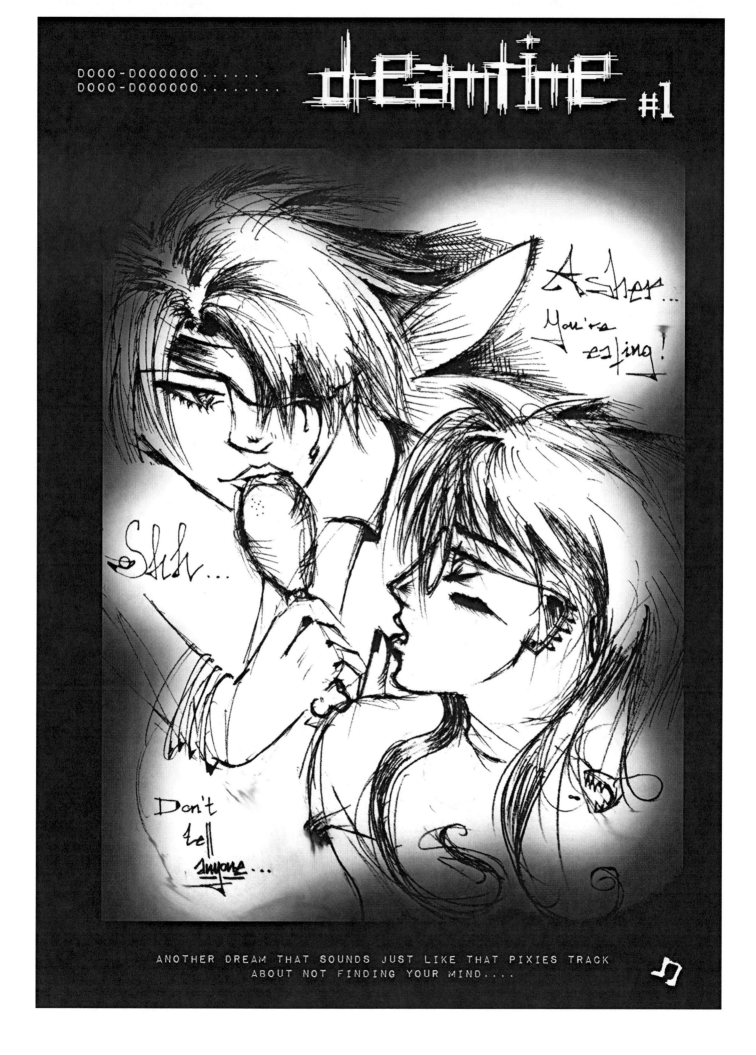

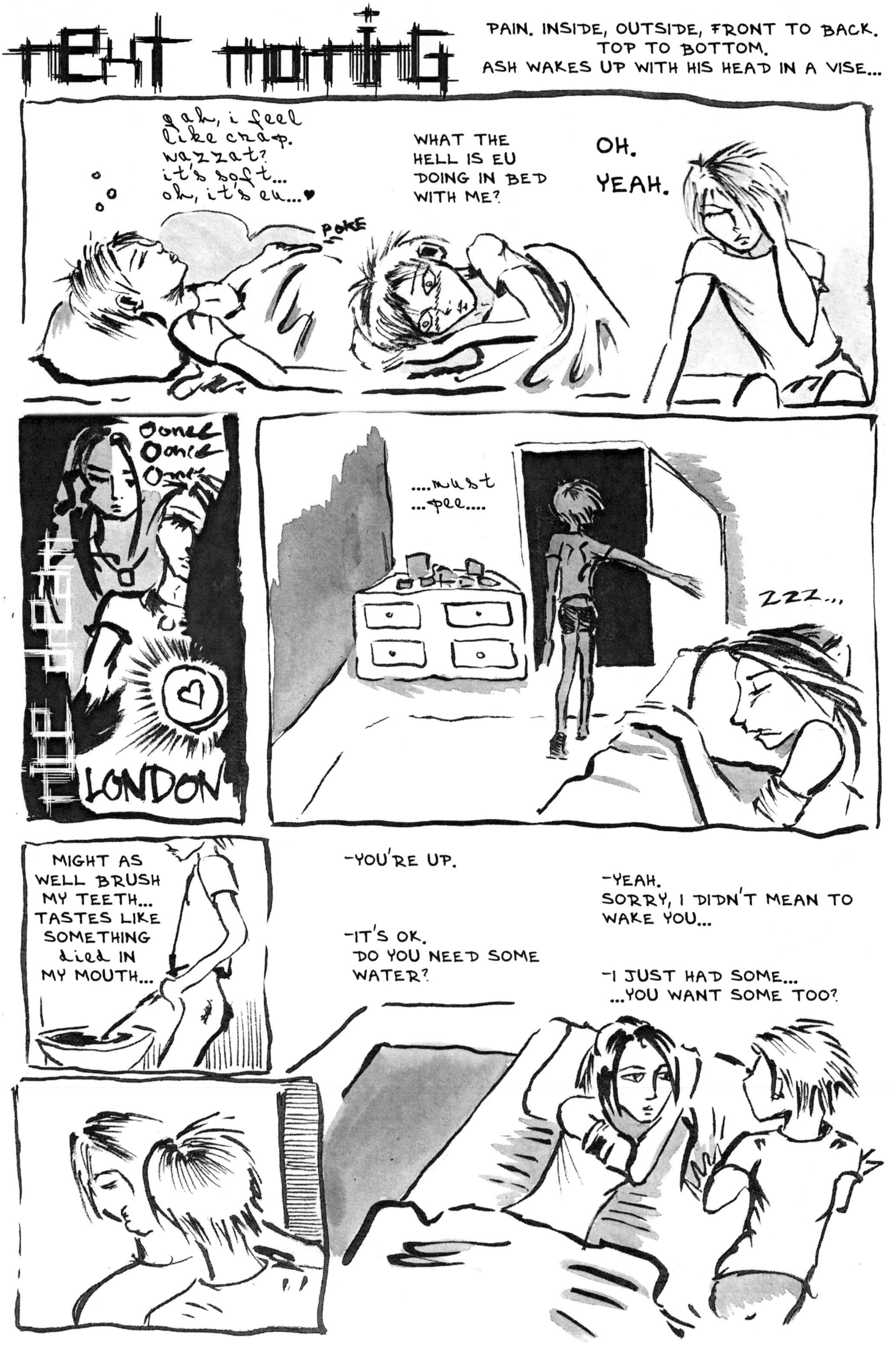
NEXT MORNING
PAIN. INSIDE, OUTSIDE, FRONT TO BACK. TOP TO BOTTOM.
ASH WAKES UP WITH HIS HEAD IN A VISE...
gah, i feel like crap. wazzat? it's soft... oh, it's eu...♥
POKE
WHAT THE HELL IS EU DOING IN BED WITH ME?
OH.
YEAH.
Oonce Oonce Oonce
LONDON
....must ...pee....
ZZZ...
MIGHT AS WELL BRUSH MY TEETH... TASTES LIKE SOMETHING died IN MY MOUTH...
-YOU'RE UP.
-YEAH. SORRY, I DIDN'T MEAN TO WAKE YOU...
-IT'S OK. DO YOU NEED SOME WATER?
-I JUST HAD SOME... ...YOU WANT SOME TOO?

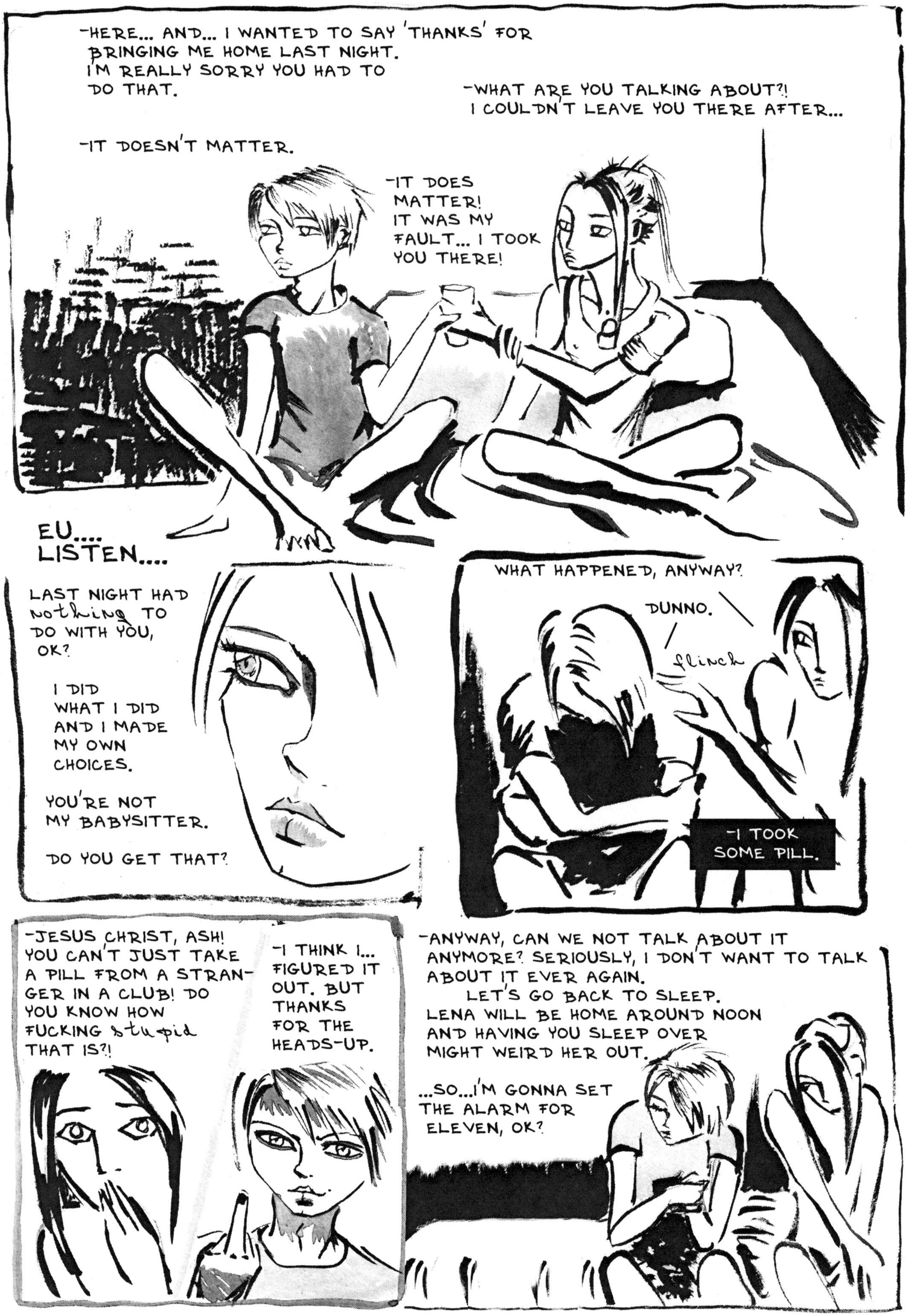

-HERE... AND... I WANTED TO SAY 'THANKS' FOR BRINGING ME HOME LAST NIGHT. I'M REALLY SORRY YOU HAD TO DO THAT.
-WHAT ARE YOU TALKING ABOUT?! I COULDN'T LEAVE YOU THERE AFTER...
-IT DOESN'T MATTER.
-IT DOES MATTER! IT WAS MY FAULT... I TOOK YOU THERE!
EU.... LISTEN....
LAST NIGHT HAD nothing TO DO WITH YOU, OK?
I DID WHAT I DID AND I MADE MY OWN CHOICES.
YOU'RE NOT MY BABYSITTER.
DO YOU GET THAT?
WHAT HAPPENED, ANYWAY?
DUNNO.
flinch
-I TOOK SOME PILL.
-JESUS CHRIST, ASH! YOU CAN'T JUST TAKE A PILL FROM A STRANGER IN A CLUB! DO YOU KNOW HOW FUCKING stupid THAT IS?!
-I THINK I... FIGURED IT OUT. BUT THANKS FOR THE HEADS-UP.
-ANYWAY, CAN WE NOT TALK ABOUT IT ANYMORE? SERIOUSLY, I DON'T WANT TO TALK ABOUT IT EVER AGAIN.
LET'S GO BACK TO SLEEP. LENA WILL BE HOME AROUND NOON AND HAVING YOU SLEEP OVER MIGHT WEIRD HER OUT.
...SO...I'M GONNA SET THE ALARM FOR ELEVEN, OK?

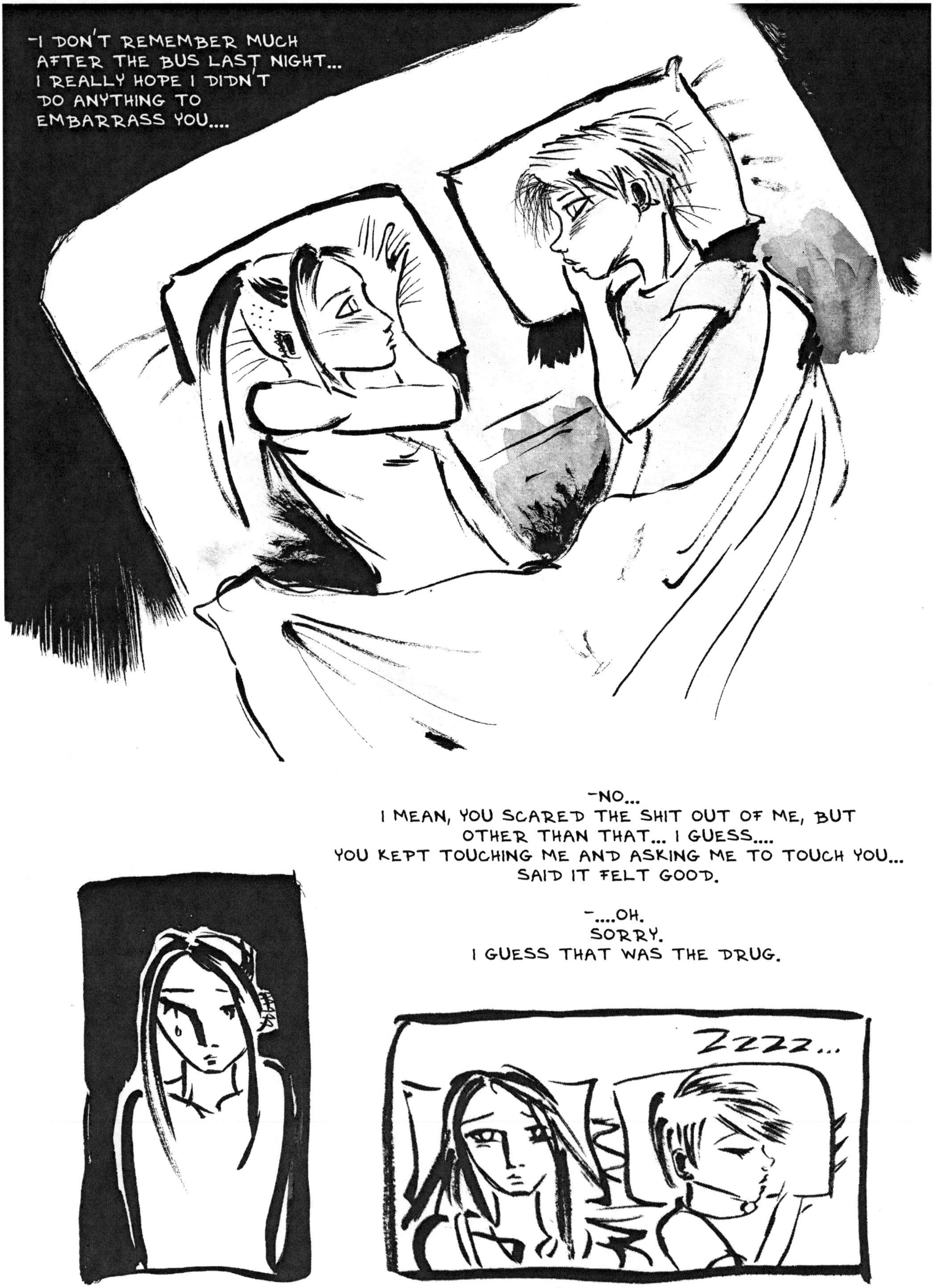

-I DON'T REMEMBER MUCH AFTER THE BUS LAST NIGHT... I REALLY HOPE I DIDN'T DO ANYTHING TO EMBARRASS YOU....
-NO... I MEAN, YOU SCARED THE SHIT OUT OF ME, BUT OTHER THAN THAT... I GUESS.... YOU KEPT TOUCHING ME AND ASKING ME TO TOUCH YOU... SAID IT FELT GOOD.
-....OH. SORRY. I GUESS THAT WAS THE DRUG.
SURE. THE DRUG.
ZZZZ...
-ANYWAY.... I'M REALLY SLEEPY SO... GOODNIGHT, EU.
-YEAH. ...GOODNIGHT.

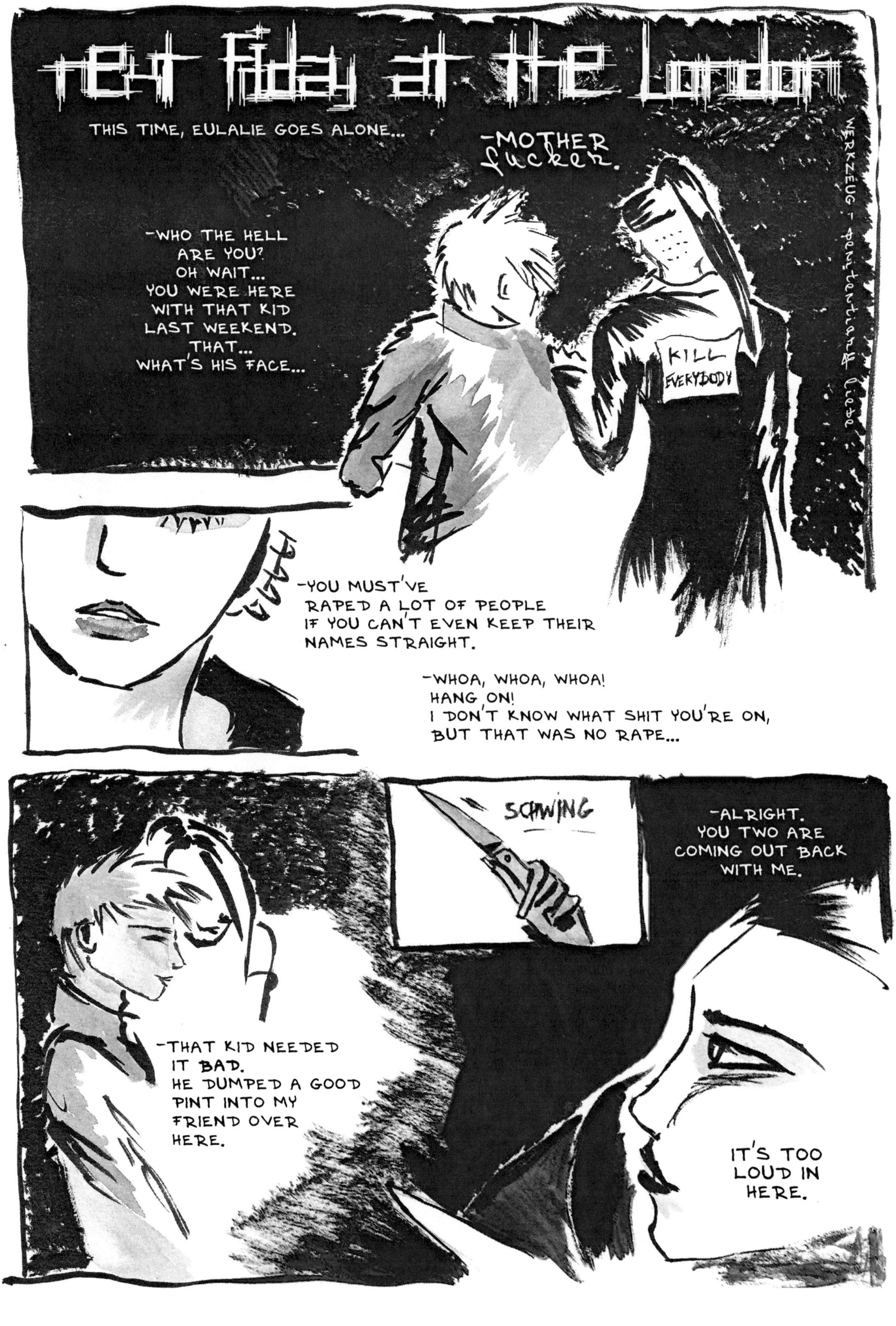
next friday at the London
THIS TIME, EULALIE GOES ALONE...
-MOTHER fucker.
WERKZEUG - penitentiary liebe
-WHO THE HELL ARE YOU? OH WAIT... YOU WERE HERE WITH THAT KID LAST WEEKEND. THAT... WHAT'S HIS FACE...
KILL EVERYBODY
-YOU MUST'VE RAPED A LOT OF PEOPLE IF YOU CAN'T EVEN KEEP THEIR NAMES STRAIGHT.
-WHOA, WHOA, WHOA! HANG ON! I DON'T KNOW WHAT SHIT YOU'RE ON, BUT THAT WAS NO RAPE...
-THAT KID NEEDED IT BAD. HE DUMPED A GOOD PINT INTO MY FRIEND OVER HERE.
SCHWING
-ALRIGHT. YOU TWO ARE COMING OUT BACK WITH ME.
IT'S TOO LOUD IN HERE.

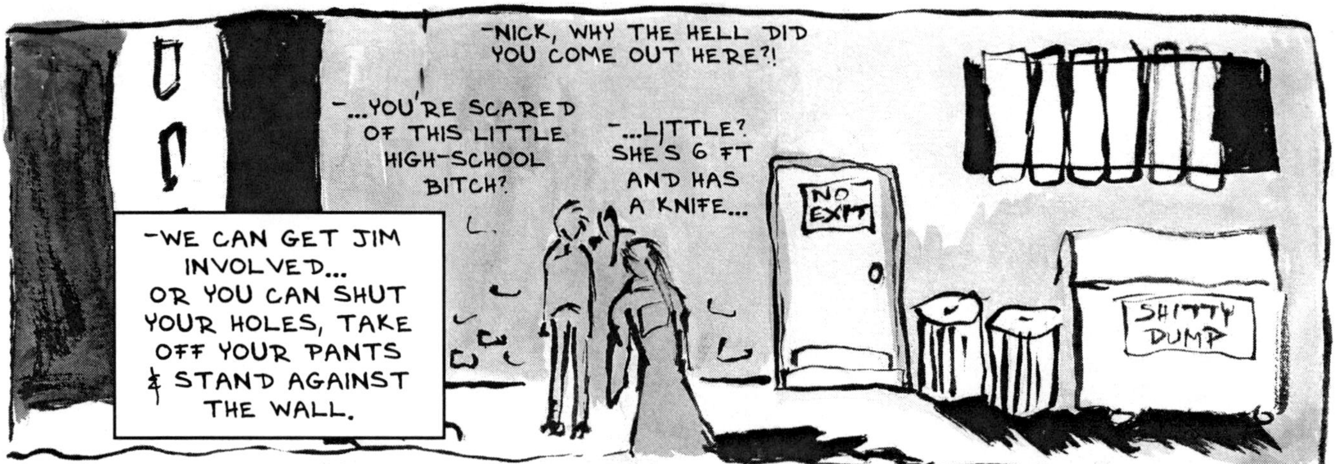
-NICK, WHY THE HELL DID YOU COME OUT HERE?!
-...YOU'RE SCARED OF THIS LITTLE HIGH-SCHOOL BITCH?
-...LITTLE? SHE'S 6 FT AND HAS A KNIFE...
NO EXIT
SHITTY DUMP
-WE CAN GET JIM INVOLVED... OR YOU CAN SHUT YOUR HOLES, TAKE OFF YOUR PANTS & STAND AGAINST THE WALL.

-SHIT MAN, SHE'S GONNA castrate US. I told YOU WE SHOULD'VE LEFT THAT KID ALONE!
-LOOK DUDE, UH, GIRL... WE DIDN'T KNOW HE WAS WITH YOU. COME ON, YOU DON'T WANT TO DO SOMETHING STUPID. WE WON'T GO NEAR HIM AGAIN, WE SWEAR.
-...HAHA, ...ALL RIGHT. BUT YOU BETTER REMEMBER, BECAUSE I SWEAR TO GOD, ...THE NEXT TIME YOU PULL SOME FUCKED UP SHIT, THIS SIX INCHES IS GOING INTO you.

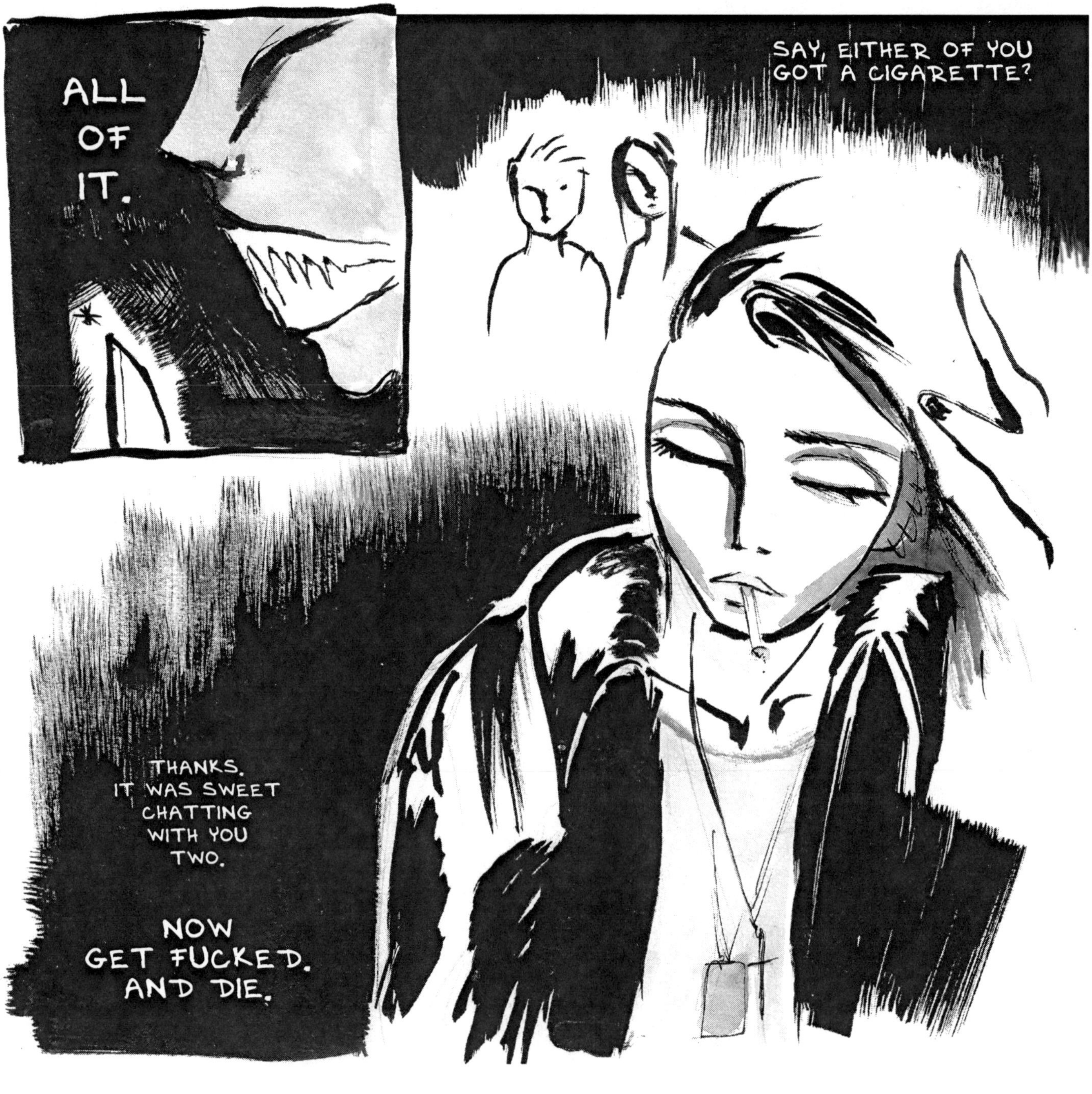
ALL OF IT.
SAY, EITHER OF YOU GOT A CIGARETTE?
THANKS. IT WAS SWEET CHATTING WITH YOU TWO.
NOW GET FUCKED. AND DIE.

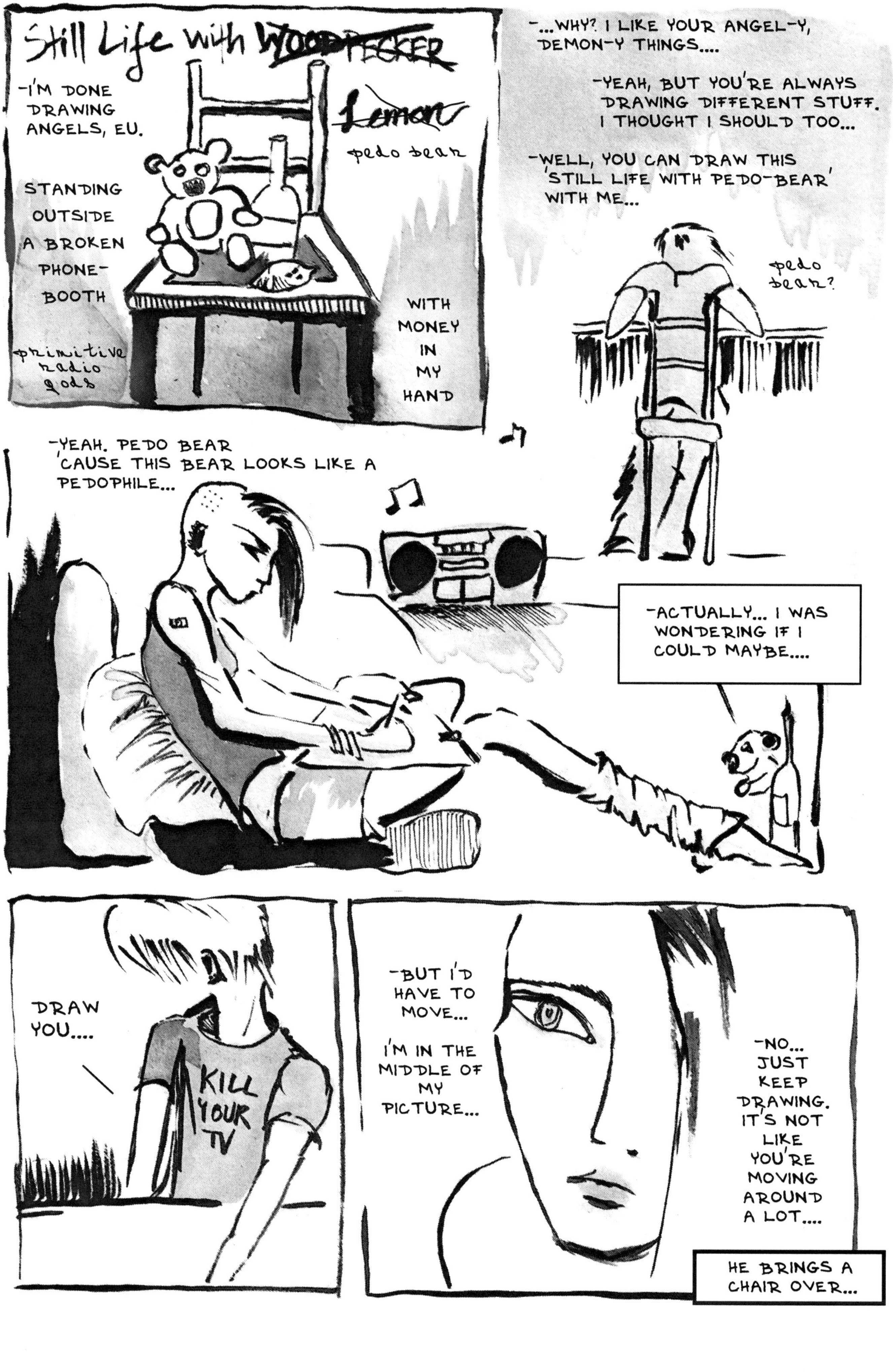
Still Life with ~~Woodpecker~~
~~Lemon~~
pedo bear
-I'M DONE DRAWING ANGELS, EU.
STANDING OUTSIDE A BROKEN PHONE-BOOTH
WITH MONEY IN MY HAND
primitive radio gods
-...WHY? I LIKE YOUR ANGEL-Y, DEMON-Y THINGS....
-YEAH, BUT YOU'RE ALWAYS DRAWING DIFFERENT STUFF. I THOUGHT I SHOULD TOO...
-WELL, YOU CAN DRAW THIS 'STILL LIFE WITH PEDO-BEAR' WITH ME...
pedo bear?
-YEAH. PEDO BEAR 'CAUSE THIS BEAR LOOKS LIKE A PEDOPHILE...
-ACTUALLY... I WAS WONDERING IF I COULD MAYBE....
DRAW YOU....
KILL YOUR TV
-BUT I'D HAVE TO MOVE...
I'M IN THE MIDDLE OF MY PICTURE...
-NO... JUST KEEP DRAWING. IT'S NOT LIKE YOU'RE MOVING AROUND A LOT....
HE BRINGS A CHAIR OVER...

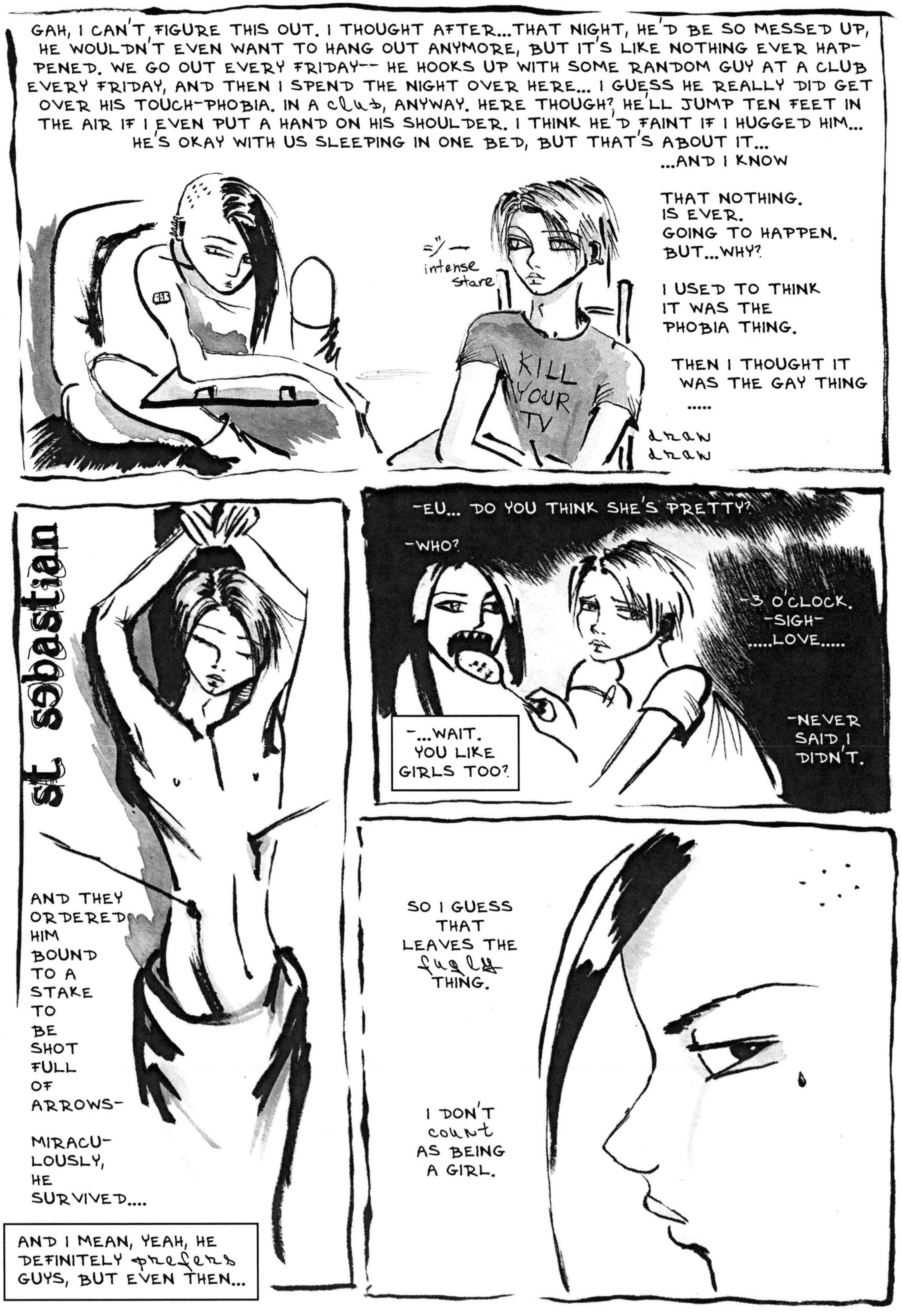
GAH, I CAN'T FIGURE THIS OUT. I THOUGHT AFTER...THAT NIGHT, HE'D BE SO MESSED UP, HE WOULDN'T EVEN WANT TO HANG OUT ANYMORE, BUT IT'S LIKE NOTHING EVER HAPPENED. WE GO OUT EVERY FRIDAY-- HE HOOKS UP WITH SOME RANDOM GUY AT A CLUB EVERY FRIDAY, AND THEN I SPEND THE NIGHT OVER HERE... I GUESS HE REALLY DID GET OVER HIS TOUCH-PHOBIA. IN A club, ANYWAY. HERE THOUGH? HE'LL JUMP TEN FEET IN THE AIR IF I EVEN PUT A HAND ON HIS SHOULDER. I THINK HE'D FAINT IF I HUGGED HIM... HE'S OKAY WITH US SLEEPING IN ONE BED, BUT THAT'S ABOUT IT...
...AND I KNOW
THAT NOTHING. IS EVER. GOING TO HAPPEN.
BUT...WHY?
intense stare
I USED TO THINK IT WAS THE PHOBIA THING.
KILL YOUR TV
THEN I THOUGHT IT WAS THE GAY THING .....
draw draw
st sebastian
AND THEY ORDERED HIM BOUND TO A STAKE TO BE SHOT FULL OF ARROWS-
MIRACULOUSLY, HE SURVIVED....
AND I MEAN, YEAH, HE DEFINITELY prefers GUYS, BUT EVEN THEN...
-EU... DO YOU THINK SHE'S PRETTY?
-WHO?
-3 O'CLOCK.
-SIGH-
.....LOVE.....
-...WAIT. YOU LIKE GIRLS TOO?
-NEVER SAID I DIDN'T.
SO I GUESS THAT LEAVES THE fugly THING.
I DON'T count AS BEING A GIRL.

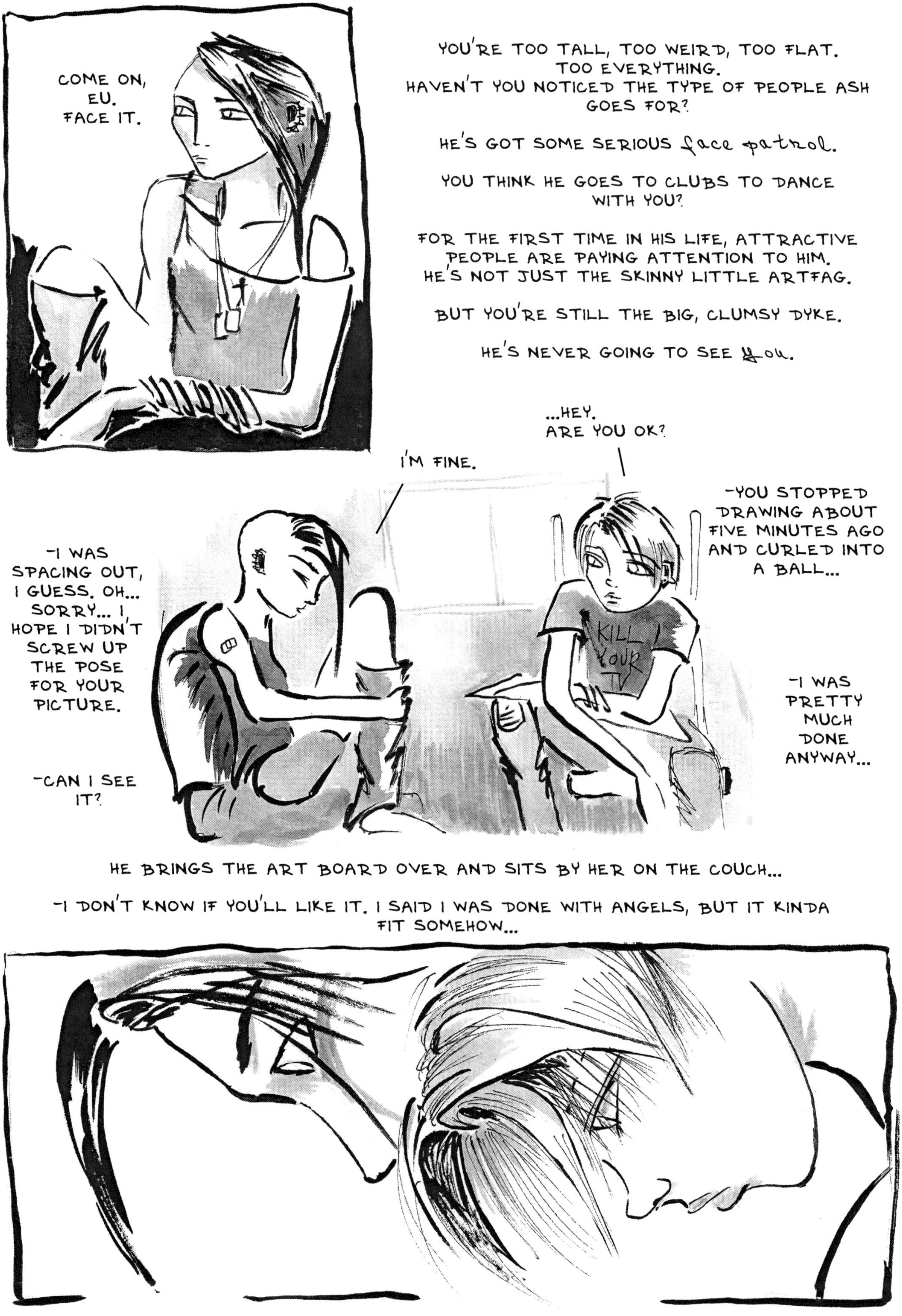
COME ON, EU. FACE IT.
YOU'RE TOO TALL, TOO WEIRD, TOO FLAT. TOO EVERYTHING.
HAVEN'T YOU NOTICED THE TYPE OF PEOPLE ASH GOES FOR?
HE'S GOT SOME SERIOUS face patrol.
YOU THINK HE GOES TO CLUBS TO DANCE WITH YOU?
FOR THE FIRST TIME IN HIS LIFE, ATTRACTIVE PEOPLE ARE PAYING ATTENTION TO HIM. HE'S NOT JUST THE SKINNY LITTLE ARTFAG.
BUT YOU'RE STILL THE BIG, CLUMSY DYKE.
HE'S NEVER GOING TO SEE you.
...HEY. ARE YOU OK?
I'M FINE.
-YOU STOPPED DRAWING ABOUT FIVE MINUTES AGO AND CURLED INTO A BALL...
-I WAS SPACING OUT, I GUESS. OH... SORRY... I HOPE I DIDN'T SCREW UP THE POSE FOR YOUR PICTURE.
-I WAS PRETTY MUCH DONE ANYWAY...
-CAN I SEE IT?
KILL YOUR TV
HE BRINGS THE ART BOARD OVER AND SITS BY HER ON THE COUCH...
-I DON'T KNOW IF YOU'LL LIKE IT. I SAID I WAS DONE WITH ANGELS, BUT IT KINDA FIT SOMEHOW...

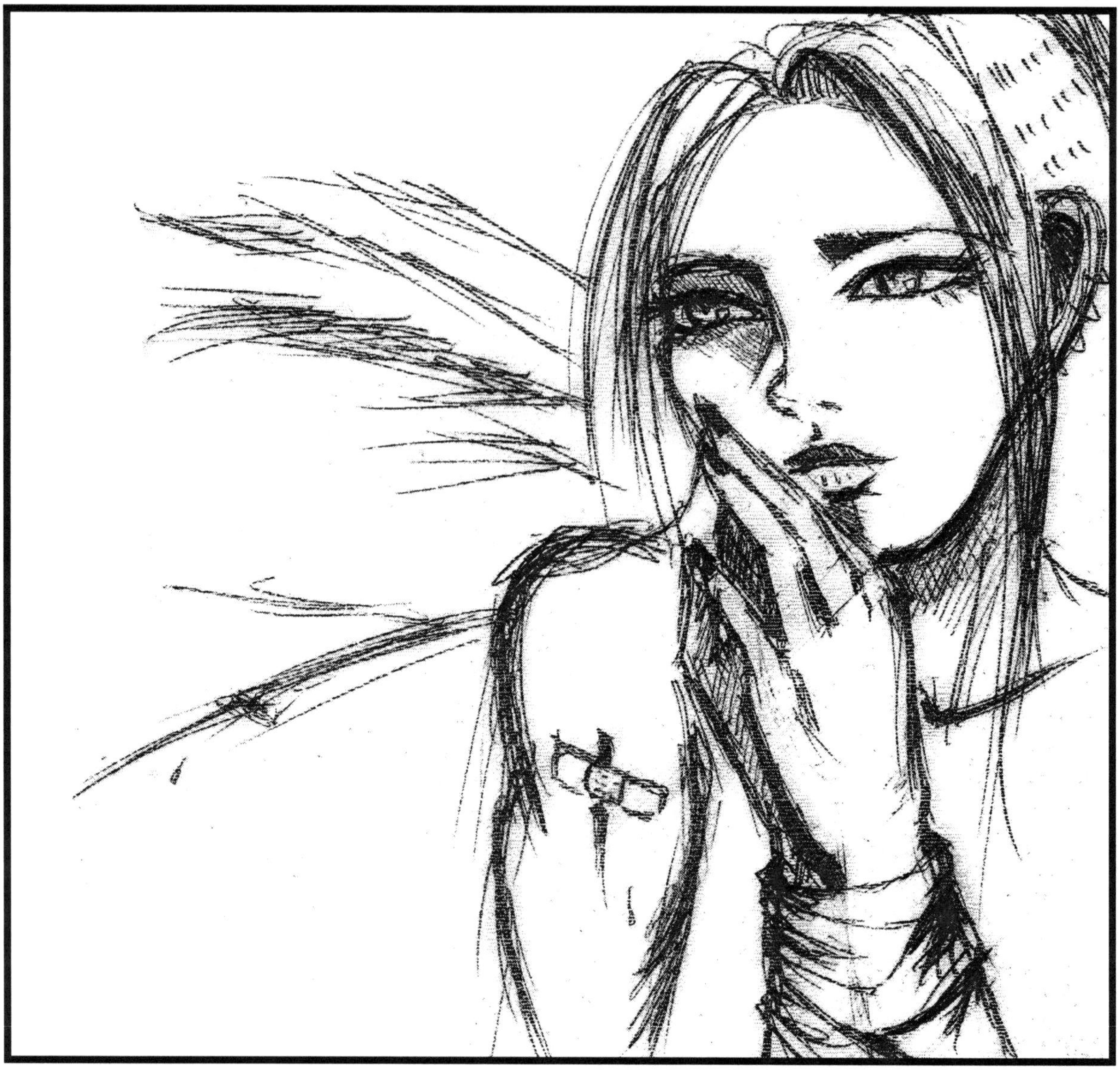

HE'S NEVER GOING TO SEE YOU.

-WOW... SHE'S BEAUTIFUL...

-WELL, YOU WERE THE MODEL...

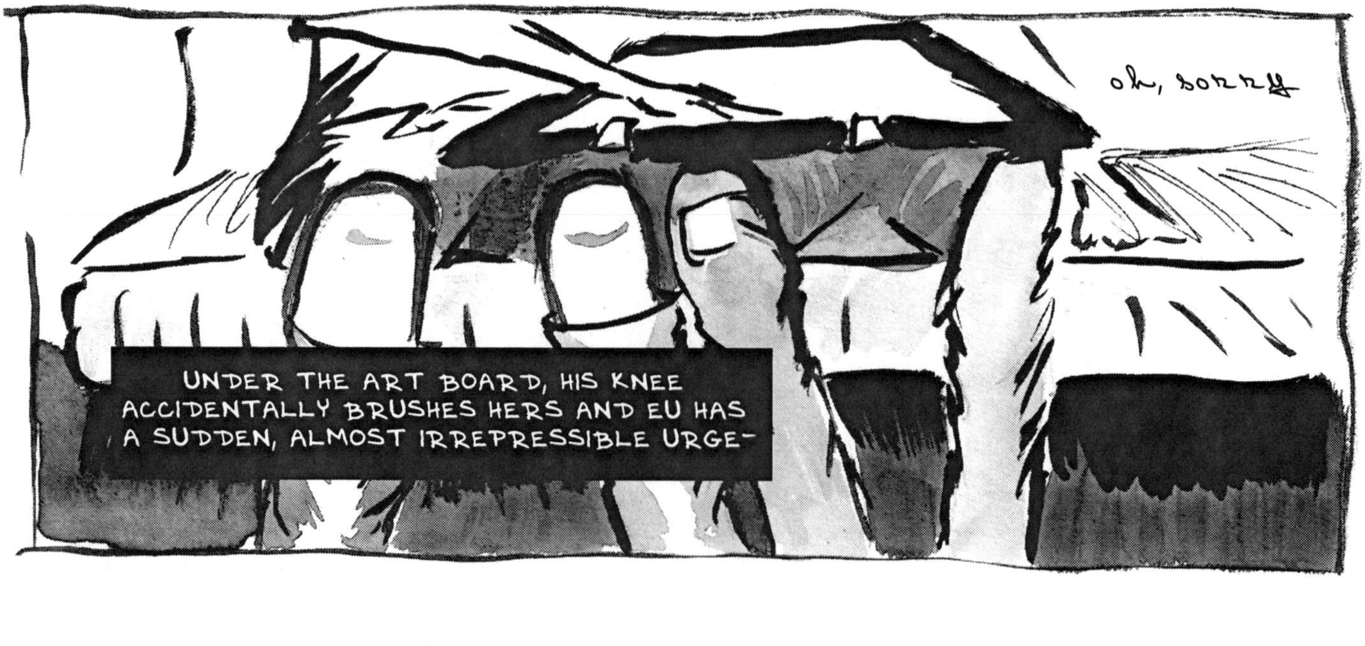

oh, sorry
UNDER THE ART BOARD, HIS KNEE ACCIDENTALLY BRUSHES HERS AND EU HAS A SUDDEN, ALMOST IRREPRESSIBLE URGE-

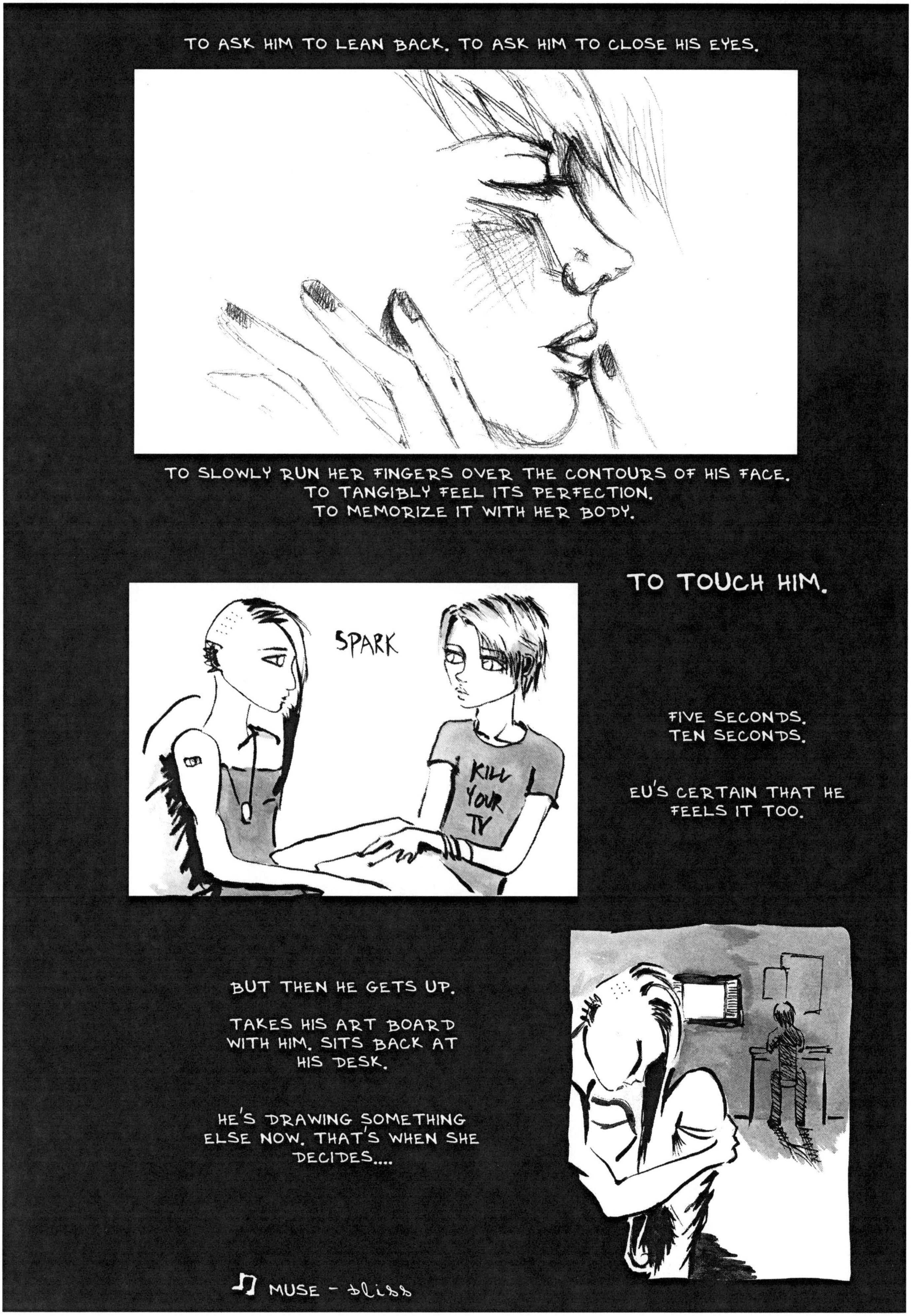
TO ASK HIM TO LEAN BACK. TO ASK HIM TO CLOSE HIS EYES.
TO SLOWLY RUN HER FINGERS OVER THE CONTOURS OF HIS FACE.
TO TANGIBLY FEEL ITS PERFECTION.
TO MEMORIZE IT WITH HER BODY.
TO TOUCH HIM.
SPARK
KILL YOUR TV
FIVE SECONDS.
TEN SECONDS.
EU'S CERTAIN THAT HE FEELS IT TOO.
BUT THEN HE GETS UP.
TAKES HIS ART BOARD WITH HIM. SITS BACK AT HIS DESK.
HE'S DRAWING SOMETHING ELSE NOW. THAT'S WHEN SHE DECIDES....
MUSE - bliss

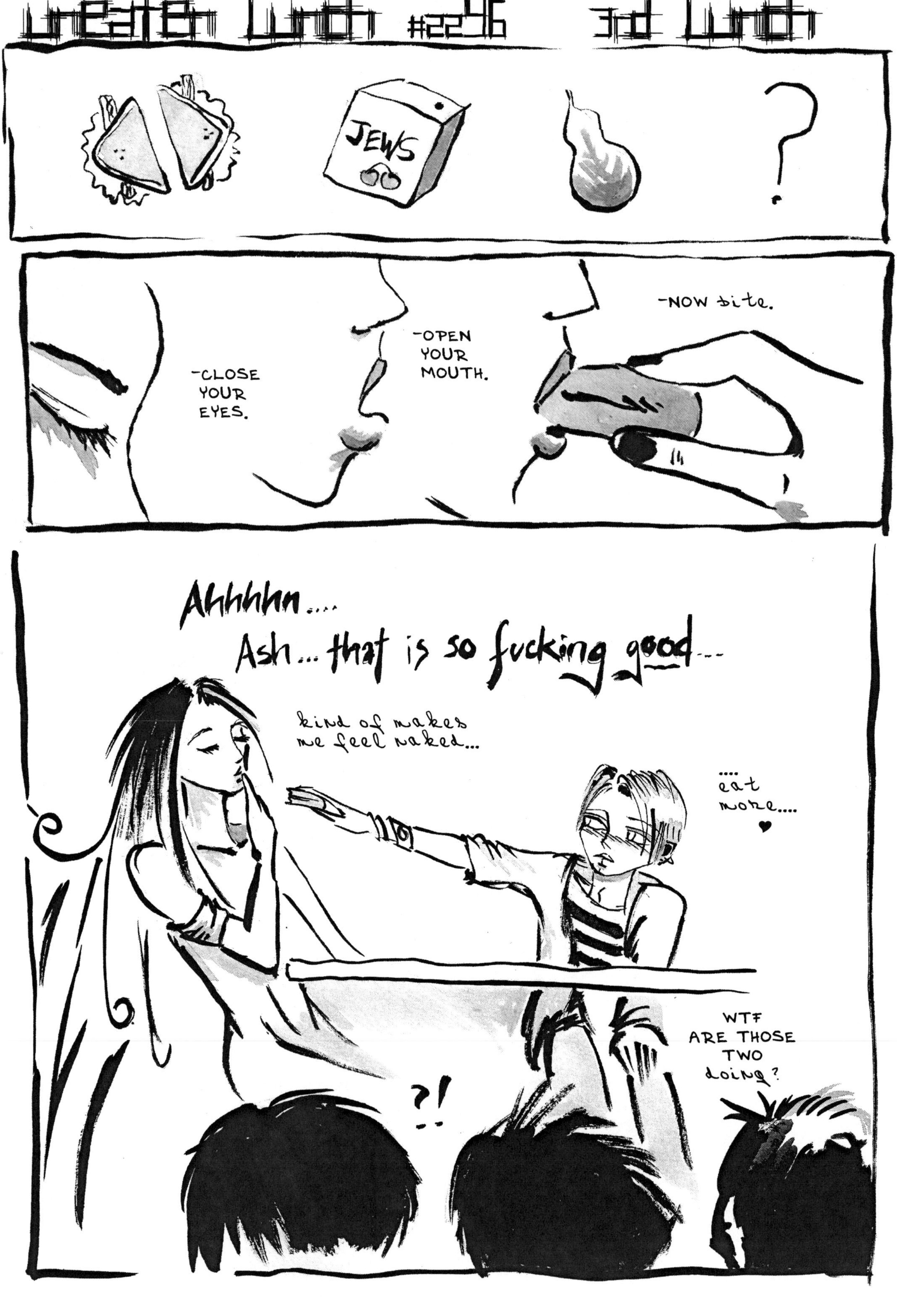
uneaten Lunch #2296 3rd Lunch
JEWS
?
-CLOSE YOUR EYES.
-OPEN YOUR MOUTH.
-NOW bite.
Ahhhhn....
Ash... that is so fucking good...
kind of makes me feel naked...
.... eat more....
?!
WTF ARE THOSE TWO doing?

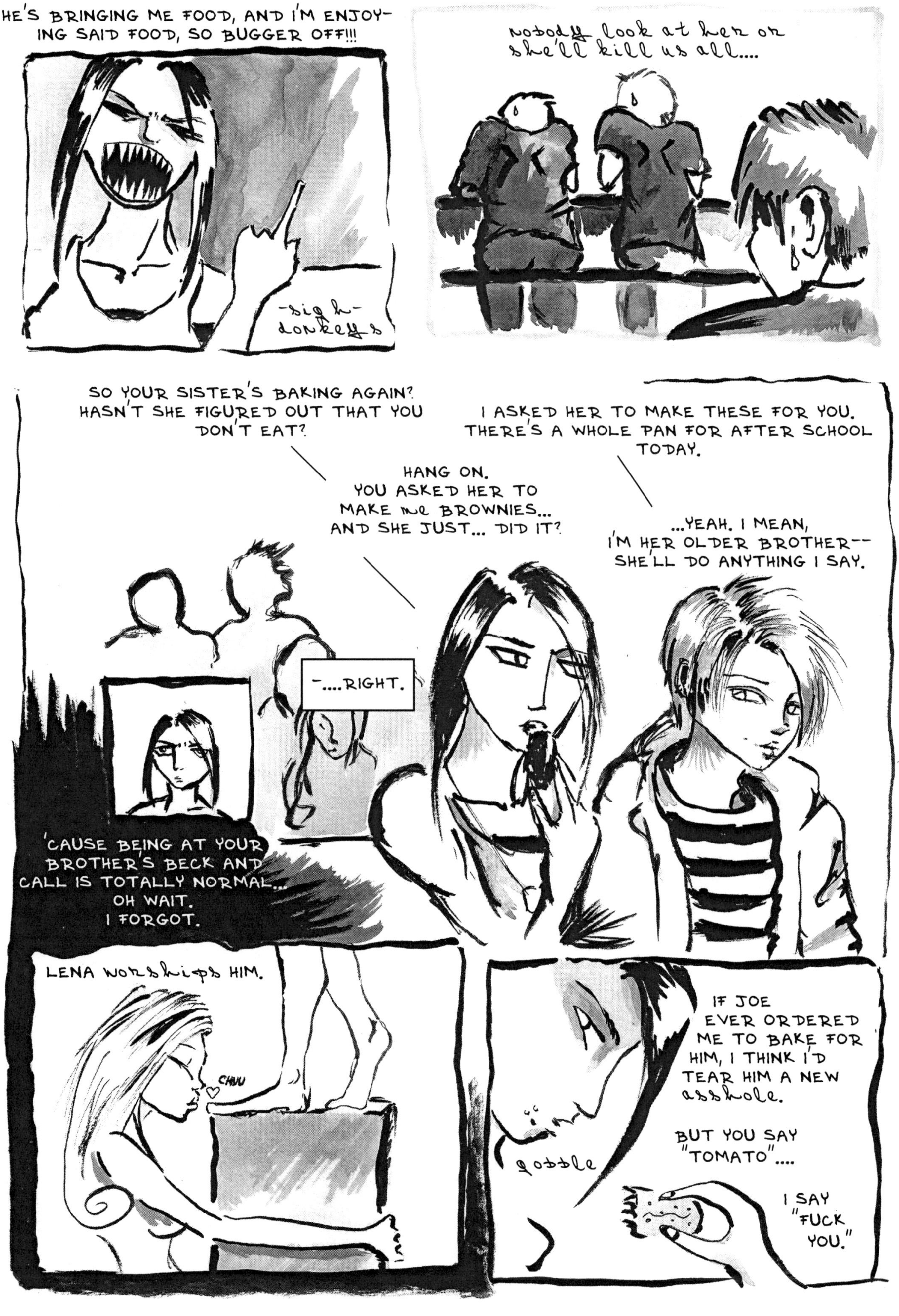
HE'S BRINGING ME FOOD, AND I'M ENJOYING SAID FOOD, SO BUGGER OFF!!!
-sigh- donkeys
nobody look at her or she'll kill us all....
SO YOUR SISTER'S BAKING AGAIN? HASN'T SHE FIGURED OUT THAT YOU DON'T EAT?
I ASKED HER TO MAKE THESE FOR YOU. THERE'S A WHOLE PAN FOR AFTER SCHOOL TODAY.
HANG ON. YOU ASKED HER TO MAKE me BROWNIES... AND SHE JUST... DID IT?
...YEAH. I MEAN, I'M HER OLDER BROTHER-- SHE'LL DO ANYTHING I SAY.
-....RIGHT.
'CAUSE BEING AT YOUR BROTHER'S BECK AND CALL IS TOTALLY NORMAL... OH WAIT. I FORGOT.
LENA worships HIM.
CHUU
IF JOE EVER ORDERED ME TO BAKE FOR HIM, I THINK I'D TEAR HIM A NEW asshole.
BUT YOU SAY "TOMATO"....
gobble
I SAY "FUCK YOU."

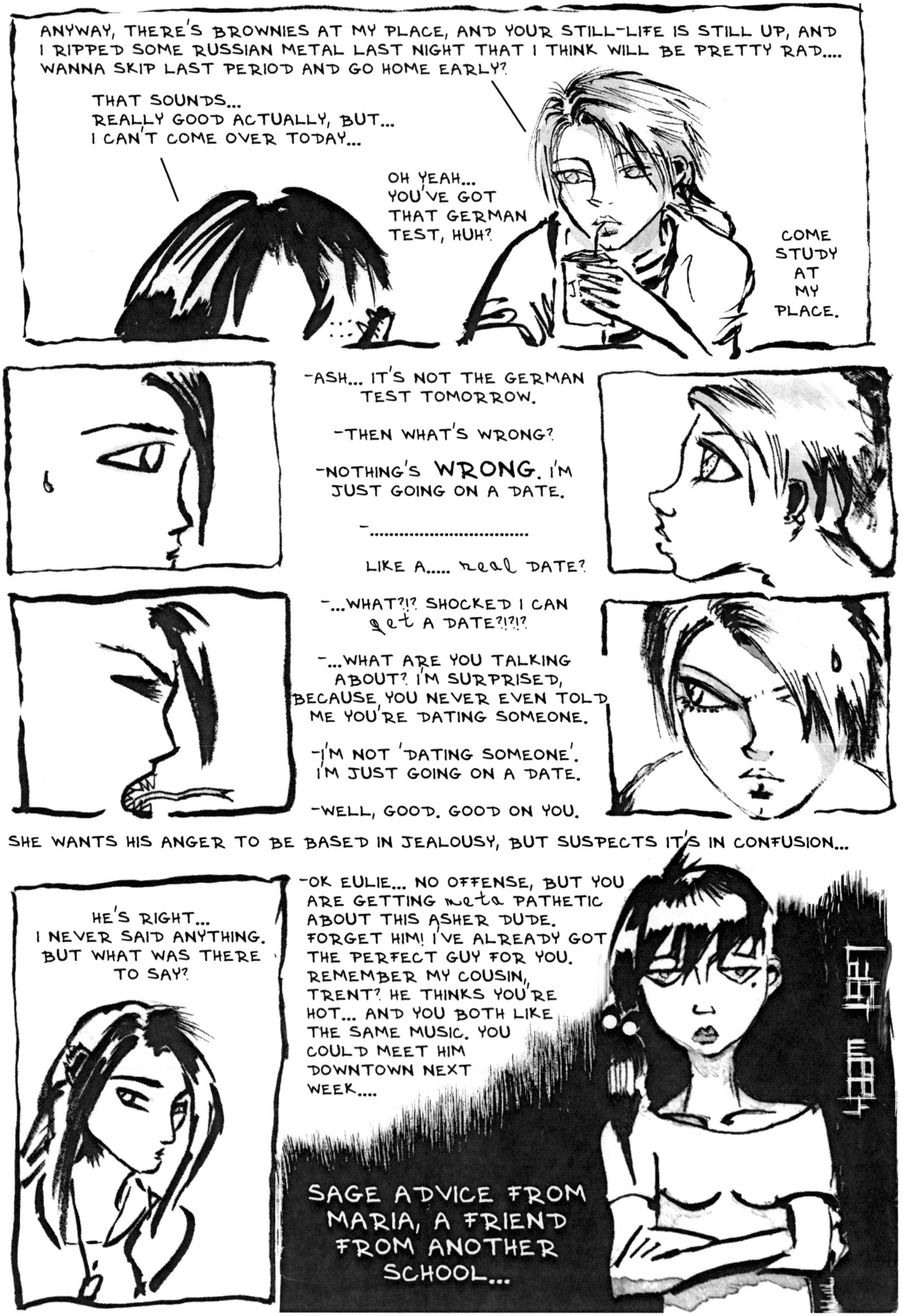
ANYWAY, THERE'S BROWNIES AT MY PLACE, AND YOUR STILL-LIFE IS STILL UP, AND I RIPPED SOME RUSSIAN METAL LAST NIGHT THAT I THINK WILL BE PRETTY RAD.... WANNA SKIP LAST PERIOD AND GO HOME EARLY?
THAT SOUNDS... REALLY GOOD ACTUALLY, BUT... I CAN'T COME OVER TODAY...
OH YEAH... YOU'VE GOT THAT GERMAN TEST, HUH?
COME STUDY AT MY PLACE.
-ASH... IT'S NOT THE GERMAN TEST TOMORROW.
-THEN WHAT'S WRONG?
-NOTHING'S WRONG. I'M JUST GOING ON A DATE.
-..............................
LIKE A..... real DATE?
-...WHAT?!? SHOCKED I CAN get A DATE?!?!?
-...WHAT ARE YOU TALKING ABOUT? I'M SURPRISED, BECAUSE YOU NEVER EVEN TOLD ME YOU'RE DATING SOMEONE.
-I'M NOT 'DATING SOMEONE'. I'M JUST GOING ON A DATE.
-WELL, GOOD. GOOD ON YOU.
SHE WANTS HIS ANGER TO BE BASED IN JEALOUSY, BUT SUSPECTS IT'S IN CONFUSION...
HE'S RIGHT... I NEVER SAID ANYTHING. BUT WHAT WAS THERE TO SAY?
-OK EULIE... NO OFFENSE, BUT YOU ARE GETTING meta PATHETIC ABOUT THIS ASHER DUDE. FORGET HIM! I'VE ALREADY GOT THE PERFECT GUY FOR YOU. REMEMBER MY COUSIN, TRENT? HE THINKS YOU'RE HOT... AND YOU BOTH LIKE THE SAME MUSIC. YOU COULD MEET HIM DOWNTOWN NEXT WEEK....
SAGE ADVICE FROM MARIA, A FRIEND FROM ANOTHER SCHOOL...

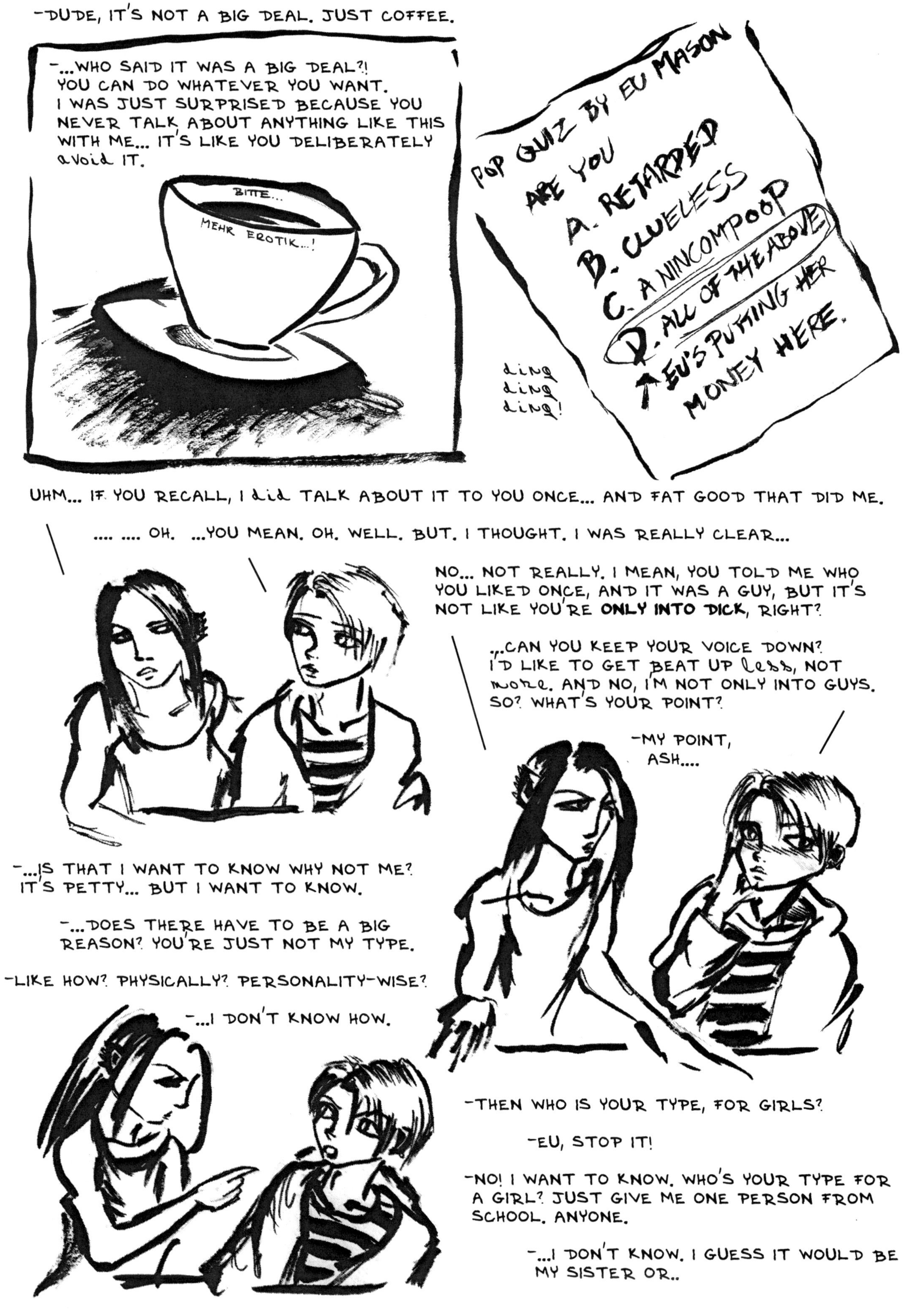
-DUDE, IT'S NOT A BIG DEAL. JUST COFFEE.
-...WHO SAID IT WAS A BIG DEAL?! YOU CAN DO WHATEVER YOU WANT. I WAS JUST SURPRISED BECAUSE YOU NEVER TALK ABOUT ANYTHING LIKE THIS WITH ME... IT'S LIKE YOU DELIBERATELY avoid IT.
BITTE...
MEHR EROTIK...!
POP QUIZ BY EU MASON
ARE YOU
A. RETARDED
B. CLUELESS
C. A NINCOMPOOP
D. ALL OF THE ABOVE
EU'S PUTTING HER MONEY HERE.
ding ding ding!
UHM... IF YOU RECALL, I did TALK ABOUT IT TO YOU ONCE... AND FAT GOOD THAT DID ME.
.... OH. ...YOU MEAN. OH. WELL. BUT. I THOUGHT. I WAS REALLY CLEAR...
NO... NOT REALLY. I MEAN, YOU TOLD ME WHO YOU LIKED ONCE, AND IT WAS A GUY, BUT IT'S NOT LIKE YOU'RE **ONLY INTO DICK**, RIGHT?
...CAN YOU KEEP YOUR VOICE DOWN? I'D LIKE TO GET BEAT UP less, NOT more. AND NO, I'M NOT ONLY INTO GUYS. SO? WHAT'S YOUR POINT?
-MY POINT, ASH....
-...IS THAT I WANT TO KNOW WHY NOT ME? IT'S PETTY... BUT I WANT TO KNOW.
-...DOES THERE HAVE TO BE A BIG REASON? YOU'RE JUST NOT MY TYPE.
-LIKE HOW? PHYSICALLY? PERSONALITY-WISE?
-...I DON'T KNOW HOW.
-THEN WHO IS YOUR TYPE, FOR GIRLS?
-EU, STOP IT!
-NO! I WANT TO KNOW. WHO'S YOUR TYPE FOR A GIRL? JUST GIVE ME ONE PERSON FROM SCHOOL. ANYONE.
-...I DON'T KNOW. I GUESS IT WOULD BE MY SISTER OR..

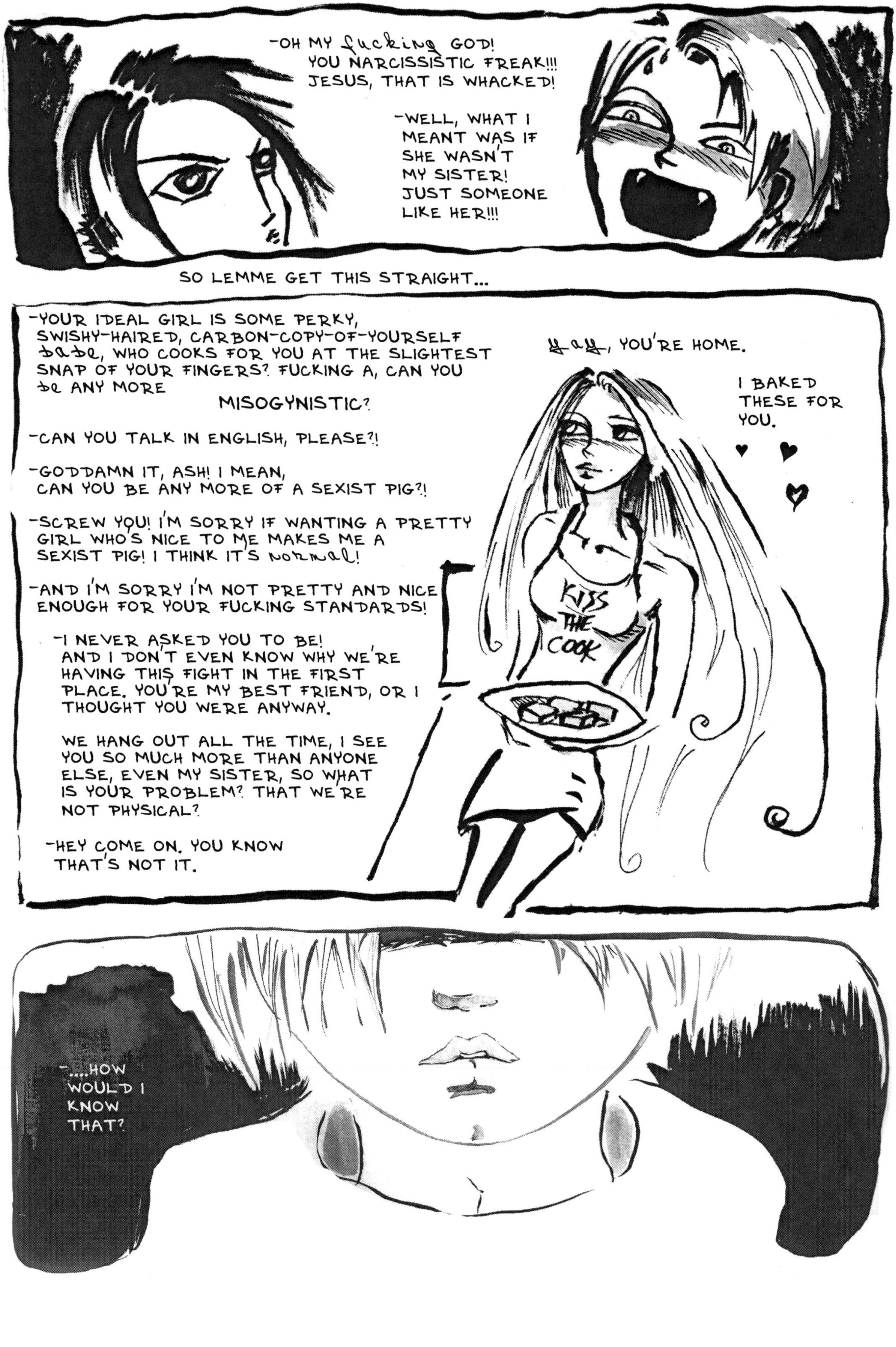
-OH MY fucking GOD! YOU NARCISSISTIC FREAK!!! JESUS, THAT IS WHACKED!
-WELL, WHAT I MEANT WAS IF SHE WASN'T MY SISTER! JUST SOMEONE LIKE HER!!!
SO LEMME GET THIS STRAIGHT...
-YOUR IDEAL GIRL IS SOME PERKY, SWISHY-HAIRED, CARBON-COPY-OF-YOURSELF babe, WHO COOKS FOR YOU AT THE SLIGHTEST SNAP OF YOUR FINGERS? FUCKING A, CAN YOU be ANY MORE MISOGYNISTIC?
-CAN YOU TALK IN ENGLISH, PLEASE?!
-GODDAMN IT, ASH! I MEAN, CAN YOU BE ANY MORE OF A SEXIST PIG?!
-SCREW YOU! I'M SORRY IF WANTING A PRETTY GIRL WHO'S NICE TO ME MAKES ME A SEXIST PIG! I THINK IT'S normal!
-AND I'M SORRY I'M NOT PRETTY AND NICE ENOUGH FOR YOUR FUCKING STANDARDS!
-I NEVER ASKED YOU TO BE! AND I DON'T EVEN KNOW WHY WE'RE HAVING THIS FIGHT IN THE FIRST PLACE. YOU'RE MY BEST FRIEND, OR I THOUGHT YOU WERE ANYWAY.
WE HANG OUT ALL THE TIME, I SEE YOU SO MUCH MORE THAN ANYONE ELSE, EVEN MY SISTER, SO WHAT IS YOUR PROBLEM? THAT WE'RE NOT PHYSICAL?
-HEY COME ON. YOU KNOW THAT'S NOT IT.
yay, YOU'RE HOME.
I BAKED THESE FOR YOU.
KISS THE COOK
-....HOW WOULD I KNOW THAT?

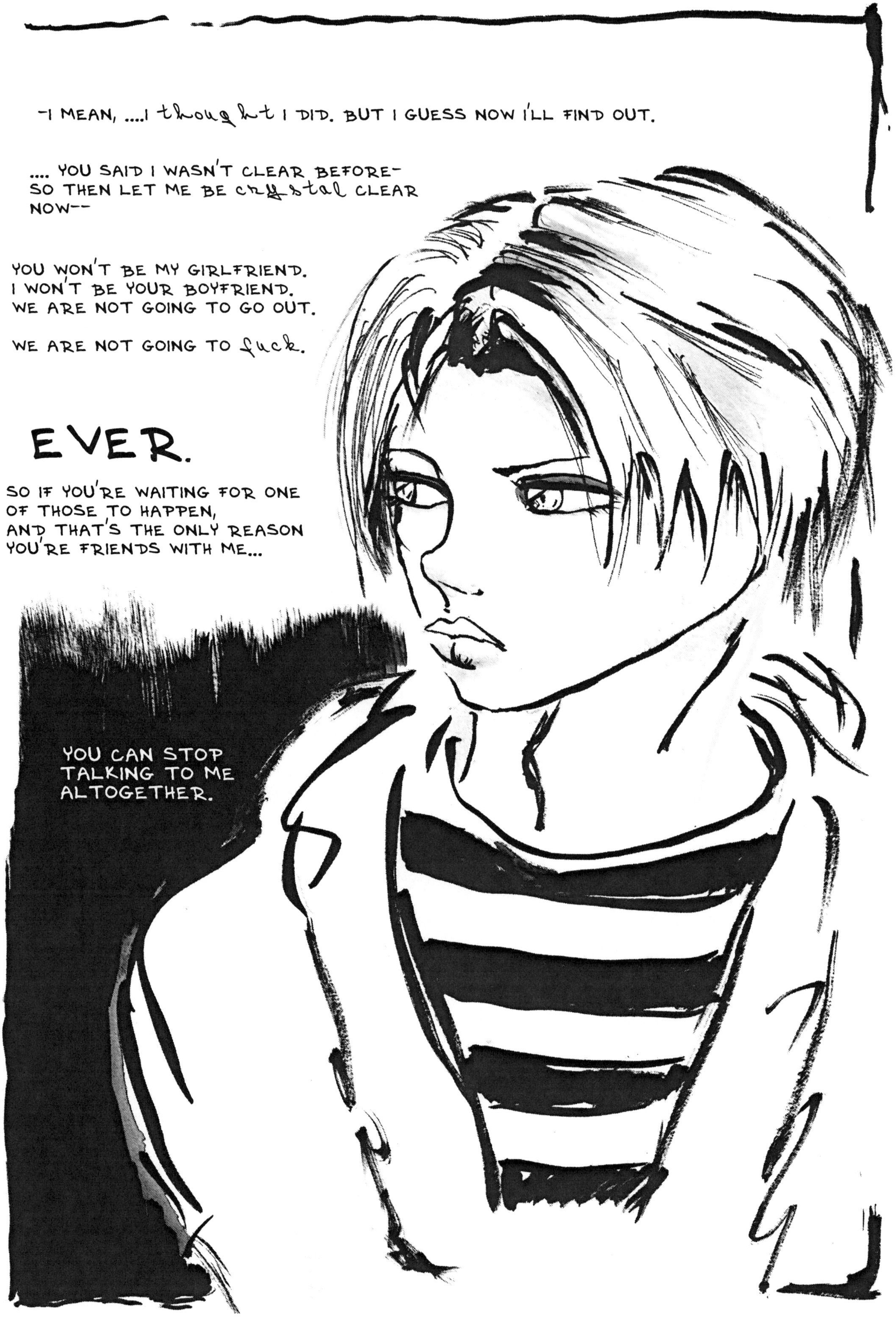
-I MEAN, ...I thought I DID. BUT I GUESS NOW I'LL FIND OUT.
.... YOU SAID I WASN'T CLEAR BEFORE- SO THEN LET ME BE crystal CLEAR NOW--
YOU WON'T BE MY GIRLFRIEND. I WON'T BE YOUR BOYFRIEND. WE ARE NOT GOING TO GO OUT.
WE ARE NOT GOING TO fuck.
EVER.
SO IF YOU'RE WAITING FOR ONE OF THOSE TO HAPPEN, AND THAT'S THE ONLY REASON YOU'RE FRIENDS WITH ME...
YOU CAN STOP TALKING TO ME ALTOGETHER.

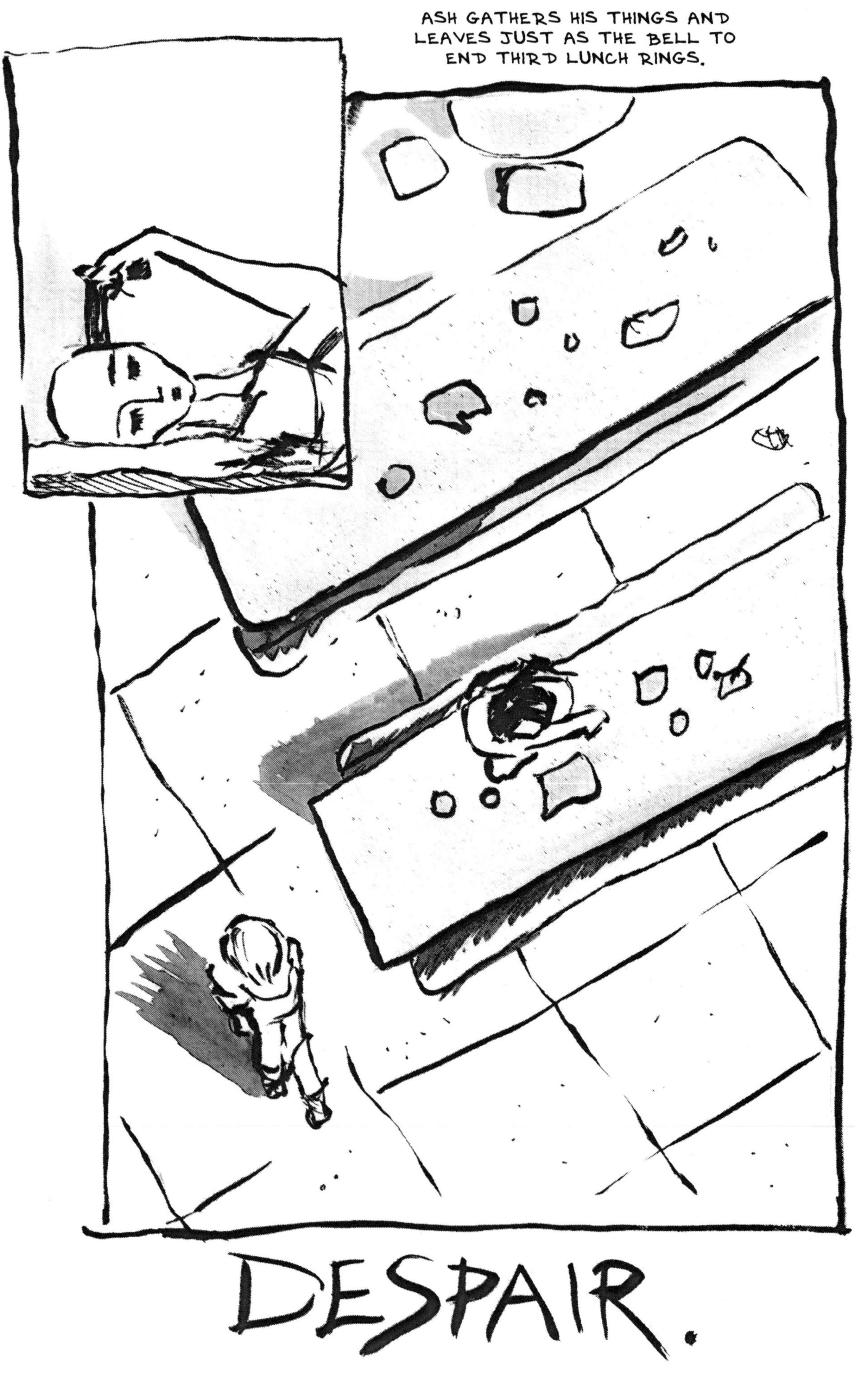
ASH GATHERS HIS THINGS AND LEAVES JUST AS THE BELL TO END THIRD LUNCH RINGS.
DESPAIR.

ein romantisches date mit... trent foreman

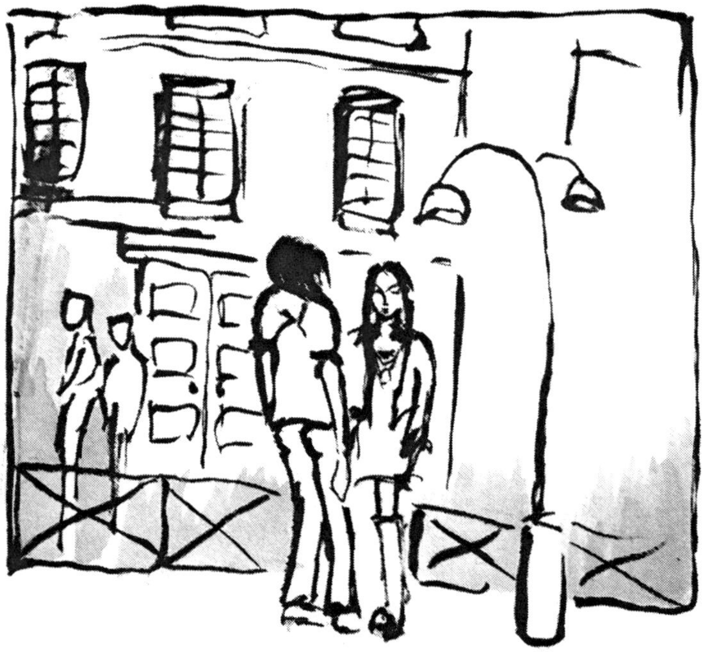

THAT AFTERNOON, EU MEETS TRENT FOREMAN DOWNTOWN FOR THEIR DATE.

TRENT IS TALLER THAN HER, PRETTY, AND DOESN'T LIKE ANY BAND THAT MORE THAN FIVE PEOPLE HAVE HEARD OF.

THEY GO SEE A MOVIE WITH MANY EXPLOSIONS, THEN HE INVITES HER TO A TRENDY COFFEE SHOP CLOSE TO THE MOVIE THEATER.

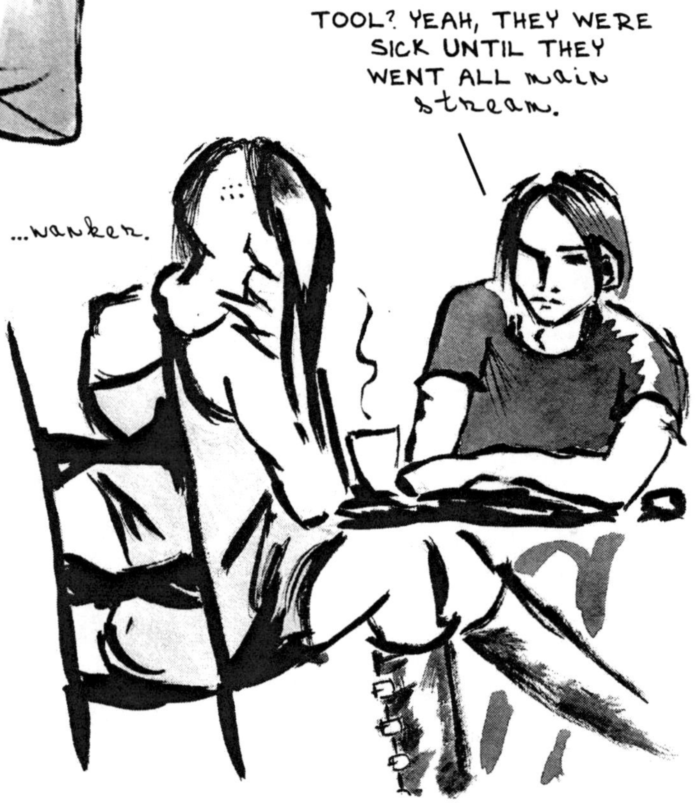
TOOL? YEAH, THEY WERE SICK UNTIL THEY WENT ALL main stream.
...wanker.

AFTER FIVE SENTENCES RELATED TO ART, SHE SEES THAT HE DOESN'T KNOW PISSARRO FROM CAMARO, AND THAT THE LETTERS B AND H HAVE NO FURTHER SIGNIFICANCE TO HIM BEYOND THE SECOND AND EIGHTH LETTERS OF THE ALPHABET, RESPECTIVELY.

STILL, SHE CAN TELL HE LIKES HER QUITE A LOT.

THE ONLY DISAPPROVAL EU INCURS ALL AFTERNOON IS WHEN SHE GETS UP TO BUY HER SECOND RASPBERRY SCONE.

EAT MUCH?, HE ASKS, ONLY A QUARTER JOKING AND EU SCOWLS AT HIM.

WHAT A BITCH, SHE THINKS.

HE DRIVES HER HOME IN HIS BATTLE-SCARRED VOLVO.

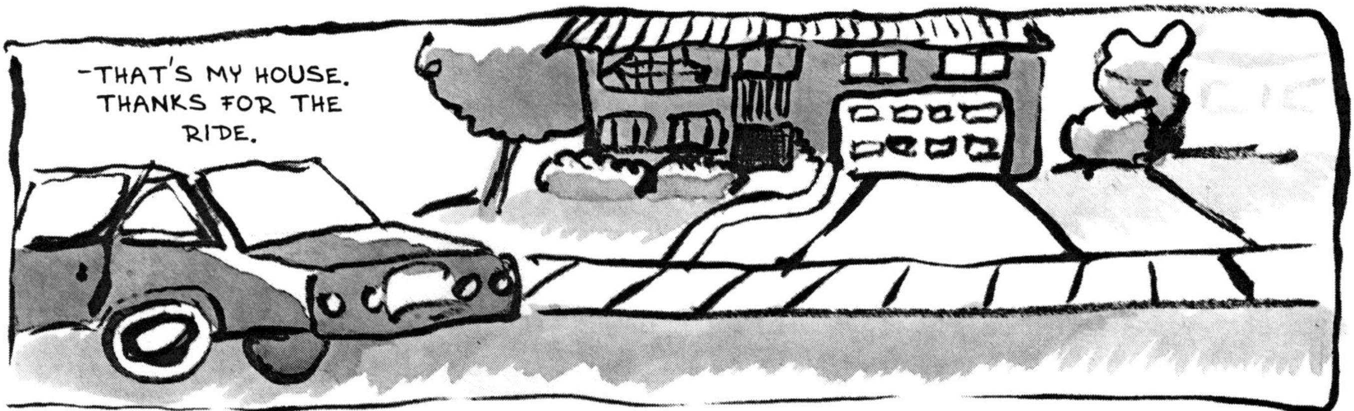
-THAT'S MY HOUSE. THANKS FOR THE RIDE.

-NO PROBLEM. I HAD A REALLY GREAT TIME WITH YOU, EULALIE. TRENT SAYS. SHE NOTICES THAT HE ALWAYS CALLS HER BY HER FULL NAME.

WHEN SHE TRIES TO LEAVE THE CAR, HE LEANS OVER AND TENTATIVELY KISSES HER NECK. HE MOVES TO HER LIPS, THEN TOUCHES HER BREASTS THROUGH HER SHIRT. EU LETS HIM, INDIFFERENT.

i guess HE doesn't mind touching me...

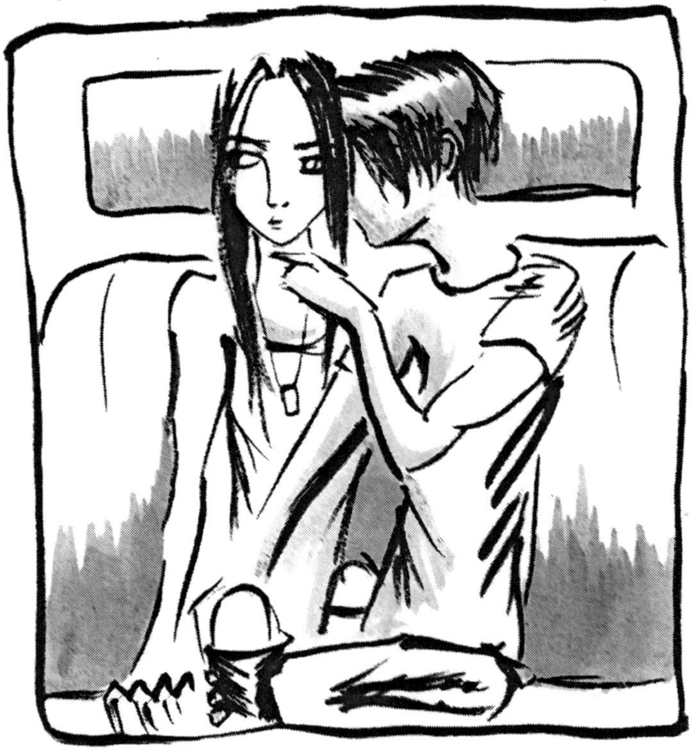

SHE SAYS SOMETHING ONLY WHEN HIS HAND GOES UNDER HER SKIRT...

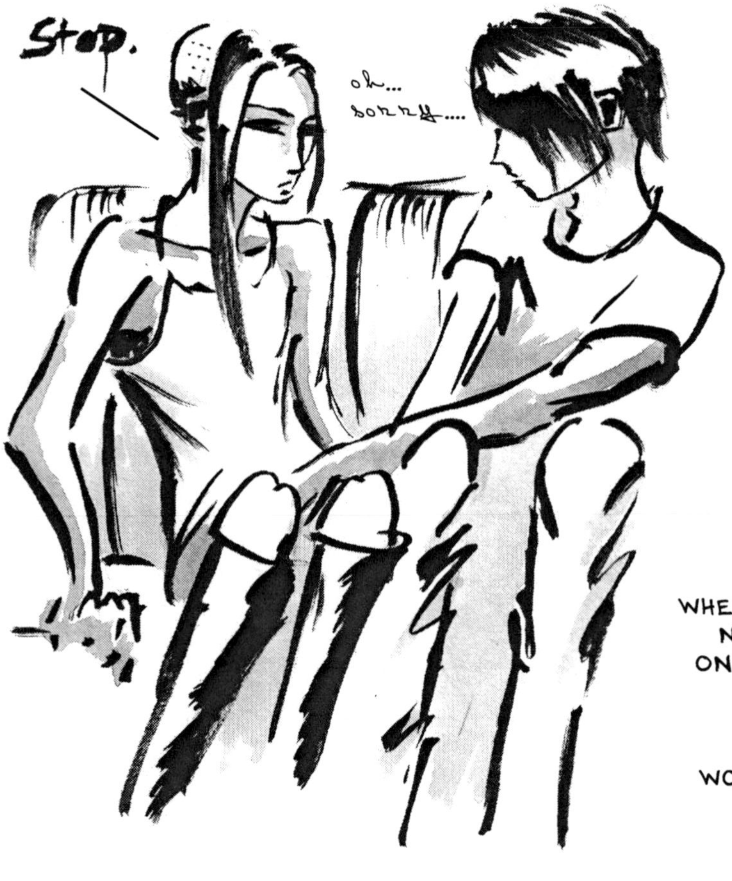
Stop.
oh... sorry....

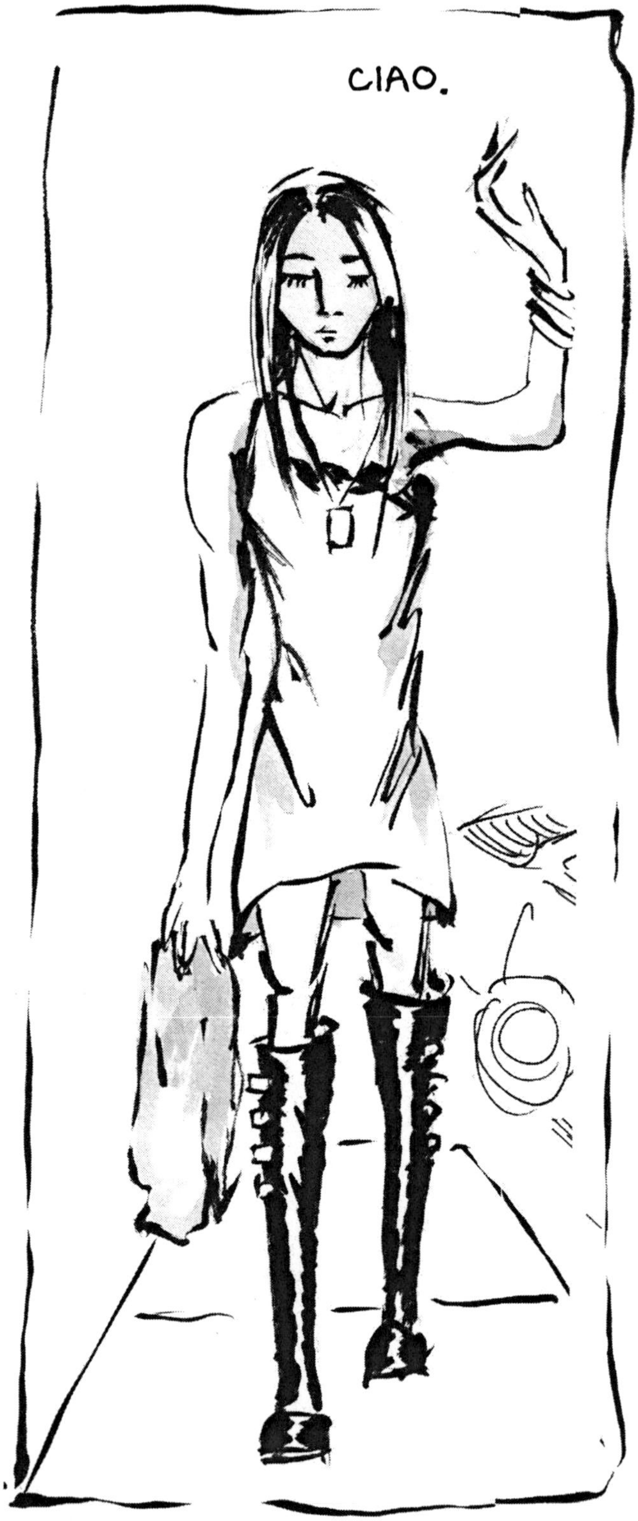
CIAO.

WHEN TRENT ASKS IF THEY CAN MEET AGAIN NEXT WEEK, SHE NODS, BUT STANDING ON THE CURB OUTSIDE HIS CAR, EU FEELS DEPRESSED.

SHE WATCHES HIM DRIVE AWAY AND WONDERS HOW SOMEONE CAN SOUND LIKE nothing.

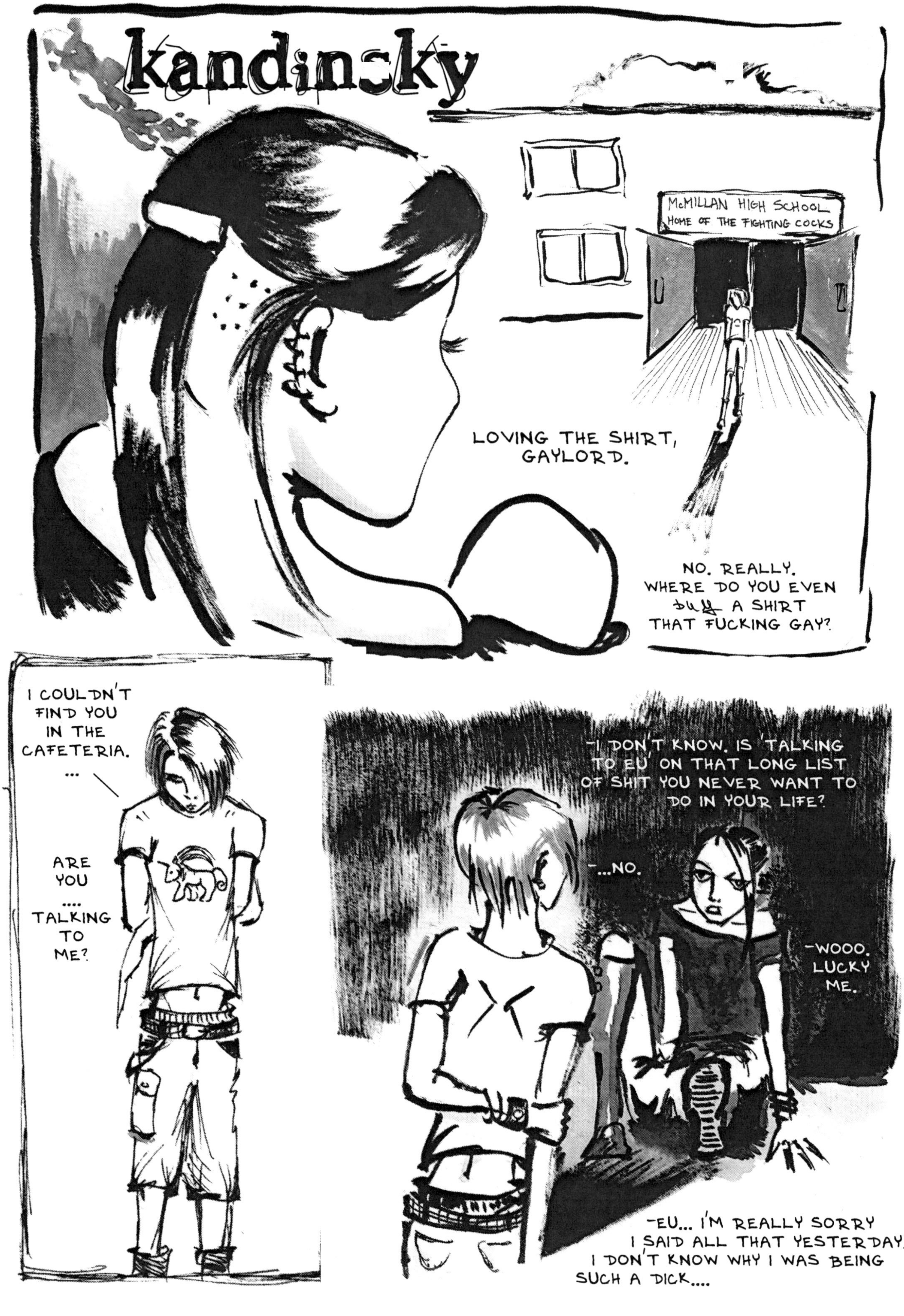
kandinsky
McMILLAN HIGH SCHOOL
HOME OF THE FIGHTING COCKS
LOVING THE SHIRT, GAYLORD.
NO. REALLY. WHERE DO YOU EVEN buy A SHIRT THAT FUCKING GAY?
I COULDN'T FIND YOU IN THE CAFETERIA. ...
ARE YOU .... TALKING TO ME?
-I DON'T KNOW. IS 'TALKING TO EU' ON THAT LONG LIST OF SHIT YOU NEVER WANT TO DO IN YOUR LIFE?
-...NO.
-WOOO. LUCKY ME.
-EU... I'M REALLY SORRY I SAID ALL THAT YESTERDAY. I DON'T KNOW WHY I WAS BEING SUCH A DICK....

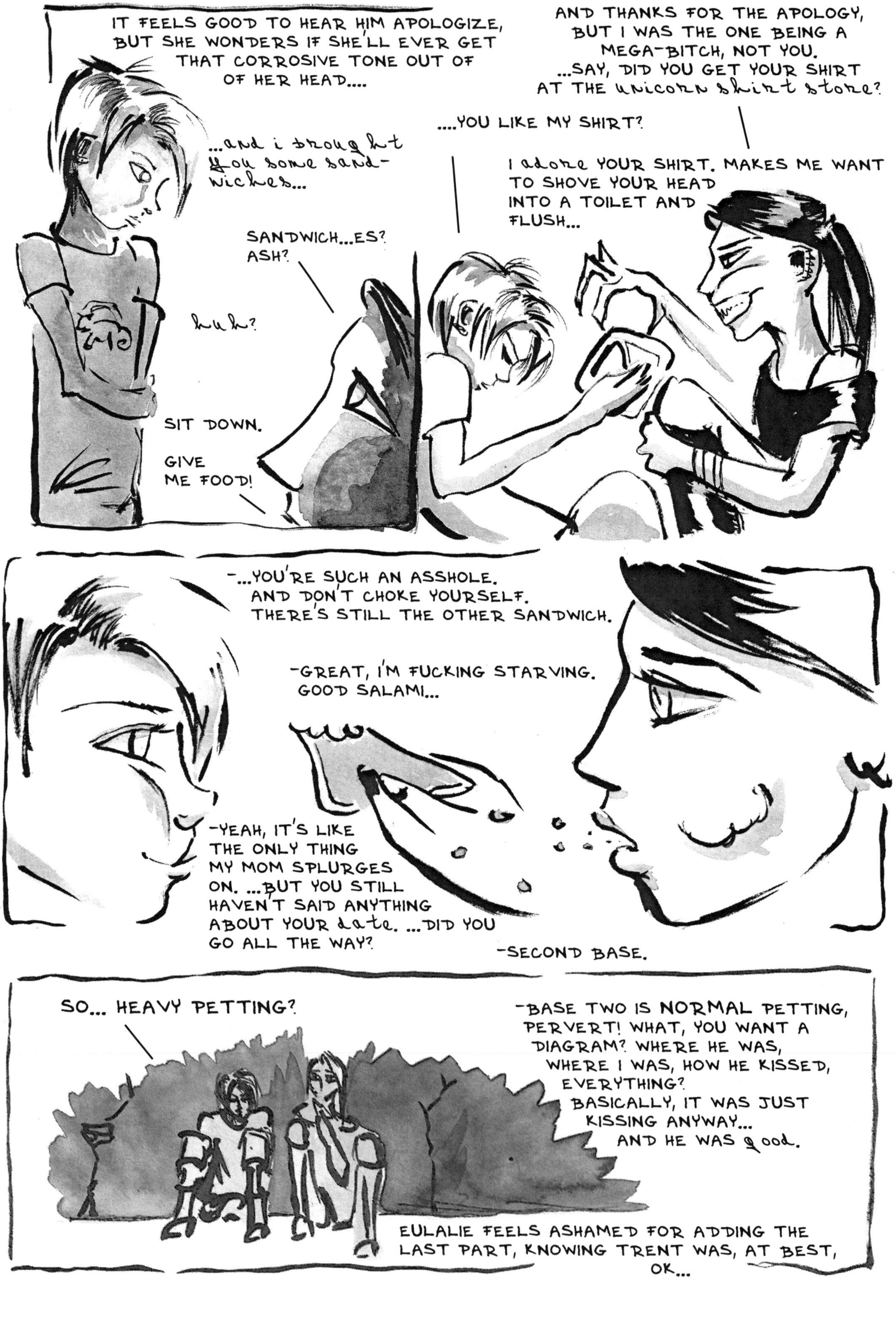

IT FEELS GOOD TO HEAR HIM APOLOGIZE, BUT SHE WONDERS IF SHE'LL EVER GET THAT CORROSIVE TONE OUT OF OF HER HEAD....
...and i brought you some sandwiches...
SANDWICH...ES? ASH?
huh?
SIT DOWN.
GIVE ME FOOD!
....YOU LIKE MY SHIRT?
I adore YOUR SHIRT. MAKES ME WANT TO SHOVE YOUR HEAD INTO A TOILET AND FLUSH...
AND THANKS FOR THE APOLOGY, BUT I WAS THE ONE BEING A MEGA-BITCH, NOT YOU. ...SAY, DID YOU GET YOUR SHIRT AT THE unicorn shirt store?
-...YOU'RE SUCH AN ASSHOLE. AND DON'T CHOKE YOURSELF. THERE'S STILL THE OTHER SANDWICH.
-GREAT, I'M FUCKING STARVING. GOOD SALAMI...
-YEAH, IT'S LIKE THE ONLY THING MY MOM SPLURGES ON. ...BUT YOU STILL HAVEN'T SAID ANYTHING ABOUT YOUR date. ...DID YOU GO ALL THE WAY?
-SECOND BASE.
SO... HEAVY PETTING?
-BASE TWO IS NORMAL PETTING, PERVERT! WHAT, YOU WANT A DIAGRAM? WHERE HE WAS, WHERE I WAS, HOW HE KISSED, EVERYTHING? BASICALLY, IT WAS JUST KISSING ANYWAY... AND HE WAS good.
EULALIE FEELS ASHAMED FOR ADDING THE LAST PART, KNOWING TRENT WAS, AT BEST, OK...

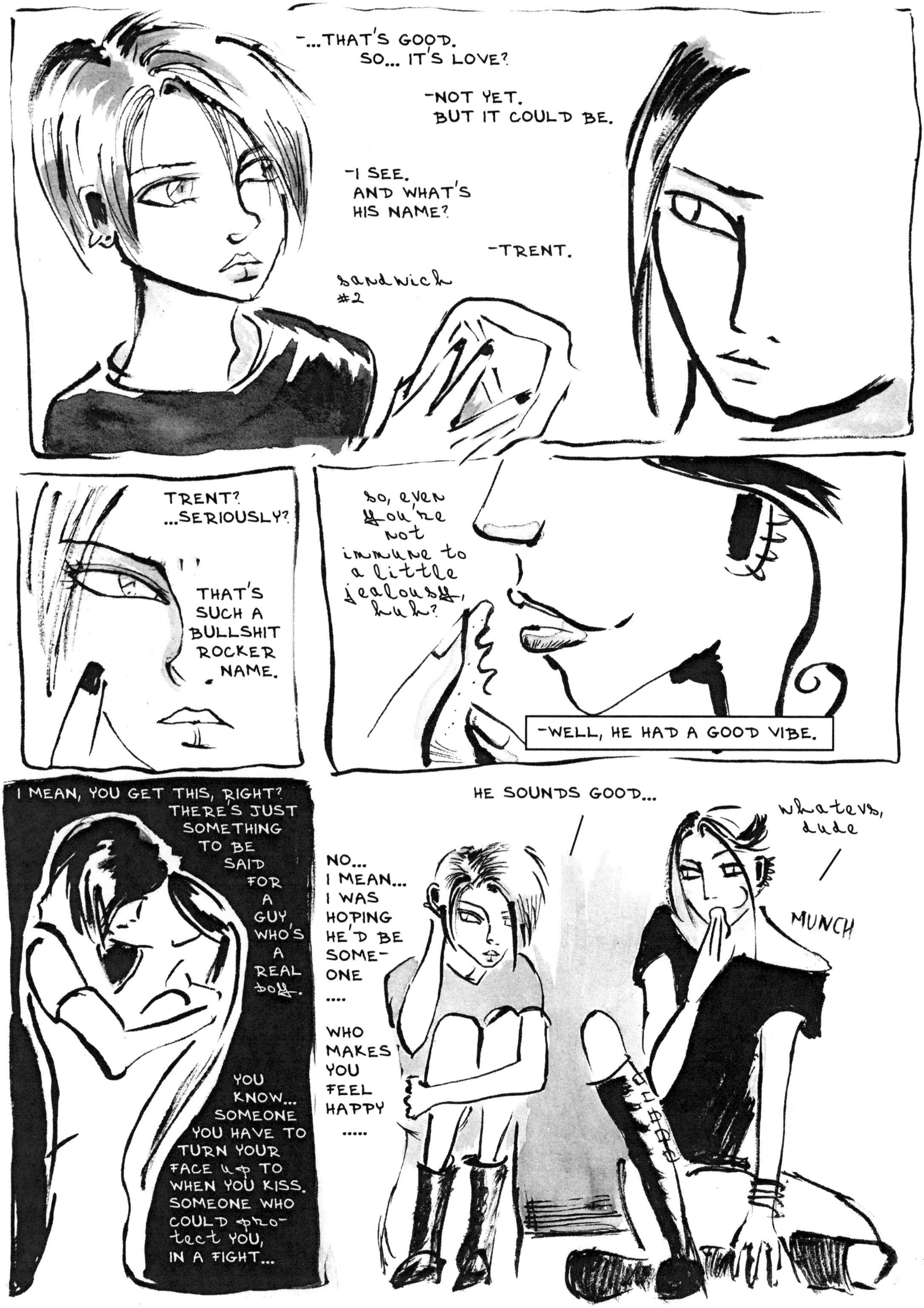
-...THAT'S GOOD.
SO... IT'S LOVE?
-NOT YET.
BUT IT COULD BE.
-I SEE.
AND WHAT'S HIS NAME?
-TRENT.
sandwich #2
TRENT?
...SERIOUSLY?
THAT'S SUCH A BULLSHIT ROCKER NAME.
so, even you're not immune to a little jealousy, huh?
-WELL, HE HAD A GOOD VIBE.
I MEAN, YOU GET THIS, RIGHT? THERE'S JUST SOMETHING TO BE SAID FOR A GUY WHO'S A REAL boy.
YOU KNOW... SOMEONE YOU HAVE TO TURN YOUR FACE up TO WHEN YOU KISS. SOMEONE WHO COULD pro-tect YOU, IN A FIGHT...
HE SOUNDS GOOD...
NO... I MEAN... I WAS HOPING HE'D BE SOME-ONE ....
WHO MAKES YOU FEEL HAPPY .....
whatevs, dude
MUNCH

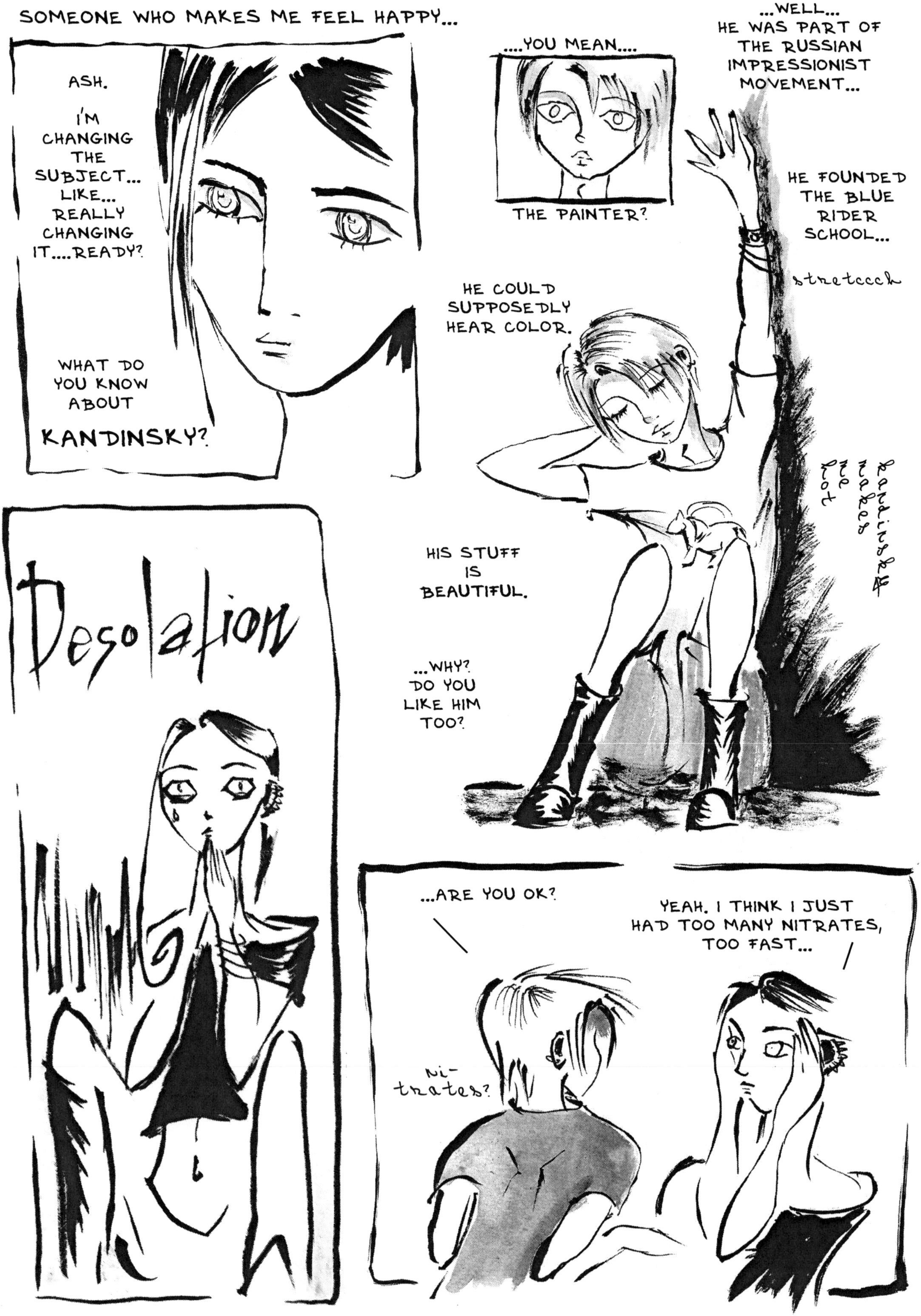
SOMEONE WHO MAKES ME FEEL HAPPY...
ASH.
I'M CHANGING THE SUBJECT... LIKE... REALLY CHANGING IT.... READY?
WHAT DO YOU KNOW ABOUT KANDINSKY?
....YOU MEAN....
THE PAINTER?
...WELL... HE WAS PART OF THE RUSSIAN IMPRESSIONIST MOVEMENT...
HE FOUNDED THE BLUE RIDER SCHOOL...
stretcccch
HE COULD SUPPOSEDLY HEAR COLOR.
kandinsky makes me hot
HIS STUFF IS BEAUTIFUL.
...WHY? DO YOU LIKE HIM TOO?
Desolation
...ARE YOU OK?
YEAH. I THINK I JUST HAD TOO MANY NITRATES, TOO FAST...
Ni-trates?

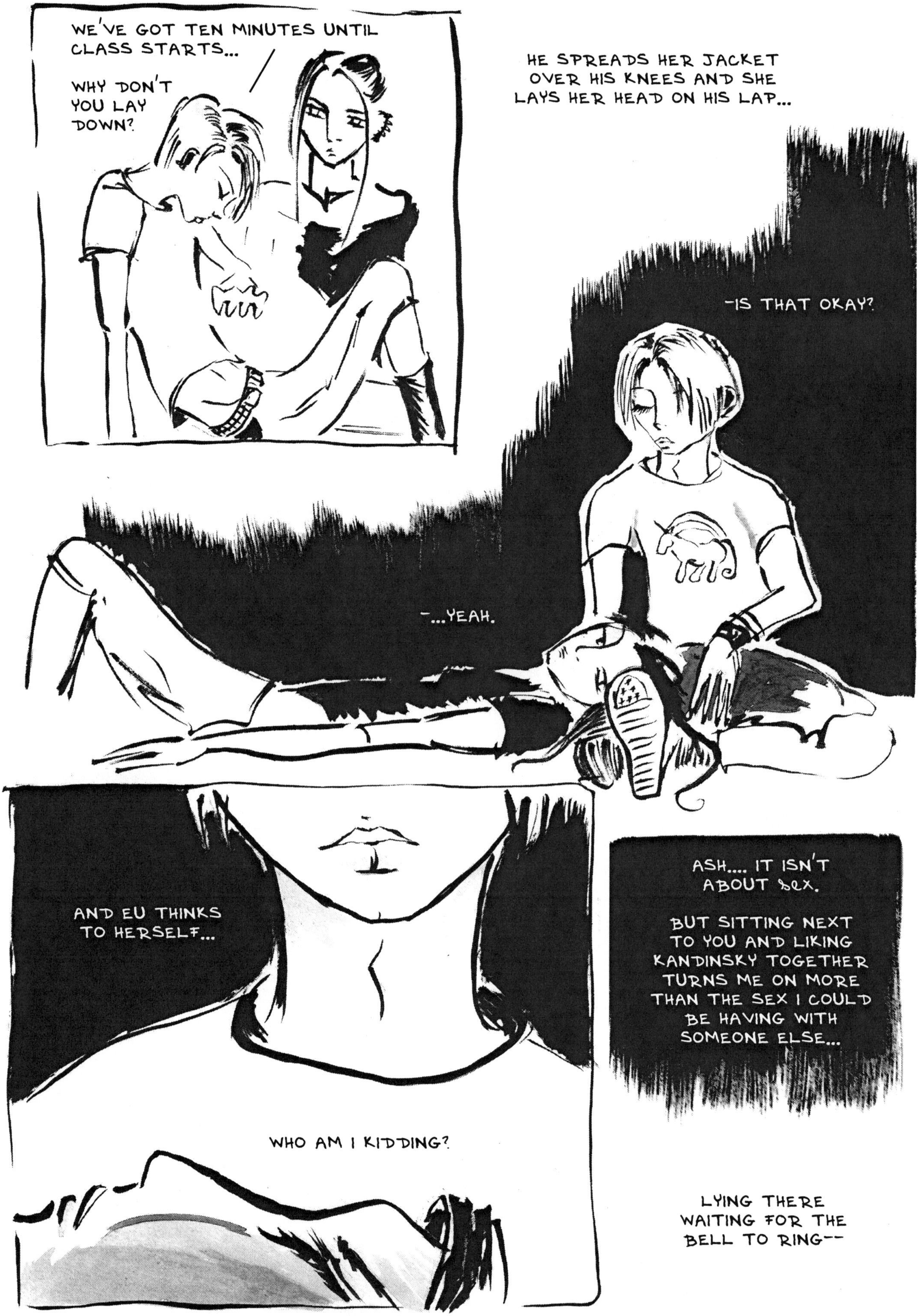
WE'VE GOT TEN MINUTES UNTIL CLASS STARTS...
WHY DON'T YOU LAY DOWN?
HE SPREADS HER JACKET OVER HIS KNEES AND SHE LAYS HER HEAD ON HIS LAP...
-IS THAT OKAY?
-...YEAH.
AND EU THINKS TO HERSELF...
ASH.... IT ISN'T ABOUT sex.
BUT SITTING NEXT TO YOU AND LIKING KANDINSKY TOGETHER TURNS ME ON MORE THAN THE SEX I COULD BE HAVING WITH SOMEONE ELSE...
WHO AM I KIDDING?
LYING THERE WAITING FOR THE BELL TO RING--

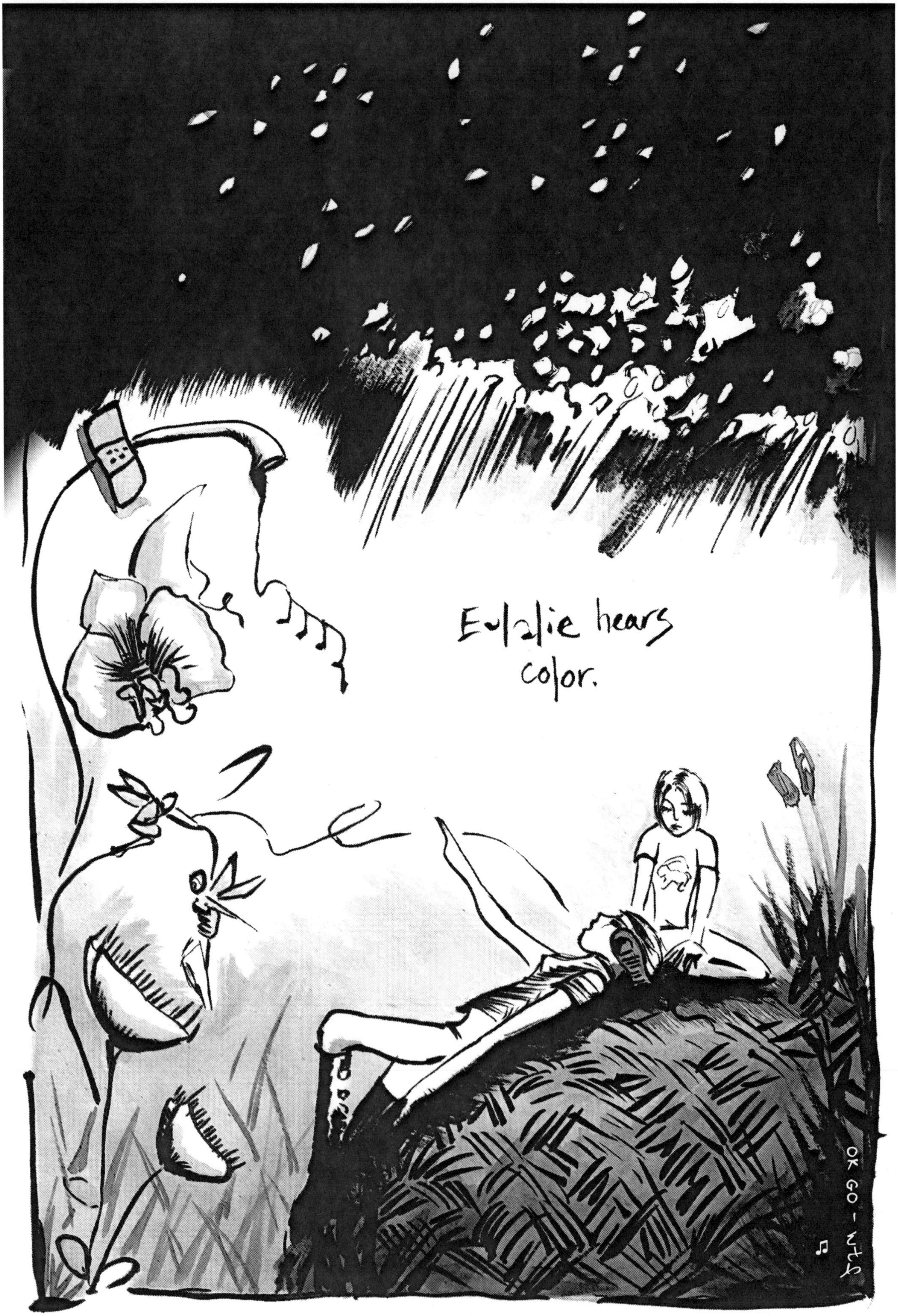
Eulalie hears color.
OK GO - WTF ♫

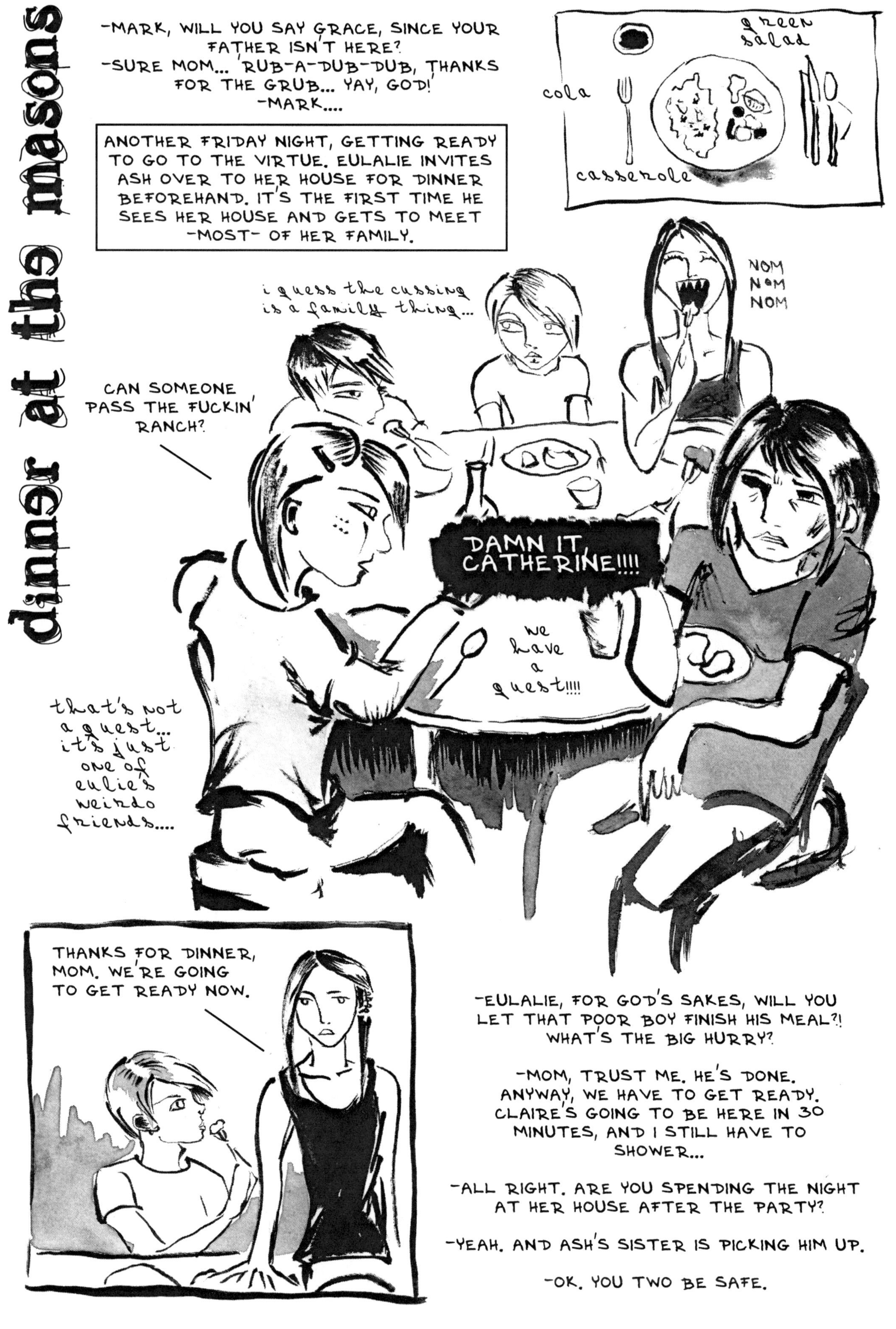
dinner at the masons
-MARK, WILL YOU SAY GRACE, SINCE YOUR FATHER ISN'T HERE?
-SURE MOM... 'RUB-A-DUB-DUB, THANKS FOR THE GRUB... YAY, GOD!'
-MARK....
ANOTHER FRIDAY NIGHT, GETTING READY TO GO TO THE VIRTUE. EULALIE INVITES ASH OVER TO HER HOUSE FOR DINNER BEFOREHAND. IT'S THE FIRST TIME HE SEES HER HOUSE AND GETS TO MEET -MOST- OF HER FAMILY.
green salad
cola
casserole
i guess the cussing is a family thing...
NOM NOM NOM
CAN SOMEONE PASS THE FUCKIN' RANCH?
DAMN IT, CATHERINE!!!!
we have a guest!!!!
that's not a guest... it's just one of eulie's weirdo friends....
THANKS FOR DINNER, MOM. WE'RE GOING TO GET READY NOW.
-EULALIE, FOR GOD'S SAKES, WILL YOU LET THAT POOR BOY FINISH HIS MEAL?! WHAT'S THE BIG HURRY?
-MOM, TRUST ME. HE'S DONE. ANYWAY, WE HAVE TO GET READY. CLAIRE'S GOING TO BE HERE IN 30 MINUTES, AND I STILL HAVE TO SHOWER...
-ALL RIGHT. ARE YOU SPENDING THE NIGHT AT HER HOUSE AFTER THE PARTY?
-YEAH. AND ASH'S SISTER IS PICKING HIM UP.
-OK. YOU TWO BE SAFE.

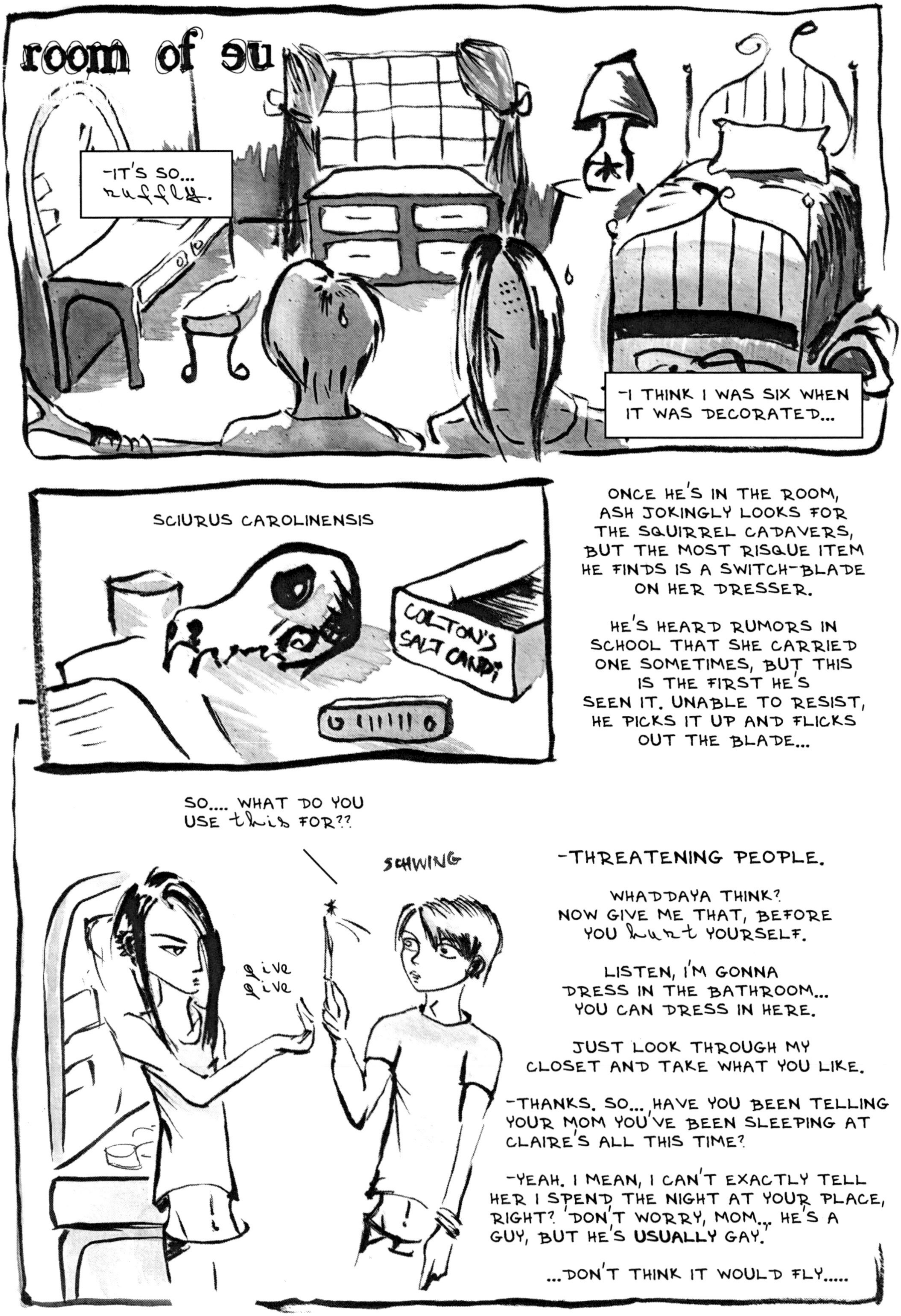
room of su
-IT'S SO... ruffly.
-I THINK I WAS SIX WHEN IT WAS DECORATED...
SCIURUS CAROLINENSIS
COLTON'S SALT CANDY
ONCE HE'S IN THE ROOM, ASH JOKINGLY LOOKS FOR THE SQUIRREL CADAVERS, BUT THE MOST RISQUE ITEM HE FINDS IS A SWITCH-BLADE ON HER DRESSER.
HE'S HEARD RUMORS IN SCHOOL THAT SHE CARRIED ONE SOMETIMES, BUT THIS IS THE FIRST HE'S SEEN IT. UNABLE TO RESIST, HE PICKS IT UP AND FLICKS OUT THE BLADE...
SO.... WHAT DO YOU USE this FOR??
SCHWING
-THREATENING PEOPLE.
WHADDAYA THINK? NOW GIVE ME THAT, BEFORE YOU hurt YOURSELF.
give give
LISTEN, I'M GONNA DRESS IN THE BATHROOM... YOU CAN DRESS IN HERE.
JUST LOOK THROUGH MY CLOSET AND TAKE WHAT YOU LIKE.
-THANKS. SO... HAVE YOU BEEN TELLING YOUR MOM YOU'VE BEEN SLEEPING AT CLAIRE'S ALL THIS TIME?
-YEAH. I MEAN, I CAN'T EXACTLY TELL HER I SPEND THE NIGHT AT YOUR PLACE, RIGHT? 'DON'T WORRY, MOM... HE'S A GUY, BUT HE'S **USUALLY** GAY.'
...DON'T THINK IT WOULD FLY.....

-OK...

I'M TAKING MY SHOWER.

SO MANY CLOTHES... ♥

WHILE SHE'S GONE, ASH RIFFLES THROUGH HER CLOSET. OTHER THAN HEIGHT, THEY ARE MORE OR LESS THE SAME SIZE AND HAVE RECENTLY STARTED TO SWAP CLOTHES. HE PICKS OUT VAMPIRE-RED VINLY PANTS, A DAY-GLO STUDDED BELT AND A SKIN-TIGHT REMY-ZERO SHIRT. HE'S STIFFENING HIS HAIR WITH WAX WHEN THE DOOR OPENS AGAIN--

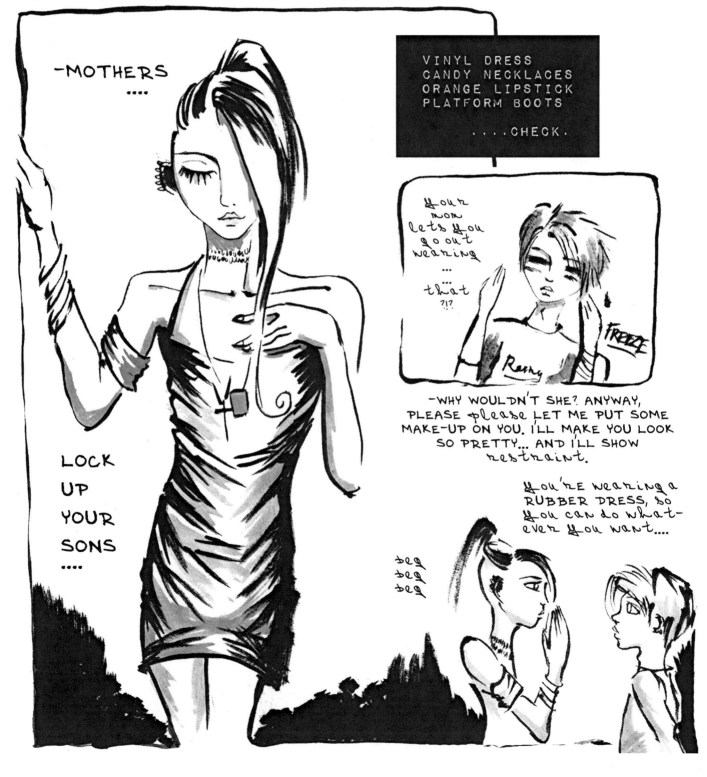

-MOTHERS
....

VINYL DRESS
CANDY NECKLACES
ORANGE LIPSTICK
PLATFORM BOOTS

.... CHECK.

your mom lets you go out wearing ... . that ?!?

-WHY WOULDN'T SHE? ANYWAY, PLEASE please LET ME PUT SOME MAKE-UP ON YOU. I'LL MAKE YOU LOOK SO PRETTY... AND I'LL SHOW restraint.

LOCK UP YOUR SONS ....

you're wearing a RUBBER DRESS, so you can do what- ever you want....

beg beg beg

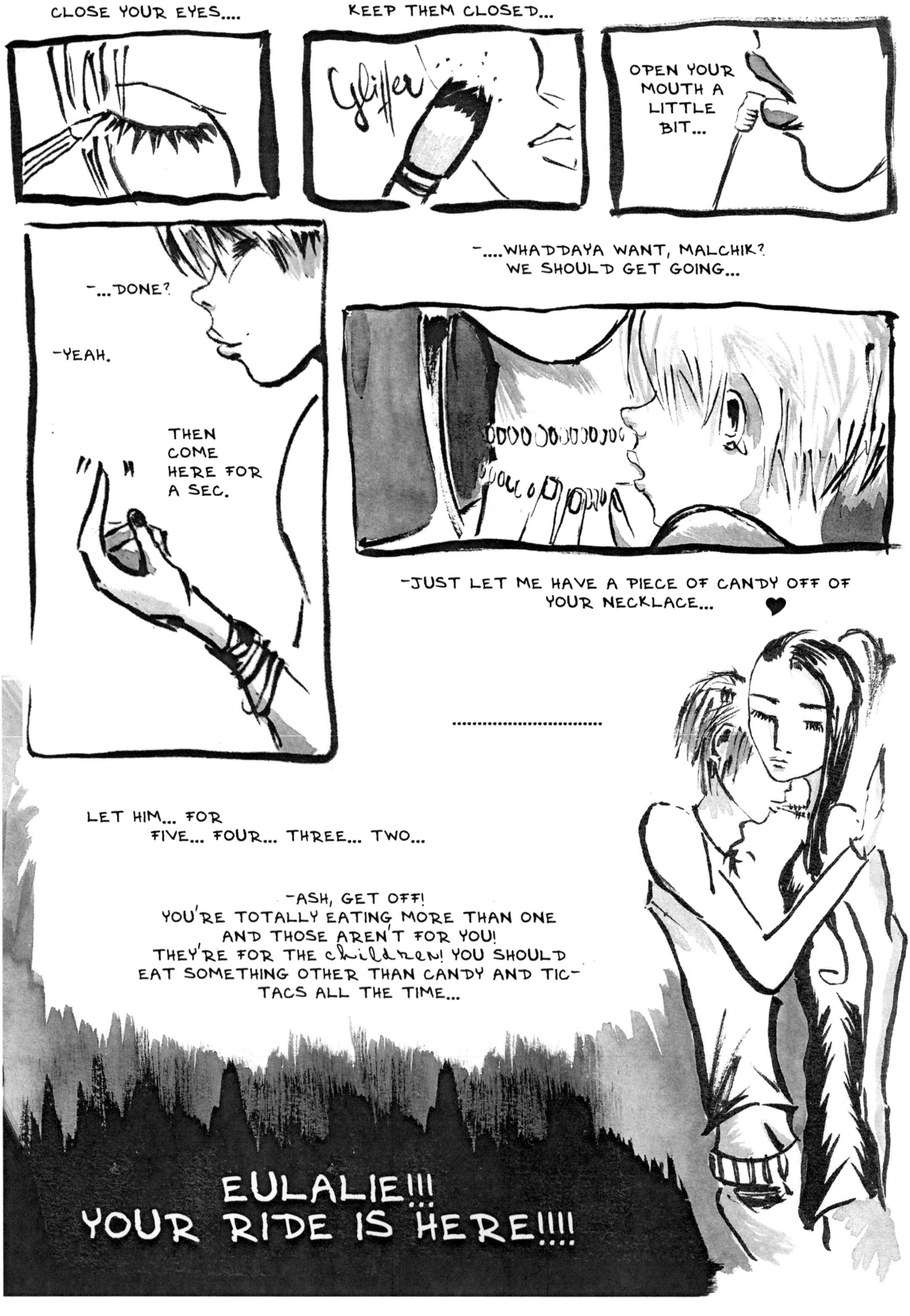

CLOSE YOUR EYES....
KEEP THEM CLOSED...
Glitter
OPEN YOUR MOUTH A LITTLE BIT...
-...DONE?
-YEAH.
THEN COME HERE FOR A SEC.
-....WHADDAYA WANT, MALCHIK? WE SHOULD GET GOING...
-JUST LET ME HAVE A PIECE OF CANDY OFF OF YOUR NECKLACE... ♥
....
LET HIM... FOR FIVE... FOUR... THREE... TWO...
-ASH, GET OFF! YOU'RE TOTALLY EATING MORE THAN ONE AND THOSE AREN'T FOR YOU! THEY'RE FOR THE children! YOU SHOULD EAT SOMETHING OTHER THAN CANDY AND TIC-TACS ALL THE TIME...
EULALIE!!! YOUR RIDE IS HERE!!!!

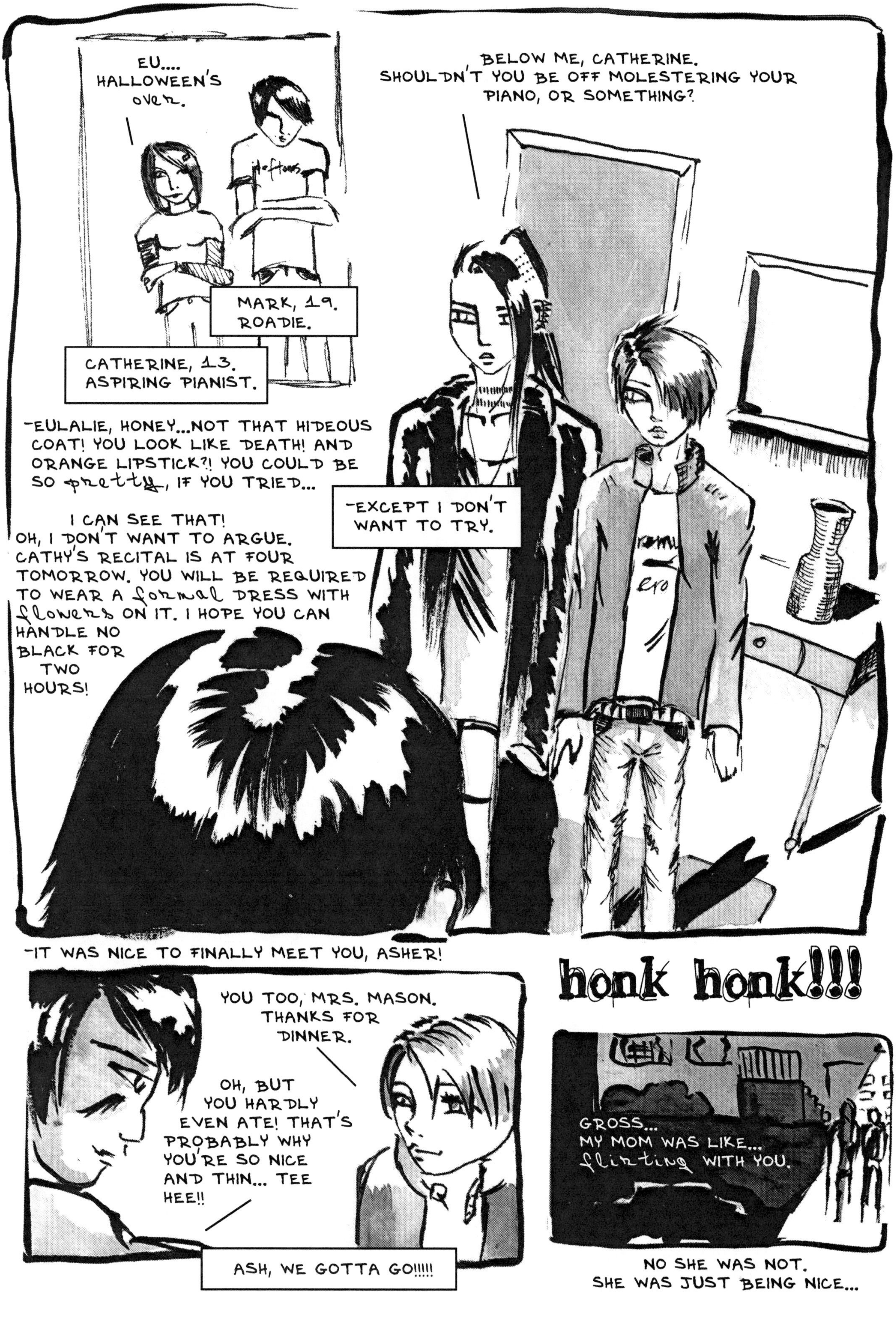
EU.... HALLOWEEN'S over.
BELOW ME, CATHERINE. SHOULDN'T YOU BE OFF MOLESTERING YOUR PIANO, OR SOMETHING?
MARK, 19. ROADIE.
CATHERINE, 13. ASPIRING PIANIST.
-EULALIE, HONEY...NOT THAT HIDEOUS COAT! YOU LOOK LIKE DEATH! AND ORANGE LIPSTICK?! YOU COULD BE SO pretty, IF YOU TRIED...
-EXCEPT I DON'T WANT TO TRY.
I CAN SEE THAT! OH, I DON'T WANT TO ARGUE. CATHY'S RECITAL IS AT FOUR TOMORROW. YOU WILL BE REQUIRED TO WEAR A formal DRESS WITH flowers ON IT. I HOPE YOU CAN HANDLE NO BLACK FOR TWO HOURS!
-IT WAS NICE TO FINALLY MEET YOU, ASHER!
YOU TOO, MRS. MASON. THANKS FOR DINNER.
OH, BUT YOU HARDLY EVEN ATE! THAT'S PROBABLY WHY YOU'RE SO NICE AND THIN... TEE HEE!!
ASH, WE GOTTA GO!!!!!
honk honk!!!
GROSS... MY MOM WAS LIKE... flirting WITH YOU.
NO SHE WAS NOT. SHE WAS JUST BEING NICE...

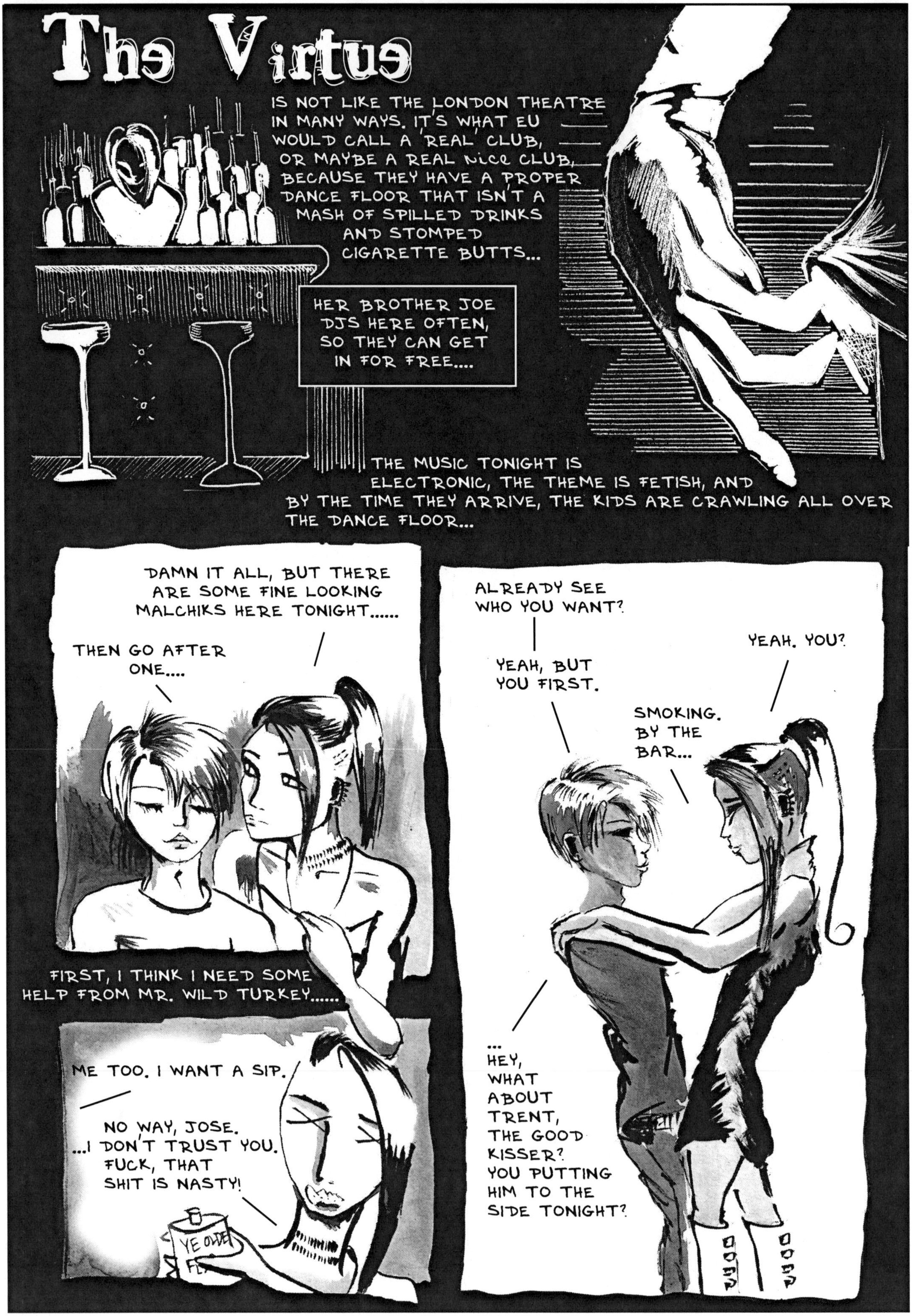
The Virtue
IS NOT LIKE THE LONDON THEATRE IN MANY WAYS. IT'S WHAT EU WOULD CALL A 'REAL' CLUB, OR MAYBE A REAL NICE CLUB, BECAUSE THEY HAVE A PROPER DANCE FLOOR THAT ISN'T A MASH OF SPILLED DRINKS AND STOMPED CIGARETTE BUTTS...
HER BROTHER JOE DJS HERE OFTEN, SO THEY CAN GET IN FOR FREE....
THE MUSIC TONIGHT IS ELECTRONIC, THE THEME IS FETISH, AND BY THE TIME THEY ARRIVE, THE KIDS ARE CRAWLING ALL OVER THE DANCE FLOOR...
DAMN IT ALL, BUT THERE ARE SOME FINE LOOKING MALCHIKS HERE TONIGHT......
THEN GO AFTER ONE....
FIRST, I THINK I NEED SOME HELP FROM MR. WILD TURKEY......
ME TOO. I WANT A SIP.
NO WAY, JOSE. ...I DON'T TRUST YOU. FUCK, THAT SHIT IS NASTY!
YE OLDE
ALREADY SEE WHO YOU WANT?
YEAH, BUT YOU FIRST.
YEAH. YOU?
SMOKING. BY THE BAR...
... HEY, WHAT ABOUT TRENT, THE GOOD KISSER? YOU PUTTING HIM TO THE SIDE TONIGHT?

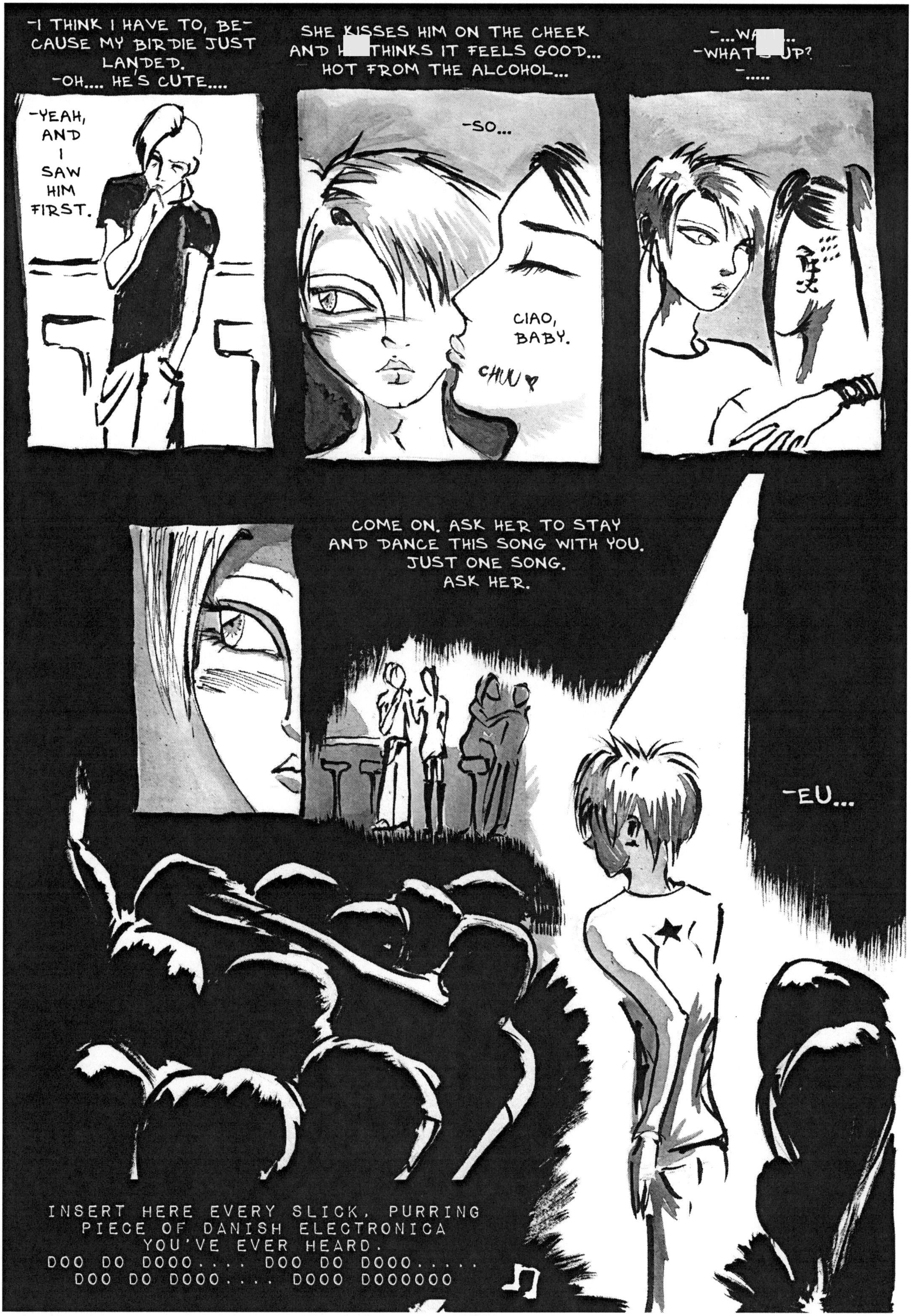
-I THINK I HAVE TO, BE-
CAUSE MY BIRDIE JUST
LANDED.
-OH.... HE'S CUTE....
-YEAH, AND I SAW HIM FIRST.
SHE KISSES HIM ON THE CHEEK
AND H THINKS IT FEELS GOOD...
HOT FROM THE ALCOHOL...
-SO...
CIAO, BABY.
CHUU
-...WA...
-WHAT UP?
-.....
COME ON. ASK HER TO STAY
AND DANCE THIS SONG WITH YOU.
JUST ONE SONG.
ASK HER.
-EU...
INSERT HERE EVERY SLICK, PURRING
PIECE OF DANISH ELECTRONICA
YOU'VE EVER HEARD.
DOO DO DOOO.... DOO DO DOOO.....
DOO DO DOOO.... DOOO DOOOOOO

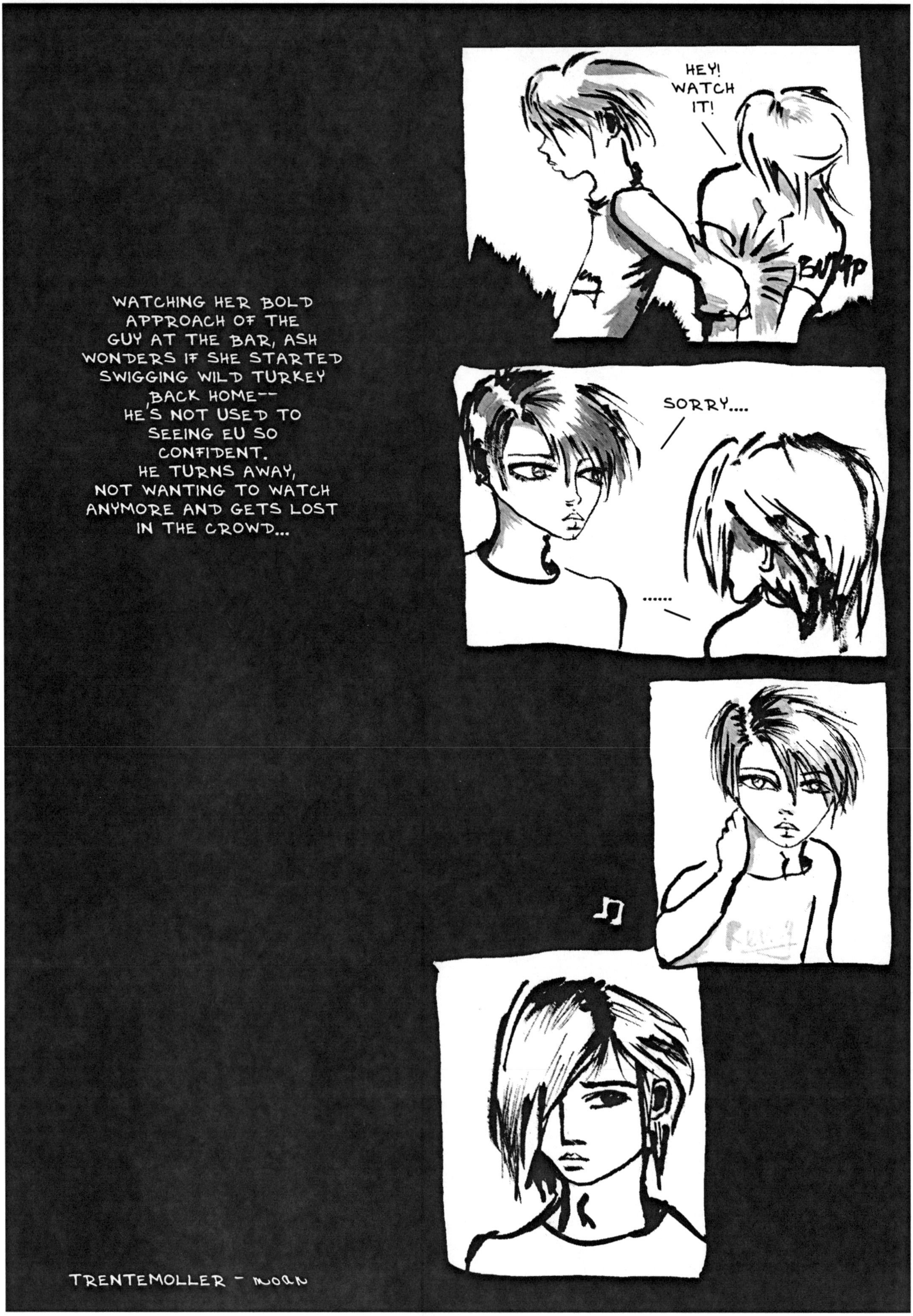
WATCHING HER BOLD APPROACH OF THE GUY AT THE BAR, ASH WONDERS IF SHE STARTED SWIGGING WILD TURKEY BACK HOME-- HE'S NOT USED TO SEEING EU SO CONFIDENT. HE TURNS AWAY, NOT WANTING TO WATCH ANYMORE AND GETS LOST IN THE CROWD...
HEY! WATCH IT!
BUMP
SORRY....
......
TRENTEMOLLER - moan

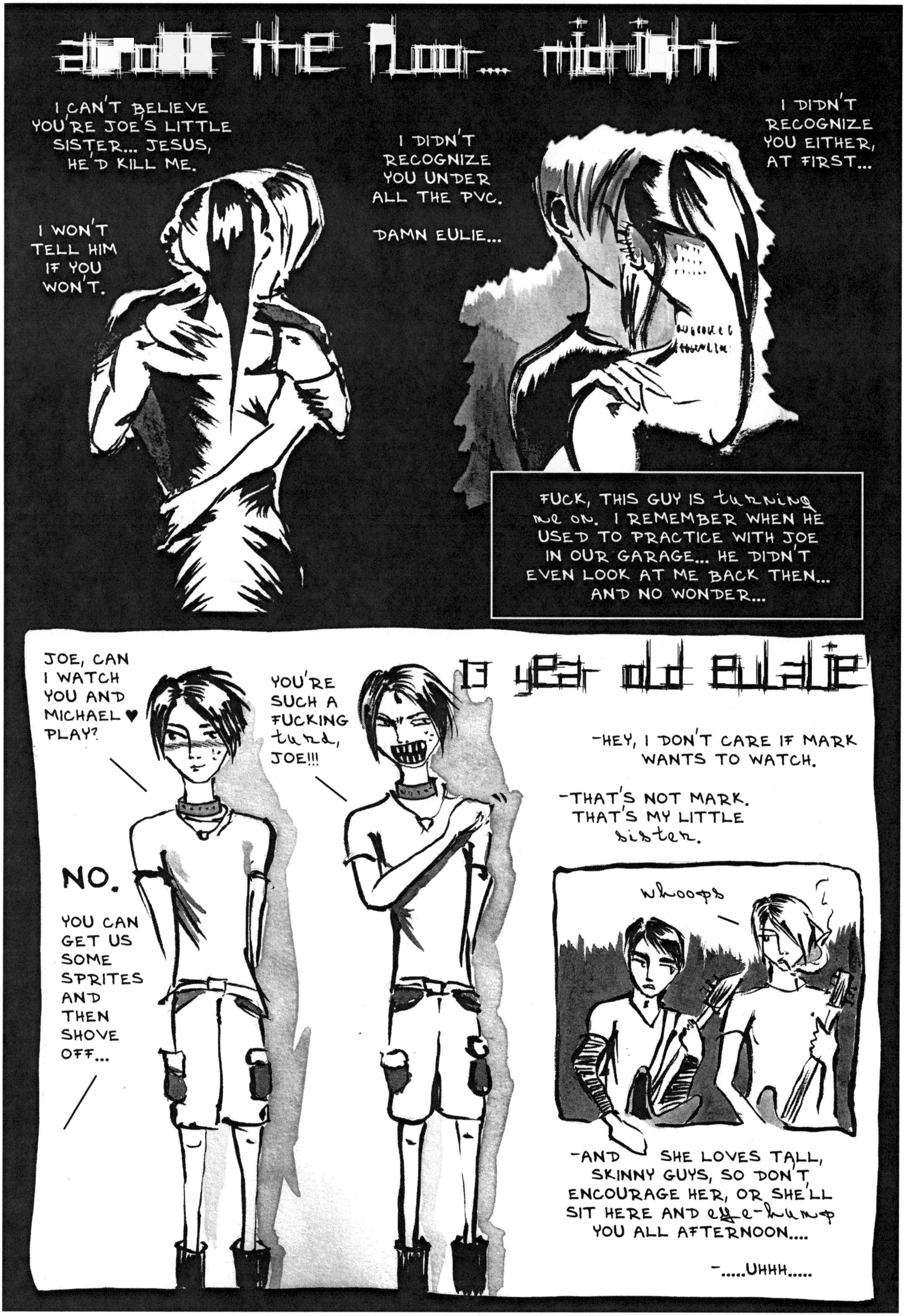

across the floor.... midnight
I CAN'T BELIEVE YOU'RE JOE'S LITTLE SISTER... JESUS, HE'D KILL ME.
I WON'T TELL HIM IF YOU WON'T.
I DIDN'T RECOGNIZE YOU UNDER ALL THE PVC.
DAMN EULIE...
I DIDN'T RECOGNIZE YOU EITHER, AT FIRST...
FUCK, THIS GUY IS turning me on. I REMEMBER WHEN HE USED TO PRACTICE WITH JOE IN OUR GARAGE... HE DIDN'T EVEN LOOK AT ME BACK THEN... AND NO WONDER...
13 year old eulalie
JOE, CAN I WATCH YOU AND MICHAEL ♥ PLAY?
NO.
YOU CAN GET US SOME SPRITES AND THEN SHOVE OFF...
YOU'RE SUCH A FUCKING turd, JOE!!!
-HEY, I DON'T CARE IF MARK WANTS TO WATCH.
-THAT'S NOT MARK. THAT'S MY LITTLE sister.
whoops
-AND SHE LOVES TALL, SKINNY GUYS, SO DON'T ENCOURAGE HER, OR SHE'LL SIT HERE AND eye-hump YOU ALL AFTERNOON....
-.....UHHH.....

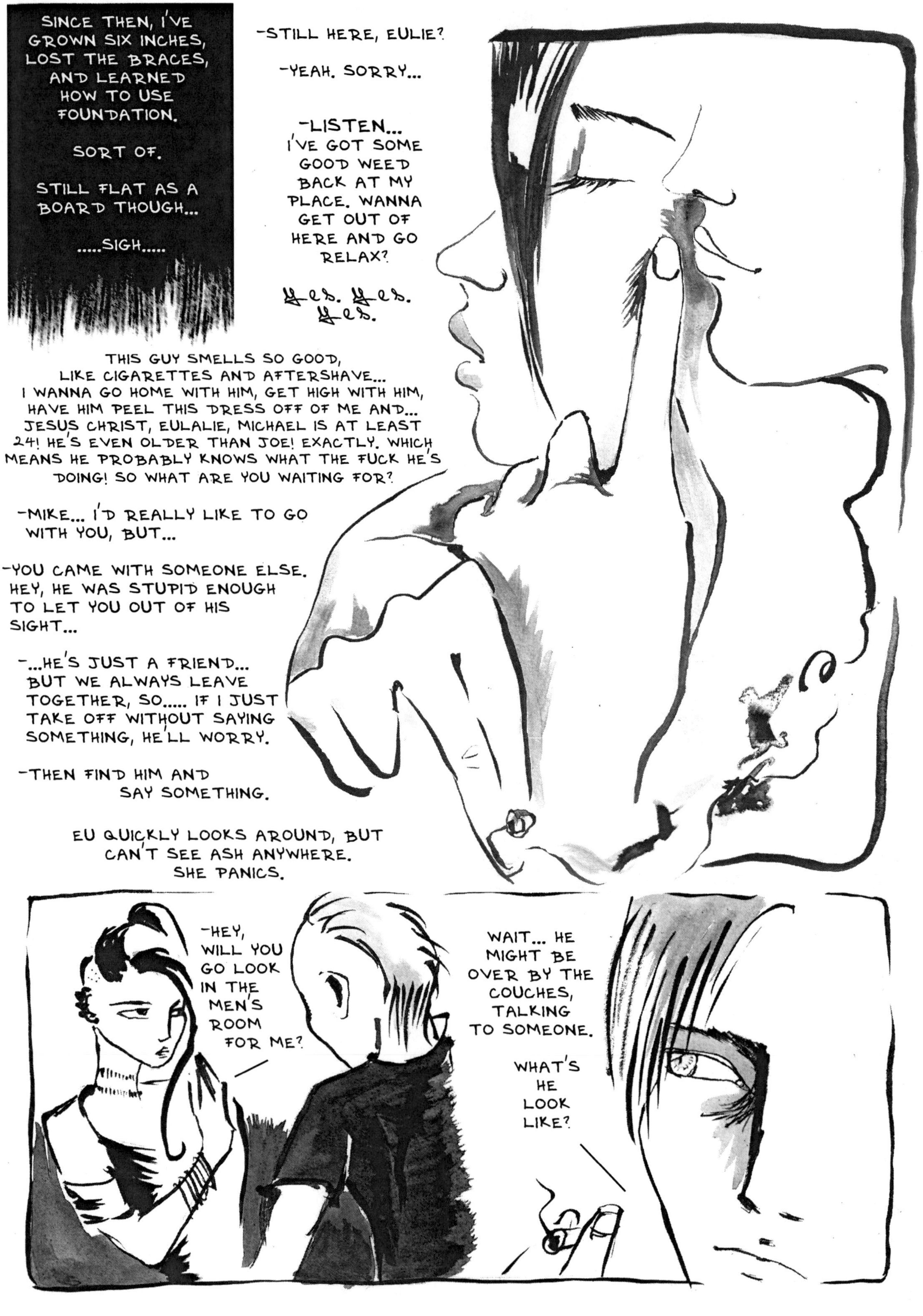
SINCE THEN, I'VE GROWN SIX INCHES, LOST THE BRACES, AND LEARNED HOW TO USE FOUNDATION.
SORT OF.
STILL FLAT AS A BOARD THOUGH...
.....SIGH.....
-STILL HERE, EULIE?
-YEAH. SORRY...
-LISTEN... I'VE GOT SOME GOOD WEED BACK AT MY PLACE. WANNA GET OUT OF HERE AND GO RELAX?
Yes. Yes. Yes.
THIS GUY SMELLS SO GOOD, LIKE CIGARETTES AND AFTERSHAVE... I WANNA GO HOME WITH HIM, GET HIGH WITH HIM, HAVE HIM PEEL THIS DRESS OFF OF ME AND... JESUS CHRIST, EULALIE, MICHAEL IS AT LEAST 24! HE'S EVEN OLDER THAN JOE! EXACTLY. WHICH MEANS HE PROBABLY KNOWS WHAT THE FUCK HE'S DOING! SO WHAT ARE YOU WAITING FOR?
-MIKE... I'D REALLY LIKE TO GO WITH YOU, BUT...
-YOU CAME WITH SOMEONE ELSE. HEY, HE WAS STUPID ENOUGH TO LET YOU OUT OF HIS SIGHT...
-...HE'S JUST A FRIEND... BUT WE ALWAYS LEAVE TOGETHER, SO..... IF I JUST TAKE OFF WITHOUT SAYING SOMETHING, HE'LL WORRY.
-THEN FIND HIM AND SAY SOMETHING.
EU QUICKLY LOOKS AROUND, BUT CAN'T SEE ASH ANYWHERE. SHE PANICS.
-HEY, WILL YOU GO LOOK IN THE MEN'S ROOM FOR ME?
WAIT... HE MIGHT BE OVER BY THE COUCHES, TALKING TO SOMEONE.
WHAT'S HE LOOK LIKE?

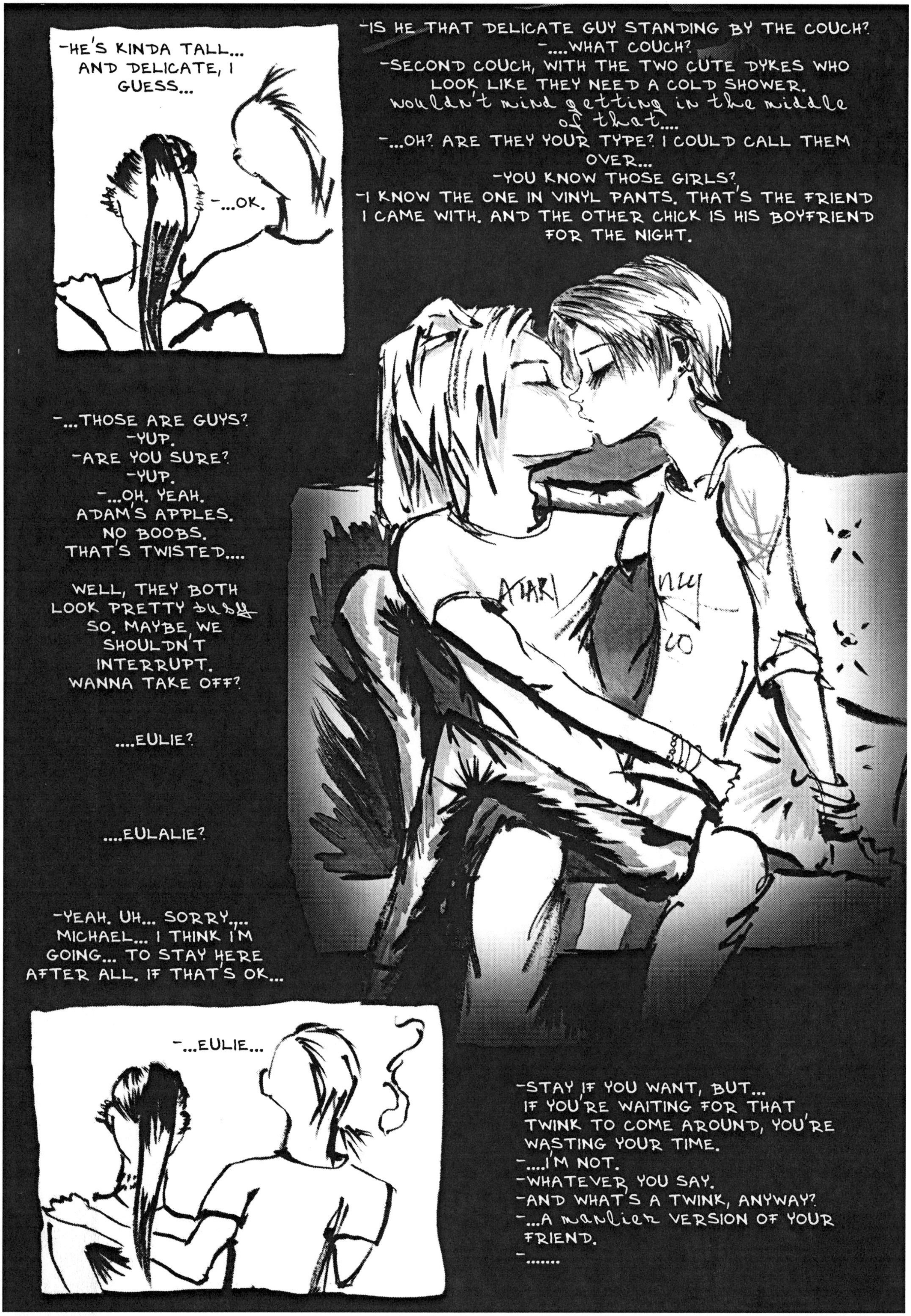
-HE'S KINDA TALL... AND DELICATE, I GUESS...
-...OK.
-IS HE THAT DELICATE GUY STANDING BY THE COUCH?
-....WHAT COUCH?
-SECOND COUCH, WITH THE TWO CUTE DYKES WHO LOOK LIKE THEY NEED A COLD SHOWER. wouldn't mind getting in the middle of that....
-...OH? ARE THEY YOUR TYPE? I COULD CALL THEM OVER...
-YOU KNOW THOSE GIRLS?
-I KNOW THE ONE IN VINYL PANTS. THAT'S THE FRIEND I CAME WITH. AND THE OTHER CHICK IS HIS BOYFRIEND FOR THE NIGHT.
-...THOSE ARE GUYS?
-YUP.
-ARE YOU SURE?
-YUP.
-...OH. YEAH. ADAM'S APPLES. NO BOOBS. THAT'S TWISTED....
WELL, THEY BOTH LOOK PRETTY busy SO. MAYBE, WE SHOULDN'T INTERRUPT. WANNA TAKE OFF?
....EULIE?
....EULALIE?
-YEAH. UH... SORRY,... MICHAEL... I THINK I'M GOING... TO STAY HERE AFTER ALL. IF THAT'S OK...
-...EULIE...
-STAY IF YOU WANT, BUT... IF YOU'RE WAITING FOR THAT TWINK TO COME AROUND, YOU'RE WASTING YOUR TIME.
-....I'M NOT.
-WHATEVER YOU SAY.
-AND WHAT'S A TWINK, ANYWAY?
-...A manlier VERSION OF YOUR FRIEND.
-.......

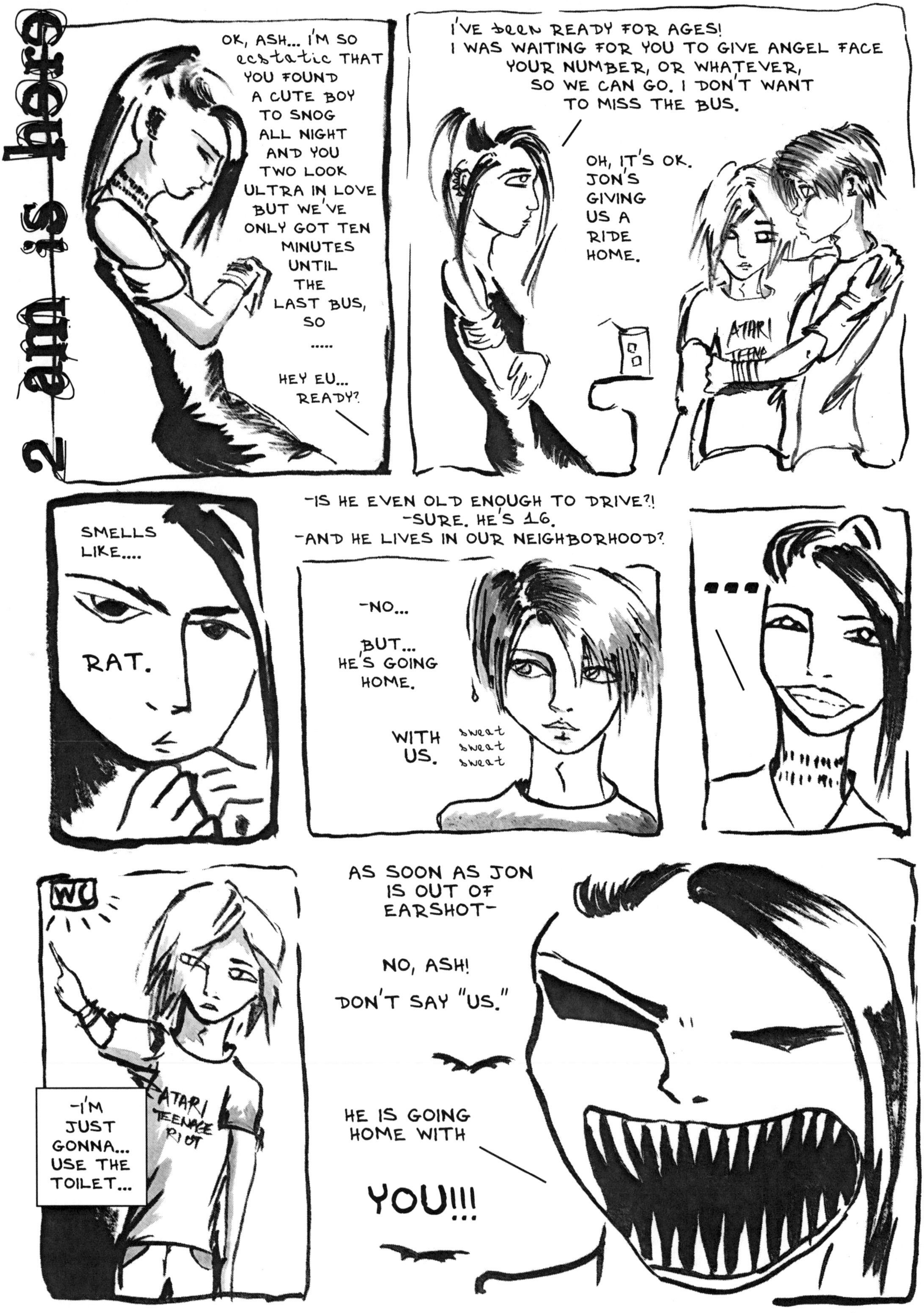
2 am is here
OK, ASH... I'M SO ecstatic THAT YOU FOUND A CUTE BOY TO SNOG ALL NIGHT AND YOU TWO LOOK ULTRA IN LOVE BUT WE'VE ONLY GOT TEN MINUTES UNTIL THE LAST BUS, SO .....
HEY EU... READY?
I'VE been READY FOR AGES! I WAS WAITING FOR YOU TO GIVE ANGEL FACE YOUR NUMBER, OR WHATEVER, SO WE CAN GO. I DON'T WANT TO MISS THE BUS.
OH, IT'S OK. JON'S GIVING US A RIDE HOME.
ATARI TEENAGE
SMELLS LIKE....
RAT.
-IS HE EVEN OLD ENOUGH TO DRIVE?!
-SURE. HE'S 16.
-AND HE LIVES IN OUR NEIGHBORHOOD?
-NO...
BUT... HE'S GOING HOME.
WITH US.
sweat sweat sweat
...
WC
-I'M JUST GONNA... USE THE TOILET...
ATARI TEENAGE RIOT
AS SOON AS JON IS OUT OF EARSHOT-
NO, ASH!
DON'T SAY "US."
HE IS GOING HOME WITH
YOU!!!

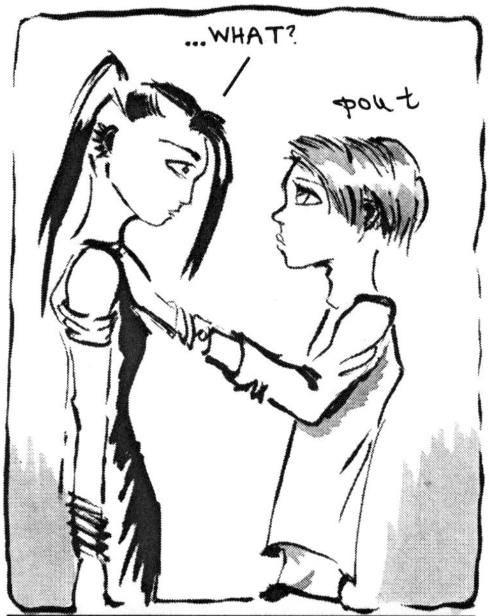
...WHAT?
pout

OH.

YOU MANIPULATIVE, LITTLE BOY-BITCH. NO, STOP TOUCHING ME, STOP FLIRTING WITH ME TO GET WHAT YOU WANT.

WHAT ANNOYS EU THE MOST IS THAT SHE CAN FEEL IT WORKING.

ALREADY, HER TONE IS SOFTER....

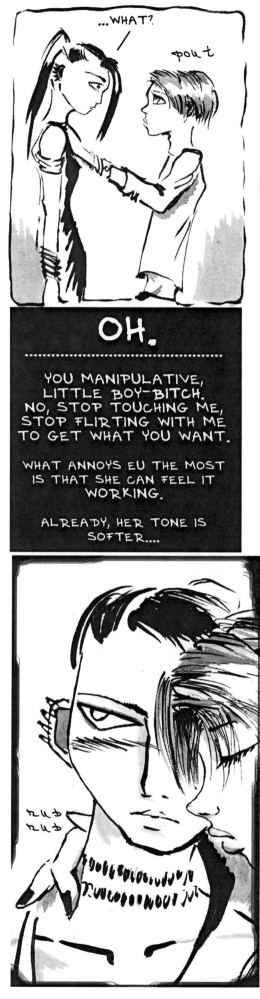

-....WHY ARE YOU LOOKING AT ME LIKE THAT?
-BECAUSE I HATE IT WHEN YOU'RE MAD AT ME....

DEVOTCHKA
....

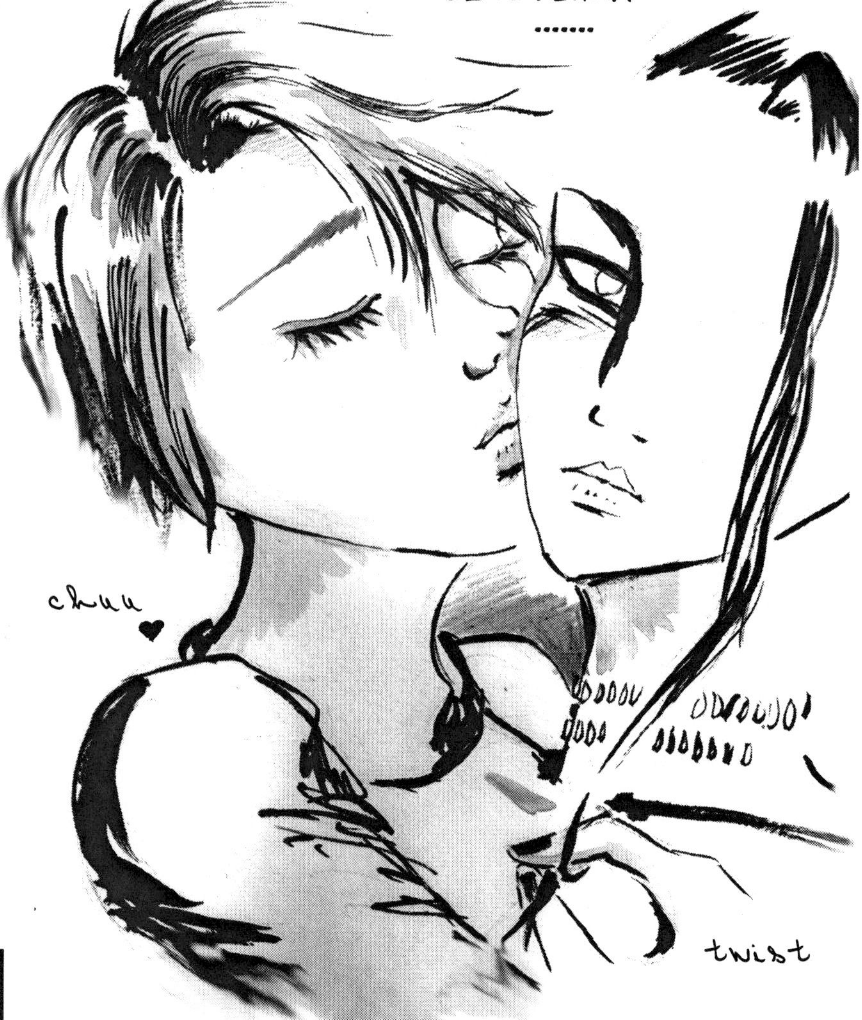
chuu
twist

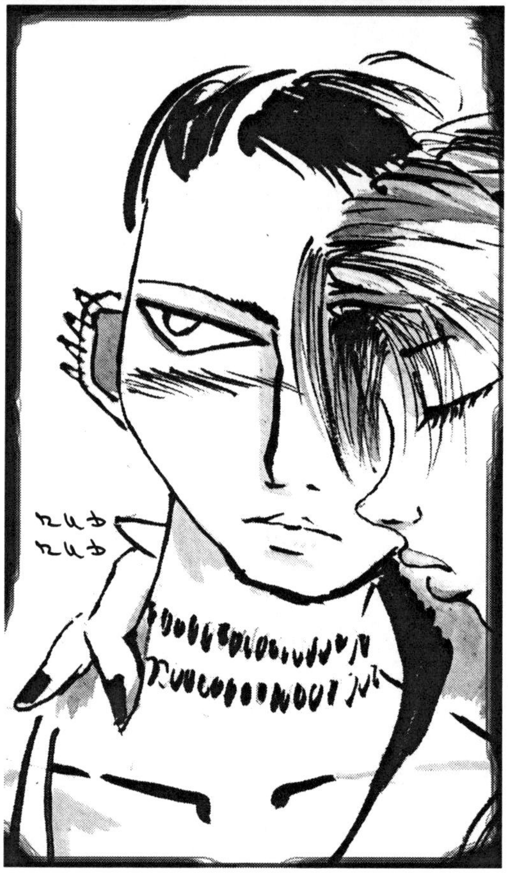
rub
rub

-DUDE, I'M NOT MAD AT YOU, BUT WHAT AM I GOING TO DO NOW? I CAN'T GO HOME THIS LATE.
-JUST COME OVER TO MY PLACE, LIKE WE PLANNED.
-AND WHERE THE HELL AM I SUPPOSED TO SLEEP?
-....
-MAYBE YOU FORGOT, BUT YOUR ROOM IS THE ONLY PLACE IN YOUR APARTMENT THAT ISN'T HELLA gross. OR WERE YOU PLANNING ON SHOVING ME IN YOUR SISTER'S BUNK WHILE YOU ....ENTERTAIN BELOW?
-...HE WON'T STAY OVER THAT LONG.
-...WAY TOO MUCH INFORMATION, MALCHIK.
-WHAT I MEAN IS...
-OH, STOP POUTING!! I'LL JUST CALL CLAIRE AND CRASH AT HER PLACE...
-NO, IT'S FINE. I'LL TELL JON IT WON'T WORK TONIGHT.
-WHY NOT? DON'T MAKE IT MY FAULT. JUST DROP ME OFF AT CLAIRE'S.
-BUT I WOULD FEEL LIKE AN ASSHOLE, KICKING YOU OUT OF MY PLACE, WHEN WE ALREADY AGREED YOU'D STAY OVER.
-OH, BUT FORCING ME TO LISTEN TO YOU SHAG YOUR UBER-CUTE LITTLE BOYFRIEND DOES NOT MAKE YOU FEEL LIKE AN ASSHOLE?!?!
-YOU WON'T HEAR ANYTHING. ...I'M QUIET.

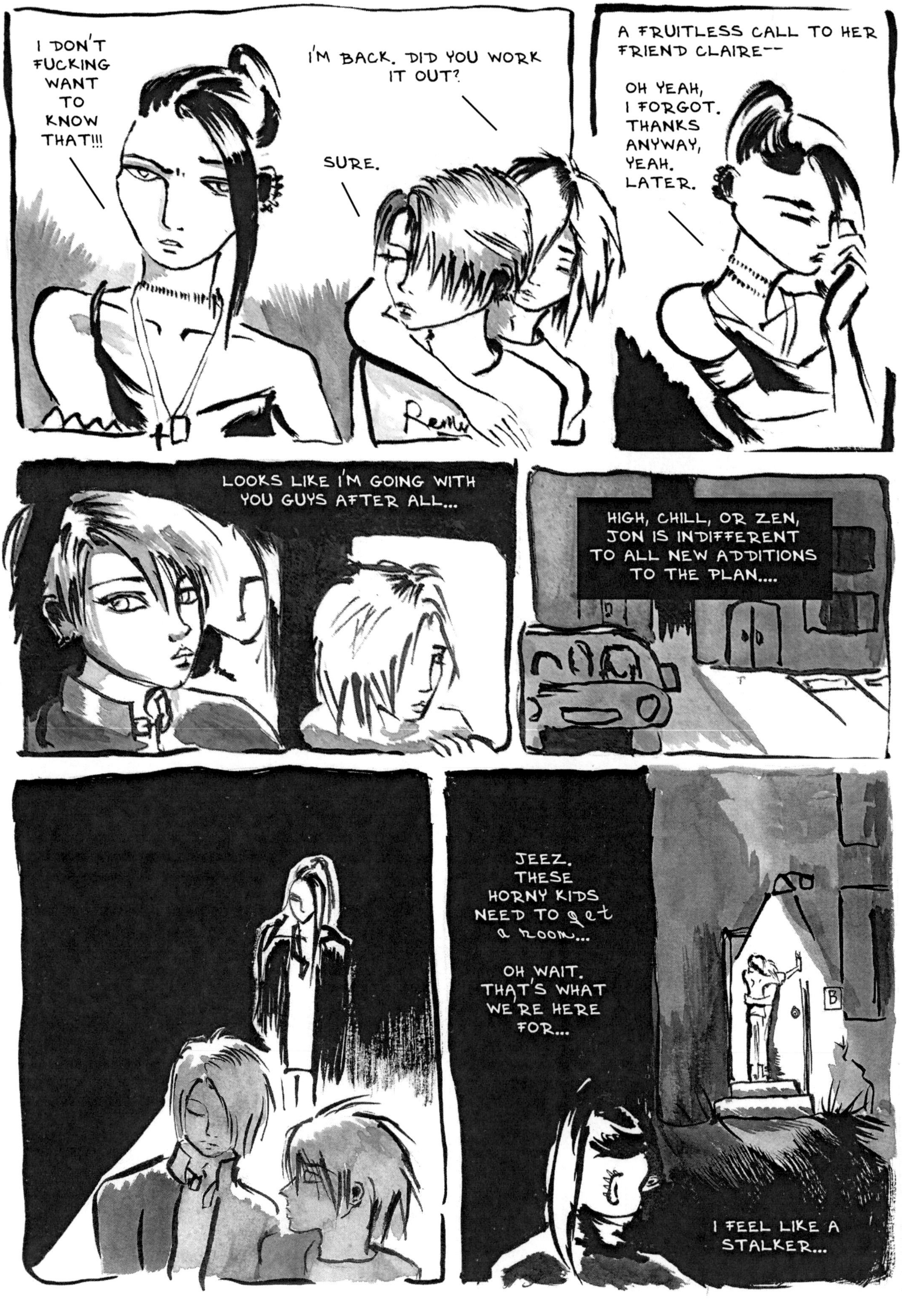
I DON'T FUCKING WANT TO KNOW THAT!!!
I'M BACK. DID YOU WORK IT OUT?
SURE.
A FRUITLESS CALL TO HER FRIEND CLAIRE--
OH YEAH, I FORGOT. THANKS ANYWAY, YEAH. LATER.
LOOKS LIKE I'M GOING WITH YOU GUYS AFTER ALL...
HIGH, CHILL, OR ZEN, JON IS INDIFFERENT TO ALL NEW ADDITIONS TO THE PLAN....
JEEZ. THESE HORNY KIDS NEED TO get a room...
OH WAIT. THAT'S WHAT WE'RE HERE FOR...
B
I FEEL LIKE A STALKER...

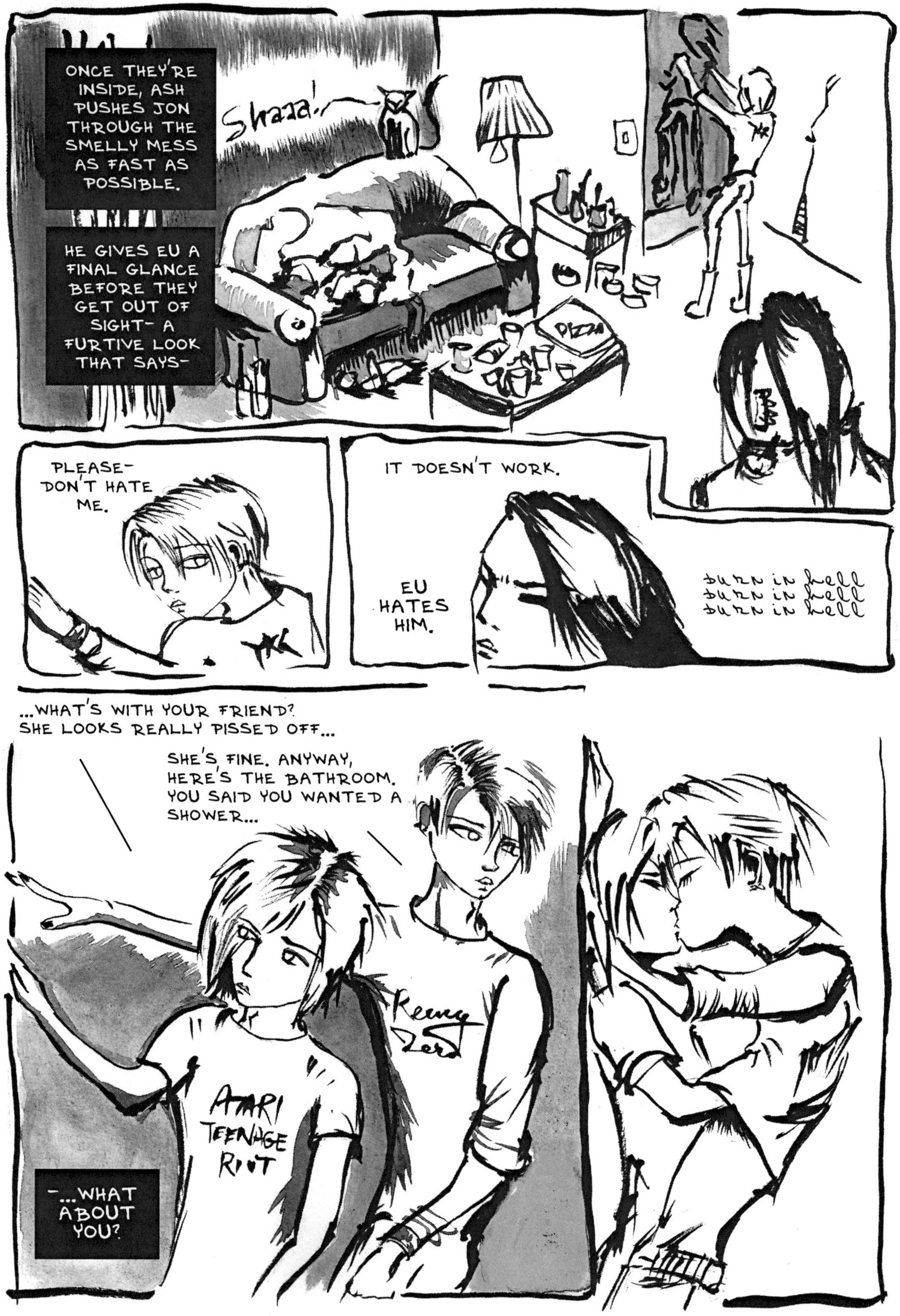

ONCE THEY'RE INSIDE, ASH PUSHES JON THROUGH THE SMELLY MESS AS FAST AS POSSIBLE.
Shaaa!
PIZZA
HE GIVES EU A FINAL GLANCE BEFORE THEY GET OUT OF SIGHT- A FURTIVE LOOK THAT SAYS-
PLEASE- DON'T HATE ME.
IT DOESN'T WORK.
EU HATES HIM.
burn in hell
burn in hell
burn in hell
...WHAT'S WITH YOUR FRIEND? SHE LOOKS REALLY PISSED OFF...
SHE'S FINE. ANYWAY, HERE'S THE BATHROOM. YOU SAID YOU WANTED A SHOWER...
ATARI TEENAGE RIOT
-...WHAT ABOUT YOU?

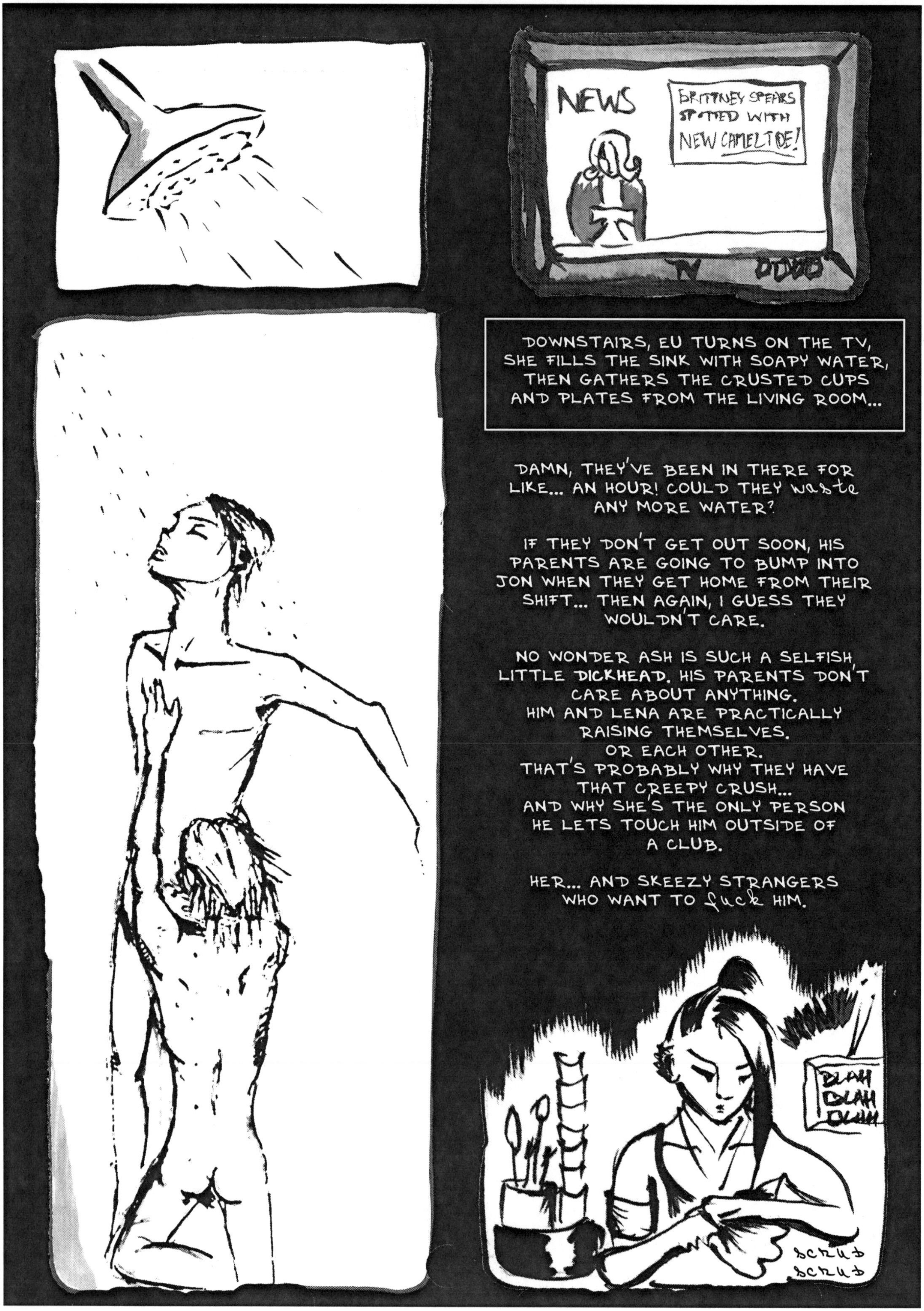
NEWS
BRITTNEY SPEARS SPOTTED WITH NEW CAMELTOE!
DOWNSTAIRS, EU TURNS ON THE TV, SHE FILLS THE SINK WITH SOAPY WATER, THEN GATHERS THE CRUSTED CUPS AND PLATES FROM THE LIVING ROOM...
DAMN, THEY'VE BEEN IN THERE FOR LIKE... AN HOUR! COULD THEY waste ANY MORE WATER?
IF THEY DON'T GET OUT SOON, HIS PARENTS ARE GOING TO BUMP INTO JON WHEN THEY GET HOME FROM THEIR SHIFT... THEN AGAIN, I GUESS THEY WOULDN'T CARE.
NO WONDER ASH IS SUCH A SELFISH, LITTLE DICKHEAD. HIS PARENTS DON'T CARE ABOUT ANYTHING.
HIM AND LENA ARE PRACTICALLY RAISING THEMSELVES.
OR EACH OTHER.
THAT'S PROBABLY WHY THEY HAVE THAT CREEPY CRUSH...
AND WHY SHE'S THE ONLY PERSON HE LETS TOUCH HIM OUTSIDE OF A CLUB.
HER... AND SKEEZY STRANGERS WHO WANT TO fuck HIM.
BLAH BLAH BLAH
SCRUB SCRUB

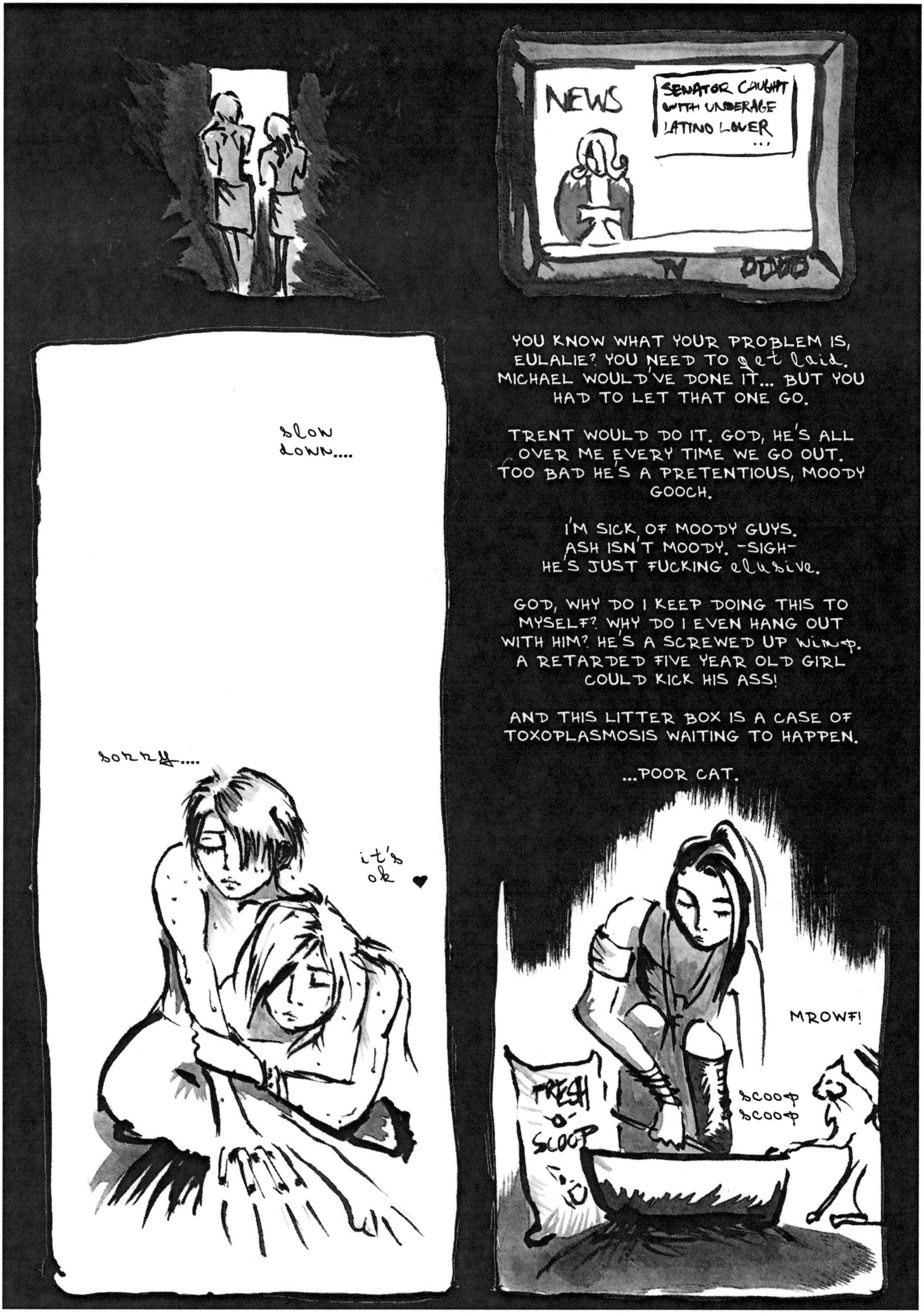
NEWS
SENATOR CAUGHT WITH UNDERAGE LATINO LOVER ...
YOU KNOW WHAT YOUR PROBLEM IS, EULALIE? YOU NEED TO get laid. MICHAEL WOULD'VE DONE IT... BUT YOU HAD TO LET THAT ONE GO.
TRENT WOULD DO IT. GOD, HE'S ALL OVER ME EVERY TIME WE GO OUT. TOO BAD HE'S A PRETENTIOUS, MOODY GOOCH.
I'M SICK OF MOODY GUYS. ASH ISN'T MOODY. -SIGH- HE'S JUST FUCKING elusive.
GOD, WHY DO I KEEP DOING THIS TO MYSELF? WHY DO I EVEN HANG OUT WITH HIM? HE'S A SCREWED UP wimp. A RETARDED FIVE YEAR OLD GIRL COULD KICK HIS ASS!
AND THIS LITTER BOX IS A CASE OF TOXOPLASMOSIS WAITING TO HAPPEN.
...POOR CAT.
slow down....
sorry....
it's ok
MROWF!
FRESH-O-SCOOP
scoop scoop

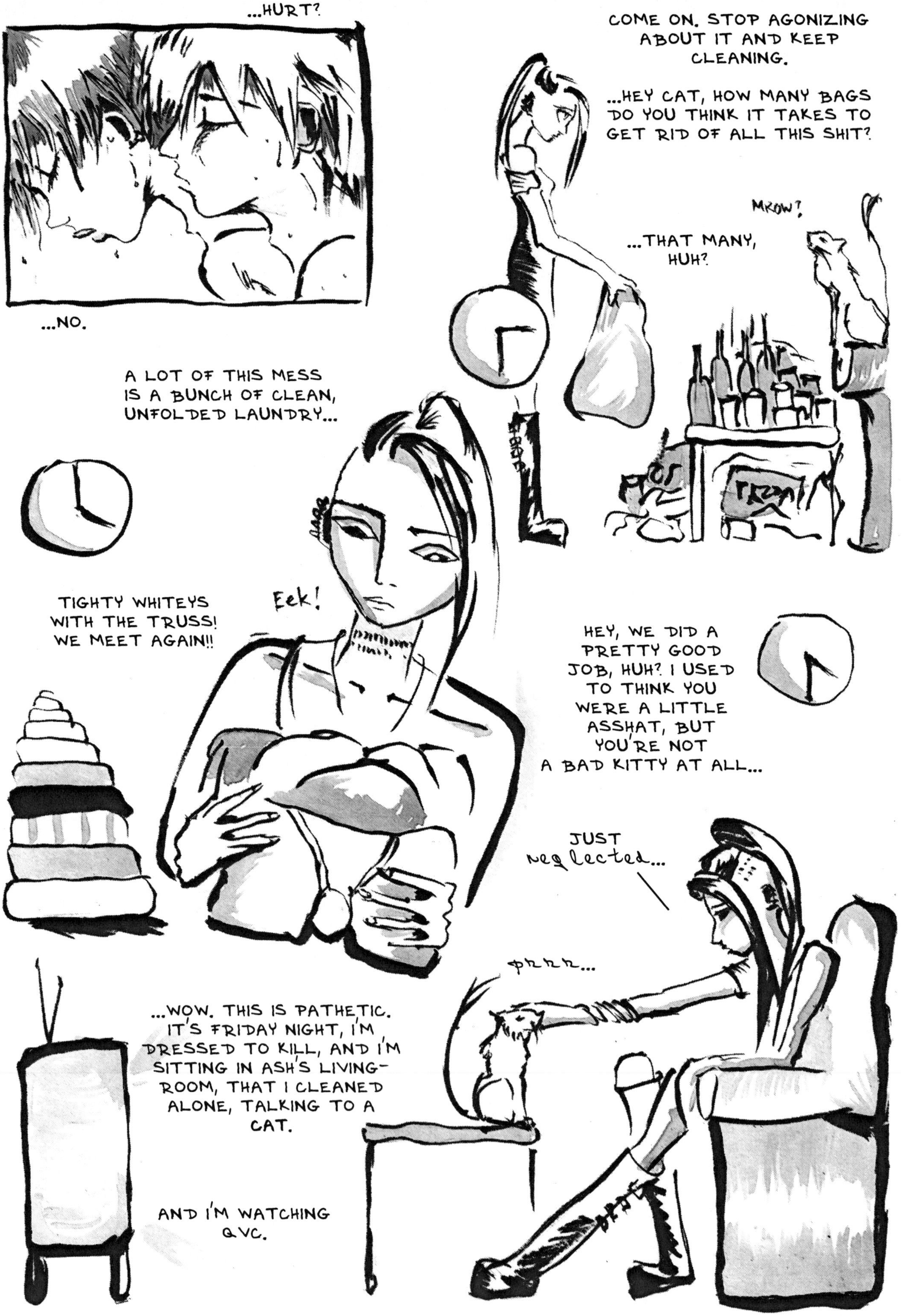
...HURT?
...NO.
COME ON. STOP AGONIZING ABOUT IT AND KEEP CLEANING.
...HEY CAT, HOW MANY BAGS DO YOU THINK IT TAKES TO GET RID OF ALL THIS SHIT?
MROW?
...THAT MANY, HUH?
A LOT OF THIS MESS IS A BUNCH OF CLEAN, UNFOLDED LAUNDRY...
TIGHTY WHITEYS WITH THE TRUSS! WE MEET AGAIN!!
Eek!
HEY, WE DID A PRETTY GOOD JOB, HUH? I USED TO THINK YOU WERE A LITTLE ASSHAT, BUT YOU'RE NOT A BAD KITTY AT ALL...
JUST neglected...
...WOW. THIS IS PATHETIC. IT'S FRIDAY NIGHT, I'M DRESSED TO KILL, AND I'M SITTING IN ASH'S LIVING-ROOM, THAT I CLEANED ALONE, TALKING TO A CAT.
AND I'M WATCHING QVC.

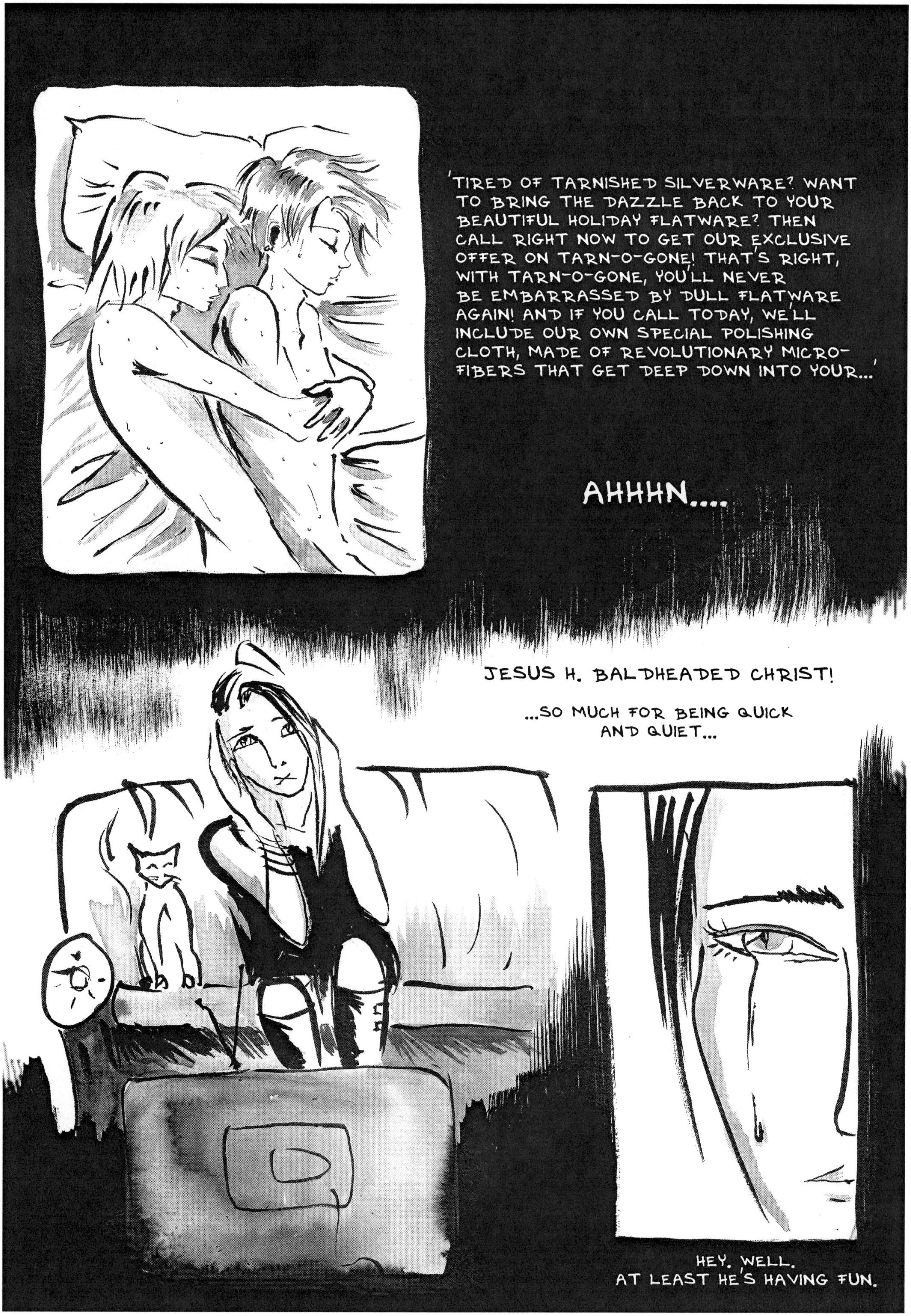
'TIRED OF TARNISHED SILVERWARE? WANT TO BRING THE DAZZLE BACK TO YOUR BEAUTIFUL HOLIDAY FLATWARE? THEN CALL RIGHT NOW TO GET OUR EXCLUSIVE OFFER ON TARN-O-GONE! THAT'S RIGHT, WITH TARN-O-GONE, YOU'LL NEVER BE EMBARRASSED BY DULL FLATWARE AGAIN! AND IF YOU CALL TODAY, WE'LL INCLUDE OUR OWN SPECIAL POLISHING CLOTH, MADE OF REVOLUTIONARY MICRO-FIBERS THAT GET DEEP DOWN INTO YOUR...'
AHHHN....
JESUS H. BALDHEADED CHRIST!
...SO MUCH FOR BEING QUICK AND QUIET...
HEY. WELL.
AT LEAST HE'S HAVING FUN.

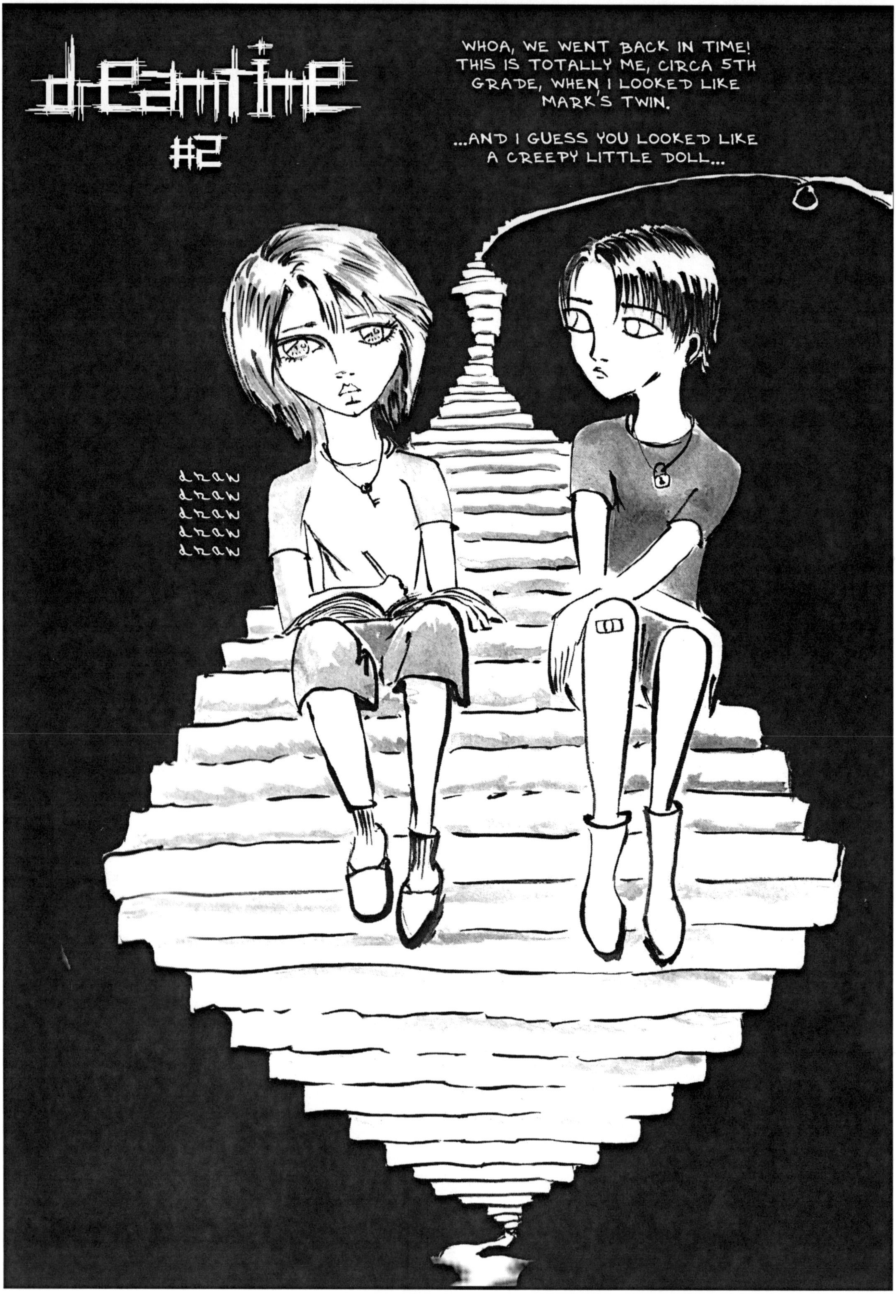
dreamtime
#2
WHOA, WE WENT BACK IN TIME! THIS IS TOTALLY ME, CIRCA 5TH GRADE, WHEN I LOOKED LIKE MARK'S TWIN.
...AND I GUESS YOU LOOKED LIKE A CREEPY LITTLE DOLL...
draw
draw
draw
draw
draw

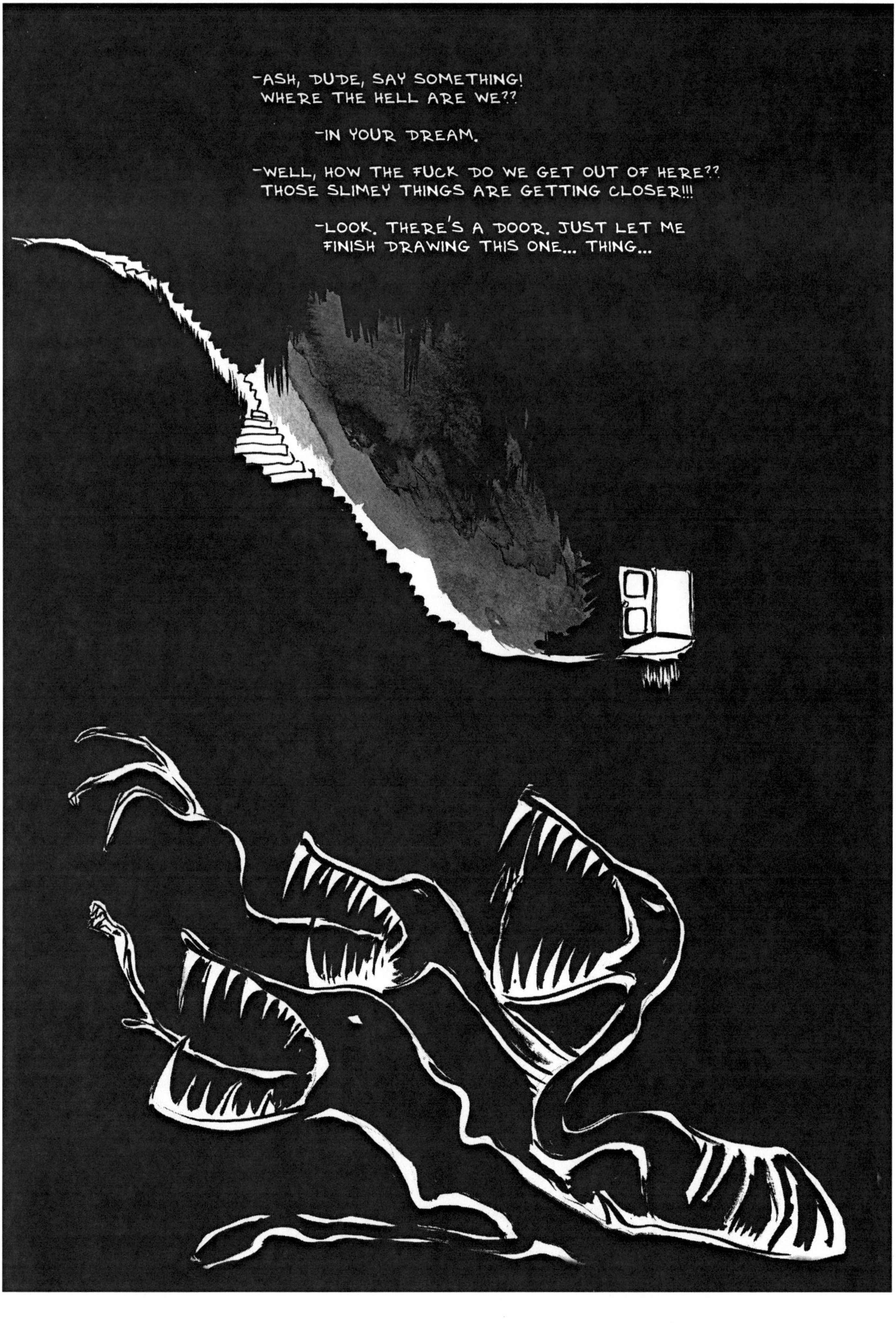
-ASH, DUDE, SAY SOMETHING! WHERE THE HELL ARE WE??
-IN YOUR DREAM.
-WELL, HOW THE FUCK DO WE GET OUT OF HERE?? THOSE SLIMEY THINGS ARE GETTING CLOSER!!!
-LOOK. THERE'S A DOOR. JUST LET ME FINISH DRAWING THIS ONE... THING...

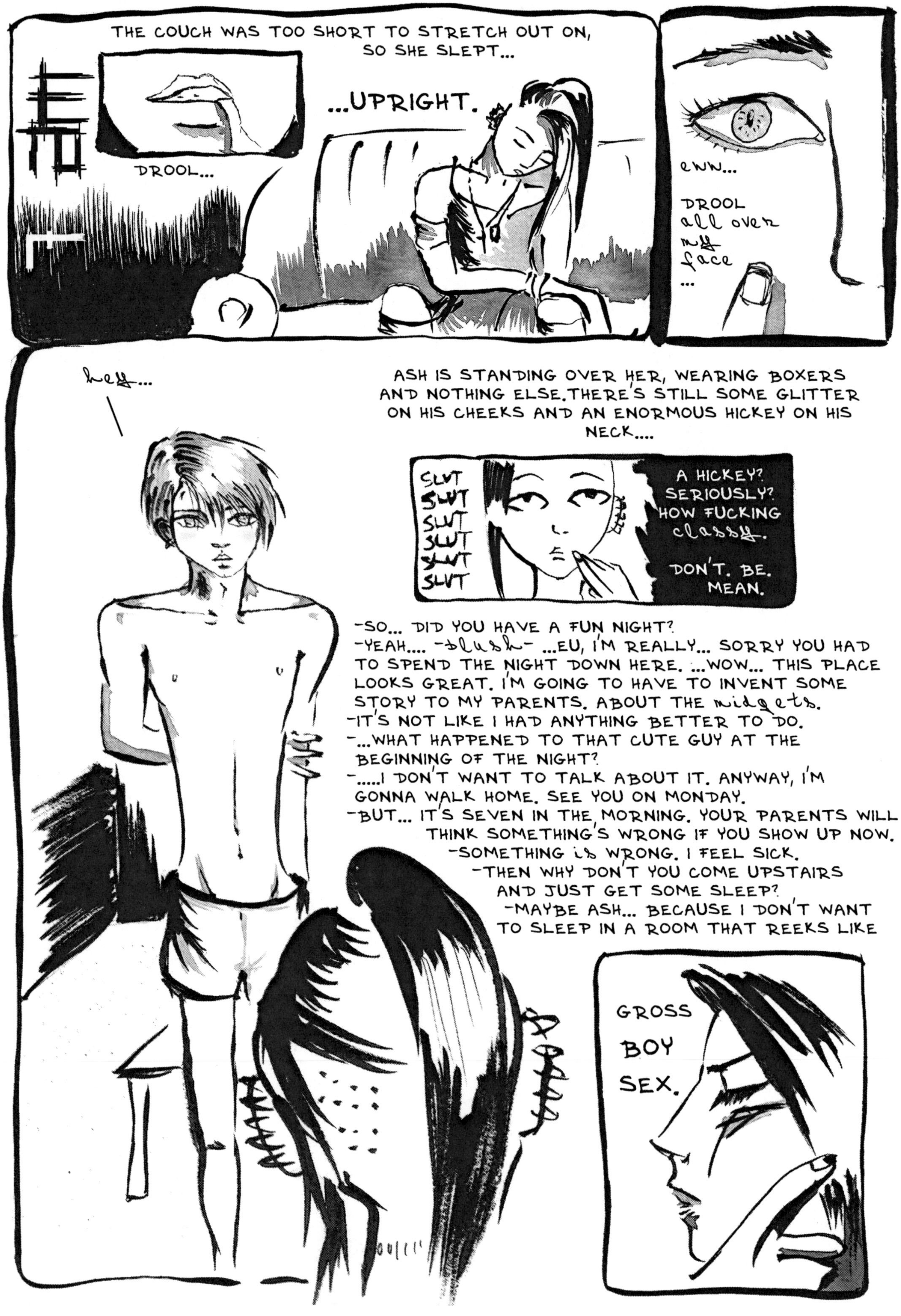
THE COUCH WAS TOO SHORT TO STRETCH OUT ON, SO SHE SLEPT...
DROOL...
...UPRIGHT.
eww...
DROOL all over my face ...
hey...
ASH IS STANDING OVER HER, WEARING BOXERS AND NOTHING ELSE. THERE'S STILL SOME GLITTER ON HIS CHEEKS AND AN ENORMOUS HICKEY ON HIS NECK....
SLUT SLUT SLUT SLUT SLUT SLUT
A HICKEY? SERIOUSLY? HOW FUCKING classy.
DON'T. BE. MEAN.
-SO... DID YOU HAVE A FUN NIGHT?
-YEAH.... -blush- ...EU, I'M REALLY... SORRY YOU HAD TO SPEND THE NIGHT DOWN HERE. ...WOW... THIS PLACE LOOKS GREAT. I'M GOING TO HAVE TO INVENT SOME STORY TO MY PARENTS. ABOUT THE midgets.
-IT'S NOT LIKE I HAD ANYTHING BETTER TO DO.
-...WHAT HAPPENED TO THAT CUTE GUY AT THE BEGINNING OF THE NIGHT?
-.....I DON'T WANT TO TALK ABOUT IT. ANYWAY, I'M GONNA WALK HOME. SEE YOU ON MONDAY.
-BUT... IT'S SEVEN IN THE MORNING. YOUR PARENTS WILL THINK SOMETHING'S WRONG IF YOU SHOW UP NOW.
-SOMETHING is WRONG. I FEEL SICK.
-THEN WHY DON'T YOU COME UPSTAIRS AND JUST GET SOME SLEEP?
-MAYBE ASH... BECAUSE I DON'T WANT TO SLEEP IN A ROOM THAT REEKS LIKE
GROSS BOY SEX.

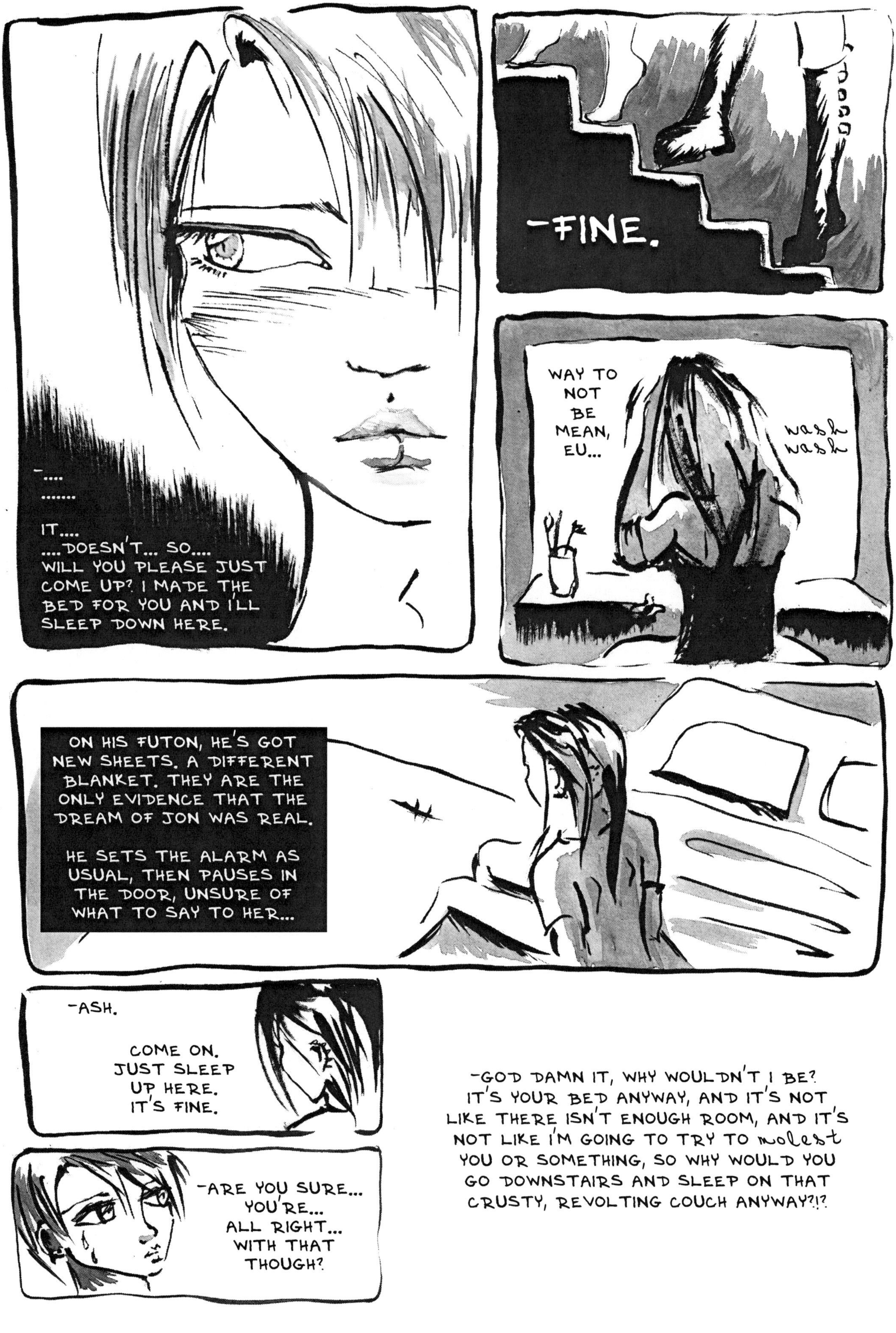
-....
....
IT....
....DOESN'T... SO....
WILL YOU PLEASE JUST COME UP? I MADE THE BED FOR YOU AND I'LL SLEEP DOWN HERE.
-FINE.
WAY TO NOT BE MEAN, EU...
wash wash
ON HIS FUTON, HE'S GOT NEW SHEETS. A DIFFERENT BLANKET. THEY ARE THE ONLY EVIDENCE THAT THE DREAM OF JON WAS REAL.
HE SETS THE ALARM AS USUAL, THEN PAUSES IN THE DOOR, UNSURE OF WHAT TO SAY TO HER...
-ASH.
COME ON. JUST SLEEP UP HERE. IT'S FINE.
-ARE YOU SURE... YOU'RE... ALL RIGHT... WITH THAT THOUGH?
-GOD DAMN IT, WHY WOULDN'T I BE? IT'S YOUR BED ANYWAY, AND IT'S NOT LIKE THERE ISN'T ENOUGH ROOM, AND IT'S NOT LIKE I'M GOING TO TRY TO molest YOU OR SOMETHING, SO WHY WOULD YOU GO DOWNSTAIRS AND SLEEP ON THAT CRUSTY, REVOLTING COUCH ANYWAY?!?

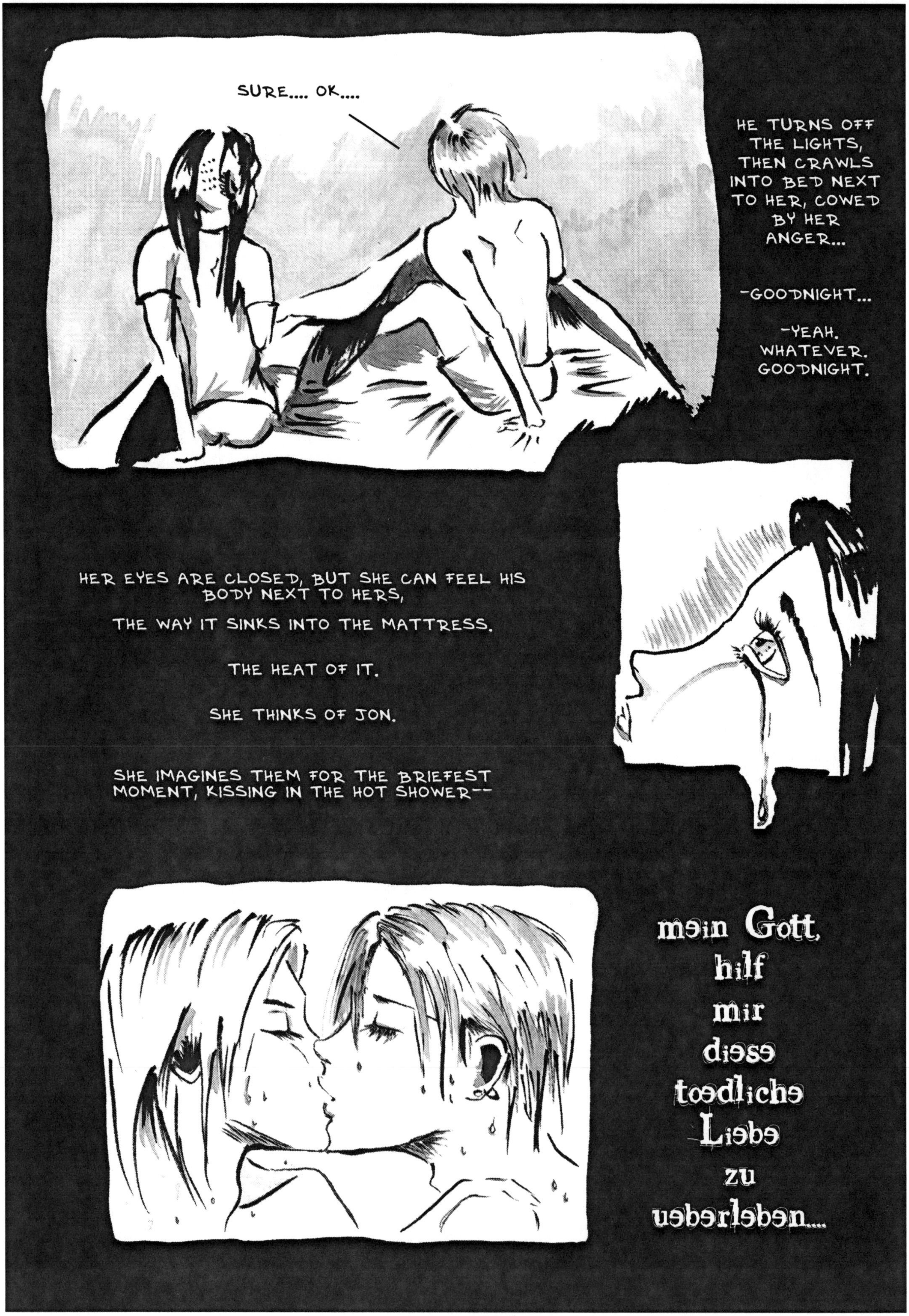
SURE.... OK....
HE TURNS OFF THE LIGHTS, THEN CRAWLS INTO BED NEXT TO HER, COWED BY HER ANGER...
-GOODNIGHT...
-YEAH. WHATEVER. GOODNIGHT.
HER EYES ARE CLOSED, BUT SHE CAN FEEL HIS BODY NEXT TO HERS,
THE WAY IT SINKS INTO THE MATTRESS.
THE HEAT OF IT.
SHE THINKS OF JON.
SHE IMAGINES THEM FOR THE BRIEFEST MOMENT, KISSING IN THE HOT SHOWER--
mein Gott, hilf mir diese toedliche Liebe zu ueberleben...

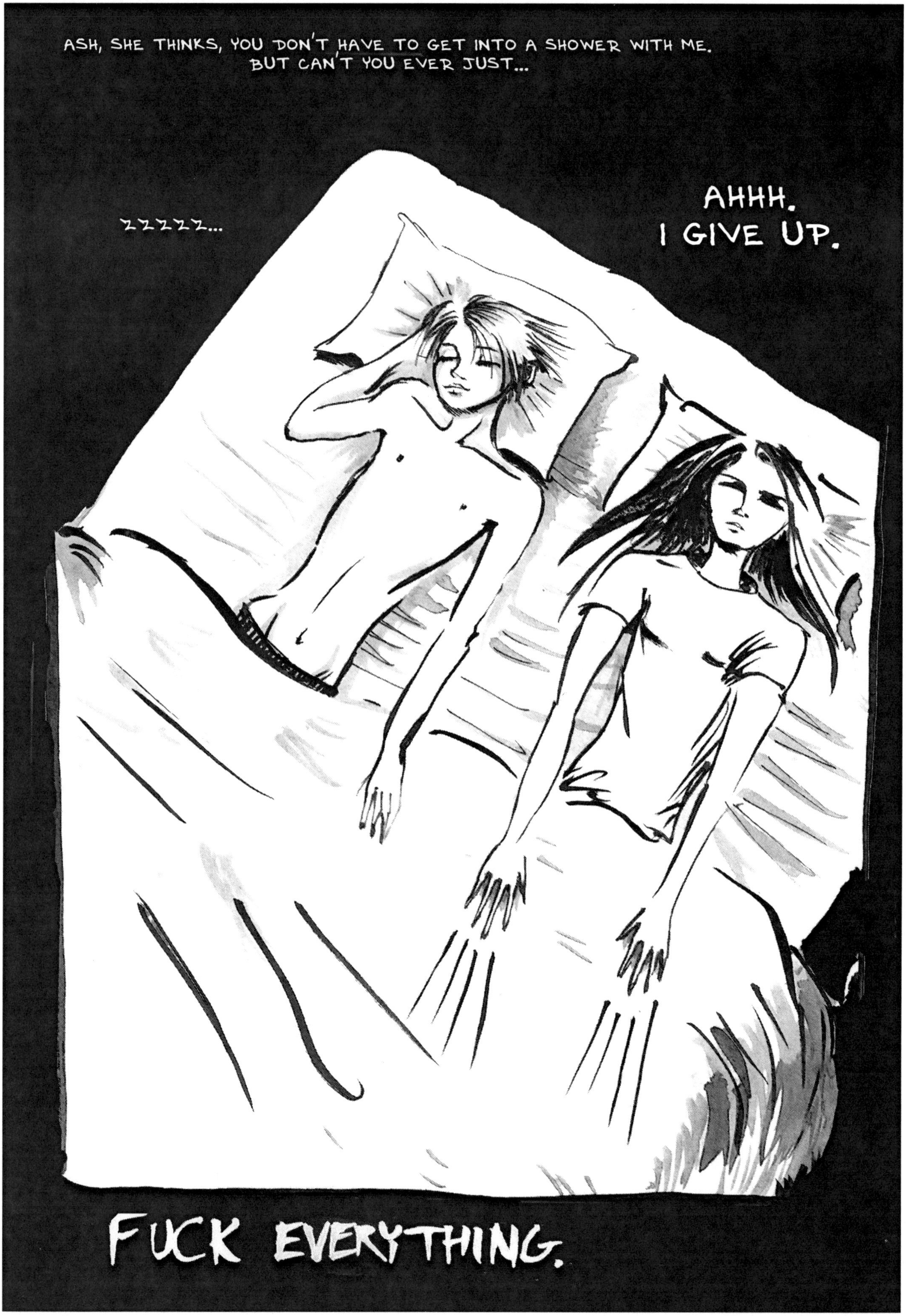
ASH, SHE THINKS, YOU DON'T HAVE TO GET INTO A SHOWER WITH ME. BUT CAN'T YOU EVER JUST...
ZZZZZ...
AHHH. I GIVE UP.
FUCK EVERYTHING.

MONDAY MORNING. THEY STAND IN A SHOWER OF HUGGING GIRLS, STARING AT THE CAST LIST. THE CAST LIST IS ANOTHER INSTRUMENT TEACHING EULALIE MASON THAT LIFE IS NOT FAIR.

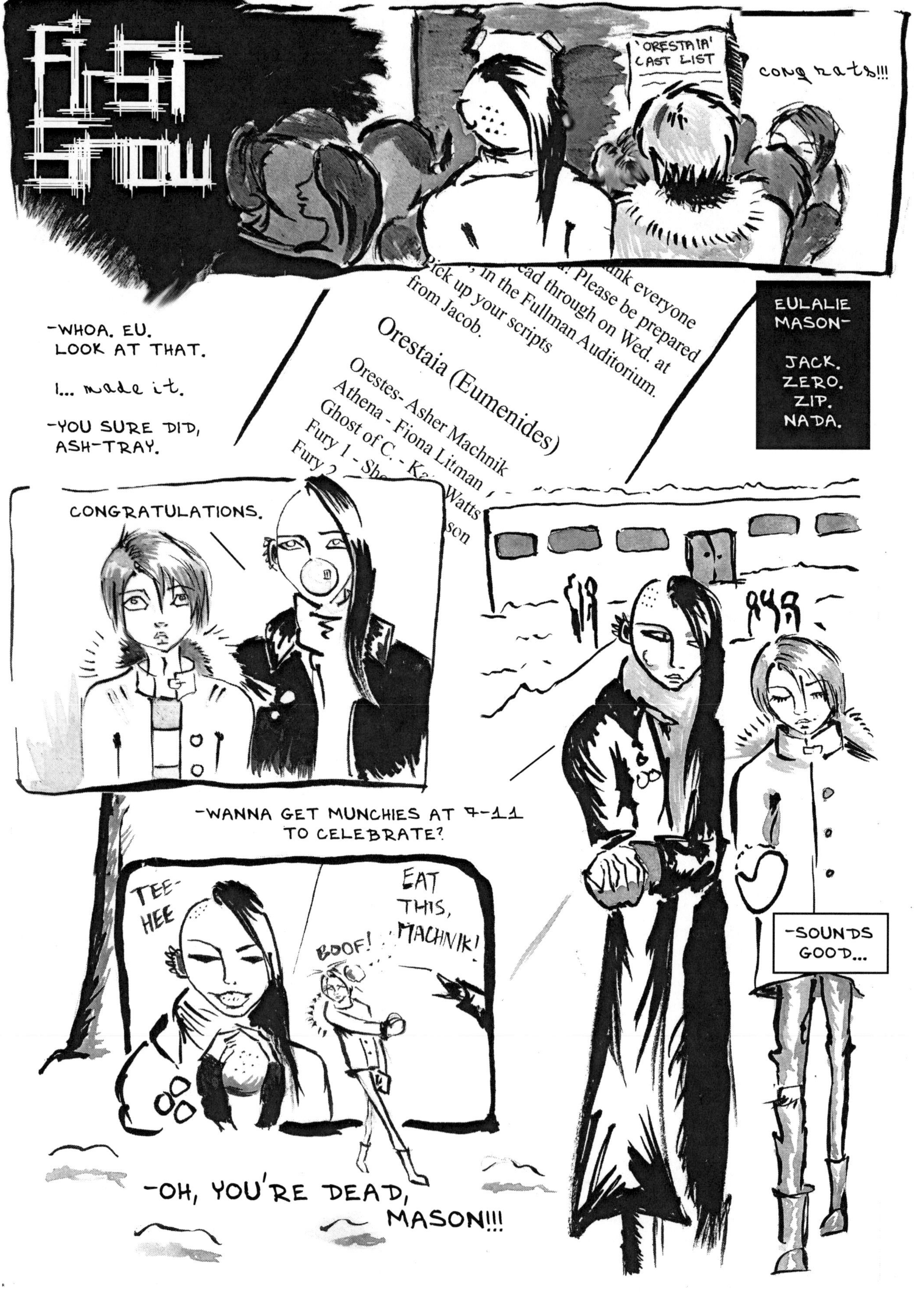

First Show
'ORESTAIA' CAST LIST
congrats!!!
-WHOA. EU. LOOK AT THAT.
I... made it.
-YOU SURE DID, ASH-TRAY.
Please be prepared
ead through on Wed. at
, in the Fullman Auditorium.
Pick up your scripts
from Jacob.
Orestaia (Eumenides)
Orestes- Asher Machnik
Athena - Fiona Litman
Ghost of C. - Ka Watts
Fury 1 - She
EULALIE MASON-
JACK. ZERO. ZIP. NADA.
CONGRATULATIONS.
-WANNA GET MUNCHIES AT 7-11 TO CELEBRATE?
-SOUNDS GOOD...
TEE-HEE
EAT THIS, MACHNIK!
BOOF!
-OH, YOU'RE DEAD, MASON!!!

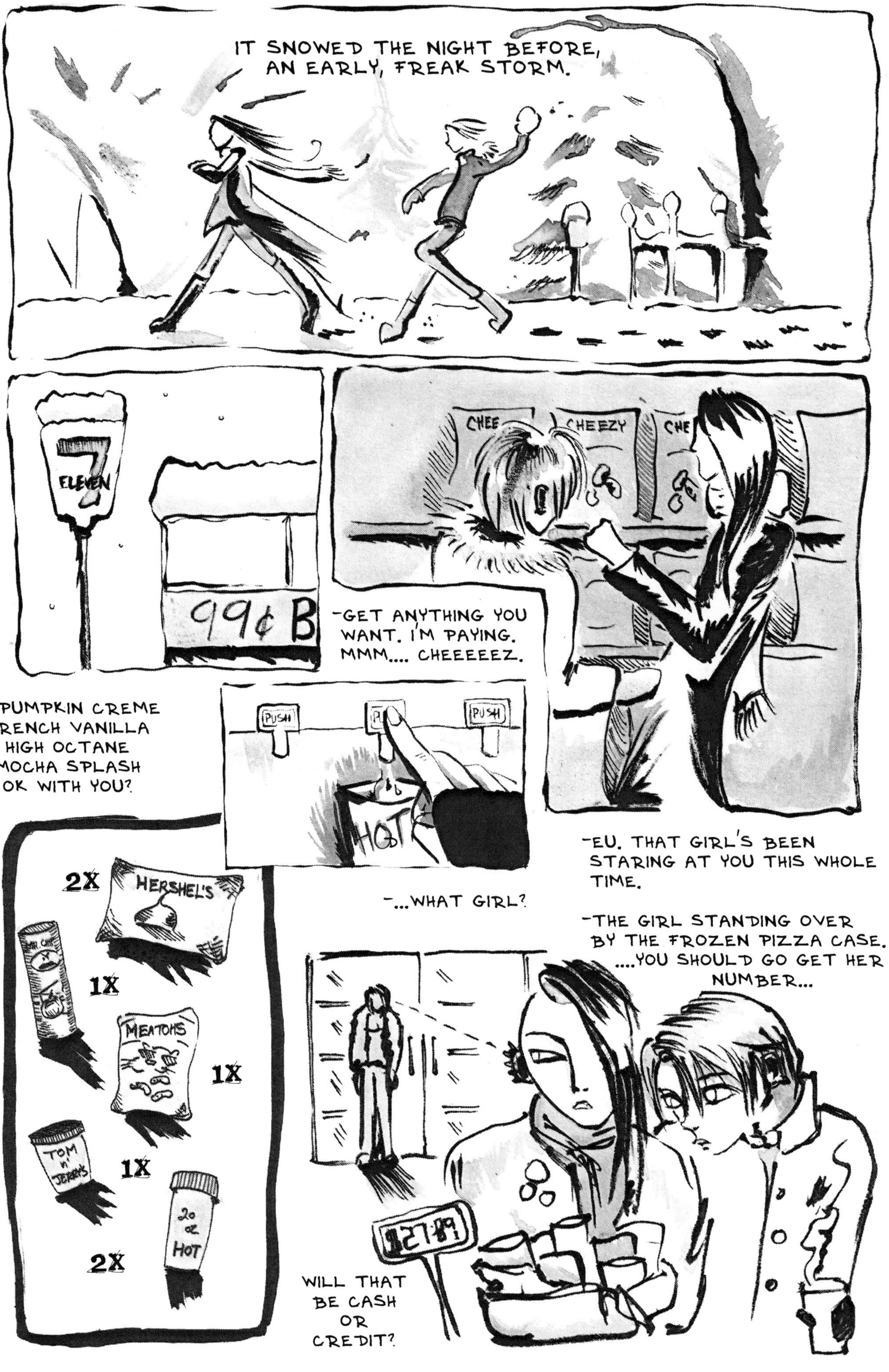
IT SNOWED THE NIGHT BEFORE, AN EARLY, FREAK STORM.
7 ELEVEN
99¢ B
CHEE
CHEEZY
CHE
-GET ANYTHING YOU WANT. I'M PAYING. MMM.... CHEEEEEZ.
-A PUMPKIN CREME FRENCH VANILLA HIGH OCTANE MOCHA SPLASH OK WITH YOU?
PUSH
PUSH
HOT
2X
HERSHEL'S
1X
MEATOHS
1X
TOM N' JERRY'S
1X
20 oz HOT
2X
-EU. THAT GIRL'S BEEN STARING AT YOU THIS WHOLE TIME.
-...WHAT GIRL?
-THE GIRL STANDING OVER BY THE FROZEN PIZZA CASE. ....YOU SHOULD GO GET HER NUMBER...
$27.89
WILL THAT BE CASH OR CREDIT?

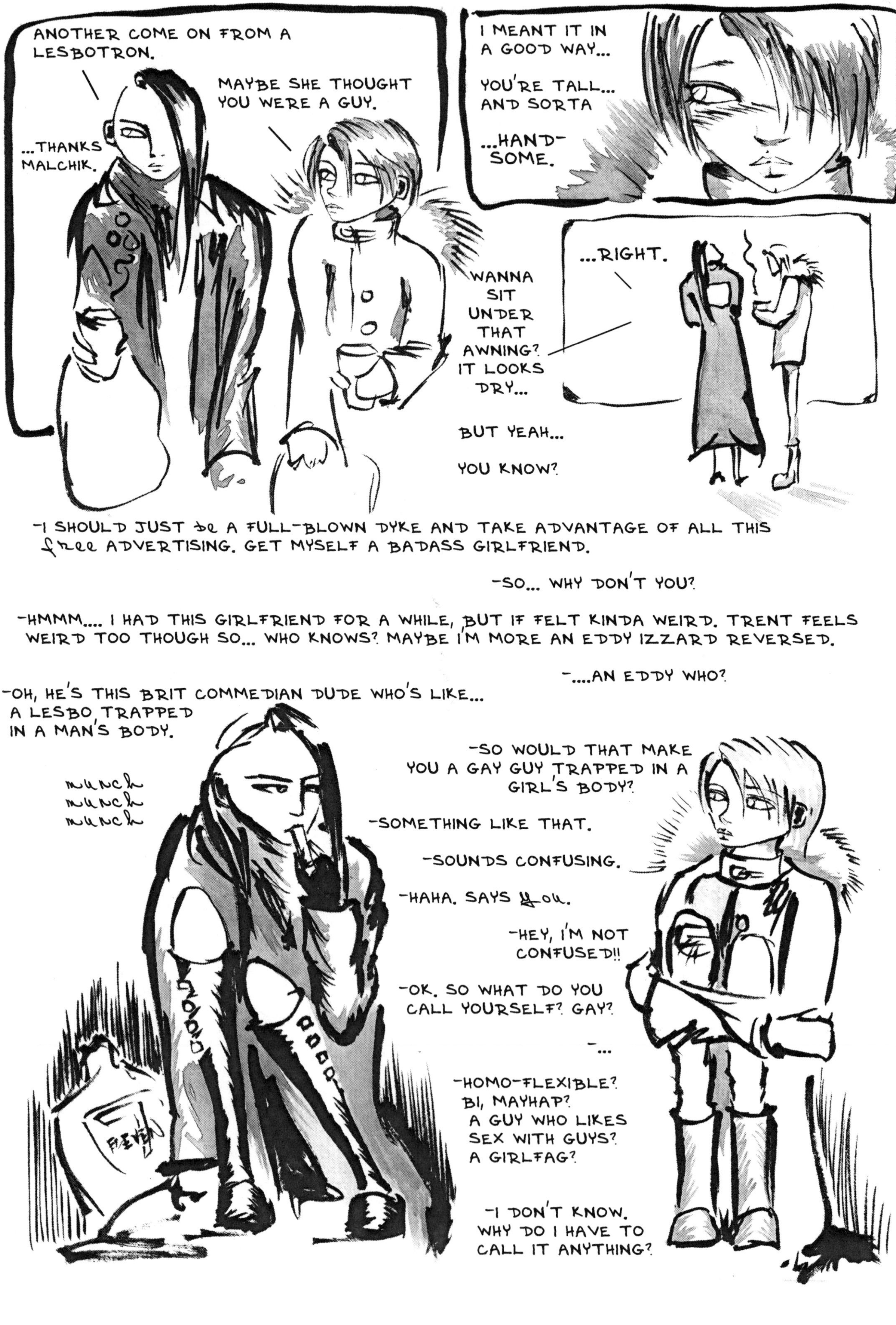
ANOTHER COME ON FROM A LESBOTRON.
...THANKS MALCHIK.
MAYBE SHE THOUGHT YOU WERE A GUY.
I MEANT IT IN A GOOD WAY...
YOU'RE TALL... AND SORTA
...HAND-SOME.
...RIGHT.
WANNA SIT UNDER THAT AWNING? IT LOOKS DRY...
BUT YEAH...
YOU KNOW?
-I SHOULD JUST be A FULL-BLOWN DYKE AND TAKE ADVANTAGE OF ALL THIS free ADVERTISING. GET MYSELF A BADASS GIRLFRIEND.
-SO... WHY DON'T YOU?
-HMMM.... I HAD THIS GIRLFRIEND FOR A WHILE, BUT IT FELT KINDA WEIRD. TRENT FEELS WEIRD TOO THOUGH SO... WHO KNOWS? MAYBE I'M MORE AN EDDY IZZARD REVERSED.
-....AN EDDY WHO?
-OH, HE'S THIS BRIT COMMEDIAN DUDE WHO'S LIKE... A LESBO TRAPPED IN A MAN'S BODY.
munch munch munch
-SO WOULD THAT MAKE YOU A GAY GUY TRAPPED IN A GIRL'S BODY?
-SOMETHING LIKE THAT.
-SOUNDS CONFUSING.
-HAHA. SAYS you.
-HEY, I'M NOT CONFUSED!!
-OK. SO WHAT DO YOU CALL YOURSELF? GAY?
-...
-HOMO-FLEXIBLE? BI, MAYHAP? A GUY WHO LIKES SEX WITH GUYS? A GIRLFAG?
-I DON'T KNOW. WHY DO I HAVE TO CALL IT ANYTHING?
ELEVEN

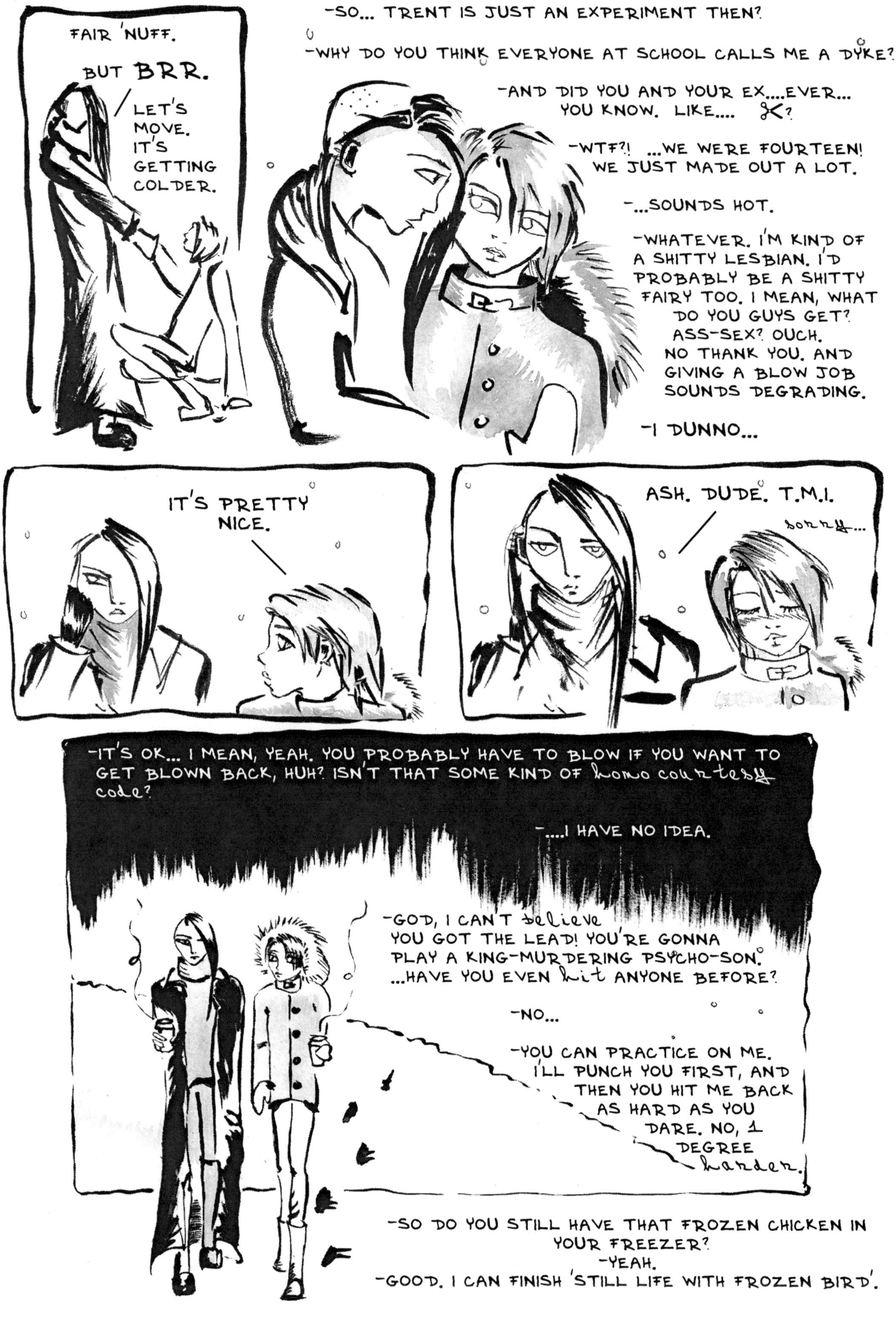
FAIR 'NUFF.
BUT BRR.
LET'S MOVE. IT'S GETTING COLDER.
-SO... TRENT IS JUST AN EXPERIMENT THEN?
-WHY DO YOU THINK EVERYONE AT SCHOOL CALLS ME A DYKE?
-AND DID YOU AND YOUR EX....EVER... YOU KNOW. LIKE.... ✂?
-WTF?! ...WE WERE FOURTEEN! WE JUST MADE OUT A LOT.
-...SOUNDS HOT.
-WHATEVER. I'M KIND OF A SHITTY LESBIAN. I'D PROBABLY BE A SHITTY FAIRY TOO. I MEAN, WHAT DO YOU GUYS GET? ASS-SEX? OUCH. NO THANK YOU. AND GIVING A BLOW JOB SOUNDS DEGRADING.
-I DUNNO...
IT'S PRETTY NICE.
ASH. DUDE. T.M.I.
sorry...
-IT'S OK... I MEAN, YEAH. YOU PROBABLY HAVE TO BLOW IF YOU WANT TO GET BLOWN BACK, HUH? ISN'T THAT SOME KIND OF homo courtesy code?
-....I HAVE NO IDEA.
-GOD, I CAN'T believe YOU GOT THE LEAD! YOU'RE GONNA PLAY A KING-MURDERING PSYCHO-SON. ...HAVE YOU EVEN hit ANYONE BEFORE?
-NO...
-YOU CAN PRACTICE ON ME. I'LL PUNCH YOU FIRST, AND THEN YOU HIT ME BACK AS HARD AS YOU DARE. NO, 1 DEGREE harder.
-SO DO YOU STILL HAVE THAT FROZEN CHICKEN IN YOUR FREEZER?
-YEAH.
-GOOD. I CAN FINISH 'STILL LIFE WITH FROZEN BIRD'.

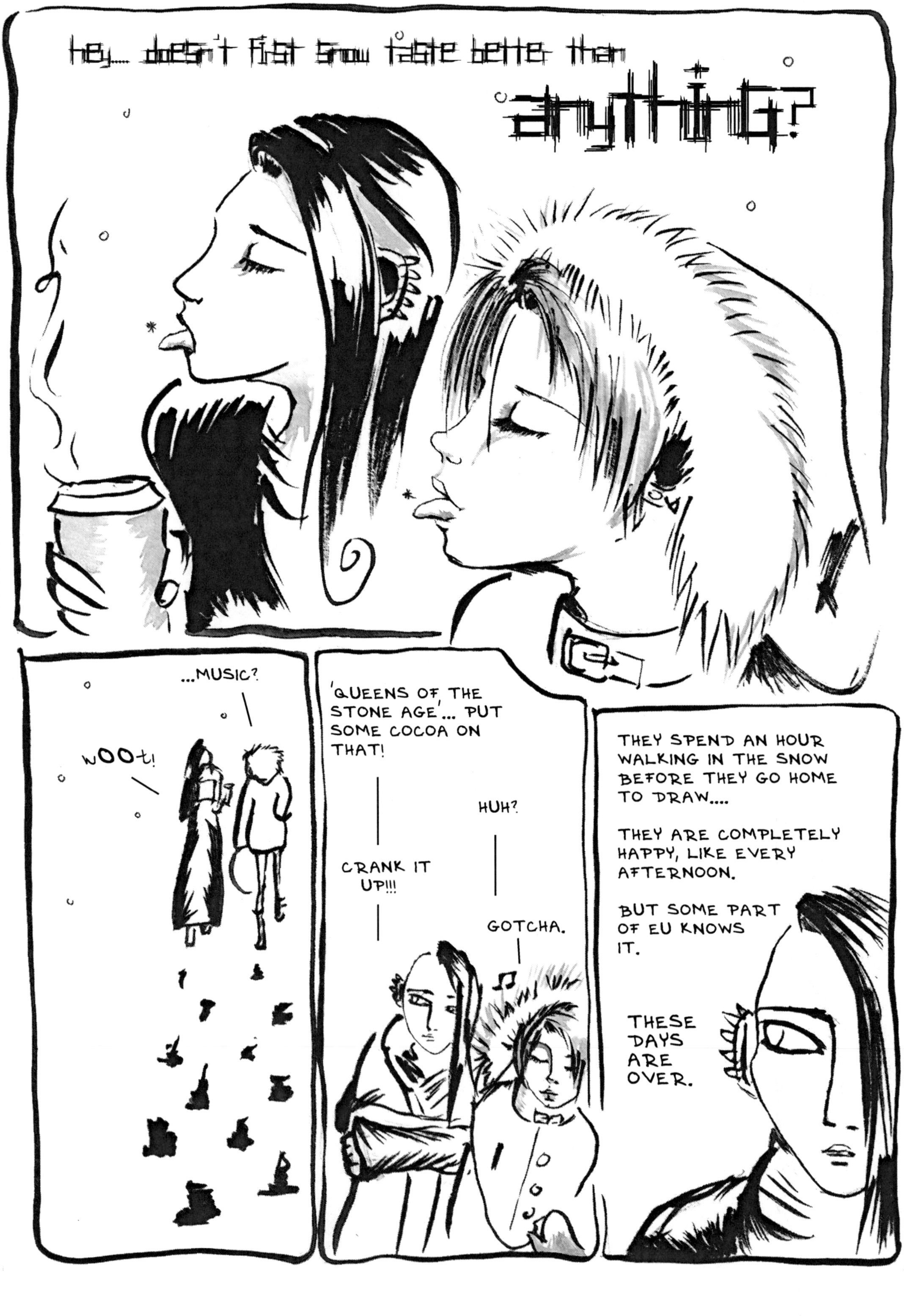
hey..... doesn't first snow taste better than
anything?
...MUSIC?
wOOt!
'QUEENS OF THE STONE AGE'... PUT SOME COCOA ON THAT!
CRANK IT UP!!!
HUH?
GOTCHA.
THEY SPEND AN HOUR WALKING IN THE SNOW BEFORE THEY GO HOME TO DRAW....
THEY ARE COMPLETELY HAPPY, LIKE EVERY AFTERNOON.
BUT SOME PART OF EU KNOWS IT.
THESE DAYS ARE OVER.

born again loser

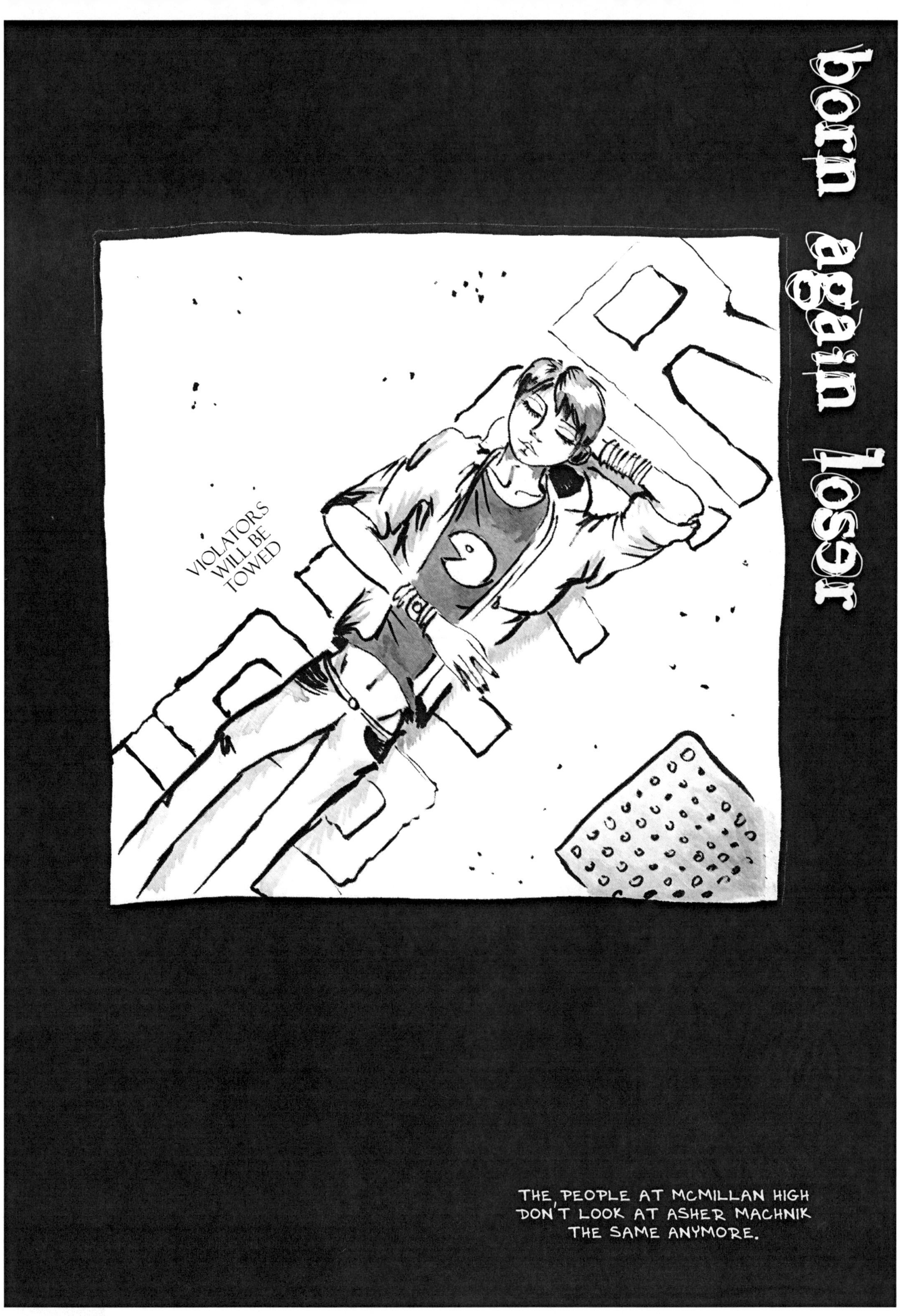
VIOLATORS WILL BE TOWED

THE PEOPLE AT MCMILLAN HIGH DON'T LOOK AT ASHER MACHNIK THE SAME ANYMORE.

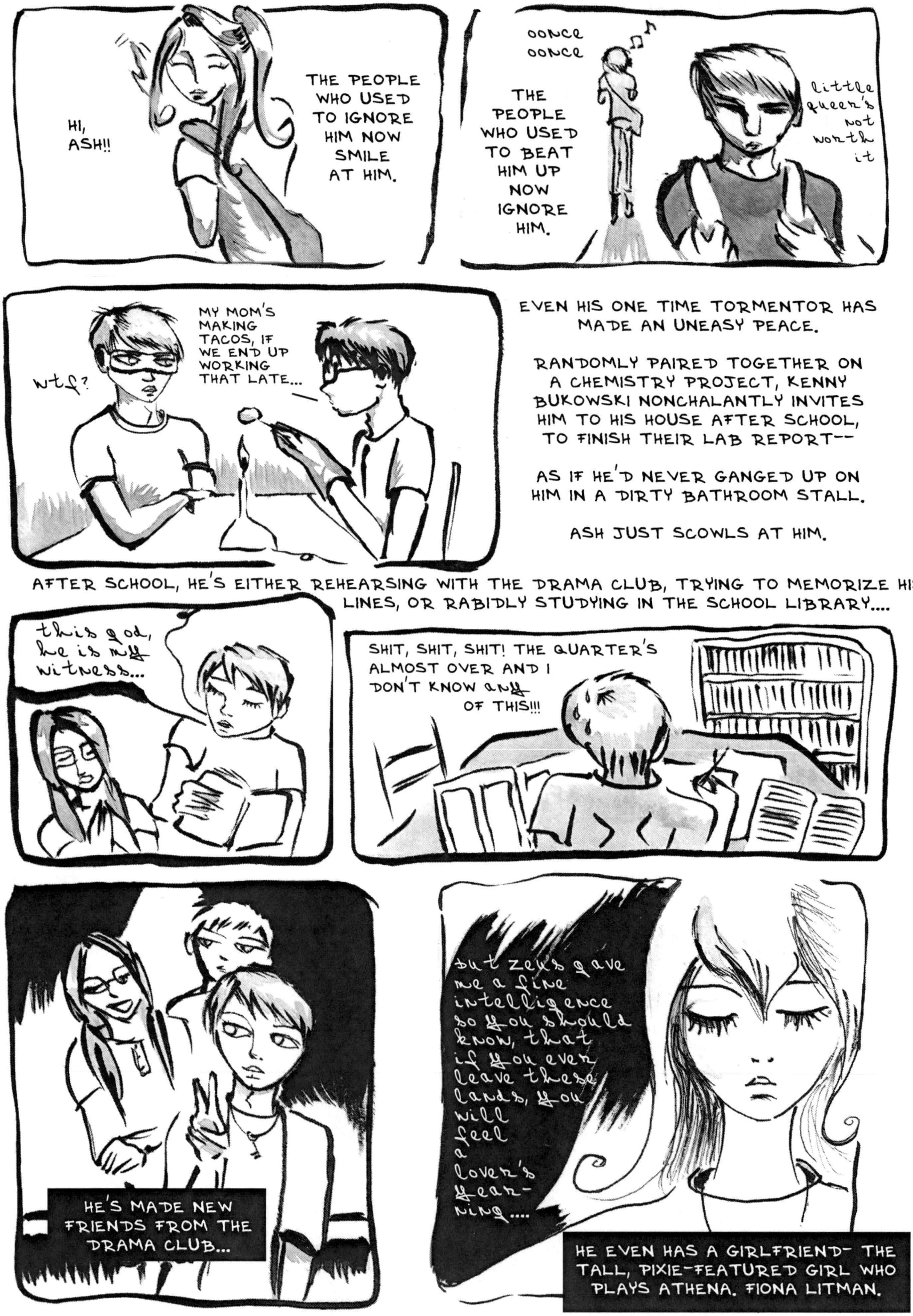
HI, ASH!!
THE PEOPLE WHO USED TO IGNORE HIM NOW SMILE AT HIM.
OONCE OONCE
THE PEOPLE WHO USED TO BEAT HIM UP NOW IGNORE HIM.
little queer's not worth it
MY MOM'S MAKING TACOS, IF WE END UP WORKING THAT LATE...
wtf?
EVEN HIS ONE TIME TORMENTOR HAS MADE AN UNEASY PEACE.
RANDOMLY PAIRED TOGETHER ON A CHEMISTRY PROJECT, KENNY BUKOWSKI NONCHALANTLY INVITES HIM TO HIS HOUSE AFTER SCHOOL, TO FINISH THEIR LAB REPORT--
AS IF HE'D NEVER GANGED UP ON HIM IN A DIRTY BATHROOM STALL.
ASH JUST SCOWLS AT HIM.
AFTER SCHOOL, HE'S EITHER REHEARSING WITH THE DRAMA CLUB, TRYING TO MEMORIZE HIS LINES, OR RABIDLY STUDYING IN THE SCHOOL LIBRARY....
this god, he is my witness...
SHIT, SHIT, SHIT! THE QUARTER'S ALMOST OVER AND I DON'T KNOW any OF THIS!!!
HE'S MADE NEW FRIENDS FROM THE DRAMA CLUB...
but zeus gave me a fine intelligence so you should know, that if you ever leave these lands, you will feel a lover's yearning....
HE EVEN HAS A GIRLFRIEND- THE TALL, PIXIE-FEATURED GIRL WHO PLAYS ATHENA. FIONA LITMAN.

FEE ISN'T COMPLICATED. SHE DOESN'T ASK HIM FOR MUCH...THEY DON'T HAVE TIME FOR MUCH EITHER, JUST SCORCHING LOOKS ACROSS THE THEATER, OR SLOW-KISSING BACK-STAGE...

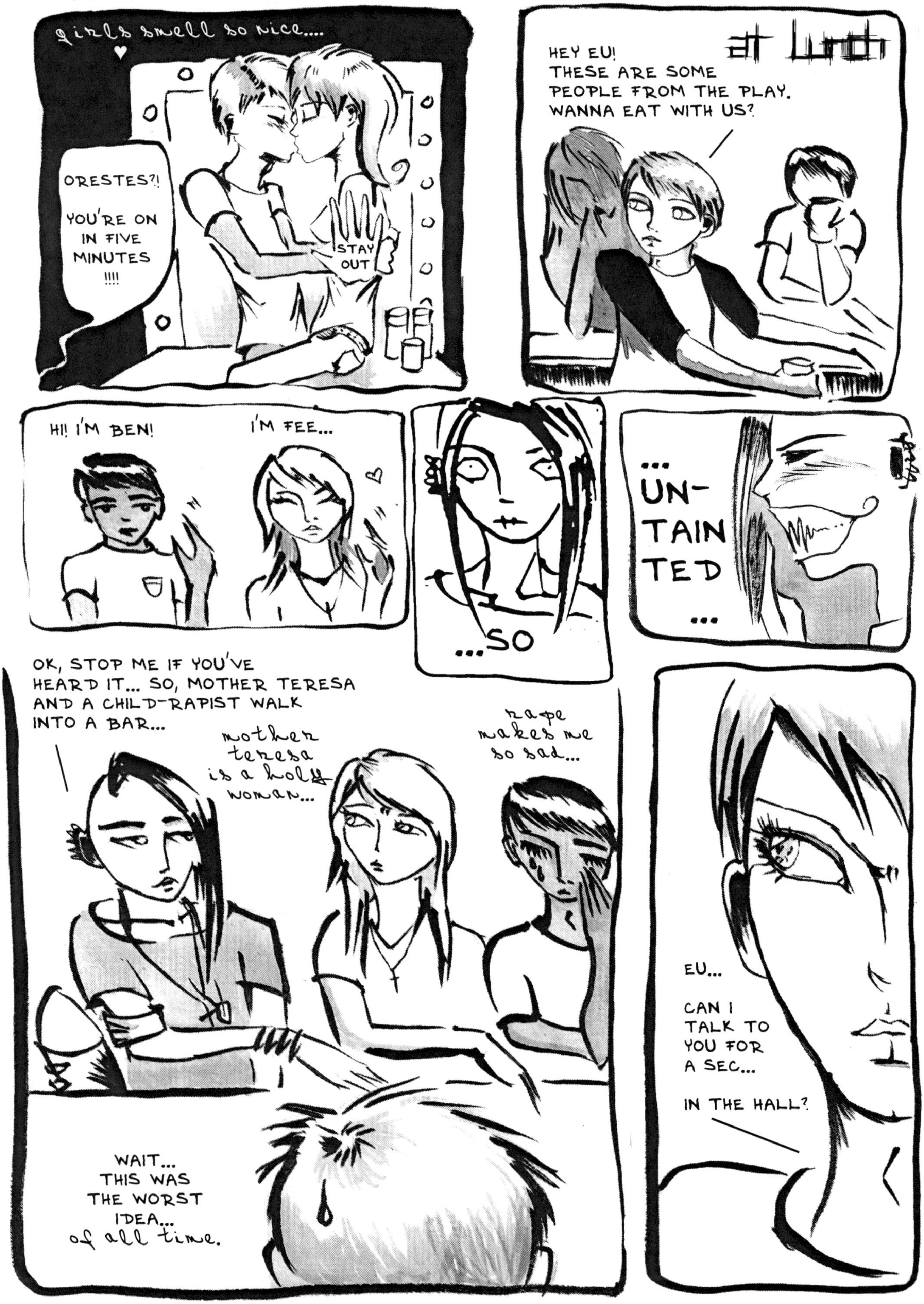

girls smell so nice....
ORESTES?! YOU'RE ON IN FIVE MINUTES !!!!
STAY OUT
at Lunch
HEY EU! THESE ARE SOME PEOPLE FROM THE PLAY. WANNA EAT WITH US?
HI! I'M BEN!
I'M FEE...
...SO
...UN-TAINTED...
OK, STOP ME IF YOU'VE HEARD IT... SO, MOTHER TERESA AND A CHILD-RAPIST WALK INTO A BAR...
mother teresa is a holy woman...
rape makes me so sad...
WAIT... THIS WAS THE WORST IDEA... of all time.
EU... CAN I TALK TO YOU FOR A SEC... IN THE HALL?

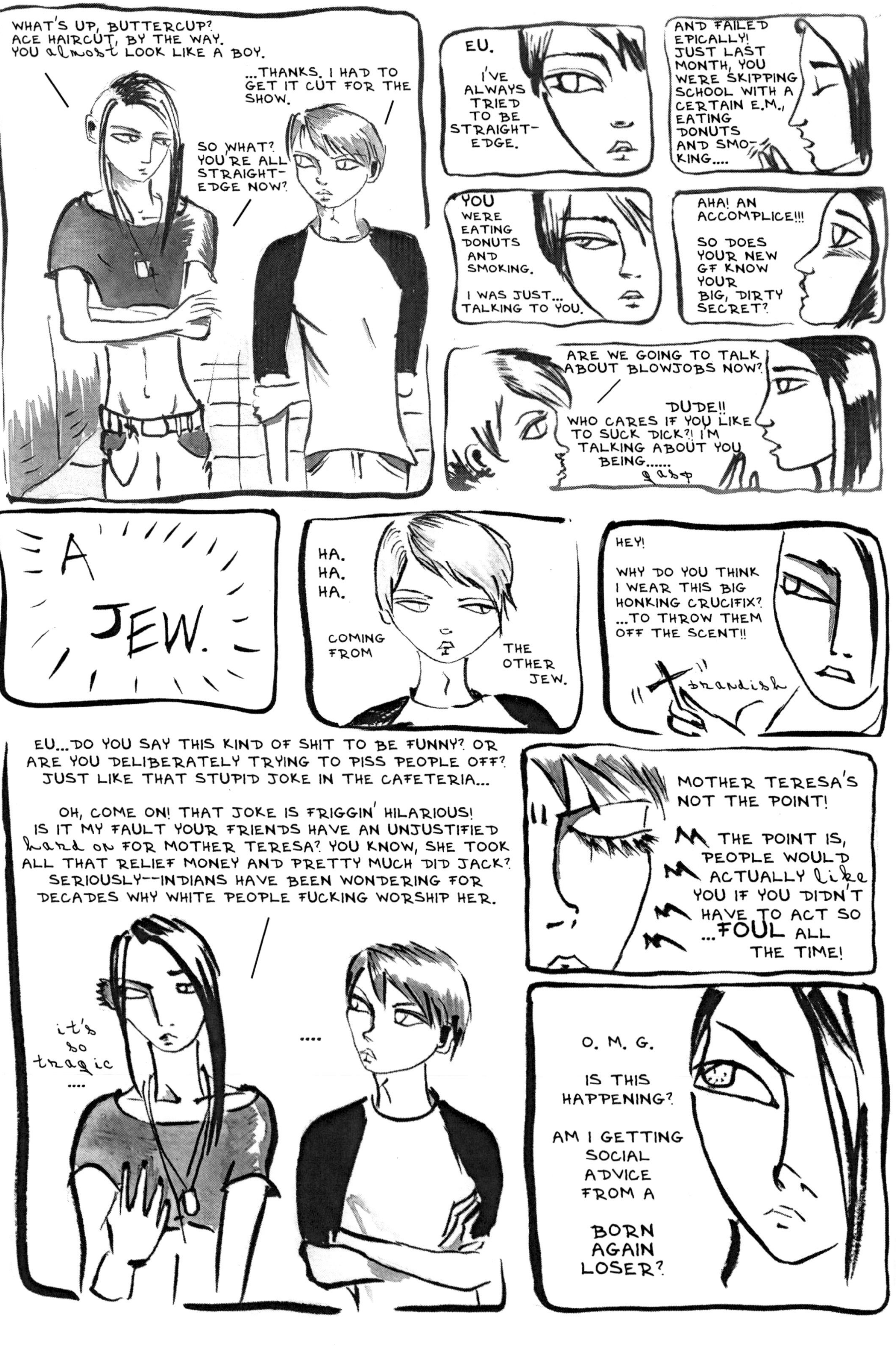
WHAT'S UP, BUTTERCUP? ACE HAIRCUT, BY THE WAY. YOU almost LOOK LIKE A BOY.
...THANKS. I HAD TO GET IT CUT FOR THE SHOW.
SO WHAT? YOU'RE ALL STRAIGHT-EDGE NOW?
EU. I'VE ALWAYS TRIED TO BE STRAIGHT-EDGE.
AND FAILED EPICALLY! JUST LAST MONTH, YOU WERE SKIPPING SCHOOL WITH A CERTAIN E.M., EATING DONUTS AND SMOKING....
YOU WERE EATING DONUTS AND SMOKING.
I WAS JUST... TALKING TO YOU.
AHA! AN ACCOMPLICE!!!
SO DOES YOUR NEW GF KNOW YOUR BIG, DIRTY SECRET?
ARE WE GOING TO TALK ABOUT BLOWJOBS NOW?
DUDE!! WHO CARES IF YOU LIKE TO SUCK DICK?! I'M TALKING ABOUT YOU BEING......
gasp
A JEW.
HA. HA. HA.
COMING FROM
THE OTHER JEW.
HEY!
WHY DO YOU THINK I WEAR THIS BIG HONKING CRUCIFIX? ...TO THROW THEM OFF THE SCENT!!
brandish
EU... DO YOU SAY THIS KIND OF SHIT TO BE FUNNY? OR ARE YOU DELIBERATELY TRYING TO PISS PEOPLE OFF? JUST LIKE THAT STUPID JOKE IN THE CAFETERIA...
OH, COME ON! THAT JOKE IS FRIGGIN' HILARIOUS! IS IT MY FAULT YOUR FRIENDS HAVE AN UNJUSTIFIED hard on FOR MOTHER TERESA? YOU KNOW, SHE TOOK ALL THAT RELIEF MONEY AND PRETTY MUCH DID JACK? SERIOUSLY--INDIANS HAVE BEEN WONDERING FOR DECADES WHY WHITE PEOPLE FUCKING WORSHIP HER.
it's so tragic ....
....
MOTHER TERESA'S NOT THE POINT!
THE POINT IS, PEOPLE WOULD ACTUALLY like YOU IF YOU DIDN'T HAVE TO ACT SO ...FOUL ALL THE TIME!
O. M. G.
IS THIS HAPPENING?
AM I GETTING SOCIAL ADVICE FROM A
BORN AGAIN LOSER?

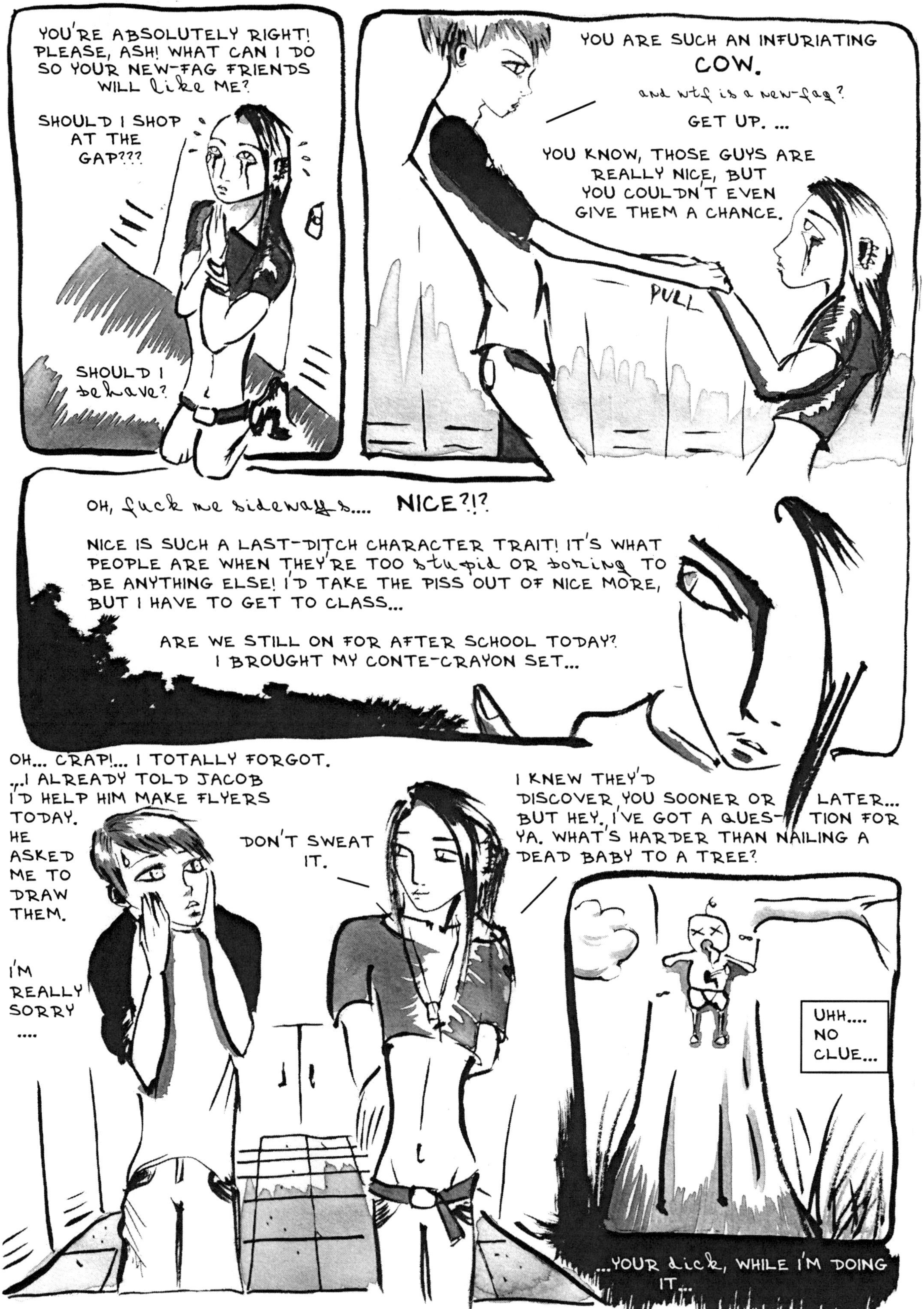
YOU'RE ABSOLUTELY RIGHT! PLEASE, ASH! WHAT CAN I DO SO YOUR NEW-FAG FRIENDS WILL like ME?
SHOULD I SHOP AT THE GAP???
SHOULD I behave?
YOU ARE SUCH AN INFURIATING COW.
and wtf is a new-fag?
GET UP. ...
YOU KNOW, THOSE GUYS ARE REALLY NICE, BUT YOU COULDN'T EVEN GIVE THEM A CHANCE.
PULL
OH, fuck me sideways.... NICE?!?
NICE IS SUCH A LAST-DITCH CHARACTER TRAIT! IT'S WHAT PEOPLE ARE WHEN THEY'RE TOO stupid OR boring TO BE ANYTHING ELSE! I'D TAKE THE PISS OUT OF NICE MORE, BUT I HAVE TO GET TO CLASS...
ARE WE STILL ON FOR AFTER SCHOOL TODAY? I BROUGHT MY CONTE-CRAYON SET...
OH... CRAP!... I TOTALLY FORGOT. ...I ALREADY TOLD JACOB I'D HELP HIM MAKE FLYERS TODAY. HE ASKED ME TO DRAW THEM.
I'M REALLY SORRY ....
DON'T SWEAT IT.
I KNEW THEY'D DISCOVER YOU SOONER OR LATER... BUT HEY, I'VE GOT A QUESTION FOR YA. WHAT'S HARDER THAN NAILING A DEAD BABY TO A TREE?
UHH.... NO CLUE...
...YOUR dick, WHILE I'M DOING IT...

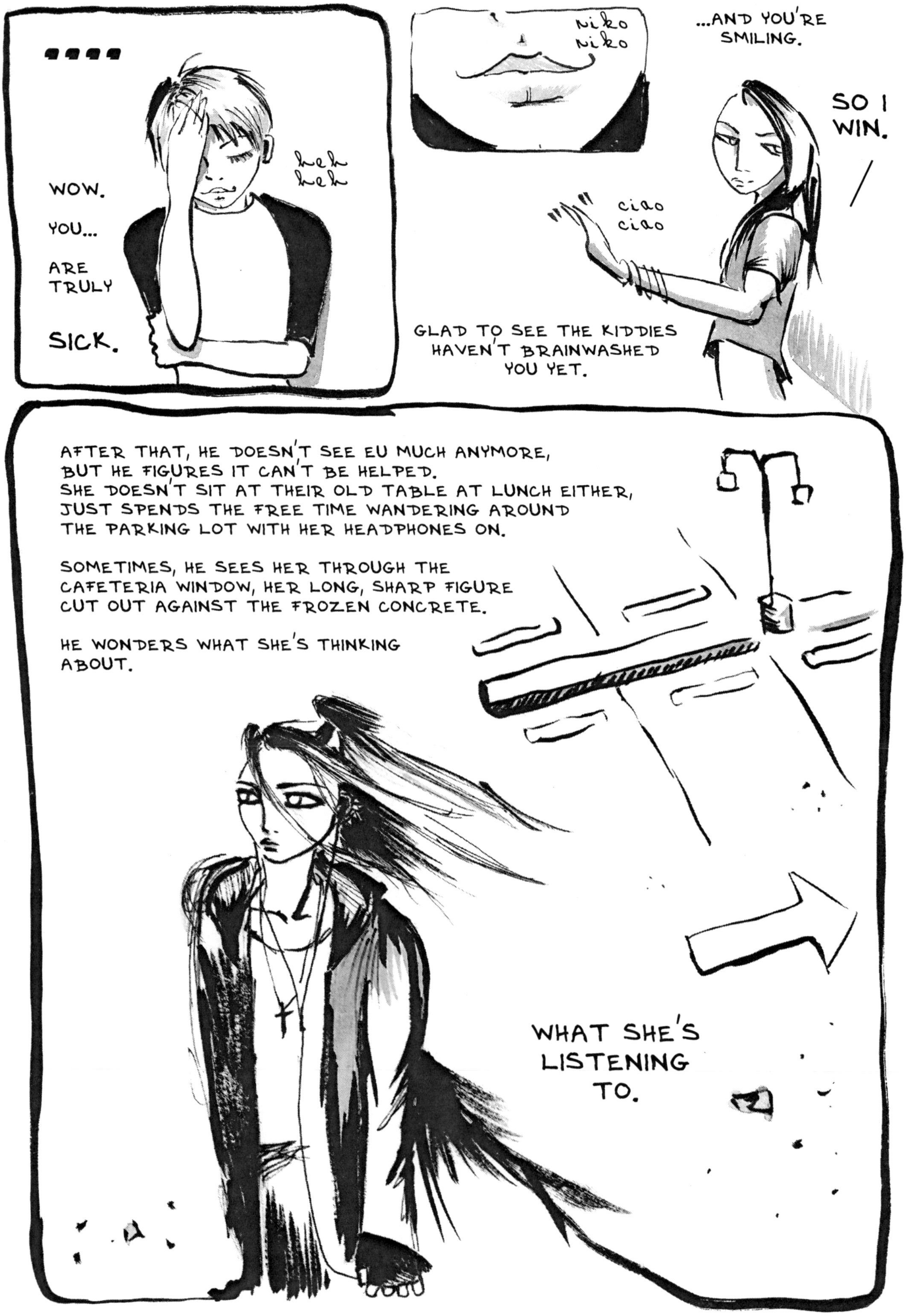
....
WOW.
YOU...
ARE TRULY
SICK.
heh heh
niko niko
...AND YOU'RE SMILING.
SO I WIN.
ciao ciao
GLAD TO SEE THE KIDDIES HAVEN'T BRAINWASHED YOU YET.
AFTER THAT, HE DOESN'T SEE EU MUCH ANYMORE, BUT HE FIGURES IT CAN'T BE HELPED. SHE DOESN'T SIT AT THEIR OLD TABLE AT LUNCH EITHER, JUST SPENDS THE FREE TIME WANDERING AROUND THE PARKING LOT WITH HER HEADPHONES ON.
SOMETIMES, HE SEES HER THROUGH THE CAFETERIA WINDOW, HER LONG, SHARP FIGURE CUT OUT AGAINST THE FROZEN CONCRETE.
HE WONDERS WHAT SHE'S THINKING ABOUT.
WHAT SHE'S LISTENING TO.

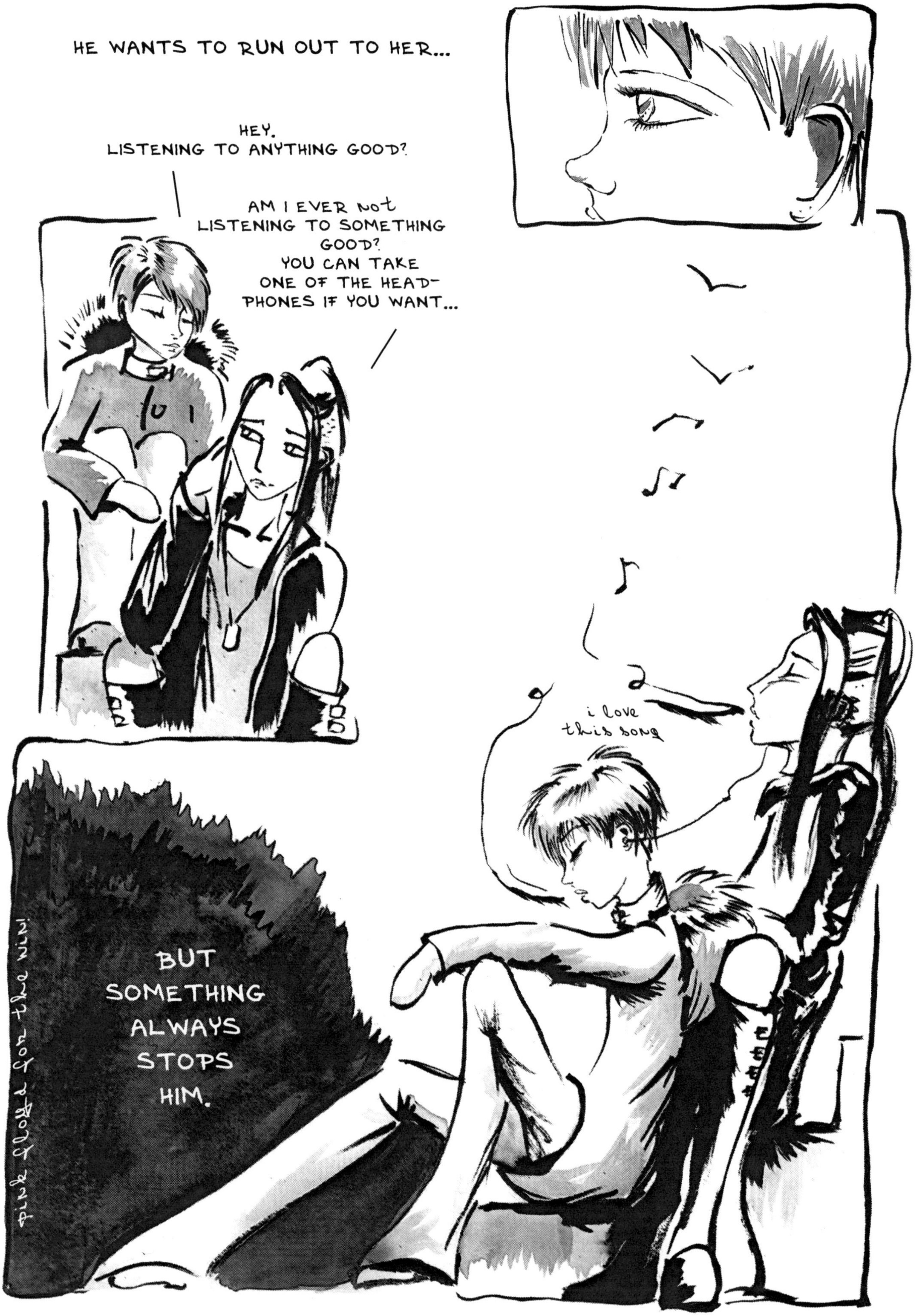
HE WANTS TO RUN OUT TO HER...
HEY. LISTENING TO ANYTHING GOOD?
AM I EVER not LISTENING TO SOMETHING GOOD? YOU CAN TAKE ONE OF THE HEAD-PHONES IF YOU WANT...
i love this song
BUT SOMETHING ALWAYS STOPS HIM.
pink floyd for the win!

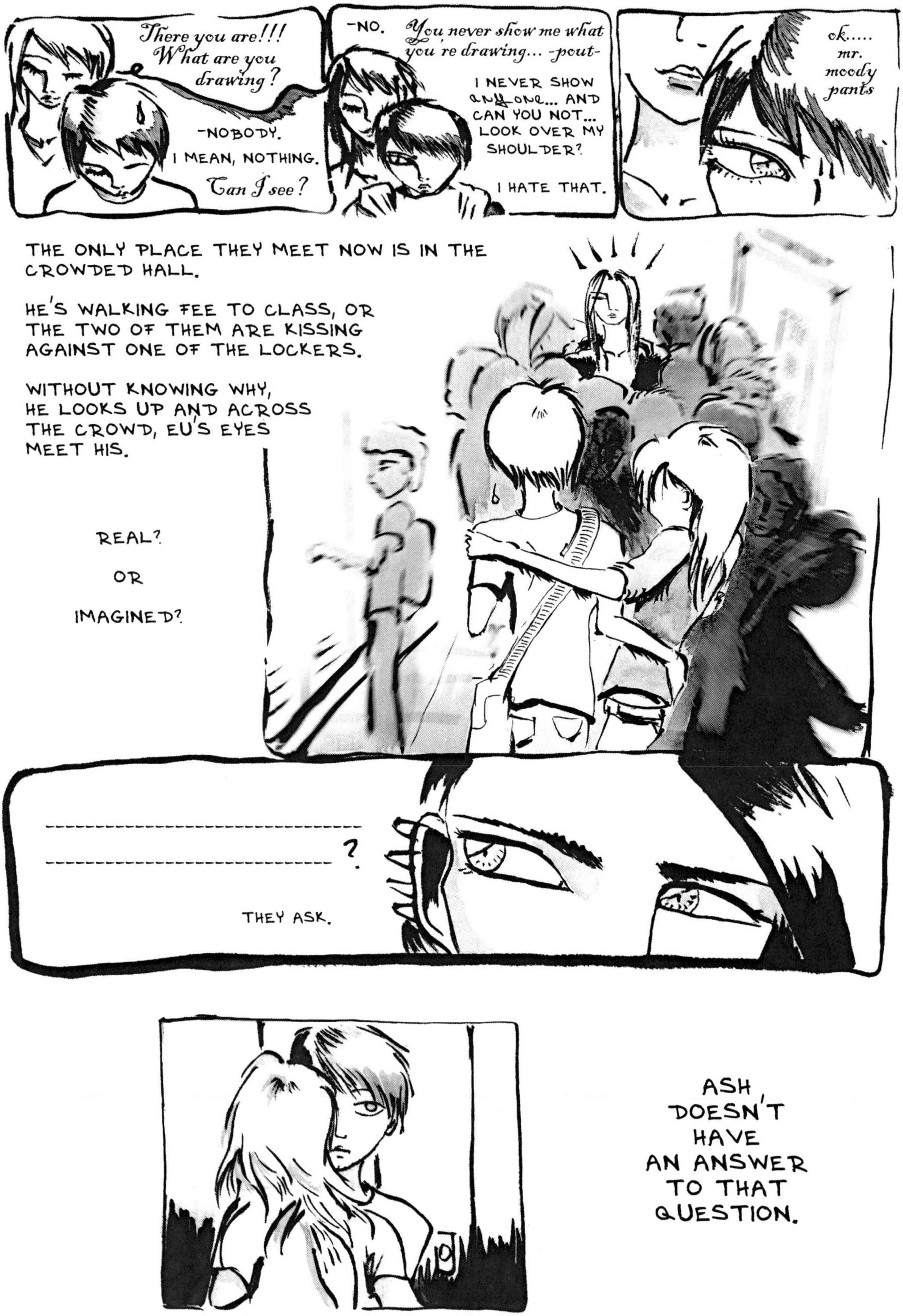

There you are!!! What are you drawing?
-NOBODY.
I MEAN, NOTHING.
Can I see?
-NO.
You never show me what you're drawing... -pout-
I NEVER SHOW anyone... AND CAN YOU NOT... LOOK OVER MY SHOULDER?
I HATE THAT.
ok..... mr. moody pants
THE ONLY PLACE THEY MEET NOW IS IN THE CROWDED HALL.
HE'S WALKING FEE TO CLASS, OR THE TWO OF THEM ARE KISSING AGAINST ONE OF THE LOCKERS.
WITHOUT KNOWING WHY, HE LOOKS UP AND ACROSS THE CROWD, EU'S EYES MEET HIS.
REAL?
OR
IMAGINED?
____
___________________________?
THEY ASK.
ASH DOESN'T HAVE AN ANSWER TO THAT QUESTION.

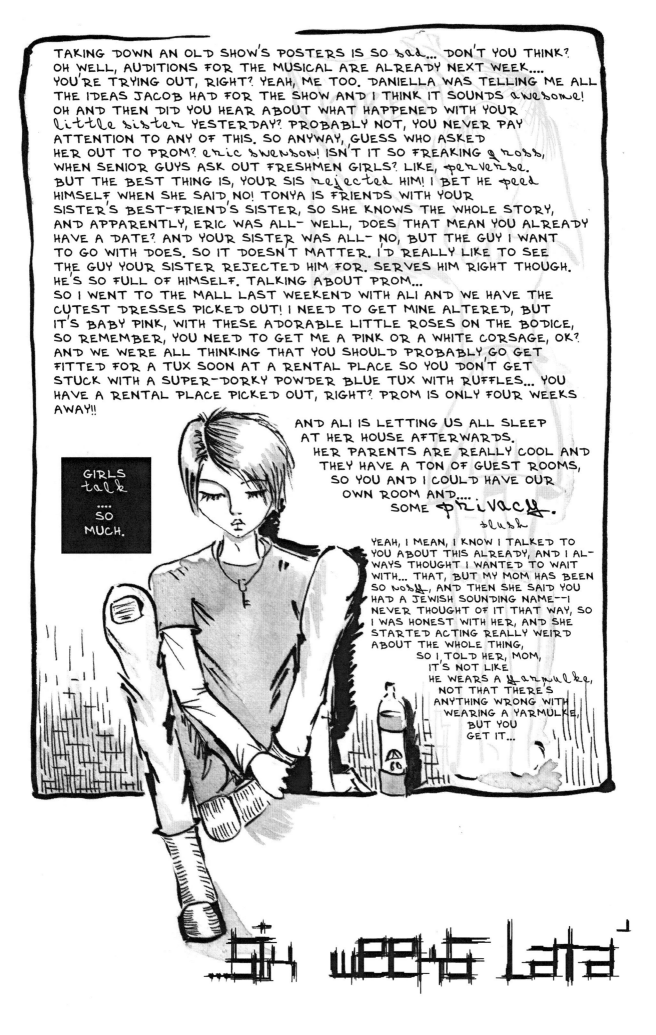

TAKING DOWN AN OLD SHOW'S POSTERS IS SO sad... DON'T YOU THINK? OH WELL, AUDITIONS FOR THE MUSICAL ARE ALREADY NEXT WEEK.... YOU'RE TRYING OUT, RIGHT? YEAH, ME TOO. DANIELLA WAS TELLING ME ALL THE IDEAS JACOB HAD FOR THE SHOW AND I THINK IT SOUNDS awesome! OH AND THEN DID YOU HEAR ABOUT WHAT HAPPENED WITH YOUR little sister YESTERDAY? PROBABLY NOT, YOU NEVER PAY ATTENTION TO ANY OF THIS. SO ANYWAY, GUESS WHO ASKED HER OUT TO PROM? eric swenson! ISN'T IT SO FREAKING gross, WHEN SENIOR GUYS ASK OUT FRESHMEN GIRLS? LIKE, perverse. BUT THE BEST THING IS, YOUR SIS rejected HIM! I BET HE peed HIMSELF WHEN SHE SAID NO! TONYA IS FRIENDS WITH YOUR SISTER'S BEST-FRIEND'S SISTER, SO SHE KNOWS THE WHOLE STORY, AND APPARENTLY, ERIC WAS ALL— WELL, DOES THAT MEAN YOU ALREADY HAVE A DATE? AND YOUR SISTER WAS ALL— NO, BUT THE GUY I WANT TO GO WITH DOES. SO IT DOESN'T MATTER. I'D REALLY LIKE TO SEE THE GUY YOUR SISTER REJECTED HIM FOR. SERVES HIM RIGHT THOUGH. HE'S SO FULL OF HIMSELF. TALKING ABOUT PROM...
SO I WENT TO THE MALL LAST WEEKEND WITH ALI AND WE HAVE THE CUTEST DRESSES PICKED OUT! I NEED TO GET MINE ALTERED, BUT IT'S BABY PINK, WITH THESE ADORABLE LITTLE ROSES ON THE BODICE, SO REMEMBER, YOU NEED TO GET ME A PINK OR A WHITE CORSAGE, OK? AND WE WERE ALL THINKING THAT YOU SHOULD PROBABLY GO GET FITTED FOR A TUX SOON AT A RENTAL PLACE SO YOU DON'T GET STUCK WITH A SUPER-DORKY POWDER BLUE TUX WITH RUFFLES... YOU HAVE A RENTAL PLACE PICKED OUT, RIGHT? PROM IS ONLY FOUR WEEKS AWAY!!

GIRLS
talk
....
SO
MUCH.

AND ALI IS LETTING US ALL SLEEP AT HER HOUSE AFTERWARDS. HER PARENTS ARE REALLY COOL AND THEY HAVE A TON OF GUEST ROOMS, SO YOU AND I COULD HAVE OUR OWN ROOM AND.... SOME privacy.
blush

YEAH, I MEAN, I KNOW I TALKED TO YOU ABOUT THIS ALREADY, AND I AL-WAYS THOUGHT I WANTED TO WAIT WITH... THAT, BUT MY MOM HAS BEEN SO nosy, AND THEN SHE SAID YOU HAD A JEWISH SOUNDING NAME—I NEVER THOUGHT OF IT THAT WAY, SO I WAS HONEST WITH HER, AND SHE STARTED ACTING REALLY WEIRD ABOUT THE WHOLE THING, SO I TOLD HER, MOM, IT'S NOT LIKE HE WEARS A yarmulke, NOT THAT THERE'S ANYTHING WRONG WITH WEARING A YARMULKE, BUT YOU GET IT...

...six weeks later

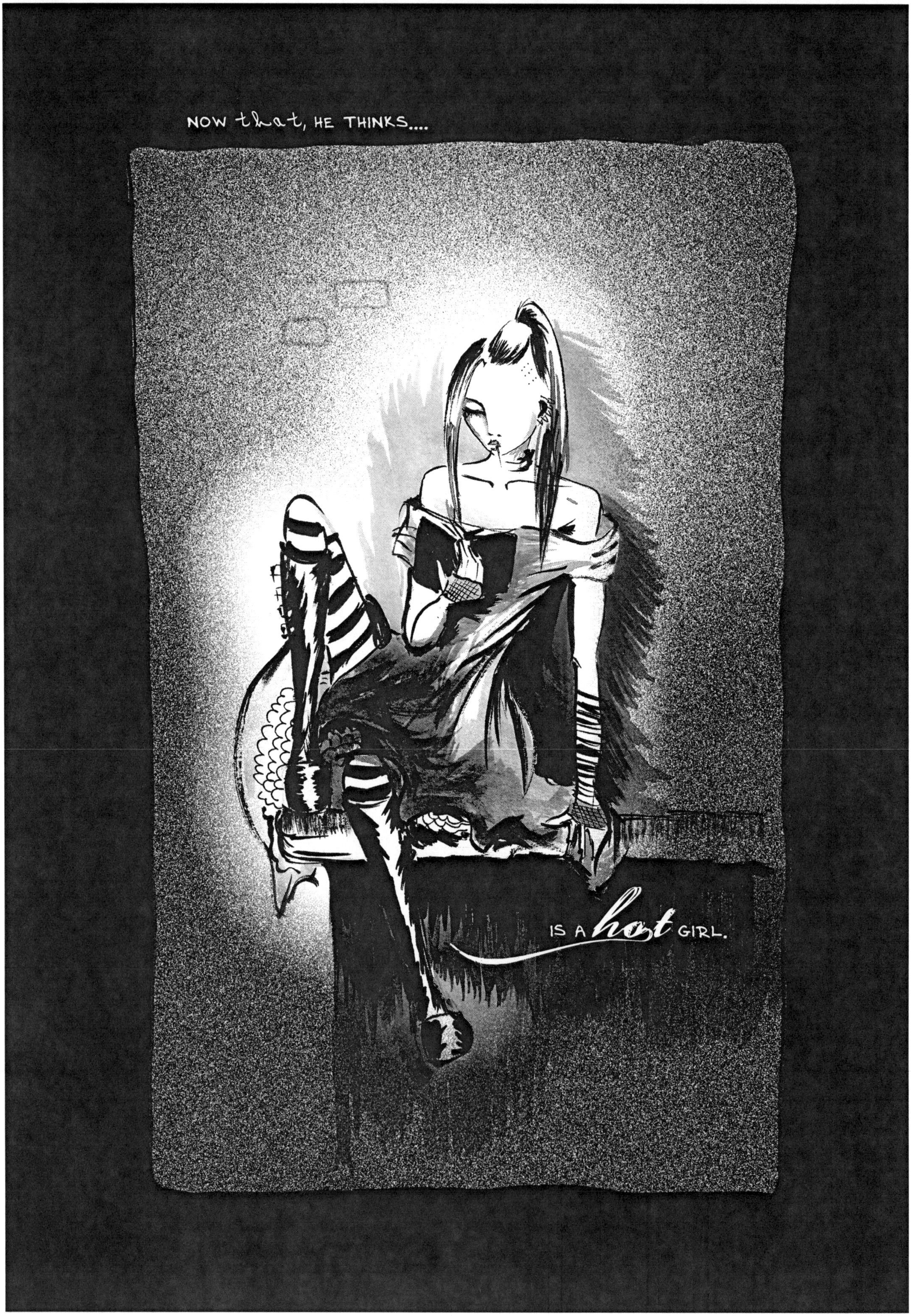
NOW that, HE THINKS....
IS A hot GIRL.

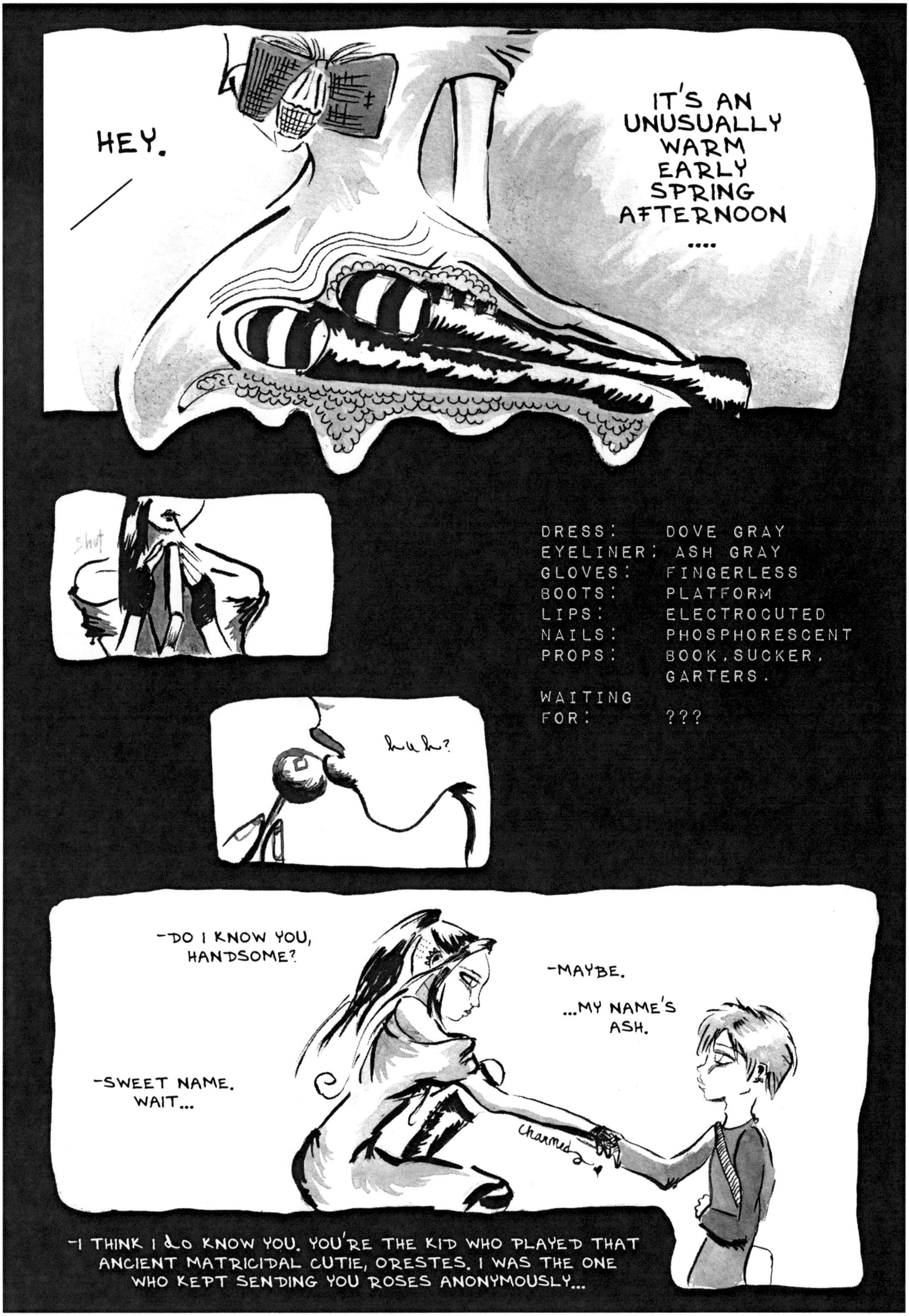
HEY.
IT'S AN UNUSUALLY WARM EARLY SPRING AFTERNOON ....
shut
DRESS: DOVE GRAY
EYELINER: ASH GRAY
GLOVES: FINGERLESS
BOOTS: PLATFORM
LIPS: ELECTROCUTED
NAILS: PHOSPHORESCENT
PROPS: BOOK, SUCKER, GARTERS.
WAITING FOR: ???
huh?
-DO I KNOW YOU, HANDSOME?
-MAYBE.
...MY NAME'S ASH.
-SWEET NAME. WAIT...
charmed
-I THINK I do KNOW YOU. YOU'RE THE KID WHO PLAYED THAT ANCIENT MATRICIDAL CUTIE, ORESTES. I WAS THE ONE WHO KEPT SENDING YOU ROSES ANONYMOUSLY...

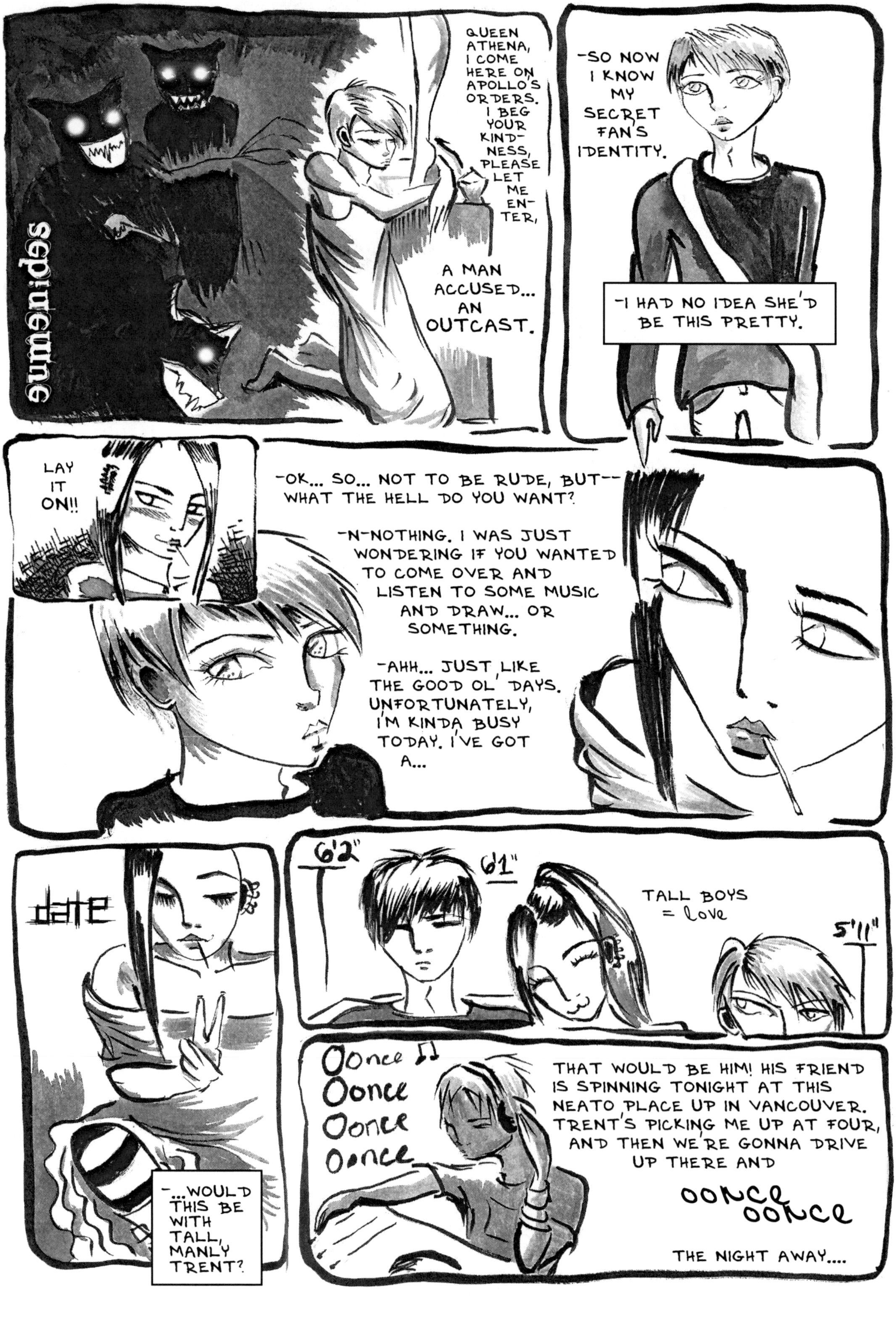
eumenides
QUEEN ATHENA, I COME HERE ON APOLLO'S ORDERS. I BEG YOUR KINDNESS, PLEASE LET ME ENTER,
A MAN ACCUSED... AN OUTCAST.
-SO NOW I KNOW MY SECRET FAN'S IDENTITY.
-I HAD NO IDEA SHE'D BE THIS PRETTY.
LAY IT ON!!
-OK... SO... NOT TO BE RUDE, BUT-- WHAT THE HELL DO YOU WANT?
-N-NOTHING. I WAS JUST WONDERING IF YOU WANTED TO COME OVER AND LISTEN TO SOME MUSIC AND DRAW... OR SOMETHING.
-AHH... JUST LIKE THE GOOD OL' DAYS. UNFORTUNATELY, I'M KINDA BUSY TODAY. I'VE GOT A...
date
-...WOULD THIS BE WITH TALL, MANLY TRENT?
6'2"
6'1"
TALL BOYS = love
5'11"
Oonce Oonce Oonce Oonce
THAT WOULD BE HIM! HIS FRIEND IS SPINNING TONIGHT AT THIS NEATO PLACE UP IN VANCOUVER. TRENT'S PICKING ME UP AT FOUR, AND THEN WE'RE GONNA DRIVE UP THERE AND
OONCE OONCE
THE NIGHT AWAY....

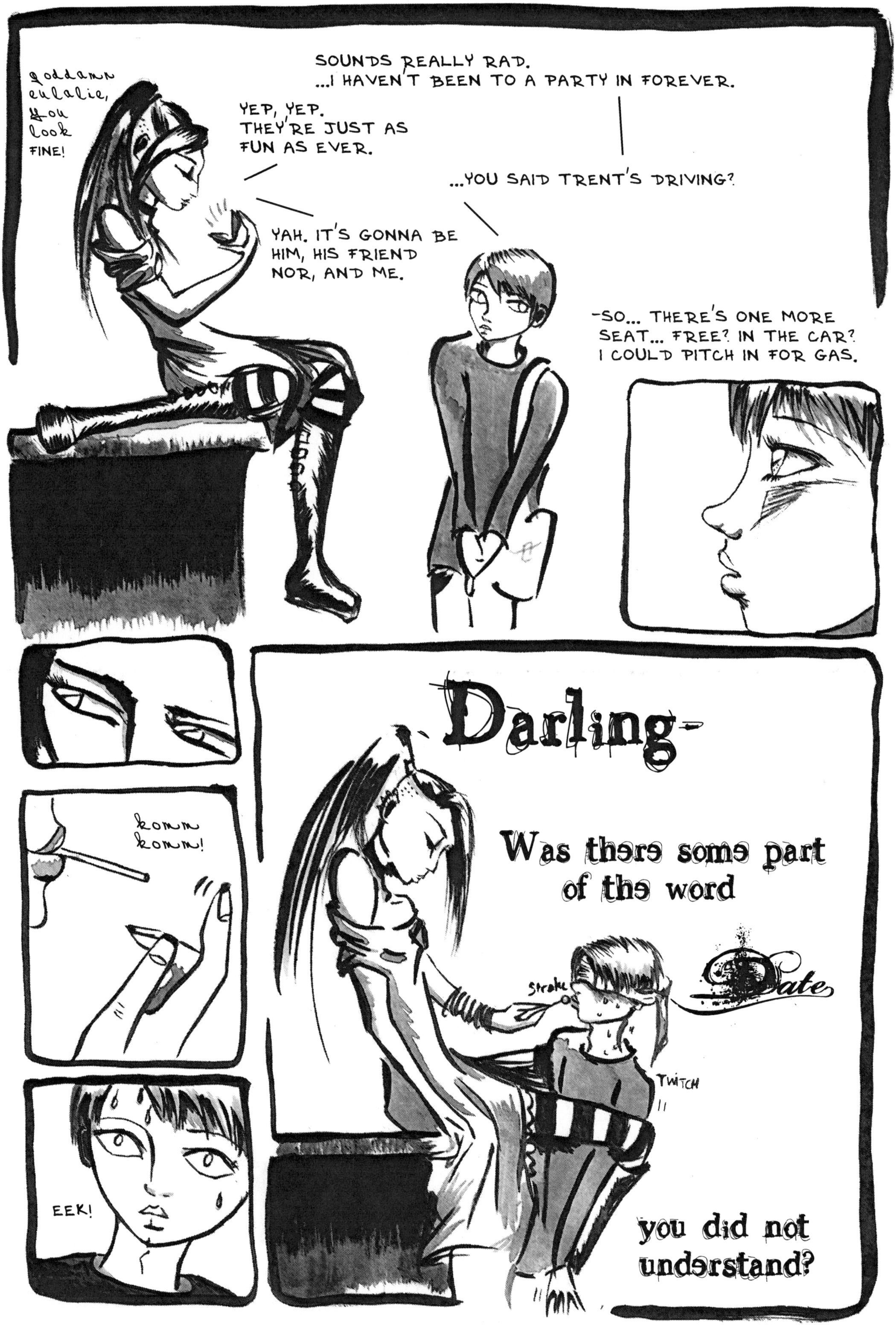

goddamn eulalie, you look FINE!
YEP, YEP. THEY'RE JUST AS FUN AS EVER.
SOUNDS REALLY RAD. ...I HAVEN'T BEEN TO A PARTY IN FOREVER.
YAH. IT'S GONNA BE HIM, HIS FRIEND NOR, AND ME.
...YOU SAID TRENT'S DRIVING?
-SO... THERE'S ONE MORE SEAT... FREE? IN THE CAR? I COULD PITCH IN FOR GAS.
komm komm!
EEK!
Darling-
Was there some part of the word
stroke
Date
TWITCH
you did not understand?

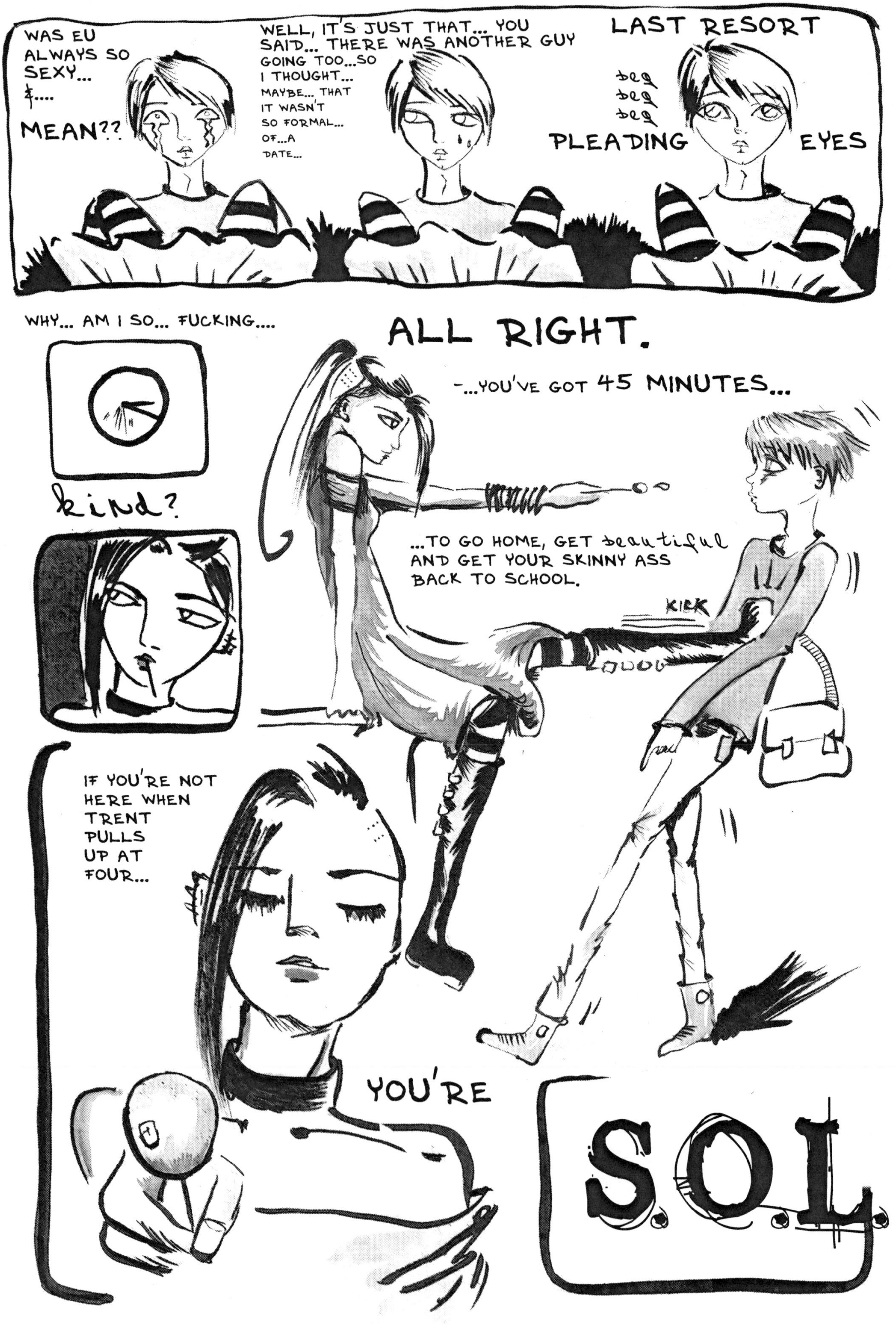

WAS EU ALWAYS SO SEXY... &.... MEAN??
WELL, IT'S JUST THAT... YOU SAID... THERE WAS ANOTHER GUY GOING TOO...SO I THOUGHT... MAYBE... THAT IT WASN'T SO FORMAL... OF...A DATE...
LAST RESORT
beg beg beg
PLEADING EYES
WHY... AM I SO... FUCKING....
kind?
ALL RIGHT.
-...YOU'VE GOT 45 MINUTES...
...TO GO HOME, GET beautiful AND GET YOUR SKINNY ASS BACK TO SCHOOL.
KICK
IF YOU'RE NOT HERE WHEN TRENT PULLS UP AT FOUR...
YOU'RE
S.O.L

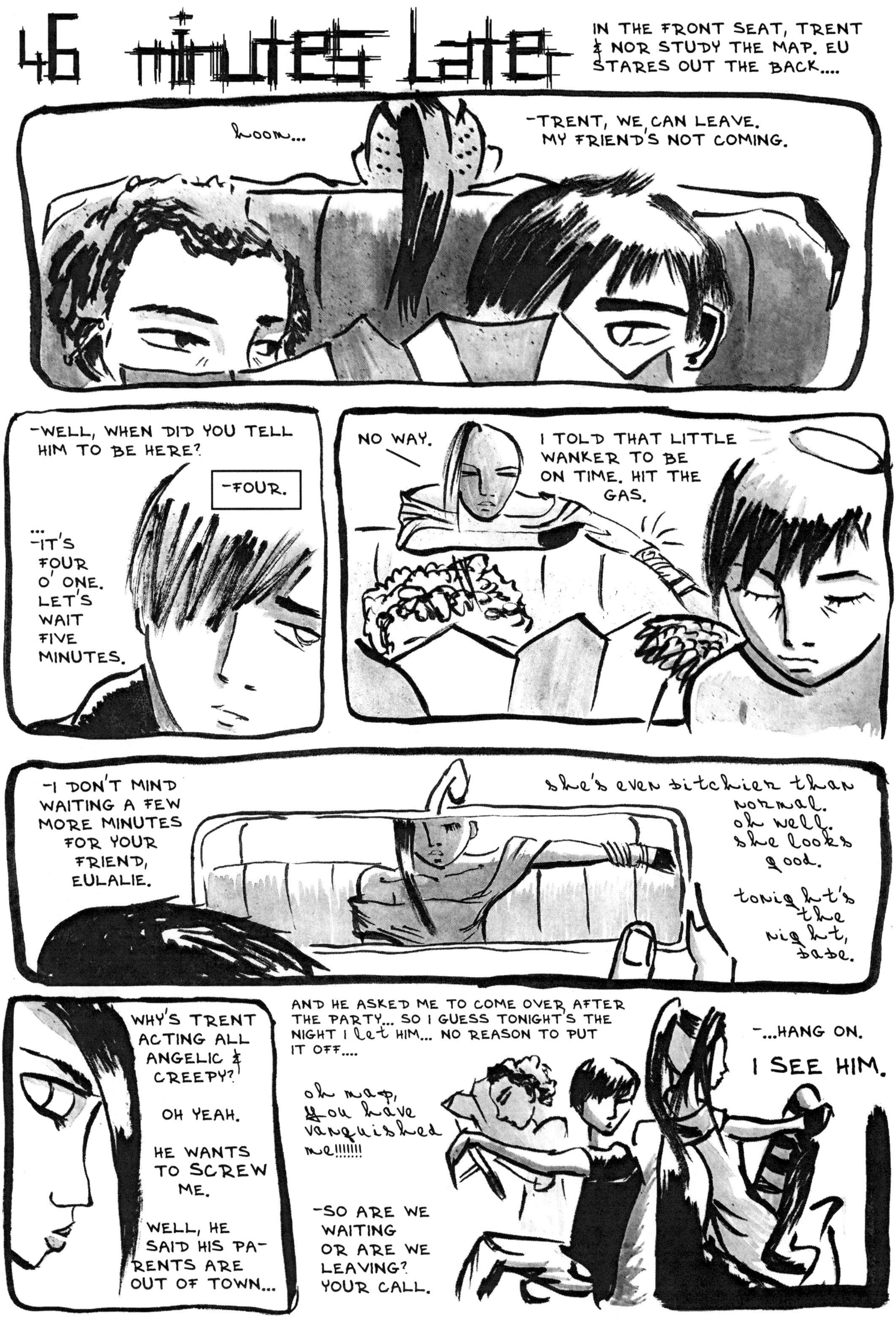
46 minutes Later
IN THE FRONT SEAT, TRENT & NOR STUDY THE MAP. EU STARES OUT THE BACK....
hoom...
-TRENT, WE CAN LEAVE. MY FRIEND'S NOT COMING.
-WELL, WHEN DID YOU TELL HIM TO BE HERE?
-FOUR.
...
-IT'S FOUR O' ONE. LET'S WAIT FIVE MINUTES.
NO WAY.
I TOLD THAT LITTLE WANKER TO BE ON TIME. HIT THE GAS.
-I DON'T MIND WAITING A FEW MORE MINUTES FOR YOUR FRIEND, EULALIE.
she's even bitchier than normal. oh well. she looks good.
tonight's the night, babe.
WHY'S TRENT ACTING ALL ANGELIC & CREEPY?
OH YEAH.
HE WANTS TO SCREW ME.
WELL, HE SAID HIS PARENTS ARE OUT OF TOWN...
AND HE ASKED ME TO COME OVER AFTER THE PARTY... SO I GUESS TONIGHT'S THE NIGHT I let HIM... NO REASON TO PUT IT OFF....
oh map, you have vanquished me!!!!!!!
-SO ARE WE WAITING OR ARE WE LEAVING? YOUR CALL.
-...HANG ON.
I SEE HIM.

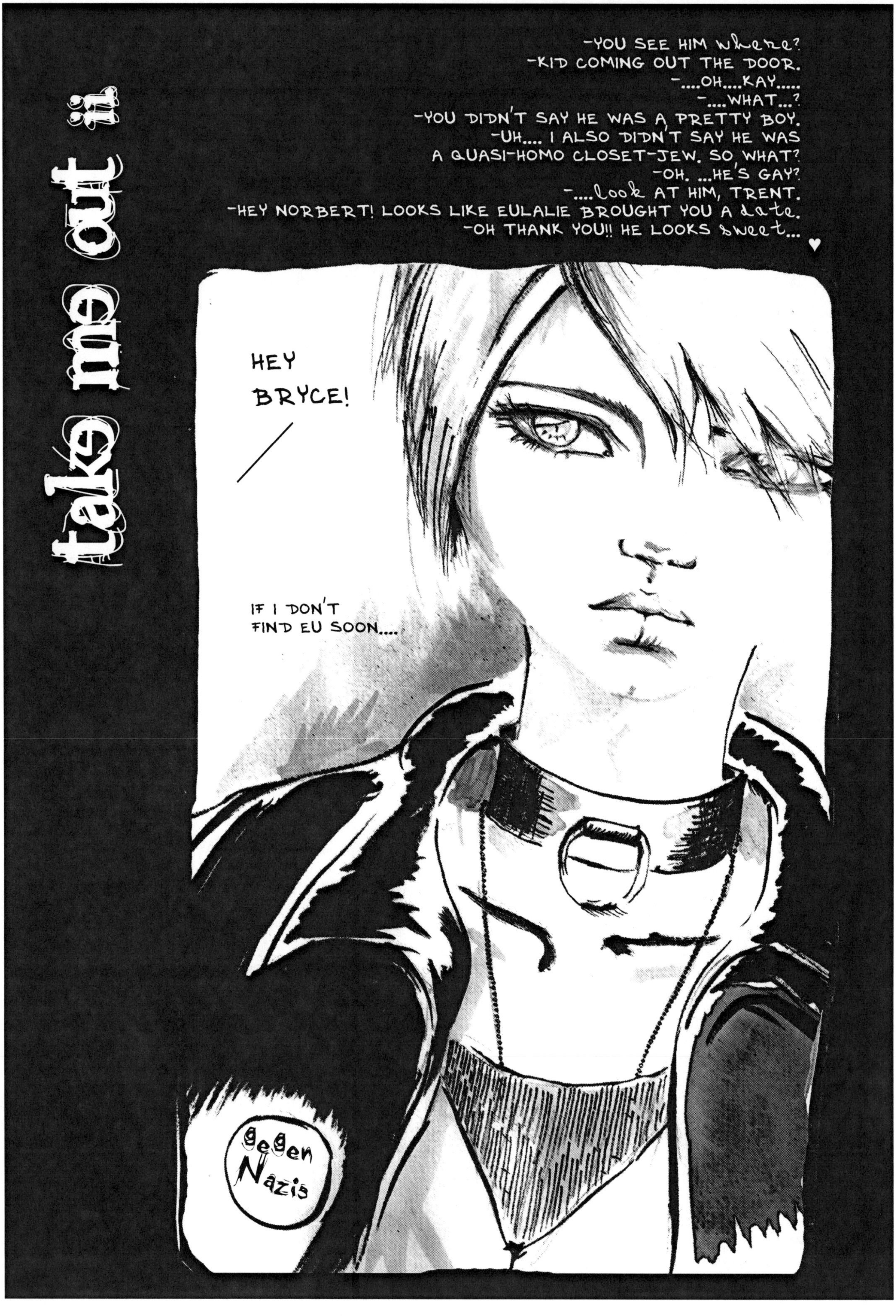
take me out ii
-YOU SEE HIM where?
-KID COMING OUT THE DOOR.
-....OH....KAY.....
-....WHAT...?
-YOU DIDN'T SAY HE WAS A PRETTY BOY.
-UH.... I ALSO DIDN'T SAY HE WAS A QUASI-HOMO CLOSET-JEW. SO WHAT?
-OH. ...HE'S GAY?
-....look AT HIM, TRENT.
-HEY NORBERT! LOOKS LIKE EULALIE BROUGHT YOU A date.
-OH THANK YOU!! HE LOOKS sweet... ♥
HEY BRYCE!
IF I DON'T FIND EU SOON....
gegen Nazis

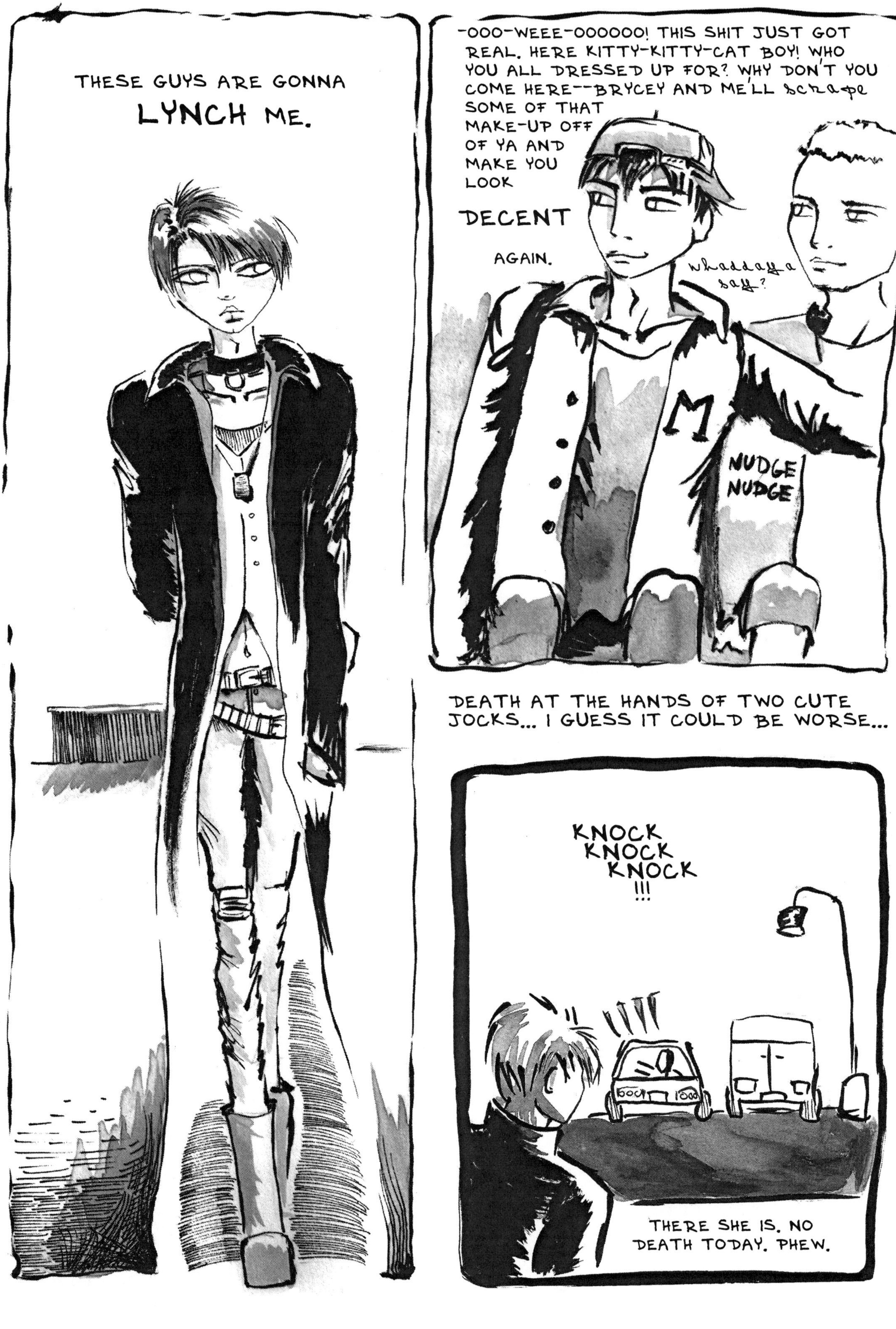

THESE GUYS ARE GONNA LYNCH ME.
-OOO-WEEE-OOOOOO! THIS SHIT JUST GOT REAL. HERE KITTY-KITTY-CAT BOY! WHO YOU ALL DRESSED UP FOR? WHY DON'T YOU COME HERE--BRYCEY AND ME'LL scrape SOME OF THAT MAKE-UP OFF OF YA AND MAKE YOU LOOK DECENT AGAIN.
whaddaya say?
NUDGE NUDGE
DEATH AT THE HANDS OF TWO CUTE JOCKS... I GUESS IT COULD BE WORSE...
KNOCK KNOCK KNOCK !!!
THERE SHE IS. NO DEATH TODAY. PHEW.

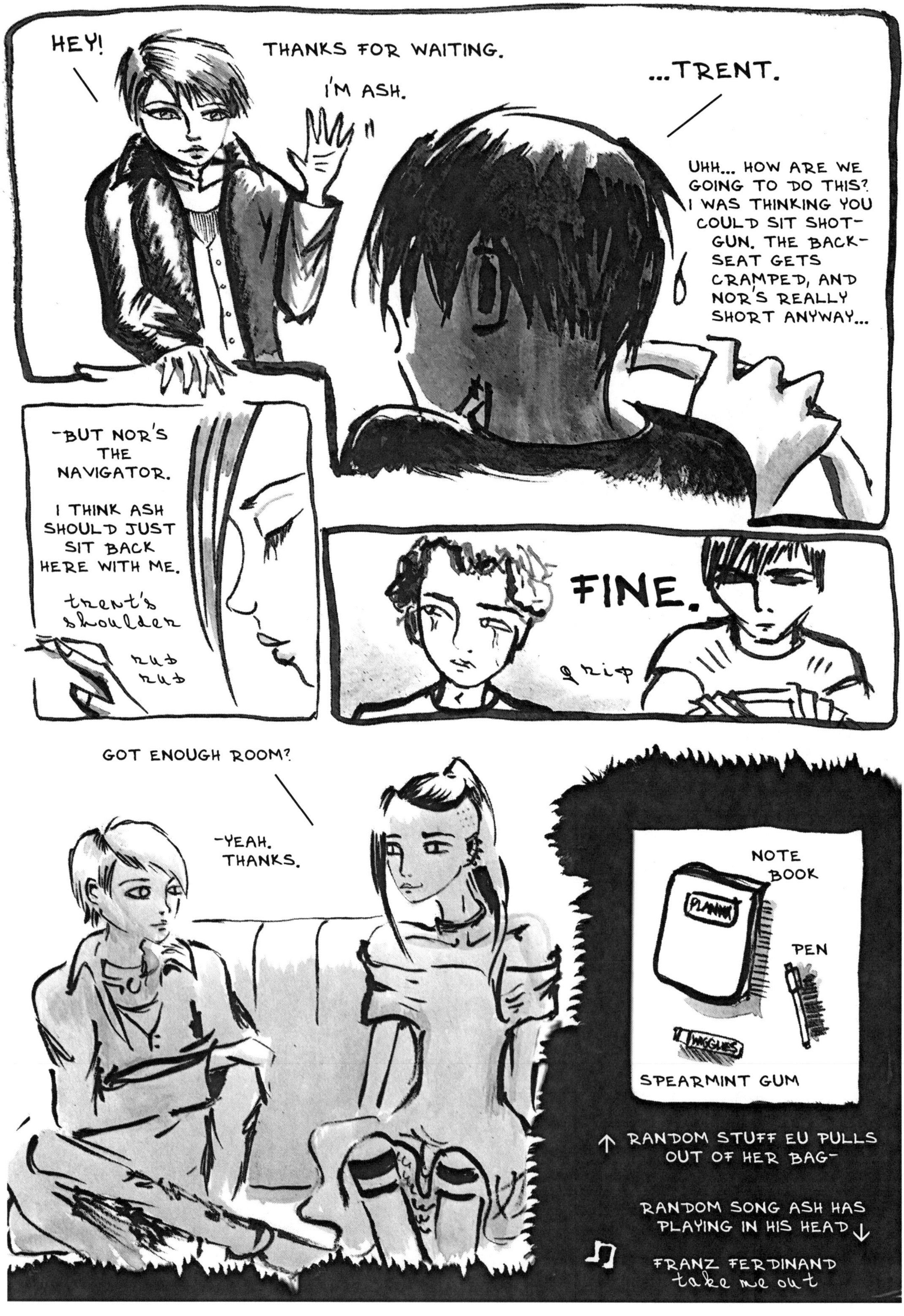
HEY!
THANKS FOR WAITING.
I'M ASH.
...TRENT.
UHH... HOW ARE WE GOING TO DO THIS? I WAS THINKING YOU COULD SIT SHOT-GUN. THE BACK-SEAT GETS CRAMPED, AND NOR'S REALLY SHORT ANYWAY...
-BUT NOR'S THE NAVIGATOR.
I THINK ASH SHOULD JUST SIT BACK HERE WITH ME.
trent's shoulder
rub rub
FINE.
grip
GOT ENOUGH ROOM?
-YEAH. THANKS.
NOTE BOOK
PLANNR
PEN
WAGGLIES
SPEARMINT GUM
↑ RANDOM STUFF EU PULLS OUT OF HER BAG-
RANDOM SONG ASH HAS PLAYING IN HIS HEAD ↓
FRANZ FERDINAND
take me out

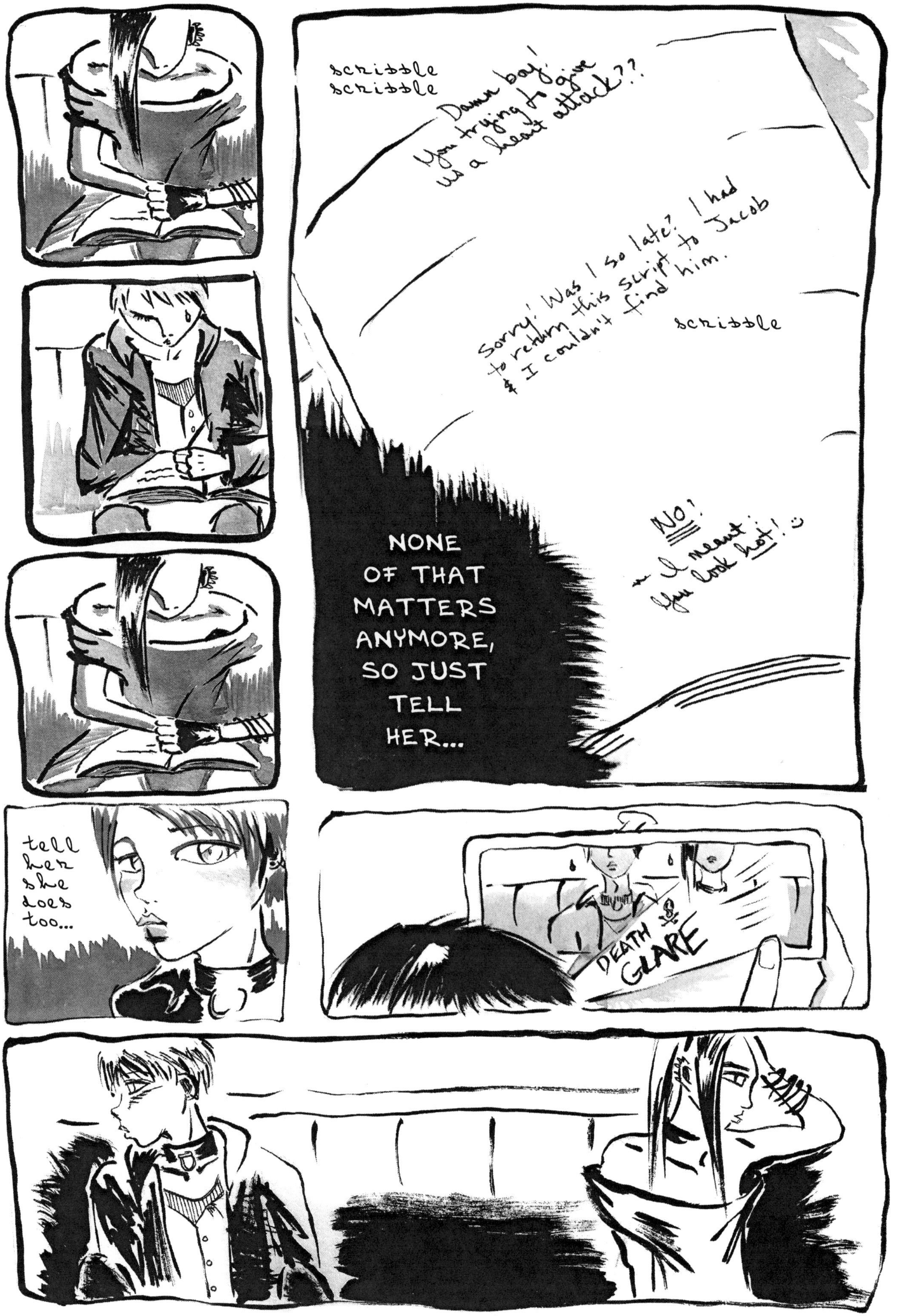
scribble scribble
Damn boy! You trying to give us a heart attack??
Sorry! Was I so late? I had to return this script to Jacob & I couldn't find him.
scribble
NONE OF THAT MATTERS ANYMORE, SO JUST TELL HER...
NO! I meant: You look hot!
tell her she does too...
DEATH GLARE

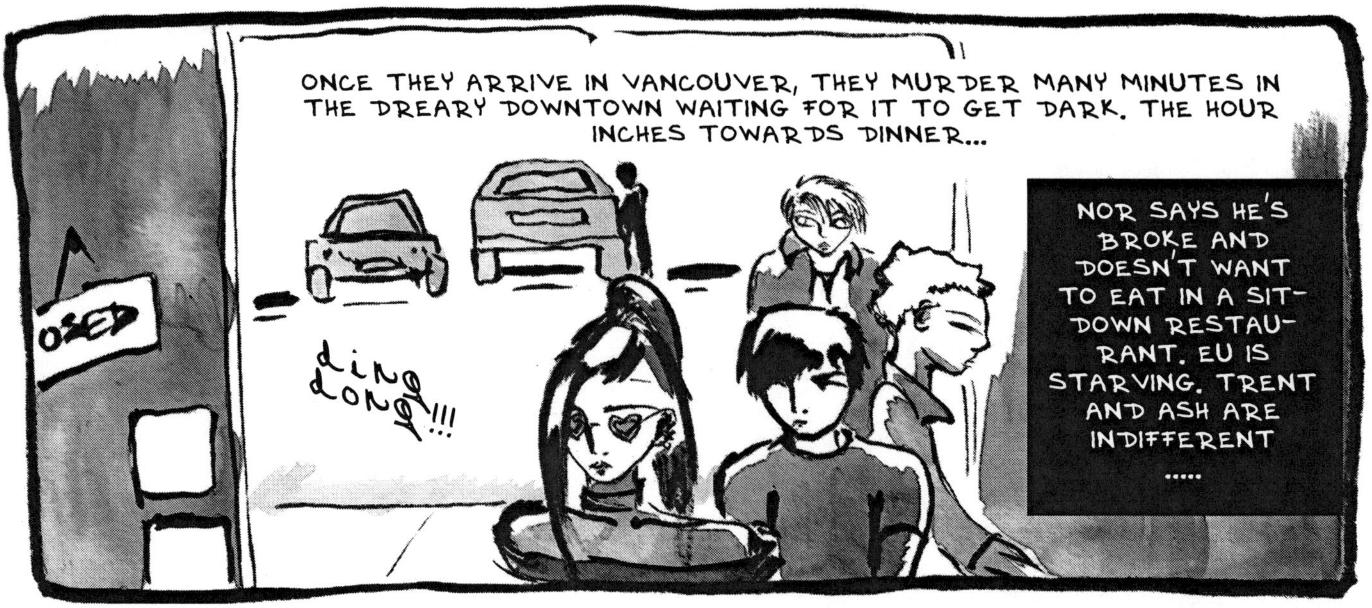
ONCE THEY ARRIVE IN VANCOUVER, THEY MURDER MANY MINUTES IN THE DREARY DOWNTOWN WAITING FOR IT TO GET DARK. THE HOUR INCHES TOWARDS DINNER...
OSED
ding dong!!!
NOR SAYS HE'S BROKE AND DOESN'T WANT TO EAT IN A SIT-DOWN RESTAURANT. EU IS STARVING. TRENT AND ASH ARE INDIFFERENT .....

THEY COMPROMIZE ON A PLAID PANTY AND EULALIE ATTEMPTS TO SUGAR-TALK THEIR JADED CASHIER INTO LETTING THEM BUY CIGARETTES FOR AN AFTER DINNER PUFF... THEY TAKE THEIR BOOTY OUT INTO THE PARKING LOT...

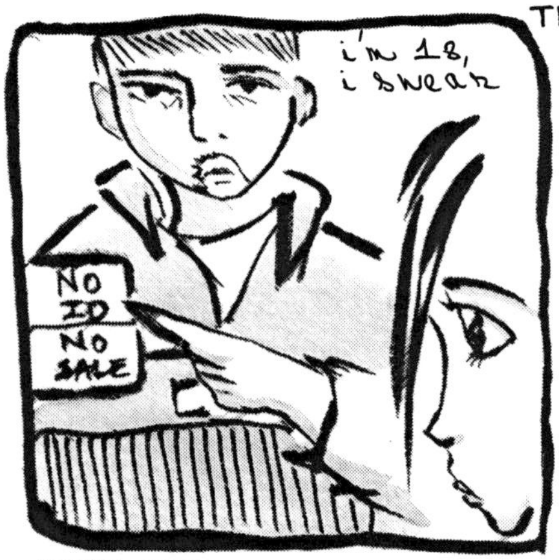
i'm 18, i swear
NO ID
NO SALE

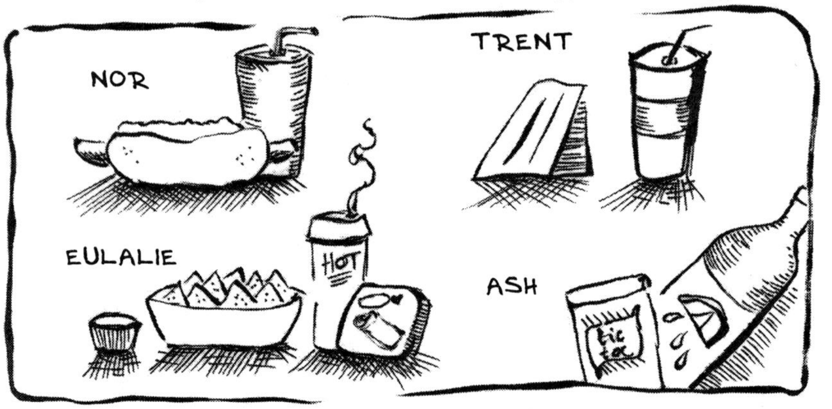
NOR
TRENT
EULALIE
HOT
ASH
tic tac

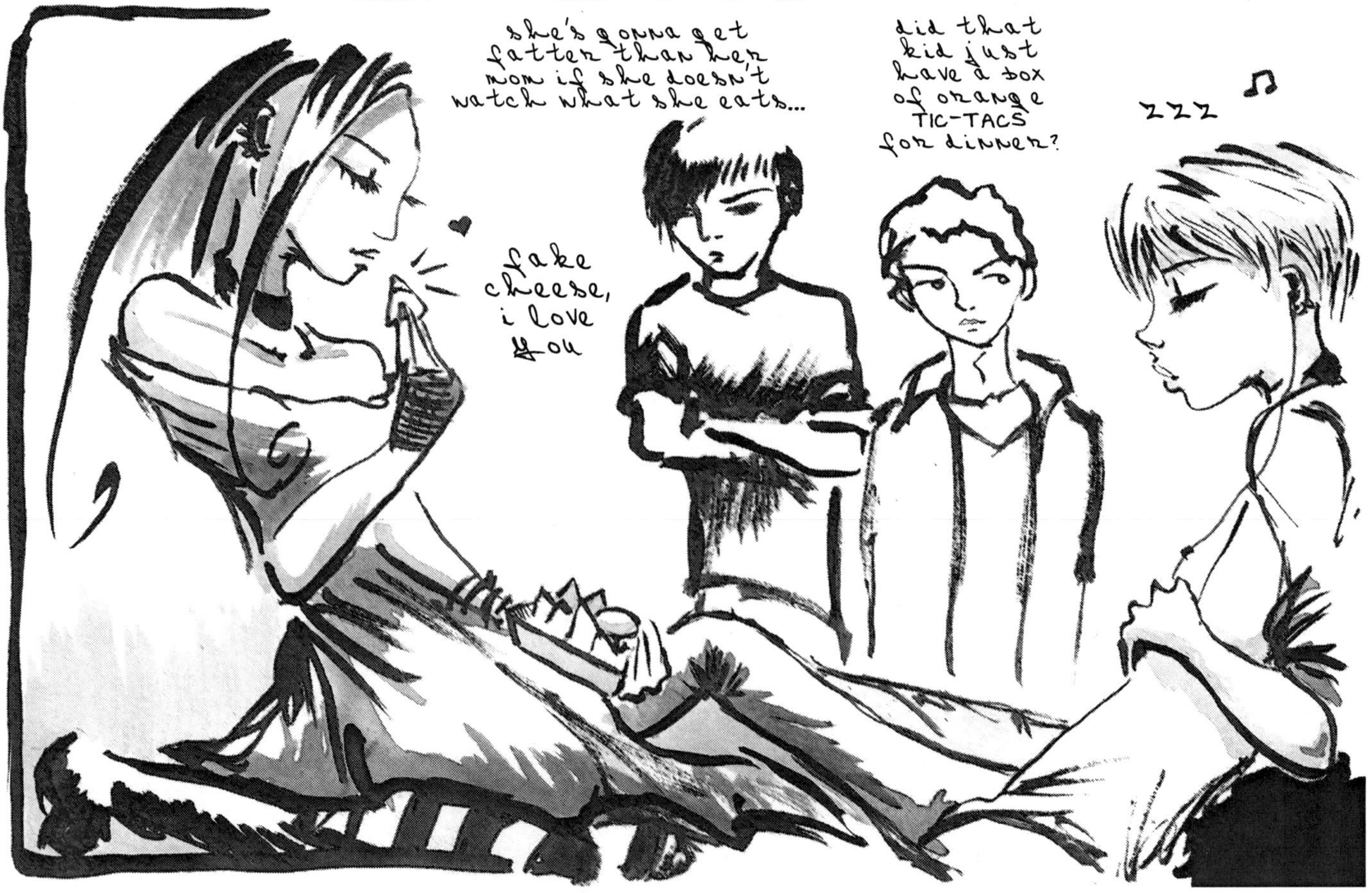
she's gonna get fatter than her mom if she doesn't watch what she eats...
did that kid just have a box of orange TIC-TACS for dinner?
zzz
fake cheese, i love you

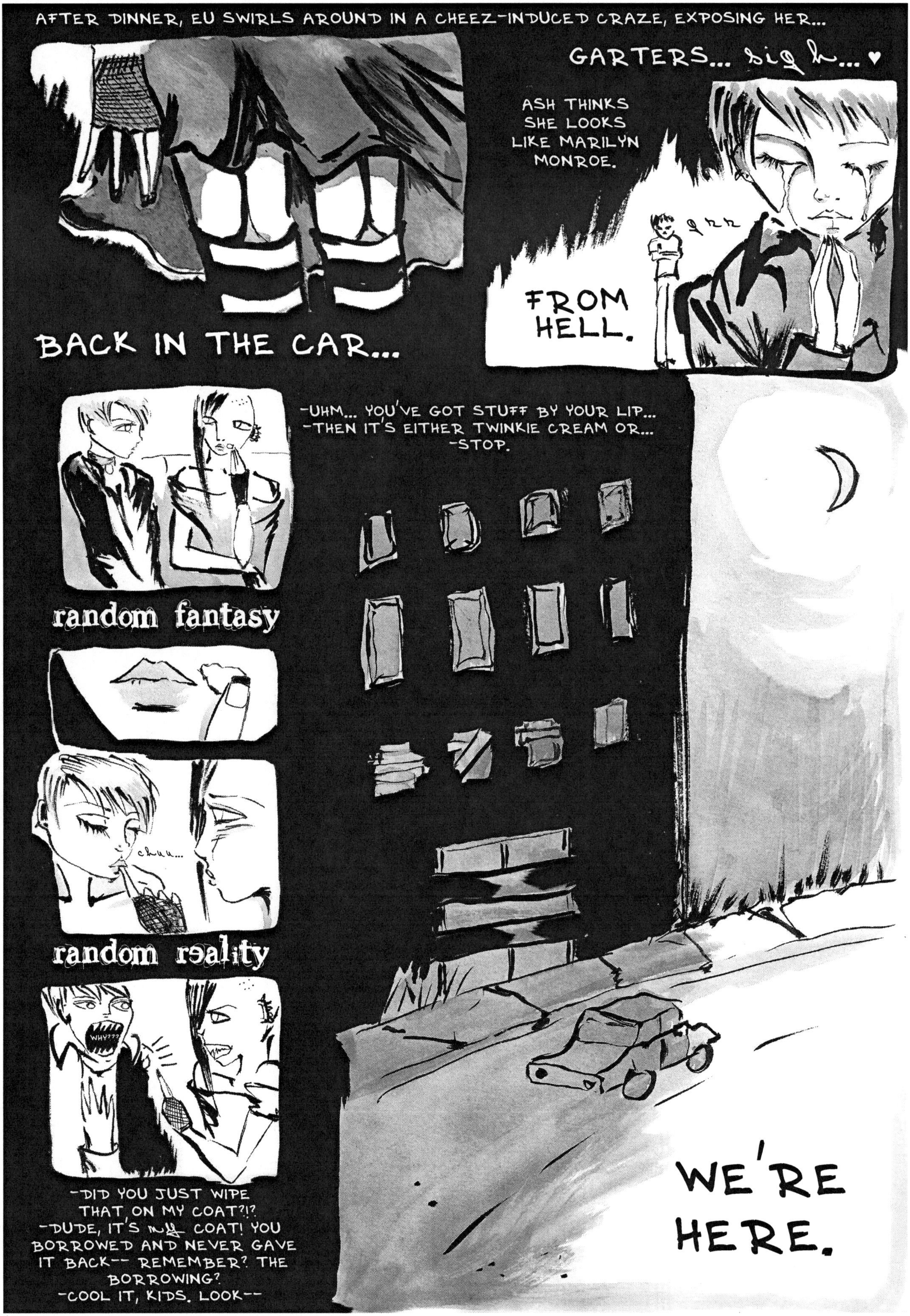
AFTER DINNER, EU SWIRLS AROUND IN A CHEEZ-INDUCED CRAZE, EXPOSING HER...
GARTERS... sigh... ♥
ASH THINKS SHE LOOKS LIKE MARILYN MONROE.
grr
FROM HELL.
BACK IN THE CAR...
-UHM... YOU'VE GOT STUFF BY YOUR LIP...
-THEN IT'S EITHER TWINKIE CREAM OR...
-STOP.
random fantasy
chuu...
random reality
WHY???
-DID YOU JUST WIPE THAT ON MY COAT?!?
-DUDE, IT'S MY COAT! YOU BORROWED AND NEVER GAVE IT BACK-- REMEMBER? THE BORROWING?
-COOL IT, KIDS. LOOK--
WE'RE HERE.

inside

write
write
write
write
write
write
write
write
write
write

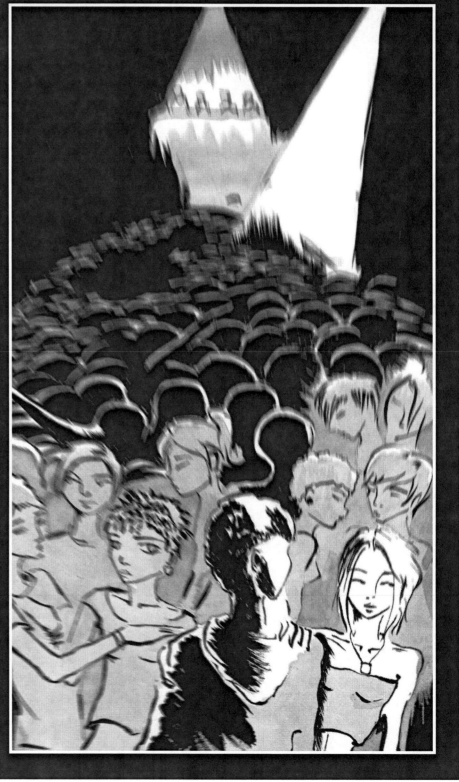

♫ BOOTY BOOTY BOOTY BOOTY

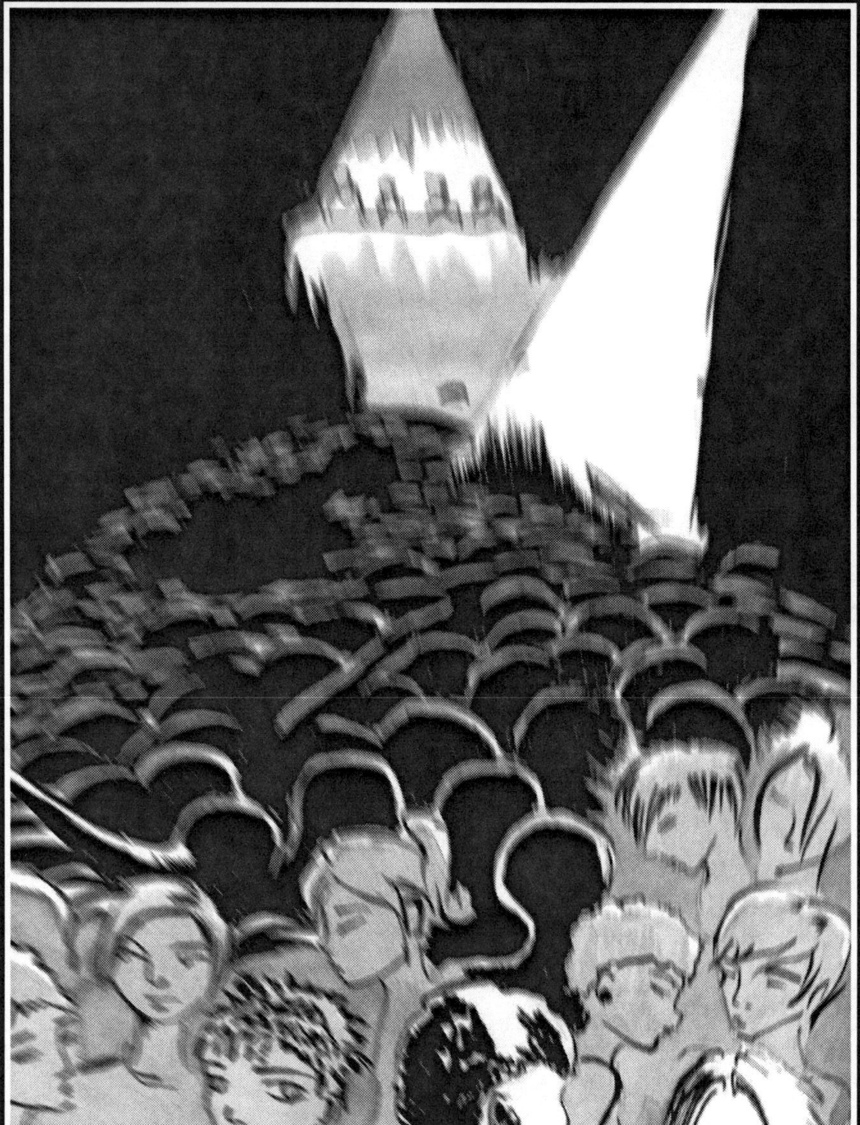

TRENT AND NOR GO TO SETTLE BRACELETS WITH THEIR FRIEND WHILE EU AND ASH WAIT JUST INSIDE THE DOOR. ASH THINKS HE'S NEVER BEEN TO A PARTY THIS BIG BEFORE...

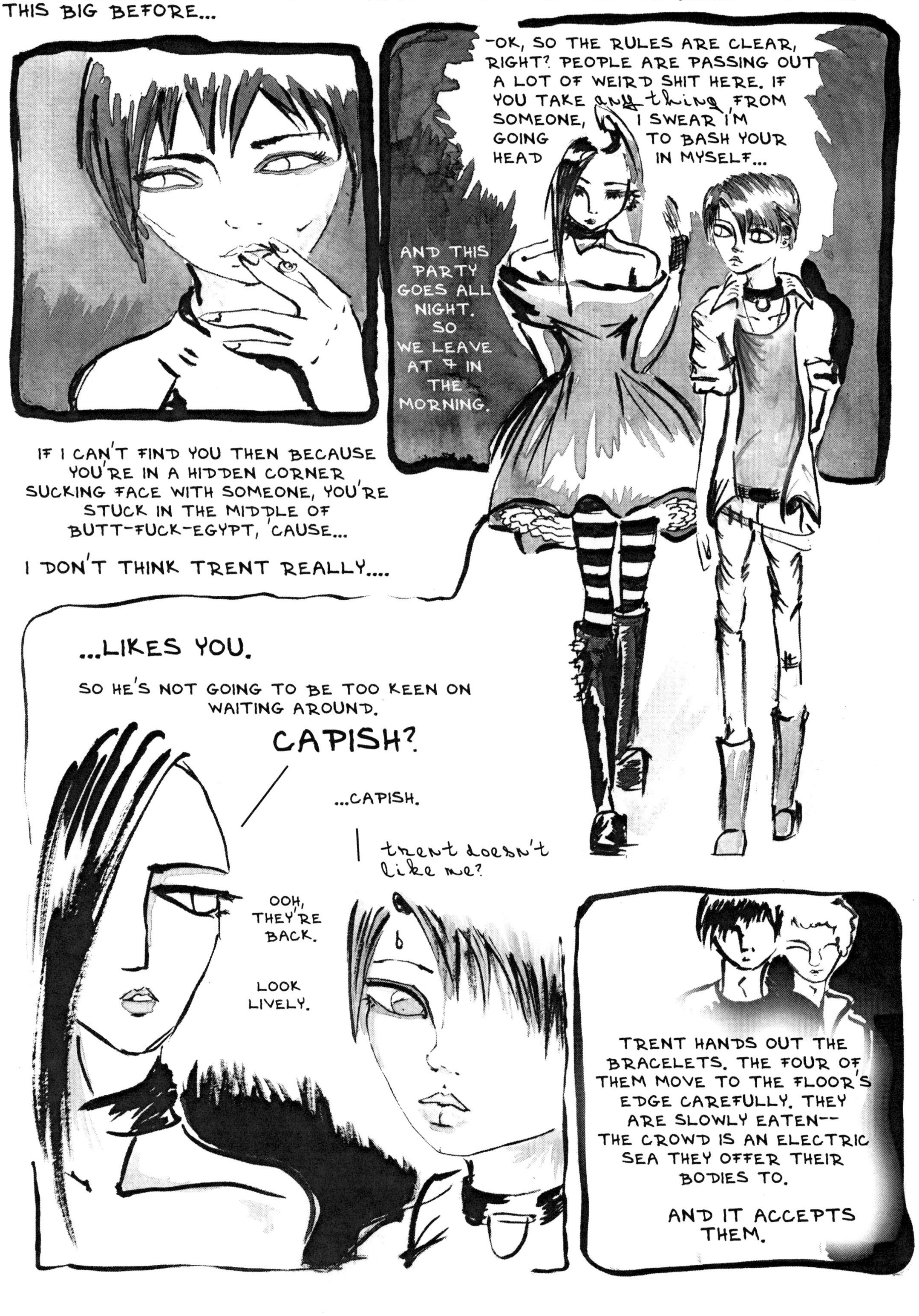
-OK, SO THE RULES ARE CLEAR, RIGHT? PEOPLE ARE PASSING OUT A LOT OF WEIRD SHIT HERE. IF YOU TAKE anything FROM SOMEONE, I SWEAR I'M GOING TO BASH YOUR HEAD IN MYSELF...
AND THIS PARTY GOES ALL NIGHT. SO WE LEAVE AT 4 IN THE MORNING.
IF I CAN'T FIND YOU THEN BECAUSE YOU'RE IN A HIDDEN CORNER SUCKING FACE WITH SOMEONE, YOU'RE STUCK IN THE MIDDLE OF BUTT-FUCK-EGYPT, 'CAUSE...
I DON'T THINK TRENT REALLY....
...LIKES YOU.
SO HE'S NOT GOING TO BE TOO KEEN ON WAITING AROUND.
CAPISH?
...CAPISH.
trent doesn't like me?
OOH, THEY'RE BACK.
LOOK LIVELY.
TRENT HANDS OUT THE BRACELETS. THE FOUR OF THEM MOVE TO THE FLOOR'S EDGE CAREFULLY. THEY ARE SLOWLY EATEN-- THE CROWD IS AN ELECTRIC SEA THEY OFFER THEIR BODIES TO.
AND IT ACCEPTS THEM.

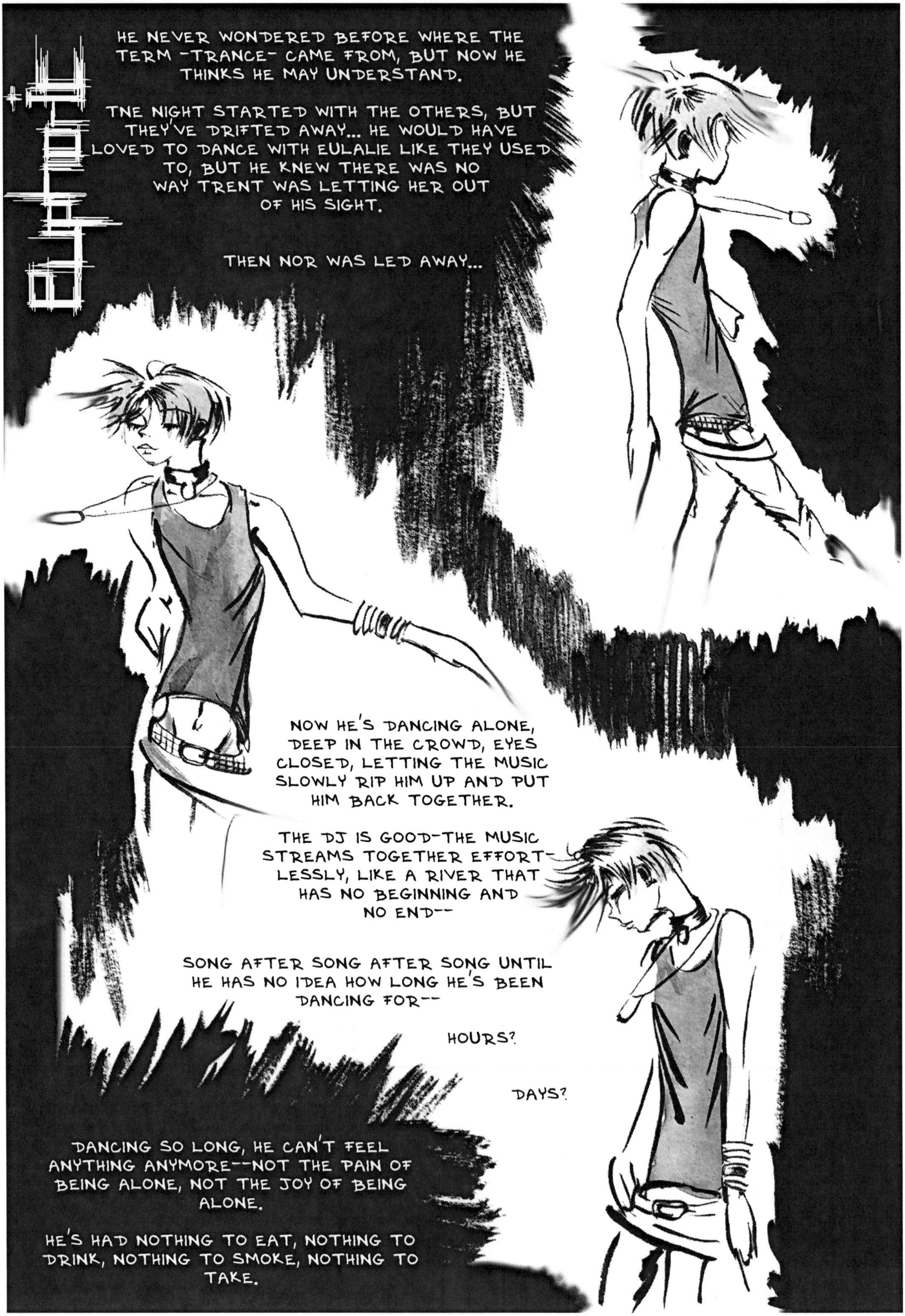
HE NEVER WONDERED BEFORE WHERE THE TERM -TRANCE- CAME FROM, BUT NOW HE THINKS HE MAY UNDERSTAND.
TNE NIGHT STARTED WITH THE OTHERS, BUT THEY'VE DRIFTED AWAY... HE WOULD HAVE LOVED TO DANCE WITH EULALIE LIKE THEY USED TO, BUT HE KNEW THERE WAS NO WAY TRENT WAS LETTING HER OUT OF HIS SIGHT.
THEN NOR WAS LED AWAY...
NOW HE'S DANCING ALONE, DEEP IN THE CROWD, EYES CLOSED, LETTING THE MUSIC SLOWLY RIP HIM UP AND PUT HIM BACK TOGETHER.
THE DJ IS GOOD-THE MUSIC STREAMS TOGETHER EFFORT-LESSLY, LIKE A RIVER THAT HAS NO BEGINNING AND NO END--
SONG AFTER SONG AFTER SONG UNTIL HE HAS NO IDEA HOW LONG HE'S BEEN DANCING FOR--
HOURS?
DAYS?
DANCING SO LONG, HE CAN'T FEEL ANYTHING ANYMORE--NOT THE PAIN OF BEING ALONE, NOT THE JOY OF BEING ALONE.
HE'S HAD NOTHING TO EAT, NOTHING TO DRINK, NOTHING TO SMOKE, NOTHING TO TAKE.

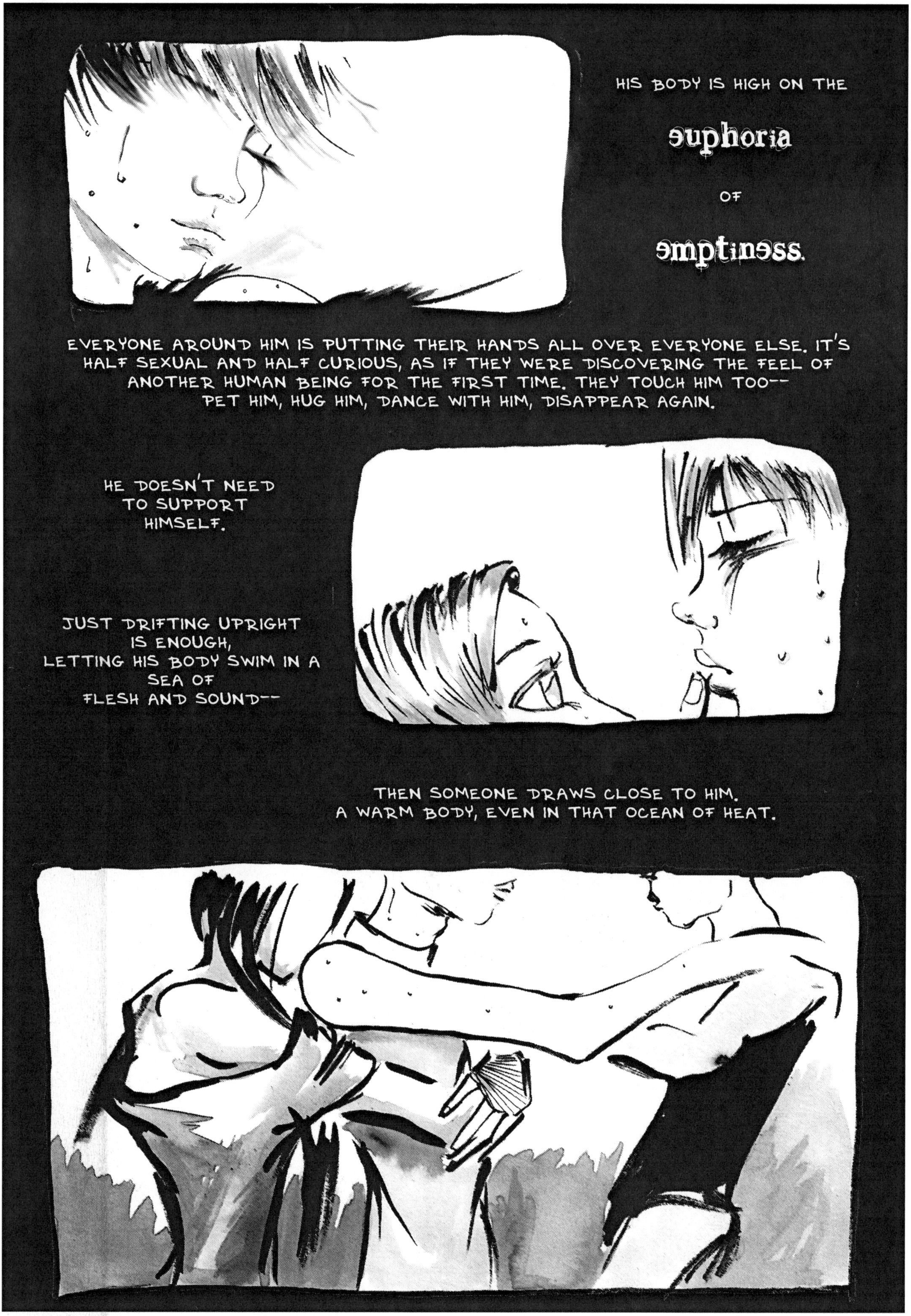
HIS BODY IS HIGH ON THE
euphoria
OF
emptiness.
EVERYONE AROUND HIM IS PUTTING THEIR HANDS ALL OVER EVERYONE ELSE. IT'S HALF SEXUAL AND HALF CURIOUS, AS IF THEY WERE DISCOVERING THE FEEL OF ANOTHER HUMAN BEING FOR THE FIRST TIME. THEY TOUCH HIM TOO-- PET HIM, HUG HIM, DANCE WITH HIM, DISAPPEAR AGAIN.
HE DOESN'T NEED TO SUPPORT HIMSELF.
JUST DRIFTING UPRIGHT IS ENOUGH, LETTING HIS BODY SWIM IN A SEA OF FLESH AND SOUND--
THEN SOMEONE DRAWS CLOSE TO HIM. A WARM BODY, EVEN IN THAT OCEAN OF HEAT.

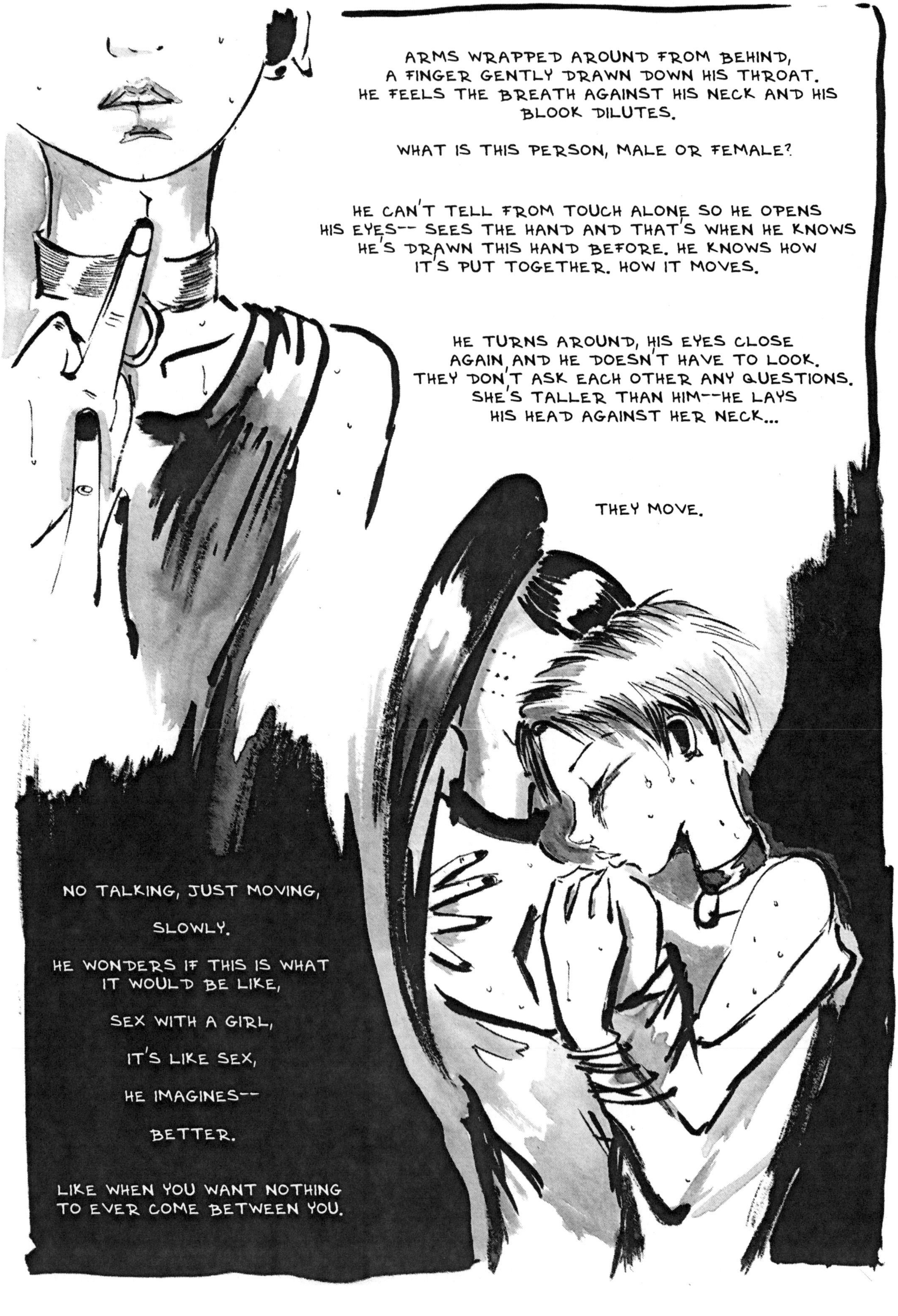
ARMS WRAPPED AROUND FROM BEHIND, A FINGER GENTLY DRAWN DOWN HIS THROAT. HE FEELS THE BREATH AGAINST HIS NECK AND HIS BLOOK DILUTES.
WHAT IS THIS PERSON, MALE OR FEMALE?
HE CAN'T TELL FROM TOUCH ALONE SO HE OPENS HIS EYES-- SEES THE HAND AND THAT'S WHEN HE KNOWS HE'S DRAWN THIS HAND BEFORE. HE KNOWS HOW IT'S PUT TOGETHER. HOW IT MOVES.
HE TURNS AROUND, HIS EYES CLOSE AGAIN AND HE DOESN'T HAVE TO LOOK. THEY DON'T ASK EACH OTHER ANY QUESTIONS. SHE'S TALLER THAN HIM--HE LAYS HIS HEAD AGAINST HER NECK...
THEY MOVE.
NO TALKING, JUST MOVING,
SLOWLY.
HE WONDERS IF THIS IS WHAT IT WOULD BE LIKE,
SEX WITH A GIRL,
IT'S LIKE SEX,
HE IMAGINES--
BETTER.
LIKE WHEN YOU WANT NOTHING TO EVER COME BETWEEN YOU.

HE PRESSES INTO HER, HE'S PAINFULLY HARD AND IT DOESN'T EMBARRASS HIM,
IT DOESN'T EMBARRASS HER, HE WANTS TO KISS HER, ALL OF HIM DOES,
BUT HE DOESN'T DARE.
THEY'RE SO CLOSE, YET HIS HOLD WEAKENS. HE CAN'T STOP IT.
WHAT IS GIVEN IS TAKEN AWAY.

THE CROWD GAVE HER TO HIM.

THE CROWD TAKES HER AWAY.

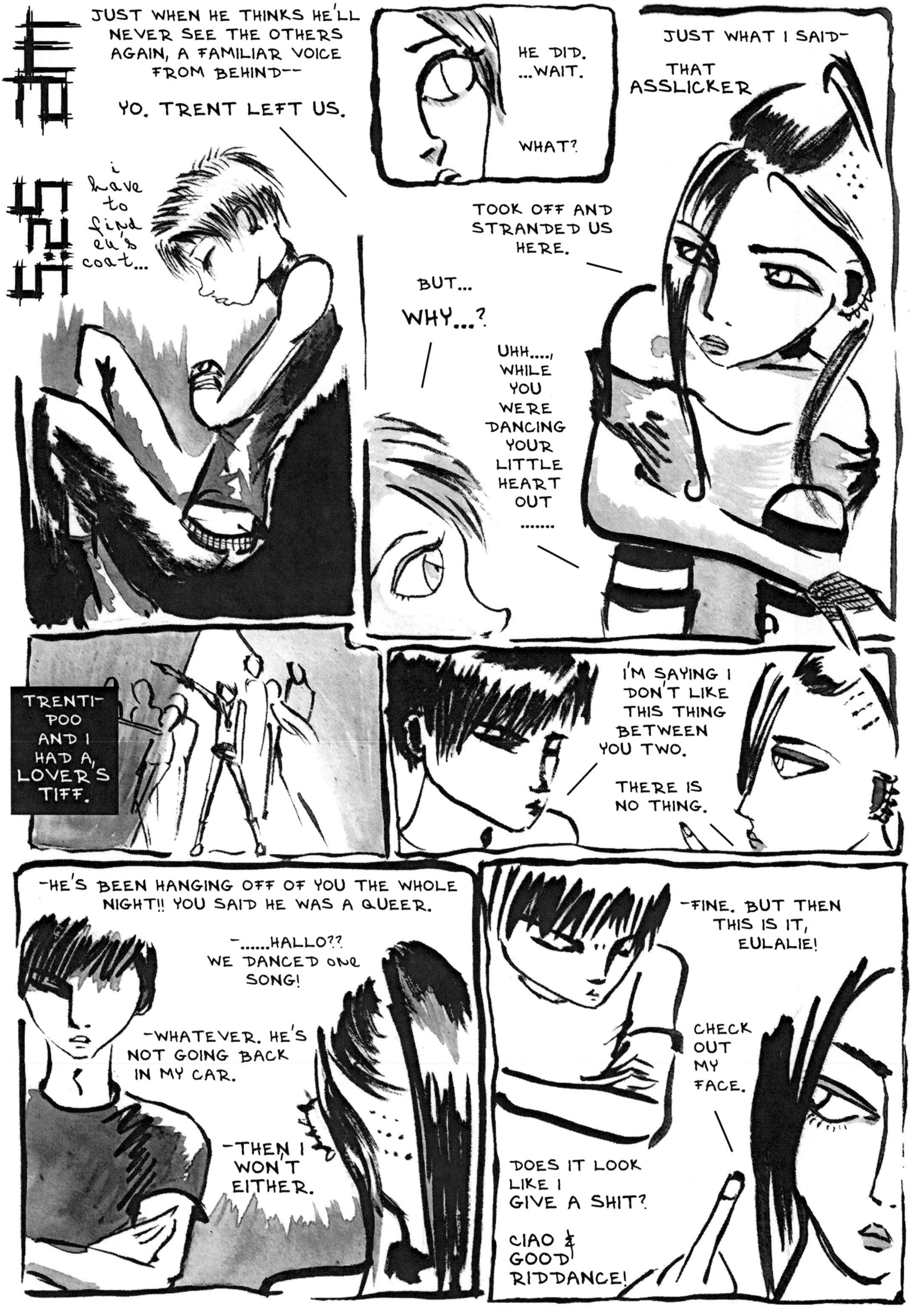

JUST WHEN HE THINKS HE'LL NEVER SEE THE OTHERS AGAIN, A FAMILIAR VOICE FROM BEHIND--
YO. TRENT LEFT US.
i have to find eu's coat...
HE DID. ...WAIT.
WHAT?
JUST WHAT I SAID-
THAT ASSLICKER
TOOK OFF AND STRANDED US HERE.
BUT... WHY...?
UHH...., WHILE YOU WERE DANCING YOUR LITTLE HEART OUT ....
TRENTI-POO AND I HAD A, LOVER'S TIFF.
I'M SAYING I DON'T LIKE THIS THING BETWEEN YOU TWO.
THERE IS NO THING.
-HE'S BEEN HANGING OFF OF YOU THE WHOLE NIGHT!! YOU SAID HE WAS A QUEER.
-......HALLO?? WE DANCED ONE SONG!
-WHATEVER. HE'S NOT GOING BACK IN MY CAR.
-THEN I WON'T EITHER.
-FINE. BUT THEN THIS IS IT, EULALIE!
CHECK OUT MY FACE.
DOES IT LOOK LIKE I GIVE A SHIT?
CIAO & GOOD RIDDANCE!

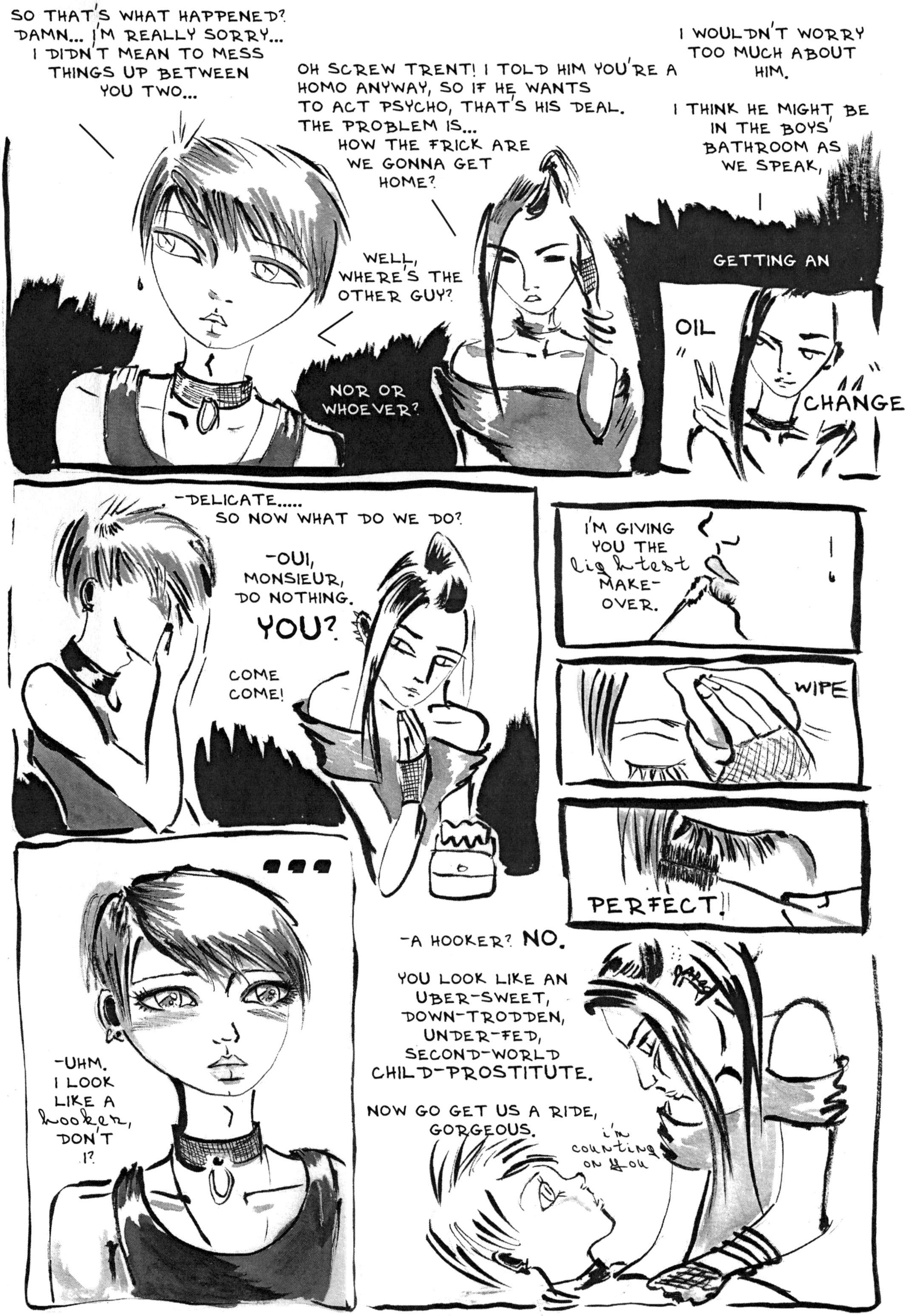
SO THAT'S WHAT HAPPENED? DAMN... I'M REALLY SORRY... I DIDN'T MEAN TO MESS THINGS UP BETWEEN YOU TWO...
OH SCREW TRENT! I TOLD HIM YOU'RE A HOMO ANYWAY, SO IF HE WANTS TO ACT PSYCHO, THAT'S HIS DEAL. THE PROBLEM IS... HOW THE FRICK ARE WE GONNA GET HOME?
WELL, WHERE'S THE OTHER GUY?
NOR OR WHOEVER?
I WOULDN'T WORRY TOO MUCH ABOUT HIM.
I THINK HE MIGHT BE IN THE BOYS' BATHROOM AS WE SPEAK,
GETTING AN
"OIL CHANGE"
-DELICATE..... SO NOW WHAT DO WE DO?
-OUI, MONSIEUR, DO NOTHING.
YOU?
COME COME!
I'M GIVING YOU THE lightest MAKE-OVER.
!
WIPE
PERFECT!
...
-UHM. I LOOK LIKE A hooker, DON'T I?
-A HOOKER? NO.
YOU LOOK LIKE AN UBER-SWEET, DOWN-TRODDEN, UNDER-FED, SECOND-WORLD CHILD-PROSTITUTE.
NOW GO GET US A RIDE, GORGEOUS.
i'm counting on you

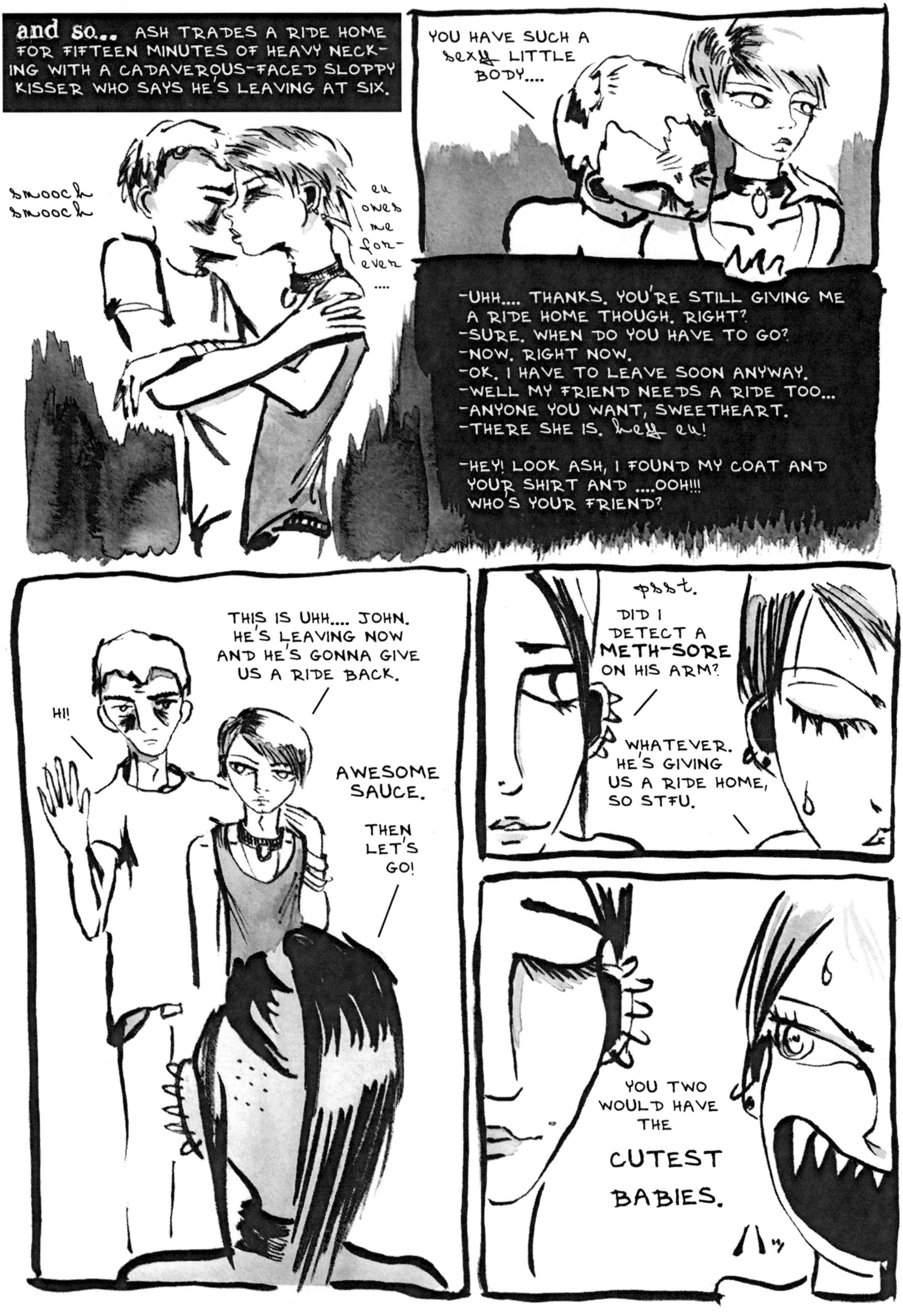
and so... ASH TRADES A RIDE HOME FOR FIFTEEN MINUTES OF HEAVY NECKING WITH A CADAVEROUS-FACED SLOPPY KISSER WHO SAYS HE'S LEAVING AT SIX.
smooch smooch
eu owes me forever....
YOU HAVE SUCH A sexy LITTLE BODY....
-UHH.... THANKS. YOU'RE STILL GIVING ME A RIDE HOME THOUGH, RIGHT?
-SURE. WHEN DO YOU HAVE TO GO?
-NOW. RIGHT NOW.
-OK. I HAVE TO LEAVE SOON ANYWAY.
-WELL MY FRIEND NEEDS A RIDE TOO...
-ANYONE YOU WANT, SWEETHEART.
-THERE SHE IS. hey eu!
-HEY! LOOK ASH, I FOUND MY COAT AND YOUR SHIRT AND ....OOH!!! WHO'S YOUR FRIEND?
THIS IS UHH.... JOHN. HE'S LEAVING NOW AND HE'S GONNA GIVE US A RIDE BACK.
HI!
AWESOME SAUCE.
THEN LET'S GO!
psst.
DID I DETECT A METH-SORE ON HIS ARM?
WHATEVER. HE'S GIVING US A RIDE HOME, SO STFU.
YOU TWO WOULD HAVE THE CUTEST BABIES.

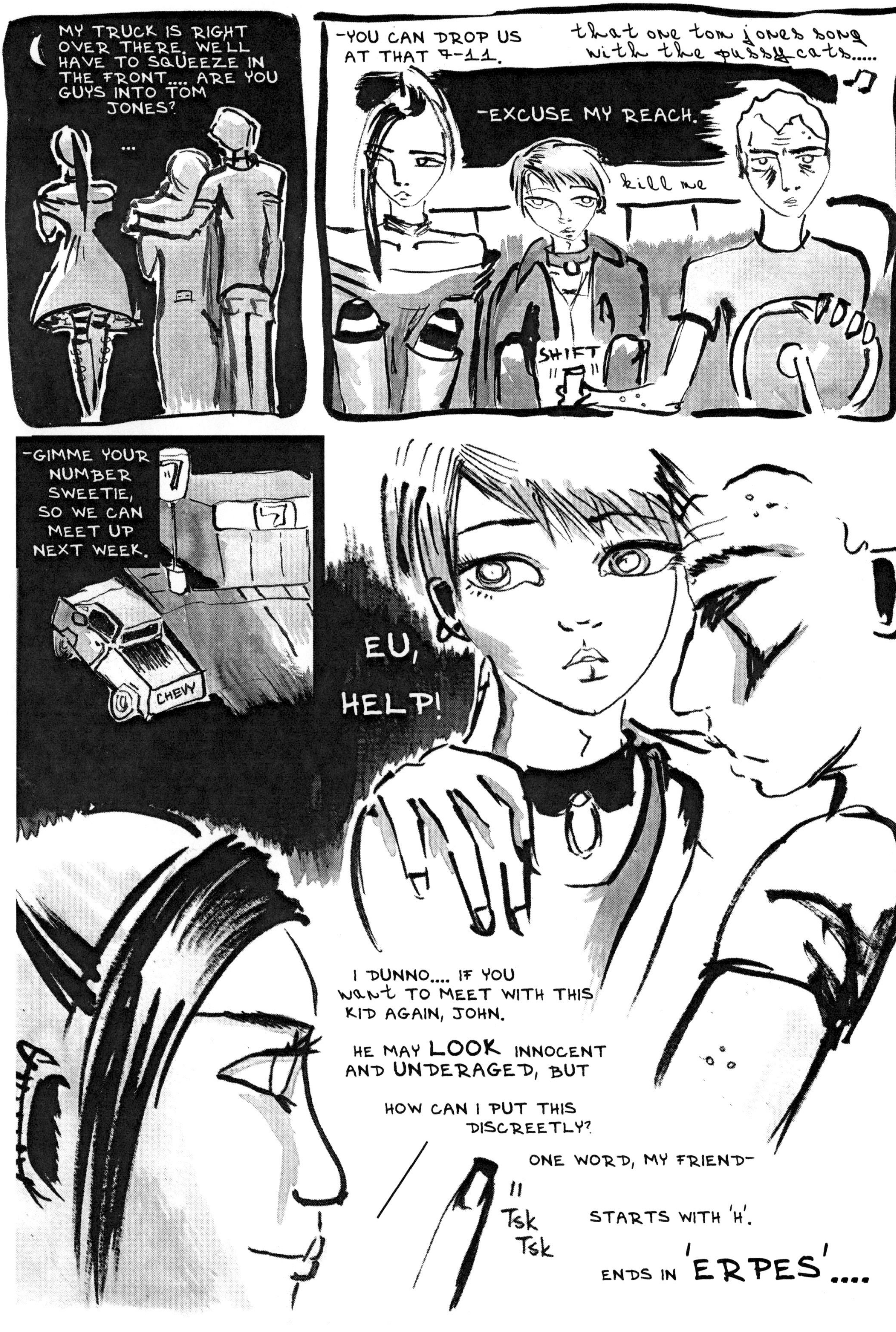
MY TRUCK IS RIGHT OVER THERE. WE'LL HAVE TO SQUEEZE IN THE FRONT.... ARE YOU GUYS INTO TOM JONES?
...
-YOU CAN DROP US AT THAT 7-11.
that one tom jones song with the pussy cats.....
-EXCUSE MY REACH.
kill me
SHIFT
-GIMME YOUR NUMBER SWEETIE, SO WE CAN MEET UP NEXT WEEK.
CHEW
EU, HELP!
I DUNNO.... IF YOU want TO MEET WITH THIS KID AGAIN, JOHN.
HE MAY LOOK INNOCENT AND UNDERAGED, BUT
HOW CAN I PUT THIS DISCREETLY?
ONE WORD, MY FRIEND-
Tsk Tsk
STARTS WITH 'H'.
ENDS IN 'ERPES'....

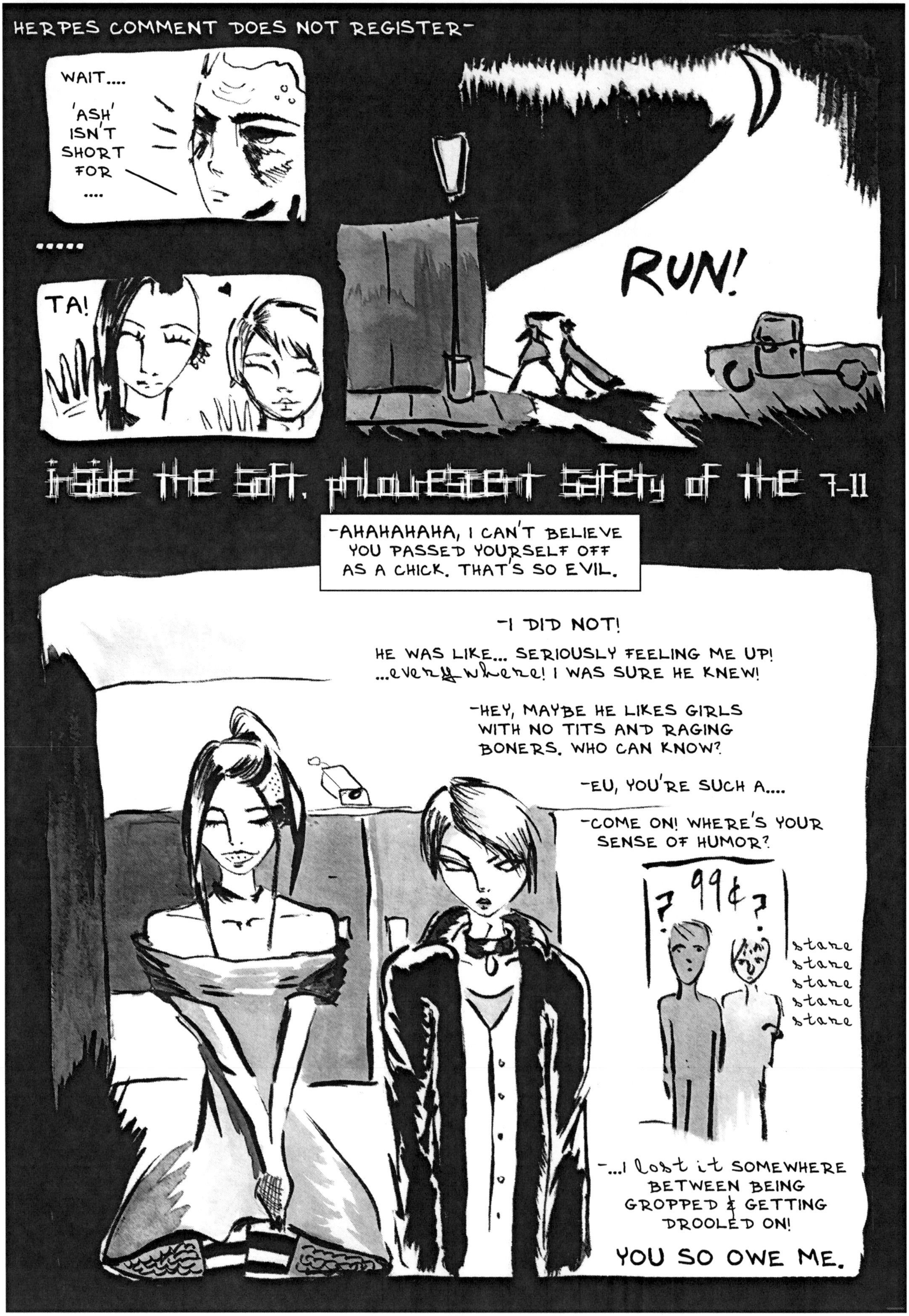
HERPES COMMENT DOES NOT REGISTER-
WAIT....
'ASH' ISN'T SHORT FOR ....
.....
TA!
RUN!
inside the soft, phlourescent safety of the 7-11
-AHAHAHAHA, I CAN'T BELIEVE YOU PASSED YOURSELF OFF AS A CHICK. THAT'S SO EVIL.
-I DID NOT!
HE WAS LIKE... SERIOUSLY FEELING ME UP! ...everywhere! I WAS SURE HE KNEW!
-HEY, MAYBE HE LIKES GIRLS WITH NO TITS AND RAGING BONERS. WHO CAN KNOW?
-EU, YOU'RE SUCH A....
-COME ON! WHERE'S YOUR SENSE OF HUMOR?
? 99¢ ?
stare stare stare stare stare
-...I lost it SOMEWHERE BETWEEN BEING GROPPED & GETTING DROOLED ON!
YOU SO OWE ME.

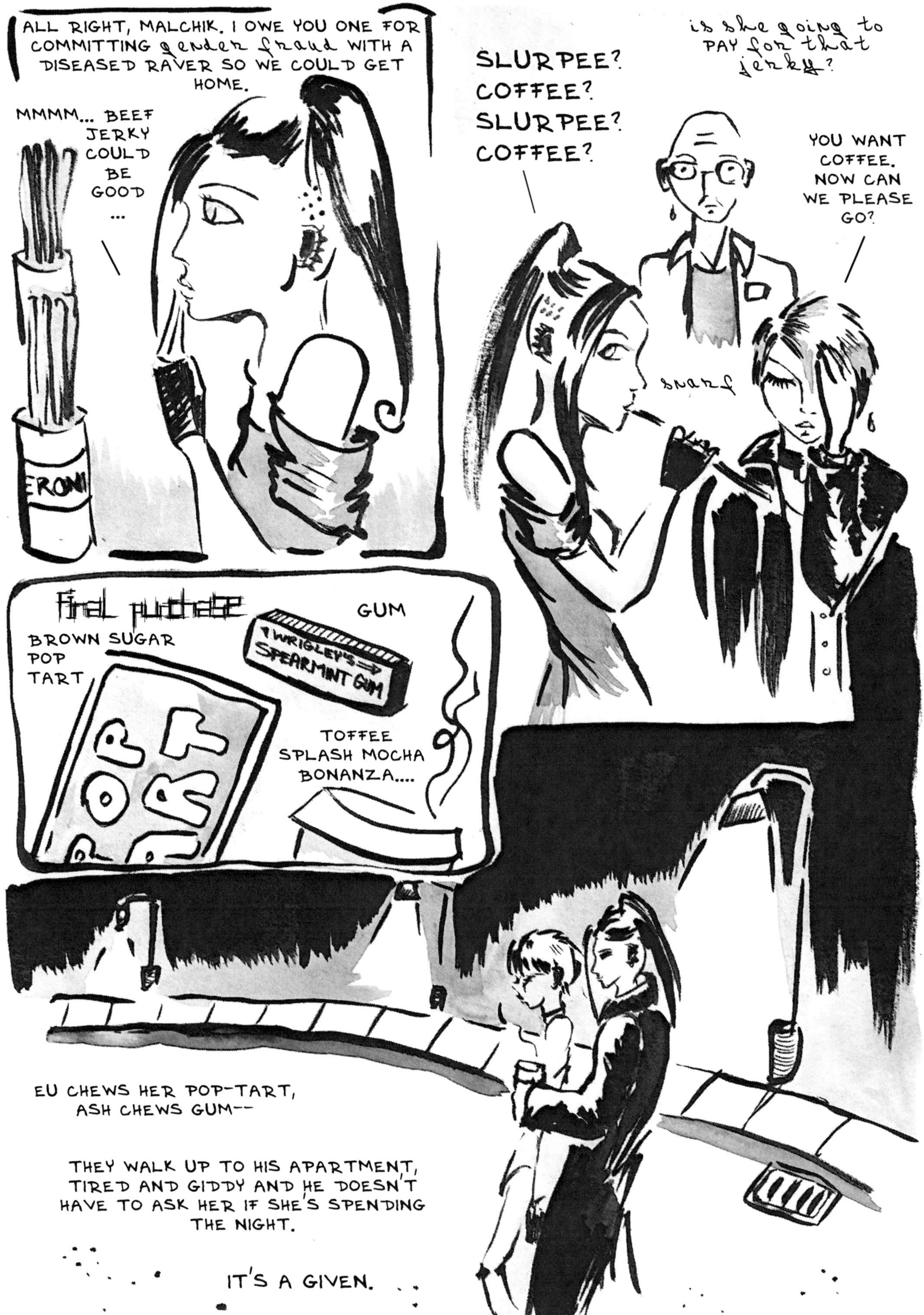
ALL RIGHT, MALCHIK. I OWE YOU ONE FOR COMMITTING gender fraud WITH A DISEASED RAVER SO WE COULD GET HOME.
MMMM... BEEF JERKY COULD BE GOOD ...
ERONI
SLURPEE? COFFEE? SLURPEE? COFFEE?
is she going to PAY for that jerky?
YOU WANT COFFEE. NOW CAN WE PLEASE GO?
snarf
Final purchase
BROWN SUGAR POP TART
GUM
WRIGLEY'S SPEARMINT GUM
POP TART
TOFFEE SPLASH MOCHA BONANZA....
EU CHEWS HER POP-TART, ASH CHEWS GUM--
THEY WALK UP TO HIS APARTMENT, TIRED AND GIDDY AND HE DOESN'T HAVE TO ASK HER IF SHE'S SPENDING THE NIGHT.
IT'S A GIVEN.

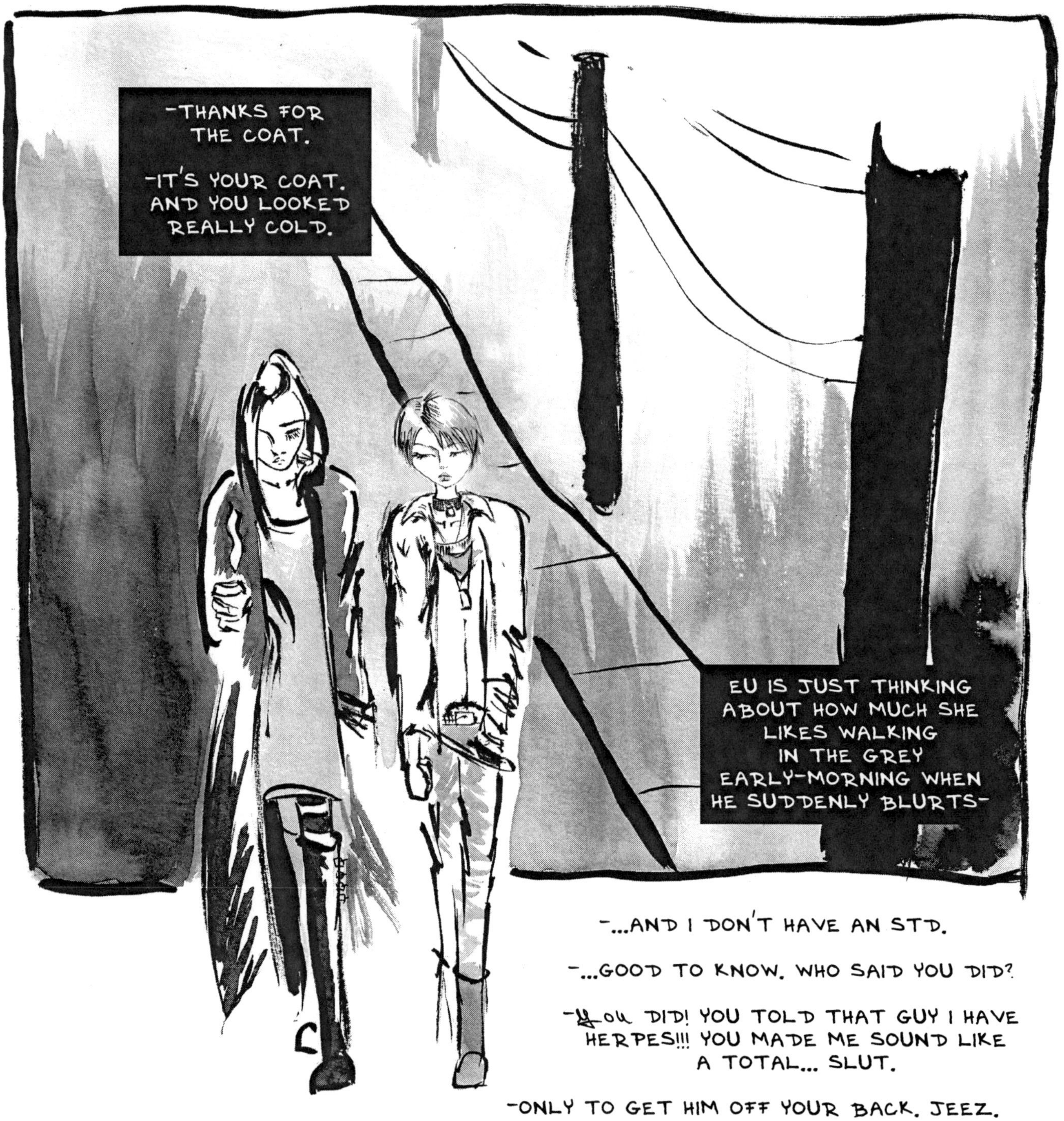
-THANKS FOR THE COAT.
-IT'S YOUR COAT. AND YOU LOOKED REALLY COLD.
EU IS JUST THINKING ABOUT HOW MUCH SHE LIKES WALKING IN THE GREY EARLY-MORNING WHEN HE SUDDENLY BLURTS-
-...AND I DON'T HAVE AN STD.
-...GOOD TO KNOW. WHO SAID YOU DID?
-You DID! YOU TOLD THAT GUY I HAVE HERPES!!! YOU MADE ME SOUND LIKE A TOTAL... SLUT.
-ONLY TO GET HIM OFF YOUR BACK. JEEZ.

-BUT YOU THINK THAT, DON'T YOU?
-THAT YOU HAVE HERPES? I DUNNO. DO YOU?
-OF COURSE NOT!
-WELL HOW SHOULD I KNOW?
-SEE? THAT PROVES IT. YOU THINK I'M SLUTTY AND DISEASED.
-DUDE. YOU'RE LIKE... THE SHYEST AND MOST AWKWARD PERSON I'VE EVER MET. I MEAN, YOU'VE GOTTEN BETTER... BUT, I DON'T THINK SOMEONE LIKE YOU CAN **BE** SLUTTY.
-...THANKS. I THINK.
-ANYWAY, WHAT DO YOU CARE ABOUT WHAT SOME STRANGER THINKS?
-I DON'T. I'M TALKING ABOUT WHAT **YOU** THINK.
-THEN FINE. I THINK YOU'RE AWESOME. IN THIS SOCIALLY RETARDED WAY.
-EU....
-WHAT?! BUT HEY. CAN WE GO HOME AND LISTEN TO ♫ SOME TOM JONES?
-............THAT'S NOT FUNNY.
-JUST GIVE IT TIME. IT'LL BE *so funny* NEXT WEEK.

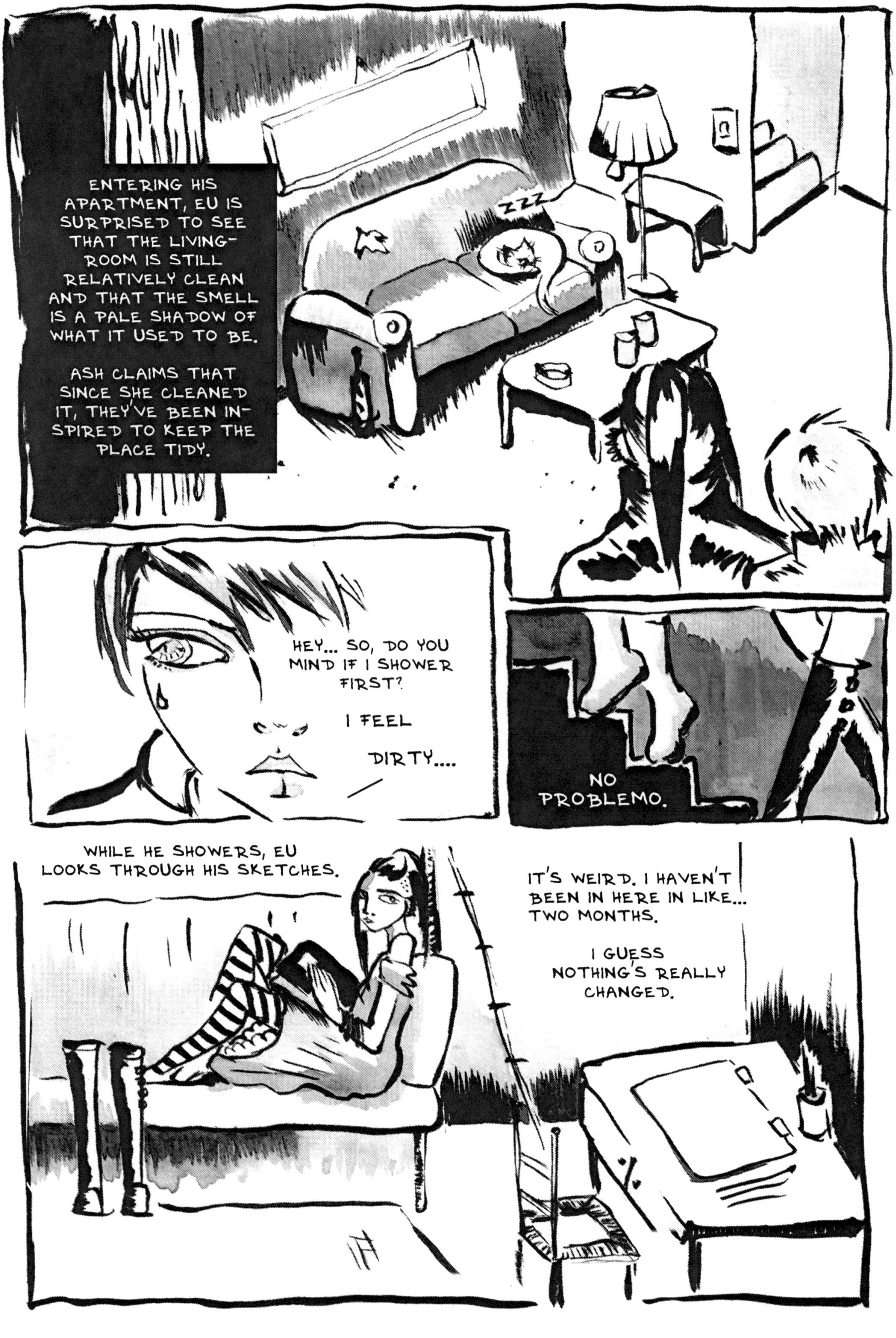
ENTERING HIS APARTMENT, EU IS SURPRISED TO SEE THAT THE LIVING-ROOM IS STILL RELATIVELY CLEAN AND THAT THE SMELL IS A PALE SHADOW OF WHAT IT USED TO BE.
ASH CLAIMS THAT SINCE SHE CLEANED IT, THEY'VE BEEN INSPIRED TO KEEP THE PLACE TIDY.
ZZZ
HEY... SO, DO YOU MIND IF I SHOWER FIRST?
I FEEL
DIRTY....
NO PROBLEMO.
WHILE HE SHOWERS, EU LOOKS THROUGH HIS SKETCHES.
IT'S WEIRD. I HAVEN'T BEEN IN HERE IN LIKE... TWO MONTHS.
I GUESS NOTHING'S REALLY CHANGED.

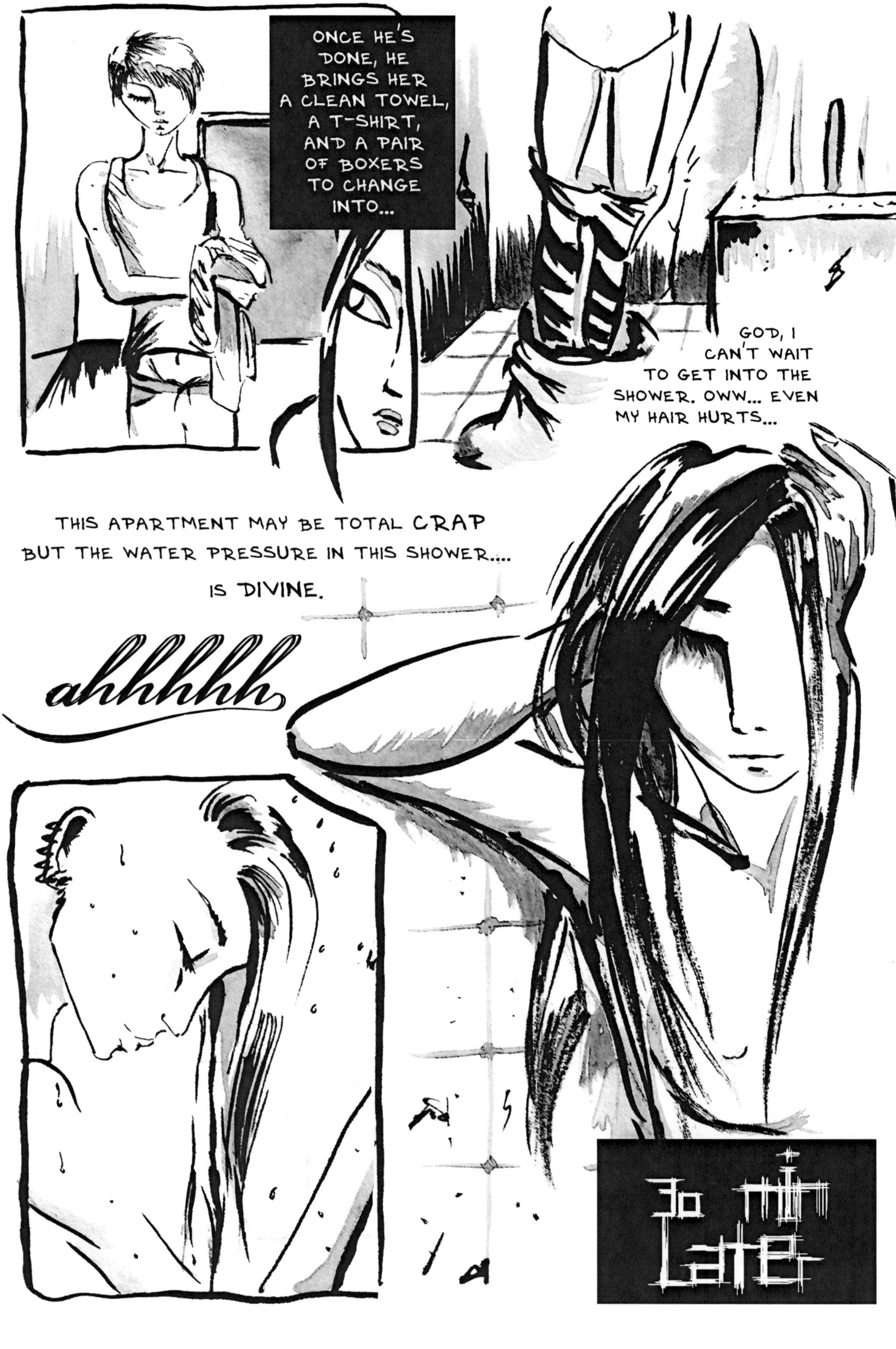
ONCE HE'S DONE, HE BRINGS HER A CLEAN TOWEL, A T-SHIRT, AND A PAIR OF BOXERS TO CHANGE INTO...
GOD, I CAN'T WAIT TO GET INTO THE SHOWER. OWW... EVEN MY HAIR HURTS...
THIS APARTMENT MAY BE TOTAL CRAP BUT THE WATER PRESSURE IN THIS SHOWER....
IS DIVINE.
ahhhhh
30 min Later

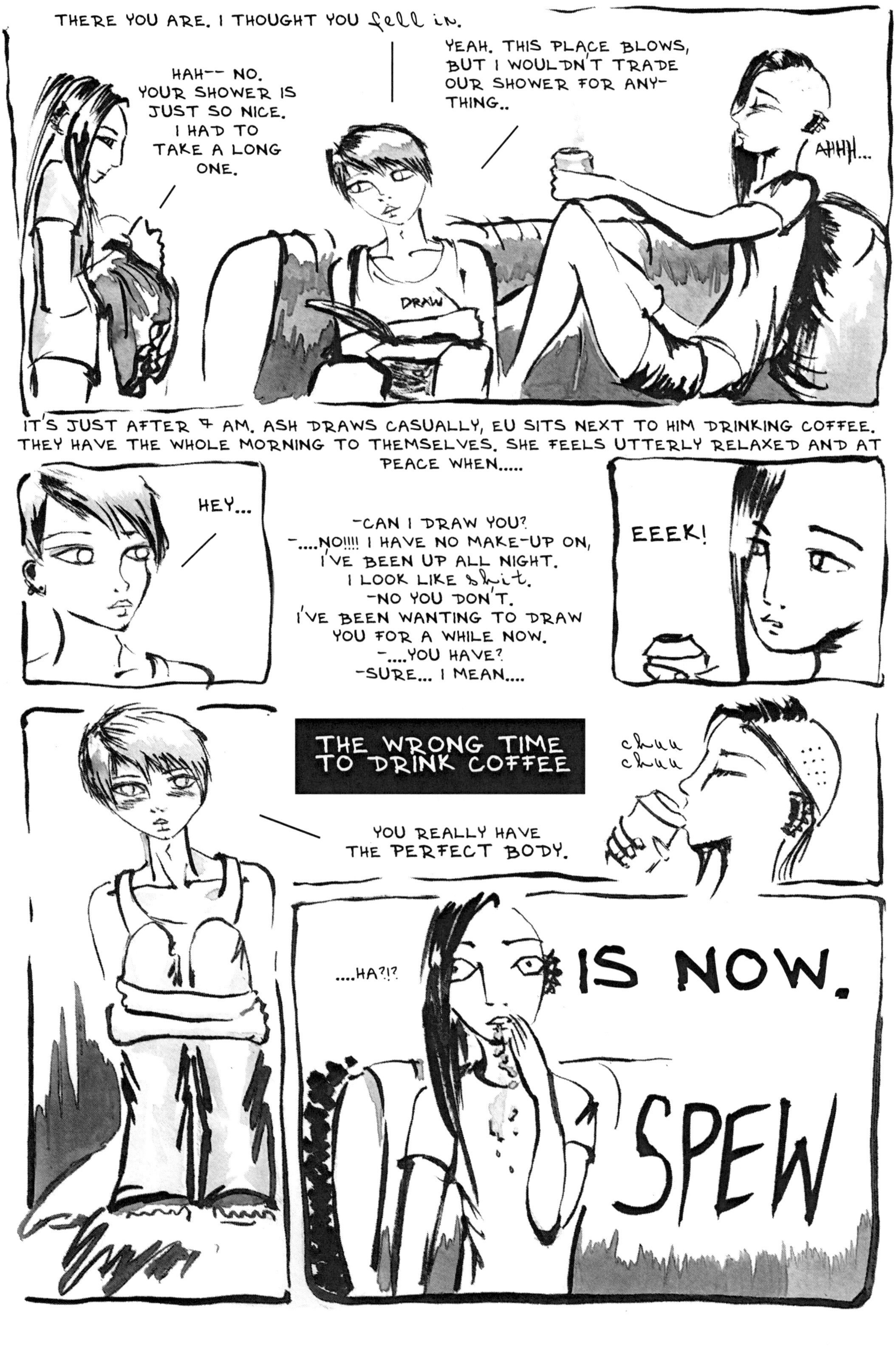
THERE YOU ARE. I THOUGHT YOU fell in.
HAH-- NO. YOUR SHOWER IS JUST SO NICE. I HAD TO TAKE A LONG ONE.
YEAH. THIS PLACE BLOWS, BUT I WOULDN'T TRADE OUR SHOWER FOR ANY-THING..
AHHH...
DRAW
IT'S JUST AFTER 7 AM. ASH DRAWS CASUALLY, EU SITS NEXT TO HIM DRINKING COFFEE. THEY HAVE THE WHOLE MORNING TO THEMSELVES. SHE FEELS UTTERLY RELAXED AND AT PEACE WHEN.....
HEY...
-CAN I DRAW YOU?
-....NO!!!! I HAVE NO MAKE-UP ON, I'VE BEEN UP ALL NIGHT. I LOOK LIKE shit.
-NO YOU DON'T. I'VE BEEN WANTING TO DRAW YOU FOR A WHILE NOW.
-....YOU HAVE?
-SURE... I MEAN....
EEEK!
THE WRONG TIME TO DRINK COFFEE
chuu chuu
YOU REALLY HAVE THE PERFECT BODY.
....HA?!?
IS NOW.
SPEW

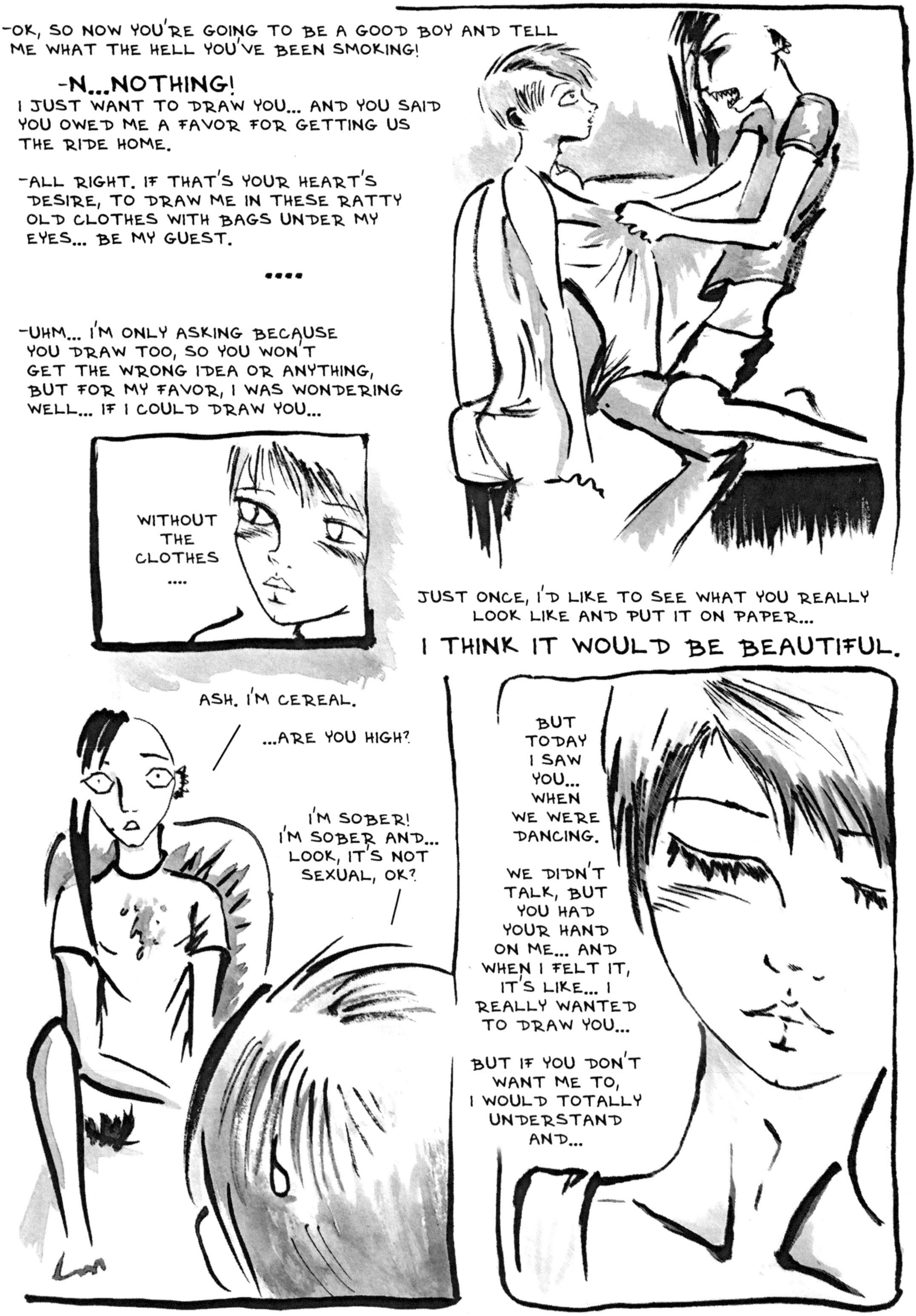
-OK, SO NOW YOU'RE GOING TO BE A GOOD BOY AND TELL ME WHAT THE HELL YOU'VE BEEN SMOKING!
-N...NOTHING!
I JUST WANT TO DRAW YOU... AND YOU SAID YOU OWED ME A FAVOR FOR GETTING US THE RIDE HOME.
-ALL RIGHT. IF THAT'S YOUR HEART'S DESIRE, TO DRAW ME IN THESE RATTY OLD CLOTHES WITH BAGS UNDER MY EYES... BE MY GUEST.
....
-UHM... I'M ONLY ASKING BECAUSE YOU DRAW TOO, SO YOU WON'T GET THE WRONG IDEA OR ANYTHING, BUT FOR MY FAVOR, I WAS WONDERING WELL... IF I COULD DRAW YOU...
WITHOUT THE CLOTHES ....
JUST ONCE, I'D LIKE TO SEE WHAT YOU REALLY LOOK LIKE AND PUT IT ON PAPER...
I THINK IT WOULD BE BEAUTIFUL.
ASH. I'M CEREAL.
...ARE YOU HIGH?
I'M SOBER! I'M SOBER AND... LOOK, IT'S NOT SEXUAL, OK?
BUT TODAY I SAW YOU... WHEN WE WERE DANCING.
WE DIDN'T TALK, BUT YOU HAD YOUR HAND ON ME... AND WHEN I FELT IT, IT'S LIKE... I REALLY WANTED TO DRAW YOU...
BUT IF YOU DON'T WANT ME TO, I WOULD TOTALLY UNDERSTAND AND...

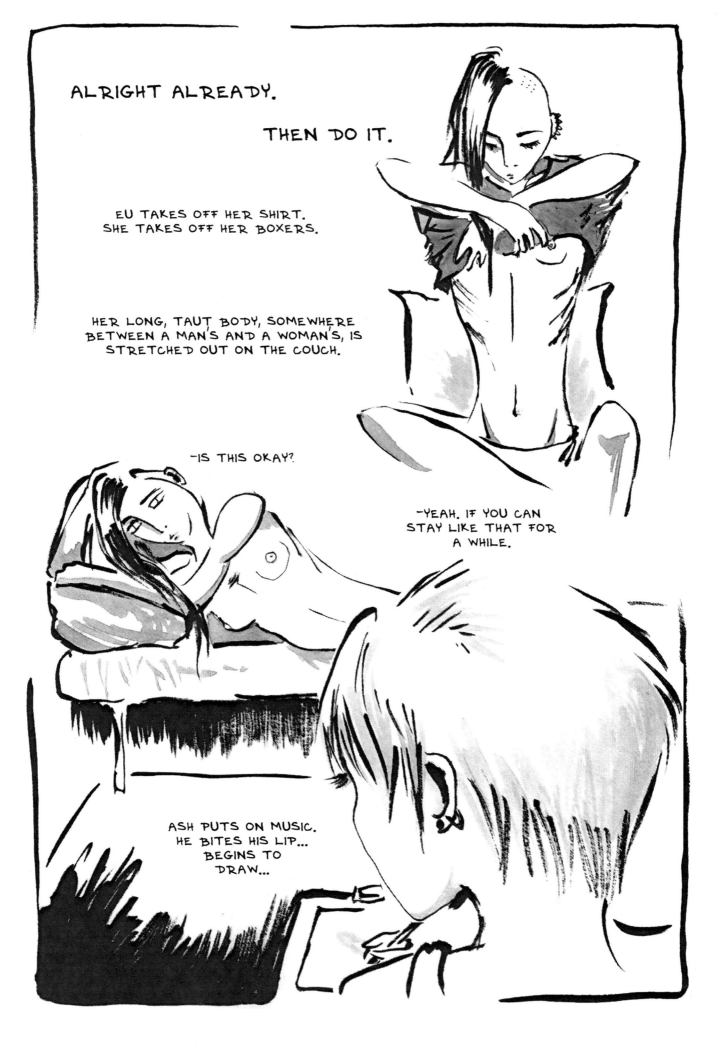

ALRIGHT ALREADY.

THEN DO IT.

EU TAKES OFF HER SHIRT.
SHE TAKES OFF HER BOXERS.

HER LONG, TAUT BODY, SOMEWHERE
BETWEEN A MAN'S AND A WOMAN'S, IS
STRETCHED OUT ON THE COUCH.

-IS THIS OKAY?

-YEAH. IF YOU CAN
STAY LIKE THAT FOR
A WHILE.

ASH PUTS ON MUSIC.
HE BITES HIS LIP...
BEGINS TO
DRAW...

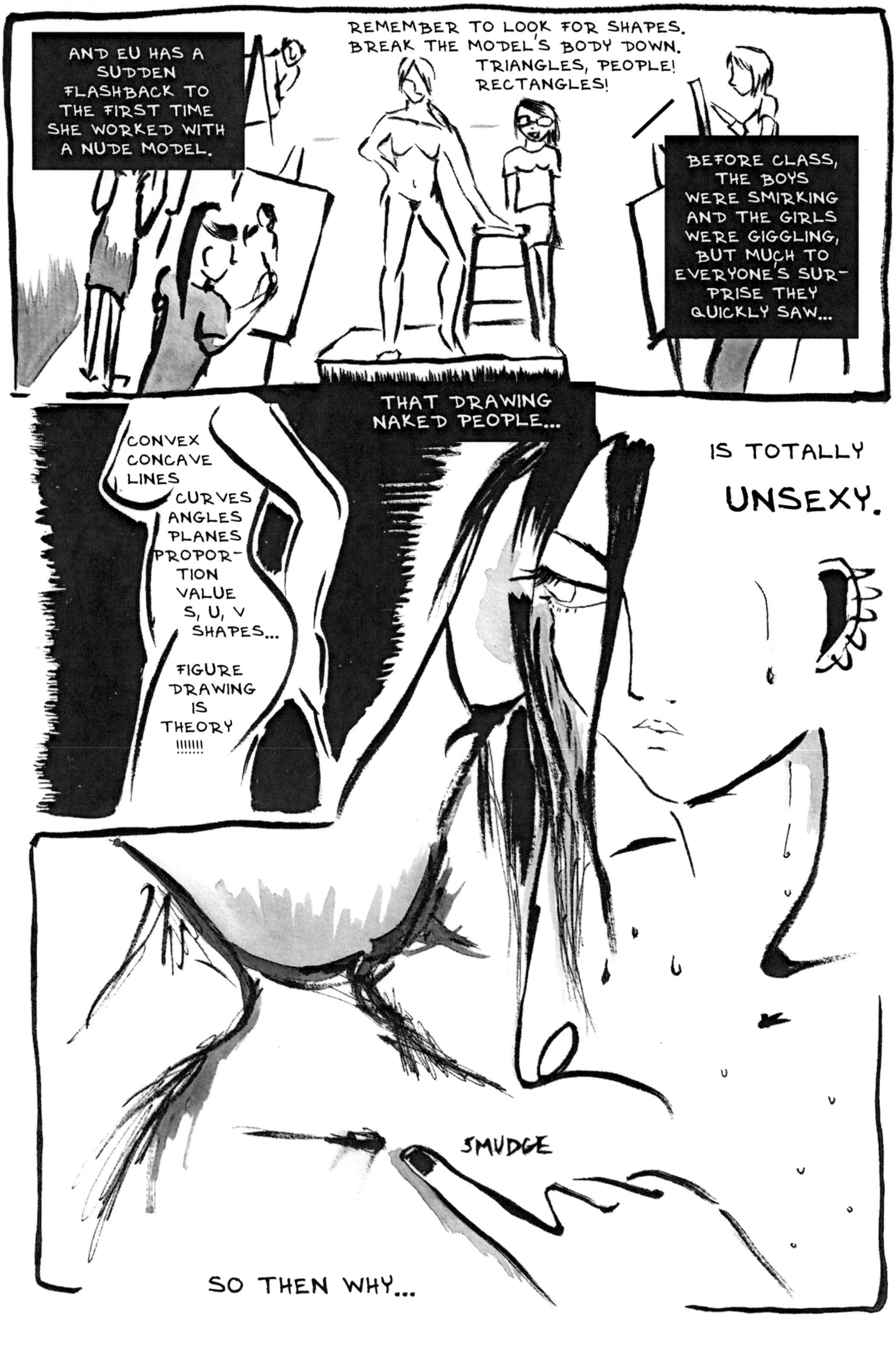
AND EU HAS A SUDDEN FLASHBACK TO THE FIRST TIME SHE WORKED WITH A NUDE MODEL.
REMEMBER TO LOOK FOR SHAPES. BREAK THE MODEL'S BODY DOWN.
TRIANGLES, PEOPLE! RECTANGLES!
BEFORE CLASS, THE BOYS WERE SMIRKING AND THE GIRLS WERE GIGGLING, BUT MUCH TO EVERYONE'S SURPRISE THEY QUICKLY SAW...
THAT DRAWING NAKED PEOPLE...
CONVEX CONCAVE LINES CURVES ANGLES PLANES PROPORTION VALUE S, U, V SHAPES...
FIGURE DRAWING IS THEORY !!!!!!!
IS TOTALLY
UNSEXY.
SMUDGE
SO THEN WHY...

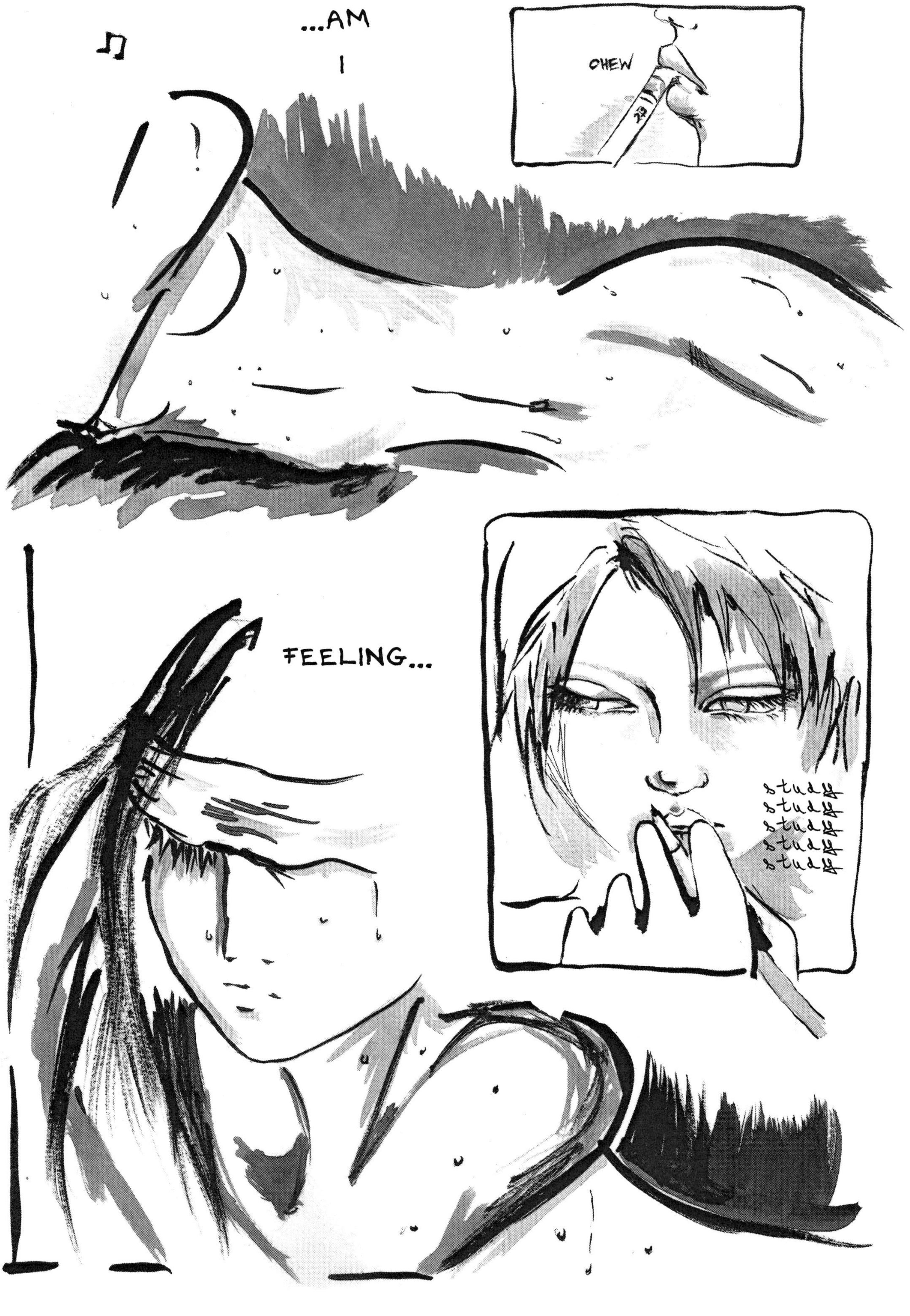
...AM
I
CHEW
FEELING...
study
study
study
study
study

A PAGE IN ASH'S SKETCHBOOK

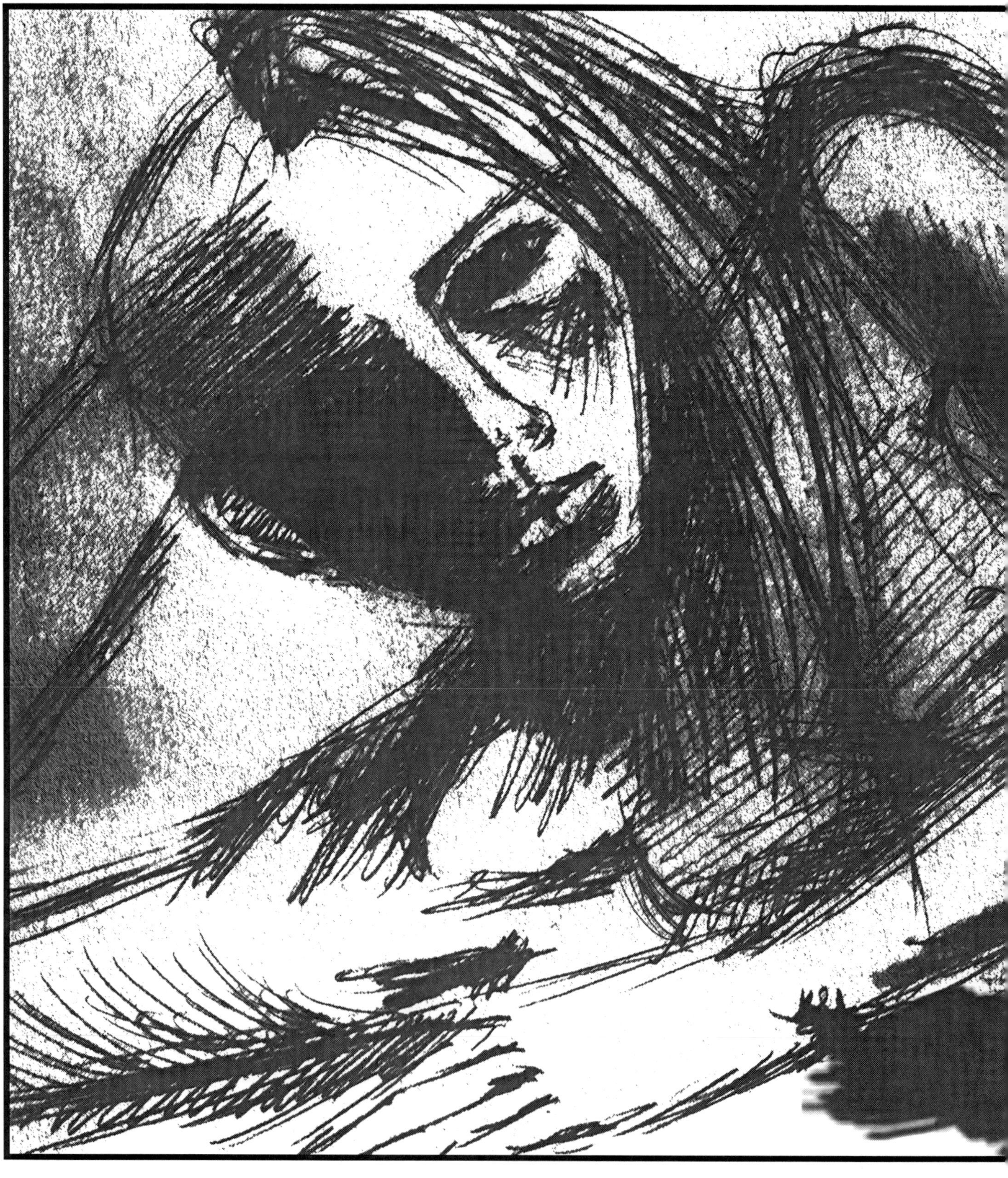

EU, AFTER THE RAVE

RADIOHEAD - all i need ♫

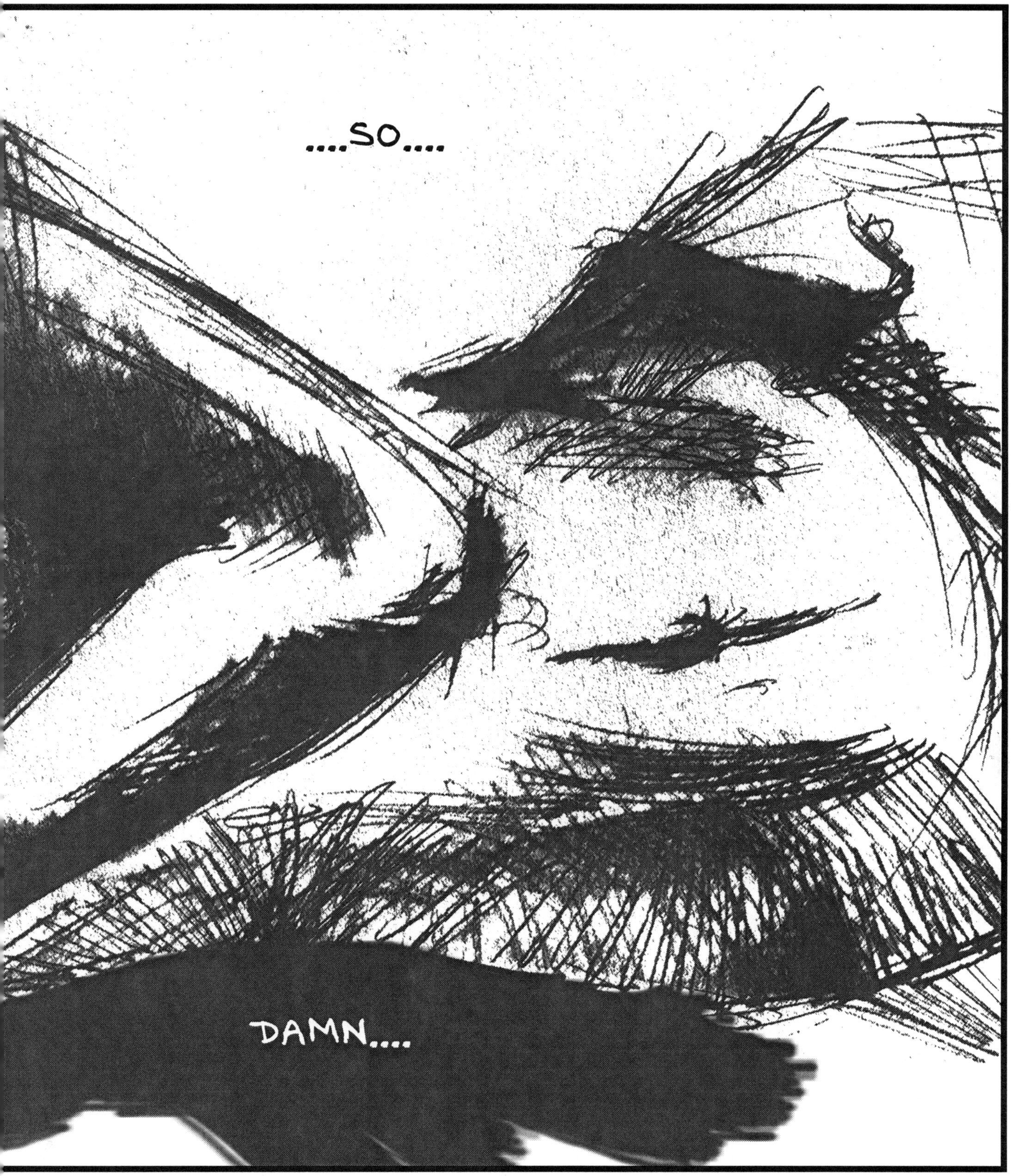

....SO....
DAMN....

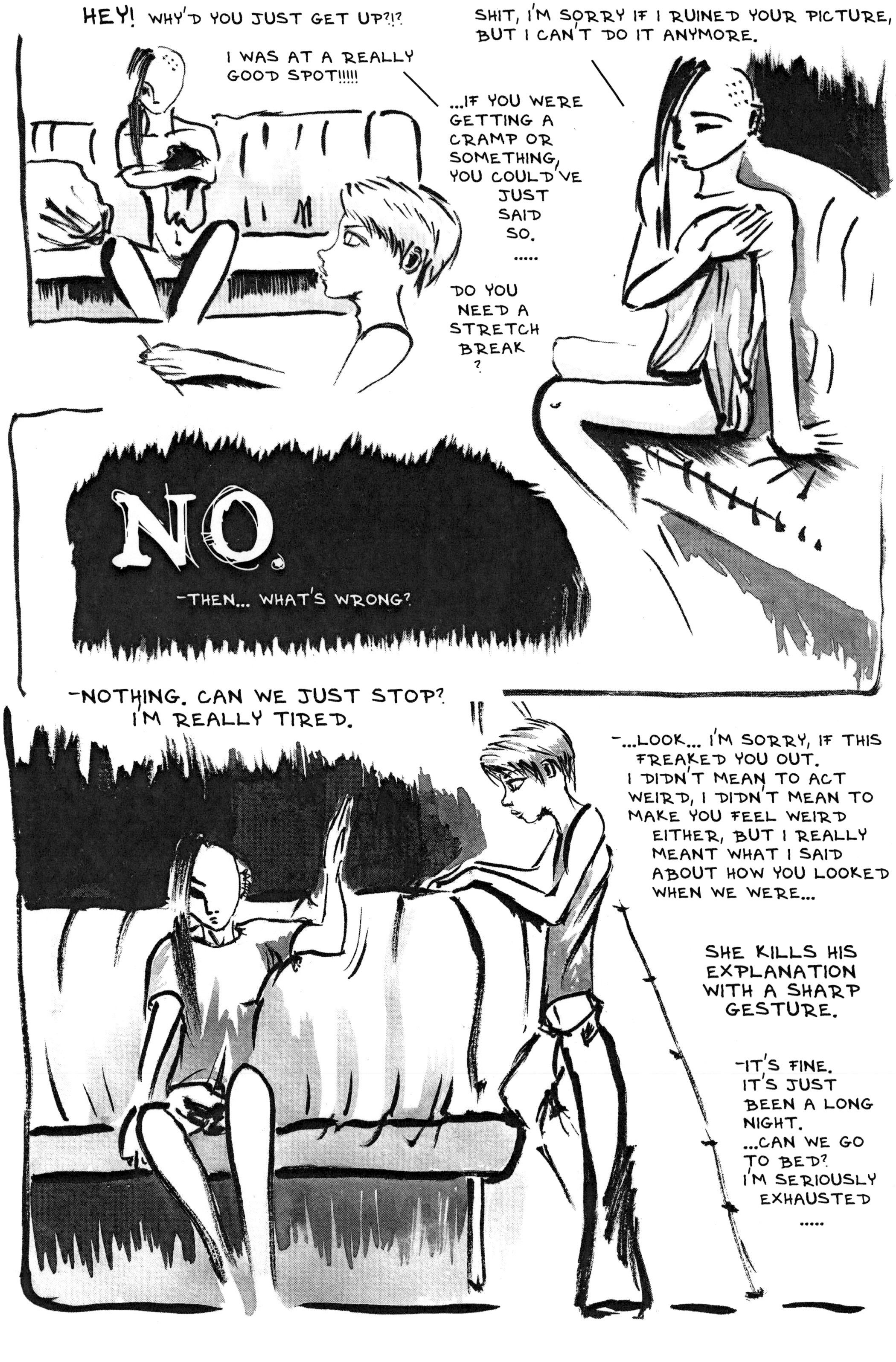
HEY! WHY'D YOU JUST GET UP?!?
I WAS AT A REALLY GOOD SPOT!!!!!
...IF YOU WERE GETTING A CRAMP OR SOMETHING, YOU COULD'VE JUST SAID SO.
.....
DO YOU NEED A STRETCH BREAK?
SHIT, I'M SORRY IF I RUINED YOUR PICTURE, BUT I CAN'T DO IT ANYMORE.
NO.
-THEN... WHAT'S WRONG?
-NOTHING. CAN WE JUST STOP? I'M REALLY TIRED.
-...LOOK... I'M SORRY, IF THIS FREAKED YOU OUT. I DIDN'T MEAN TO ACT WEIRD, I DIDN'T MEAN TO MAKE YOU FEEL WEIRD EITHER, BUT I REALLY MEANT WHAT I SAID ABOUT HOW YOU LOOKED WHEN WE WERE...
SHE KILLS HIS EXPLANATION WITH A SHARP GESTURE.
-IT'S FINE. IT'S JUST BEEN A LONG NIGHT. ...CAN WE GO TO BED? I'M SERIOUSLY EXHAUSTED
.....

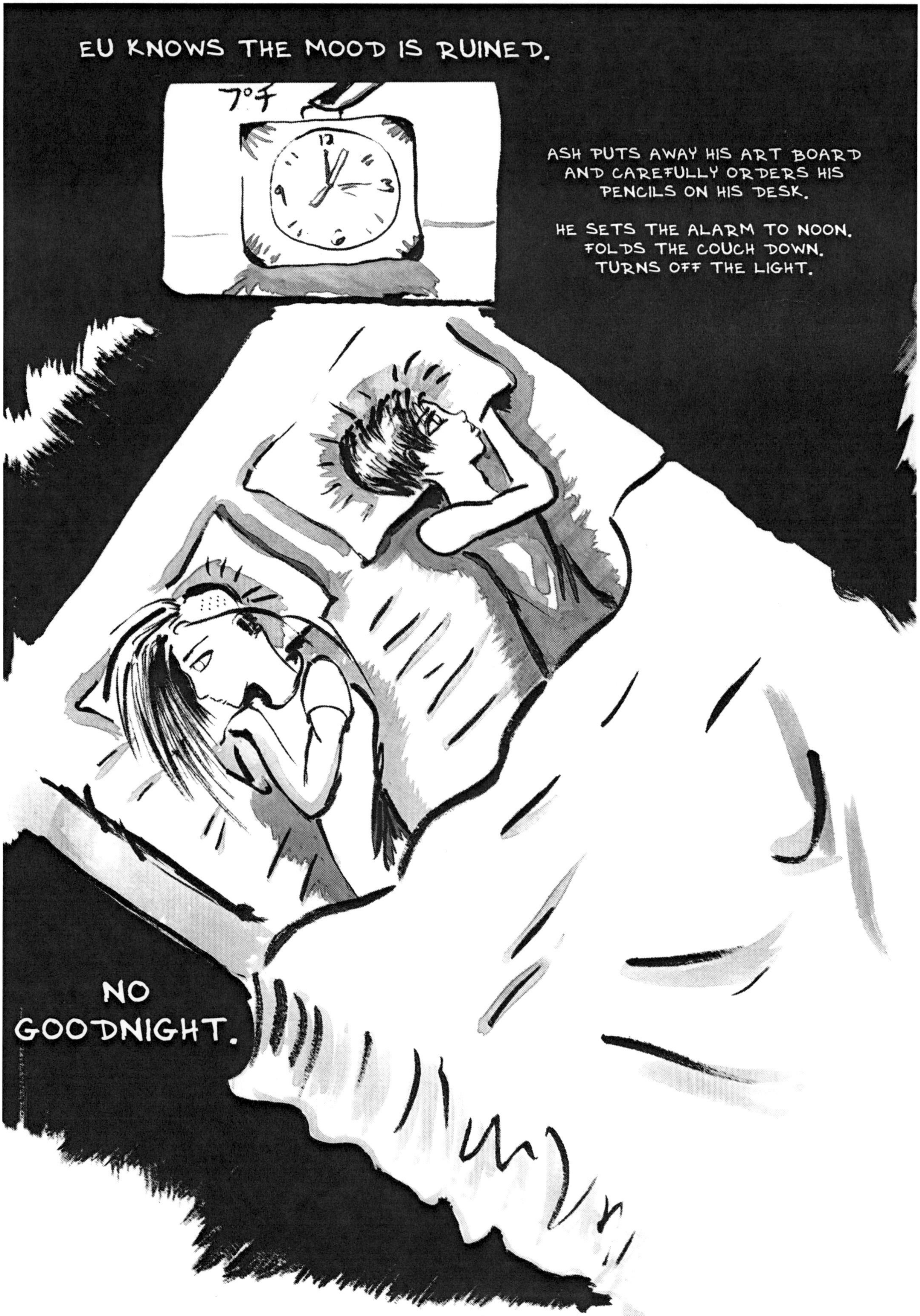
EU KNOWS THE MOOD IS RUINED.
プチ
ASH PUTS AWAY HIS ART BOARD AND CAREFULLY ORDERS HIS PENCILS ON HIS DESK.
HE SETS THE ALARM TO NOON. FOLDS THE COUCH DOWN. TURNS OFF THE LIGHT.
NO GOODNIGHT.

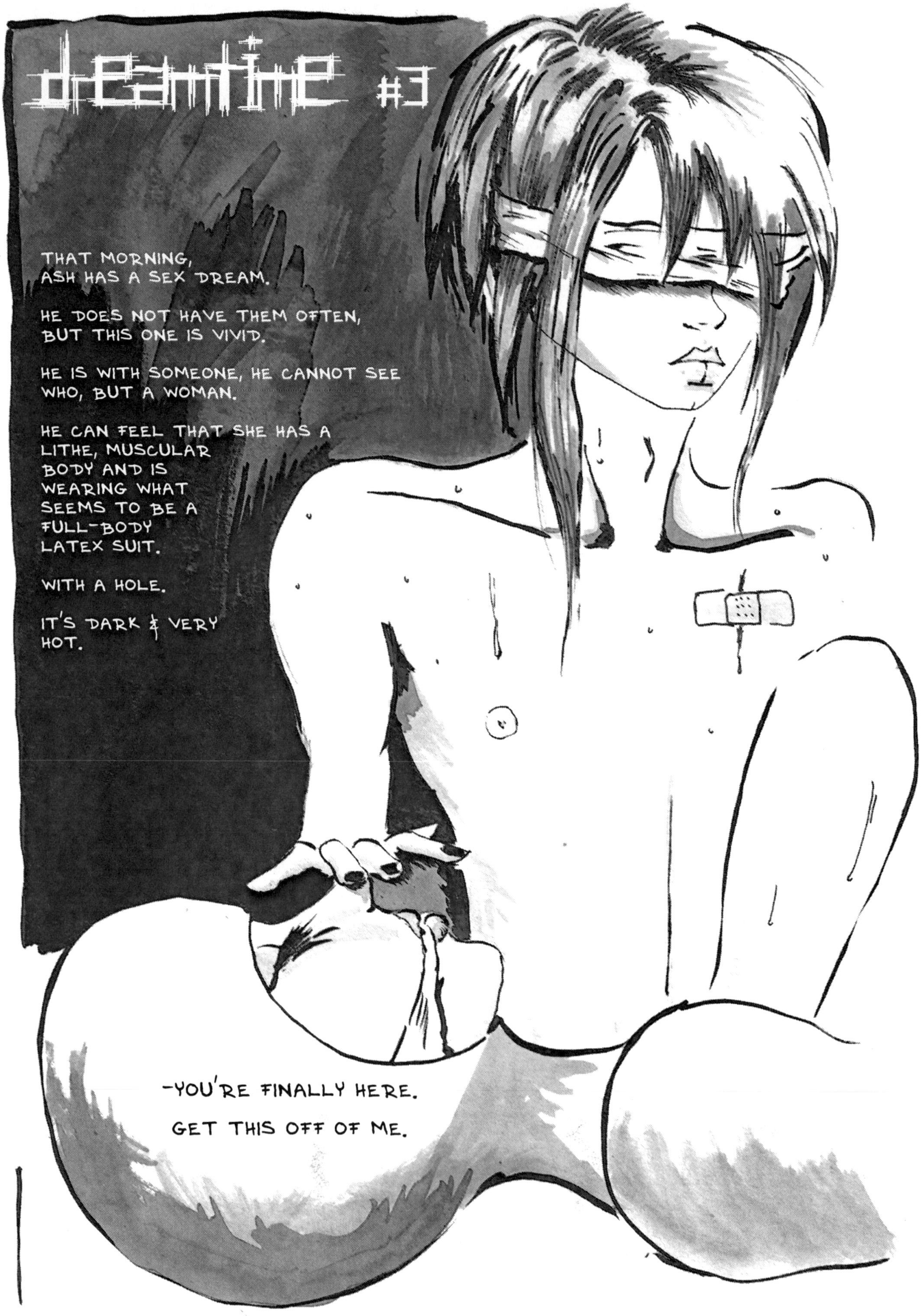
dreamtime #3
THAT MORNING, ASH HAS A SEX DREAM.
HE DOES NOT HAVE THEM OFTEN, BUT THIS ONE IS VIVID.
HE IS WITH SOMEONE, HE CANNOT SEE WHO, BUT A WOMAN.
HE CAN FEEL THAT SHE HAS A LITHE, MUSCULAR BODY AND IS WEARING WHAT SEEMS TO BE A FULL-BODY LATEX SUIT.
WITH A HOLE.
IT'S DARK & VERY HOT.
–YOU'RE FINALLY HERE.
GET THIS OFF OF ME.

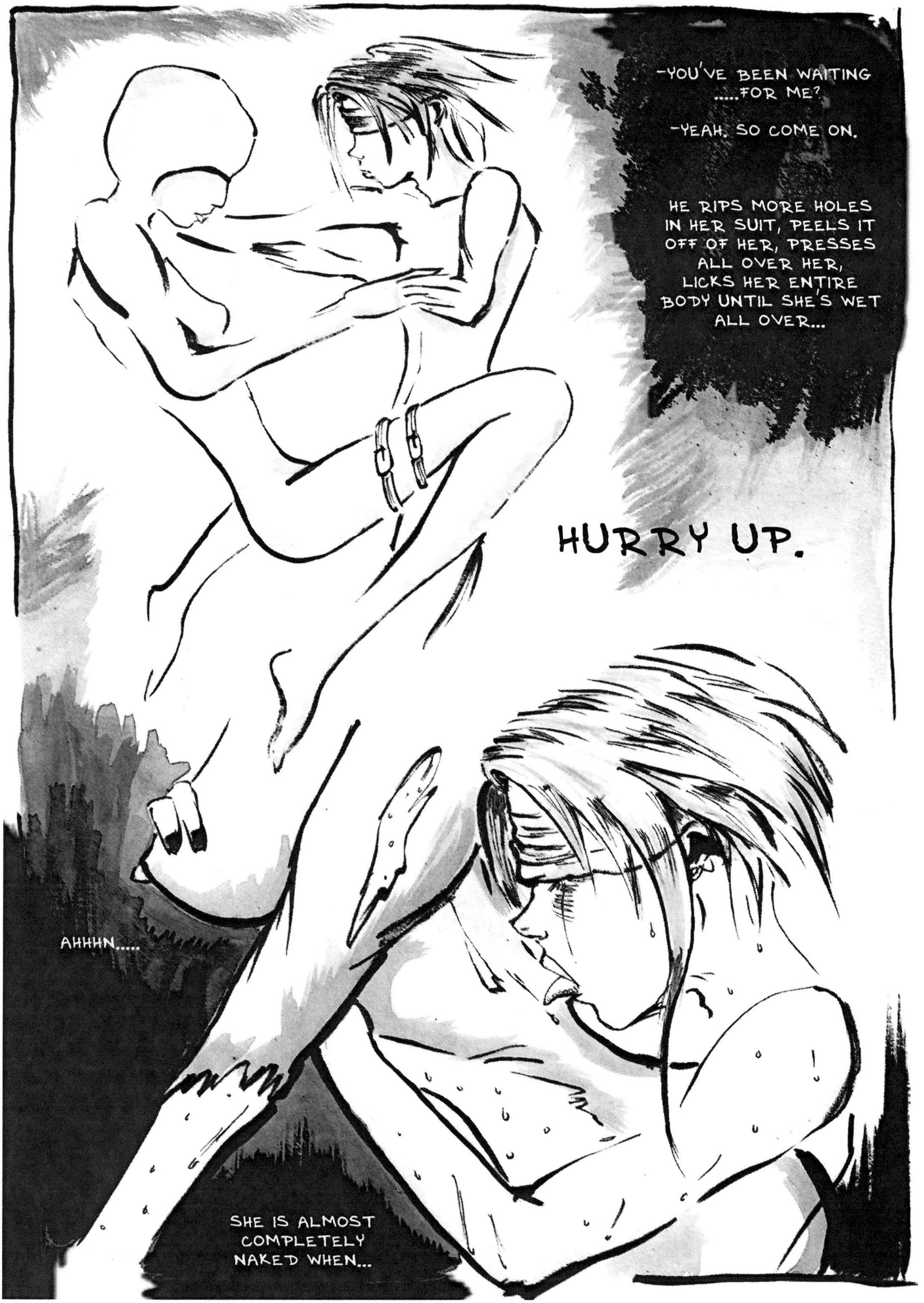
-YOU'VE BEEN WAITING .....FOR ME?
-YEAH. SO COME ON.
HE RIPS MORE HOLES IN HER SUIT, PEELS IT OFF OF HER, PRESSES ALL OVER HER, LICKS HER ENTIRE BODY UNTIL SHE'S WET ALL OVER...
HURRY UP.
AHHHN.....
SHE IS ALMOST COMPLETELY NAKED WHEN...

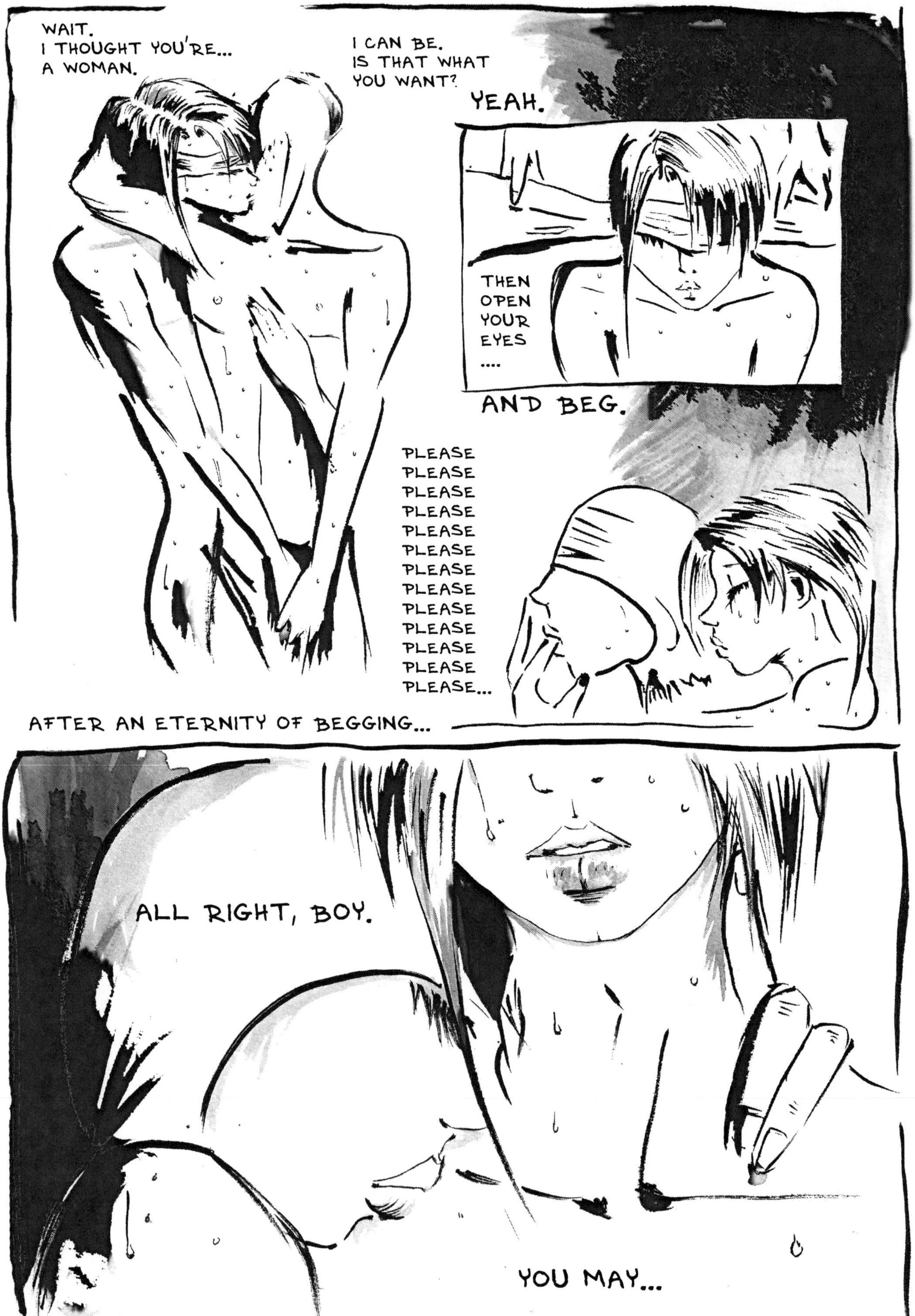
WAIT.
I THOUGHT YOU'RE...
A WOMAN.
I CAN BE.
IS THAT WHAT
YOU WANT?
YEAH.
THEN
OPEN
YOUR
EYES
....
AND BEG.
PLEASE
PLEASE
PLEASE
PLEASE
PLEASE
PLEASE
PLEASE
PLEASE
PLEASE
PLEASE
PLEASE
PLEASE
PLEASE...
AFTER AN ETERNITY OF BEGGING...
ALL RIGHT, BOY.
YOU MAY...

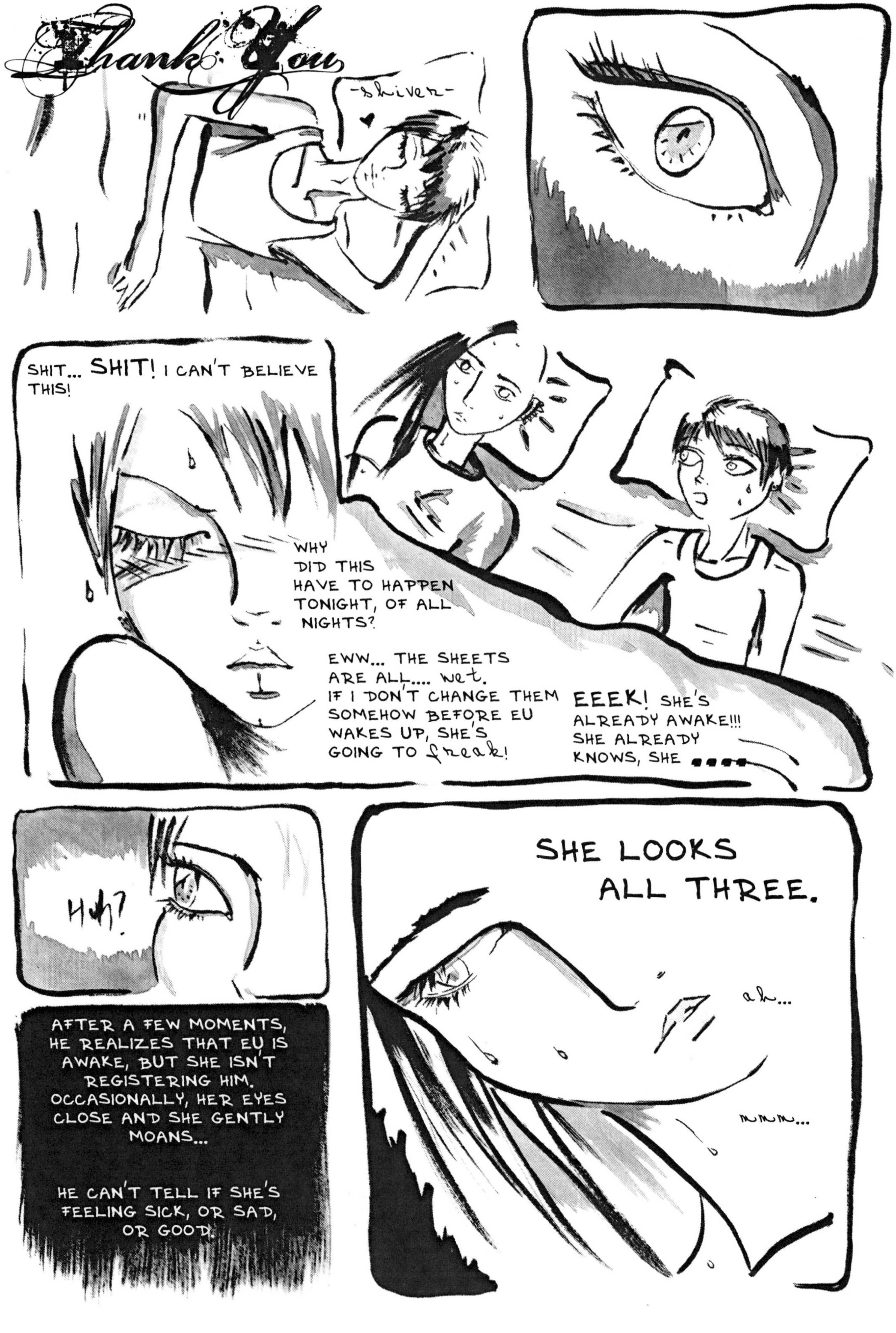
Thank You
-shiver-
SHIT... SHIT! I CAN'T BELIEVE THIS!
WHY DID THIS HAVE TO HAPPEN TONIGHT, OF ALL NIGHTS?
EWW... THE SHEETS ARE ALL.... wet. IF I DON'T CHANGE THEM SOMEHOW BEFORE EU WAKES UP, SHE'S GOING TO freak!
EEEK! SHE'S ALREADY AWAKE!!! SHE ALREADY KNOWS, SHE ....
Huh?
AFTER A FEW MOMENTS, HE REALIZES THAT EU IS AWAKE, BUT SHE ISN'T REGISTERING HIM. OCCASIONALLY, HER EYES CLOSE AND SHE GENTLY MOANS...
HE CAN'T TELL IF SHE'S FEELING SICK, OR SAD, OR GOOD.
SHE LOOKS ALL THREE.
ah...
mmm...

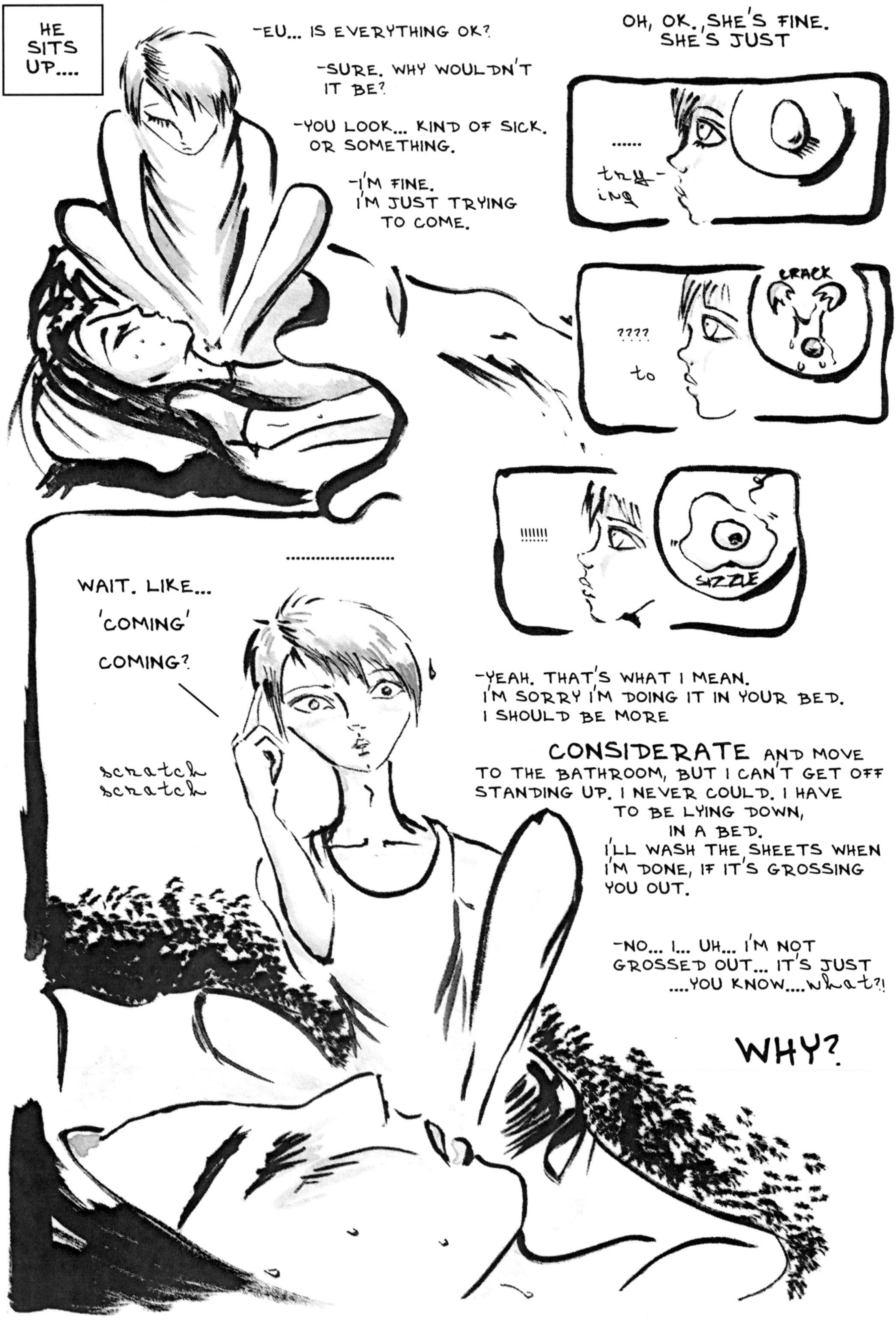
HE SITS UP....
-EU... IS EVERYTHING OK?
-SURE. WHY WOULDN'T IT BE?
-YOU LOOK... KIND OF SICK. OR SOMETHING.
-I'M FINE. I'M JUST TRYING TO COME.
OH, OK. SHE'S FINE. SHE'S JUST
......
try-ing
????
to
CRACK
!!!!!!
SIZZLE
....
WAIT. LIKE... 'COMING' COMING?
scratch scratch
-YEAH. THAT'S WHAT I MEAN. I'M SORRY I'M DOING IT IN YOUR BED. I SHOULD BE MORE
CONSIDERATE AND MOVE TO THE BATHROOM, BUT I CAN'T GET OFF STANDING UP. I NEVER COULD. I HAVE TO BE LYING DOWN, IN A BED.
I'LL WASH THE SHEETS WHEN I'M DONE, IF IT'S GROSSING YOU OUT.
-NO... I... UH... I'M NOT GROSSED OUT... IT'S JUST ....YOU KNOW....what?!
WHY?

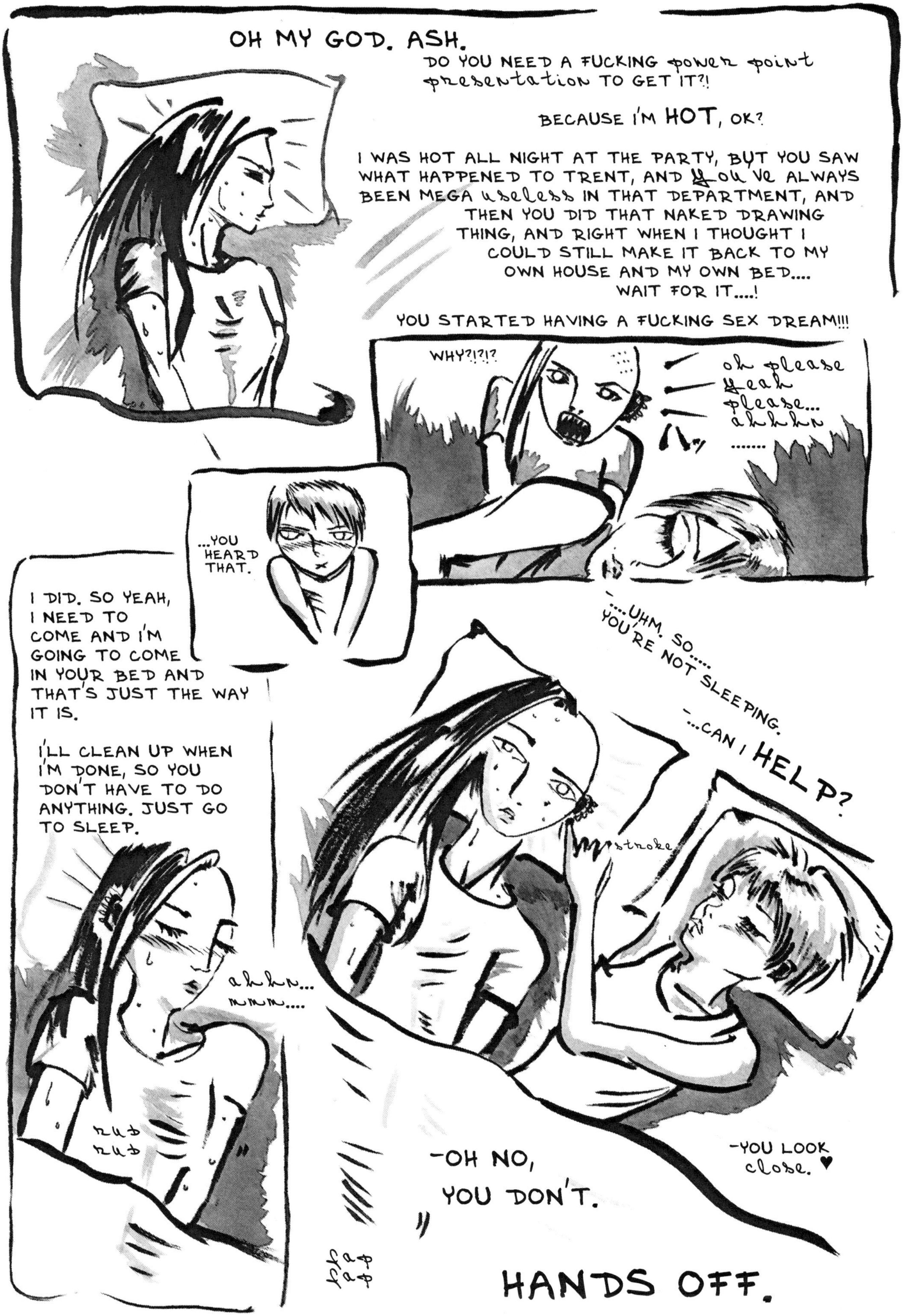
OH MY GOD. ASH.
DO YOU NEED A FUCKING power point presentation TO GET IT?!
BECAUSE I'M HOT, OK?
I WAS HOT ALL NIGHT AT THE PARTY, BUT YOU SAW WHAT HAPPENED TO TRENT, AND you've ALWAYS BEEN MEGA useless IN THAT DEPARTMENT, AND THEN YOU DID THAT NAKED DRAWING THING, AND RIGHT WHEN I THOUGHT I COULD STILL MAKE IT BACK TO MY OWN HOUSE AND MY OWN BED.... WAIT FOR IT....!
YOU STARTED HAVING A FUCKING SEX DREAM!!!
WHY?!?!?
oh please yeah please... ahhhn ....
...YOU HEARD THAT.
I DID. SO YEAH, I NEED TO COME AND I'M GOING TO COME IN YOUR BED AND THAT'S JUST THE WAY IT IS.
I'LL CLEAN UP WHEN I'M DONE, SO YOU DON'T HAVE TO DO ANYTHING. JUST GO TO SLEEP.
ahhhn... mmm....
rub rub
fap fap
-....UHM. SO..... YOU'RE NOT SLEEPING.
-...CAN I HELP?
stroke
-OH NO, YOU DON'T.
-YOU LOOK close. ♥
HANDS OFF.

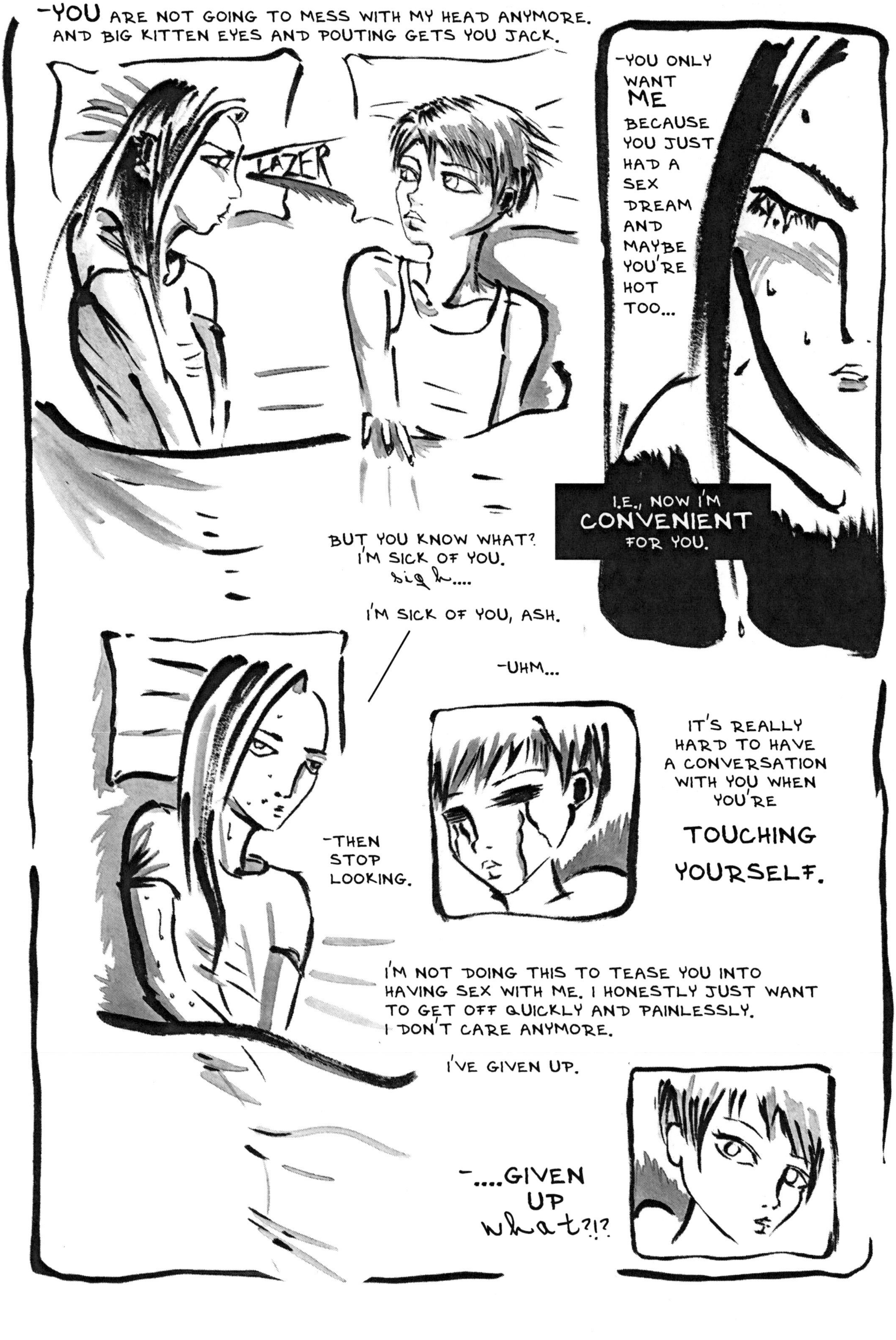

-YOU ARE NOT GOING TO MESS WITH MY HEAD ANYMORE. AND BIG KITTEN EYES AND POUTING GETS YOU JACK.
LAZER
-YOU ONLY WANT ME BECAUSE YOU JUST HAD A SEX DREAM AND MAYBE YOU'RE HOT TOO...
I.E., NOW I'M CONVENIENT FOR YOU.
BUT YOU KNOW WHAT? I'M SICK OF YOU. sigh....
I'M SICK OF YOU, ASH.
-UHM...
IT'S REALLY HARD TO HAVE A CONVERSATION WITH YOU WHEN YOU'RE TOUCHING YOURSELF.
-THEN STOP LOOKING.
I'M NOT DOING THIS TO TEASE YOU INTO HAVING SEX WITH ME. I HONESTLY JUST WANT TO GET OFF QUICKLY AND PAINLESSLY. I DON'T CARE ANYMORE.
I'VE GIVEN UP.
-....GIVEN UP what?!?

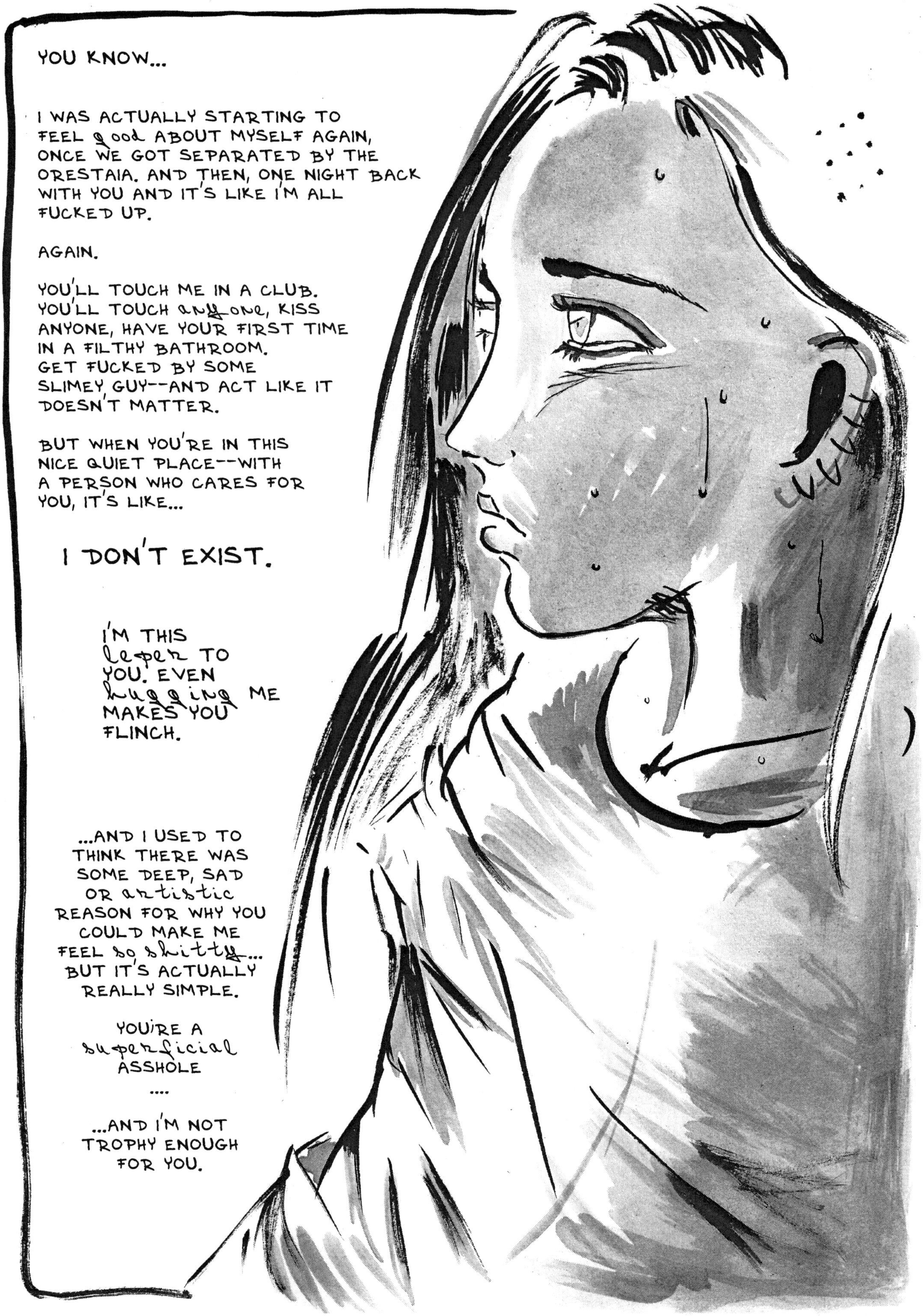
YOU KNOW...
I WAS ACTUALLY STARTING TO FEEL good ABOUT MYSELF AGAIN, ONCE WE GOT SEPARATED BY THE ORESTAIA. AND THEN, ONE NIGHT BACK WITH YOU AND IT'S LIKE I'M ALL FUCKED UP.
AGAIN.
YOU'LL TOUCH ME IN A CLUB. YOU'LL TOUCH anyone, KISS ANYONE, HAVE YOUR FIRST TIME IN A FILTHY BATHROOM. GET FUCKED BY SOME SLIMEY GUY--AND ACT LIKE IT DOESN'T MATTER.
BUT WHEN YOU'RE IN THIS NICE QUIET PLACE--WITH A PERSON WHO CARES FOR YOU, IT'S LIKE...
I DON'T EXIST.
I'M THIS leper TO YOU. EVEN hugging ME MAKES YOU FLINCH.
...AND I USED TO THINK THERE WAS SOME DEEP, SAD OR artistic REASON FOR WHY YOU COULD MAKE ME FEEL so shitty... BUT IT'S ACTUALLY REALLY SIMPLE.
YOU'RE A superficial ASSHOLE
....
...AND I'M NOT TROPHY ENOUGH FOR YOU.

-HEY THAT'S NOT... I DIDN'T KNOW I WAS...
-SHUT up. YOU KNEW. YOU always KNEW, BUT YOU DIDN'T CARE, BECAUSE I'M NOT
SOME PRETTY GUY WHO WANTS TO USE YOU OR A PERKY LITTLE CHICK WITH
big boobs.
-EU....
-JUST LEAVE ME ALONE. STAY ON YOUR SIDE AND LET ME GET OFF IN PEACE.

BUT HE CAN'T. HER BODY LOOKS LIKE A
WOUND TO HIM, LIKE SOME KIND OF OPEN
SORE...

-YOU REALLY...
DON'T WANT ME TO?

HE RESTS ONE HAND ON HER STOMACH,
AND SHE LETS HERSELF
FOR ONE MOMENT...

. . . .

OK YES
OK YES
OH
PLEASEPLEASEPLEASE
PLEASEPLEASE
OH ASH
I'VE WANTED YOU FOR
SO.
FUCKING.
LONG.
PUT YOUR
HANDS ON
ME.
YOUR
MOUTH,
ALL OVER
OH PLEASEPLEASEPLEASE
PLEASEPLEASE
ASH
PLEASE ASH
DO IT ASH
DO IT ASH
DO IT
DO IT
DO IT
DO IT
DO IT
DO IT

DO IT.

-STOP.

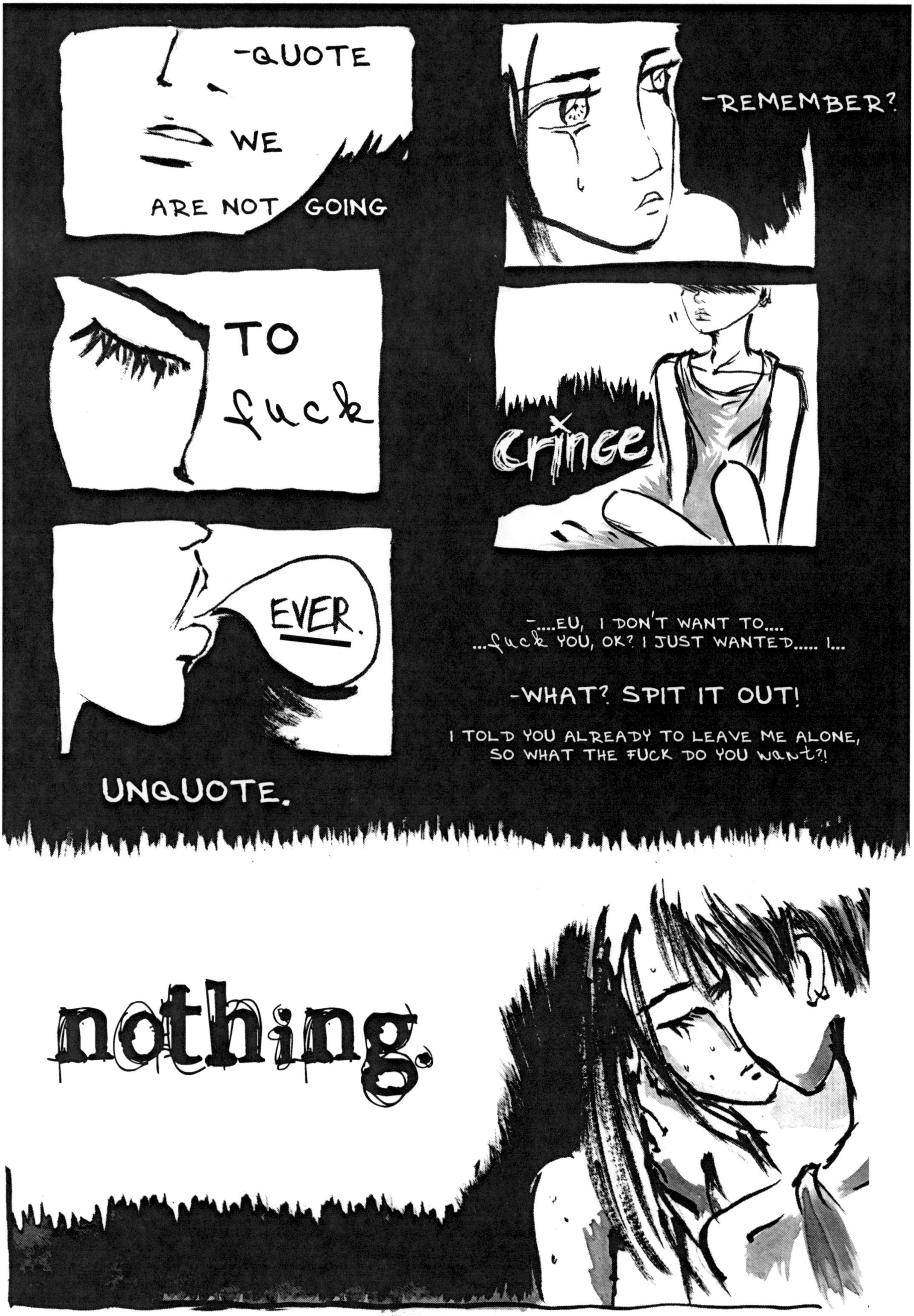

-QUOTE
WE
ARE NOT GOING
TO
fuck
EVER.
UNQUOTE.
-REMEMBER?
cringe
-....EU, I DON'T WANT TO....
...fuck YOU, OK? I JUST WANTED..... I...
-WHAT? SPIT IT OUT!
I TOLD YOU ALREADY TO LEAVE ME ALONE,
SO WHAT THE FUCK DO YOU want?!
nothing.

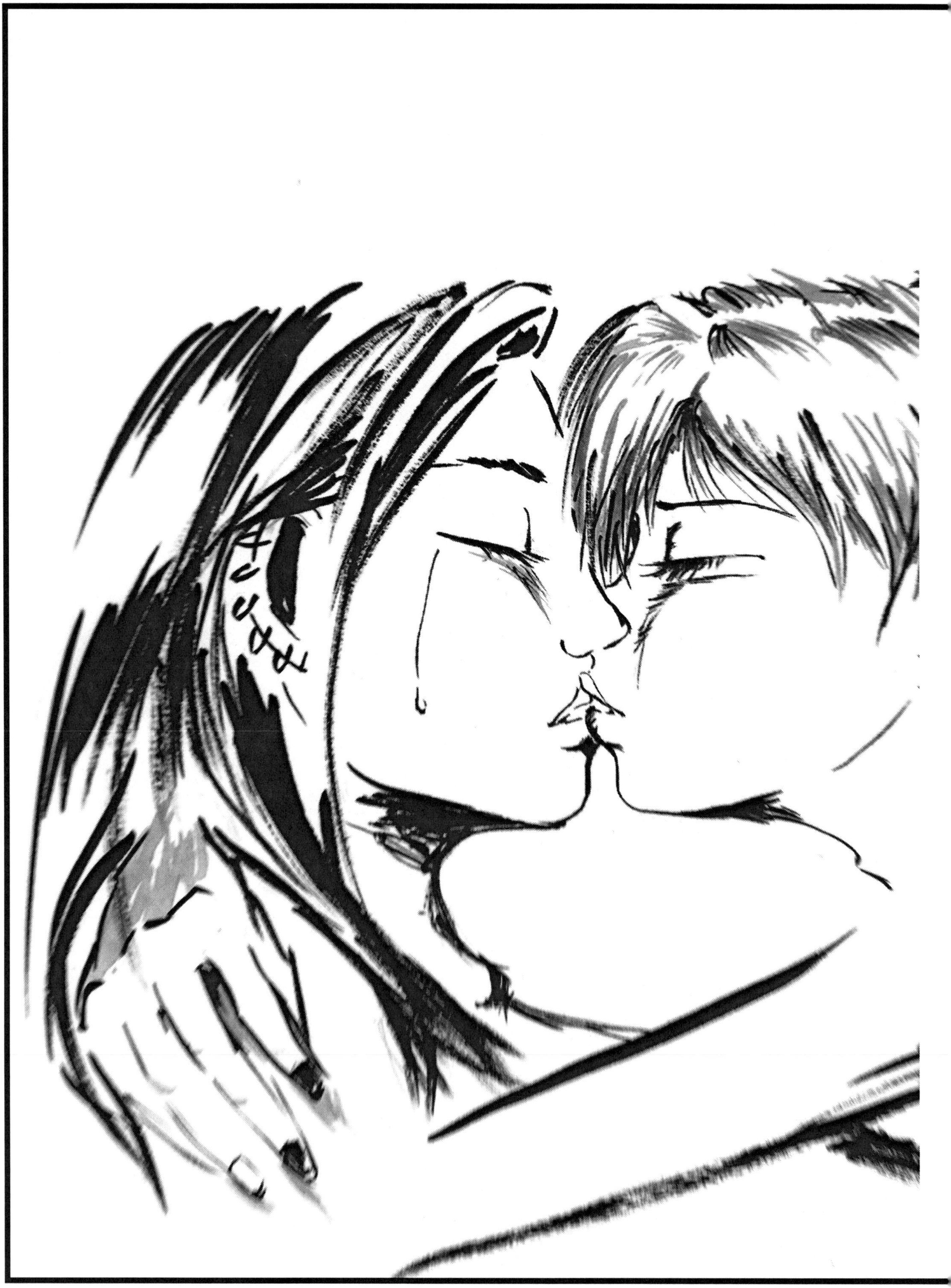

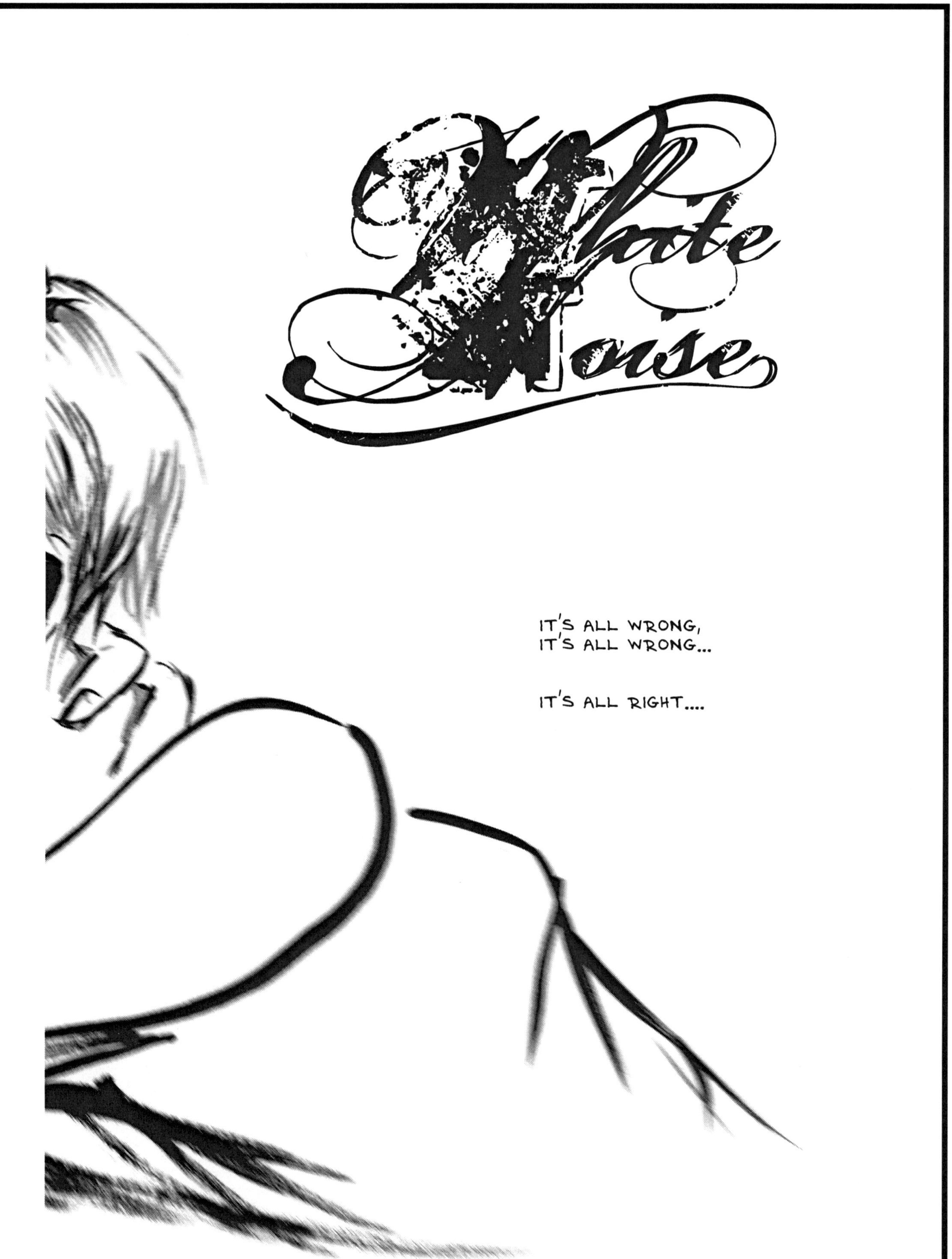
White House
IT'S ALL WRONG,
IT'S ALL WRONG...
IT'S ALL RIGHT....

DRIP
DROP
DRIP
DROP

DRIP.

-EU... ...?
-YEAH. THANKS. AND GOODNIGHT.
-YOU'RE GOING TO SLEEP NOW?
-...I DON'T HAVE A BETTER IDEA.
-DEVOTCHKA... come on.
-YOU SAID NEVER, NOT ME.

-BEG ME.

SHE'S STILL SHUDDERING AND
WATCHING IT MAKES HIM ACHE.

SHE CLOSES HER EYES AND HER
BREATHING DEEPENS.

ASH DESPAIRS.
HE KEEPS TOUCHING HER AND
WHEN SHE CAN NO LONGER
PRETEND TO BE ASLEEP...

HE BEGS HER.

he begs her.

FINALLY, SHE NODS.
THE SLIGHTEST MOVEMENT.
HE BLUSHES-

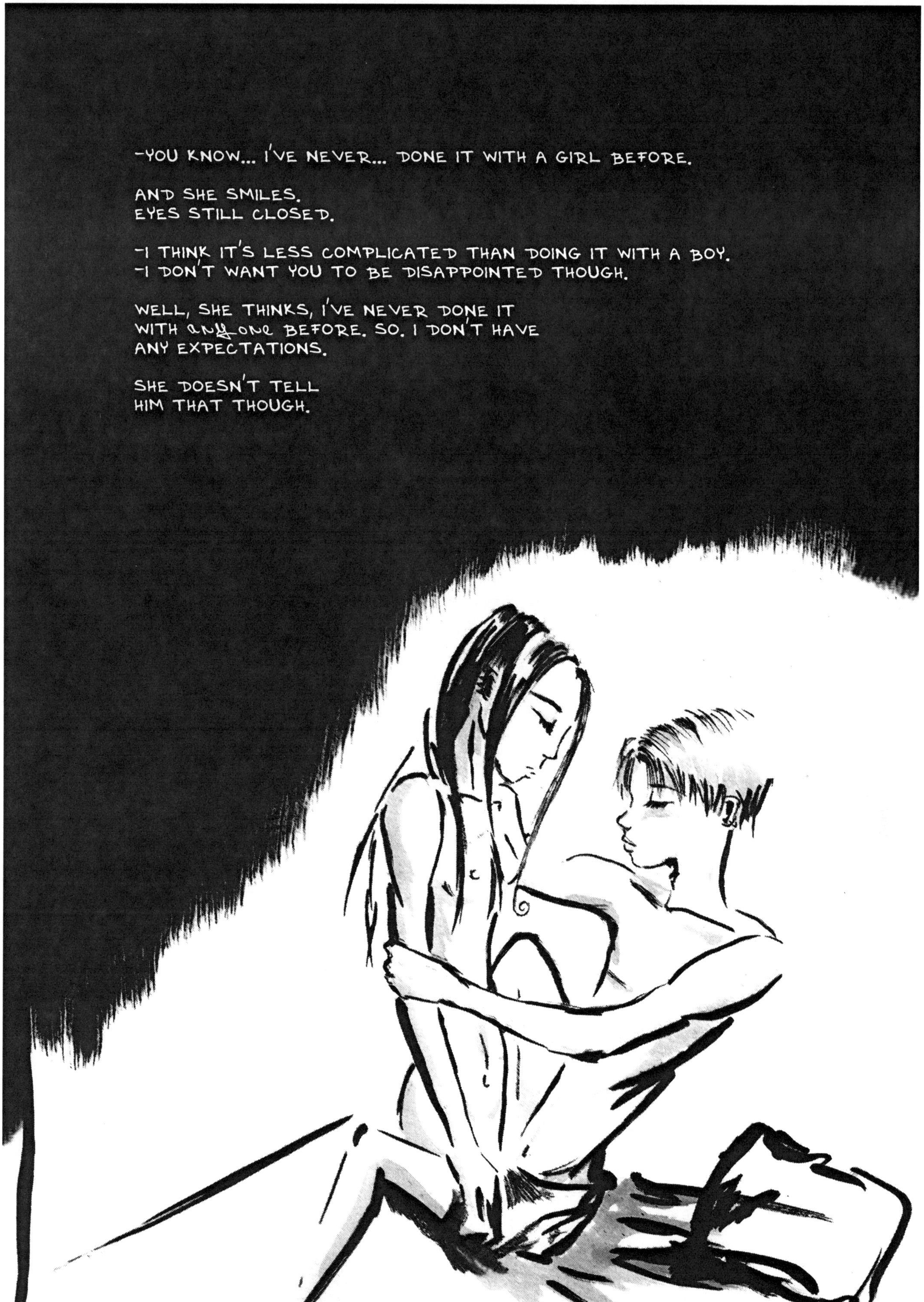
-YOU KNOW... I'VE NEVER... DONE IT WITH A GIRL BEFORE.
AND SHE SMILES.
EYES STILL CLOSED.
-I THINK IT'S LESS COMPLICATED THAN DOING IT WITH A BOY.
-I DON'T WANT YOU TO BE DISAPPOINTED THOUGH.
WELL, SHE THINKS, I'VE NEVER DONE IT WITH anyone BEFORE. SO. I DON'T HAVE ANY EXPECTATIONS.
SHE DOESN'T TELL HIM THAT THOUGH.

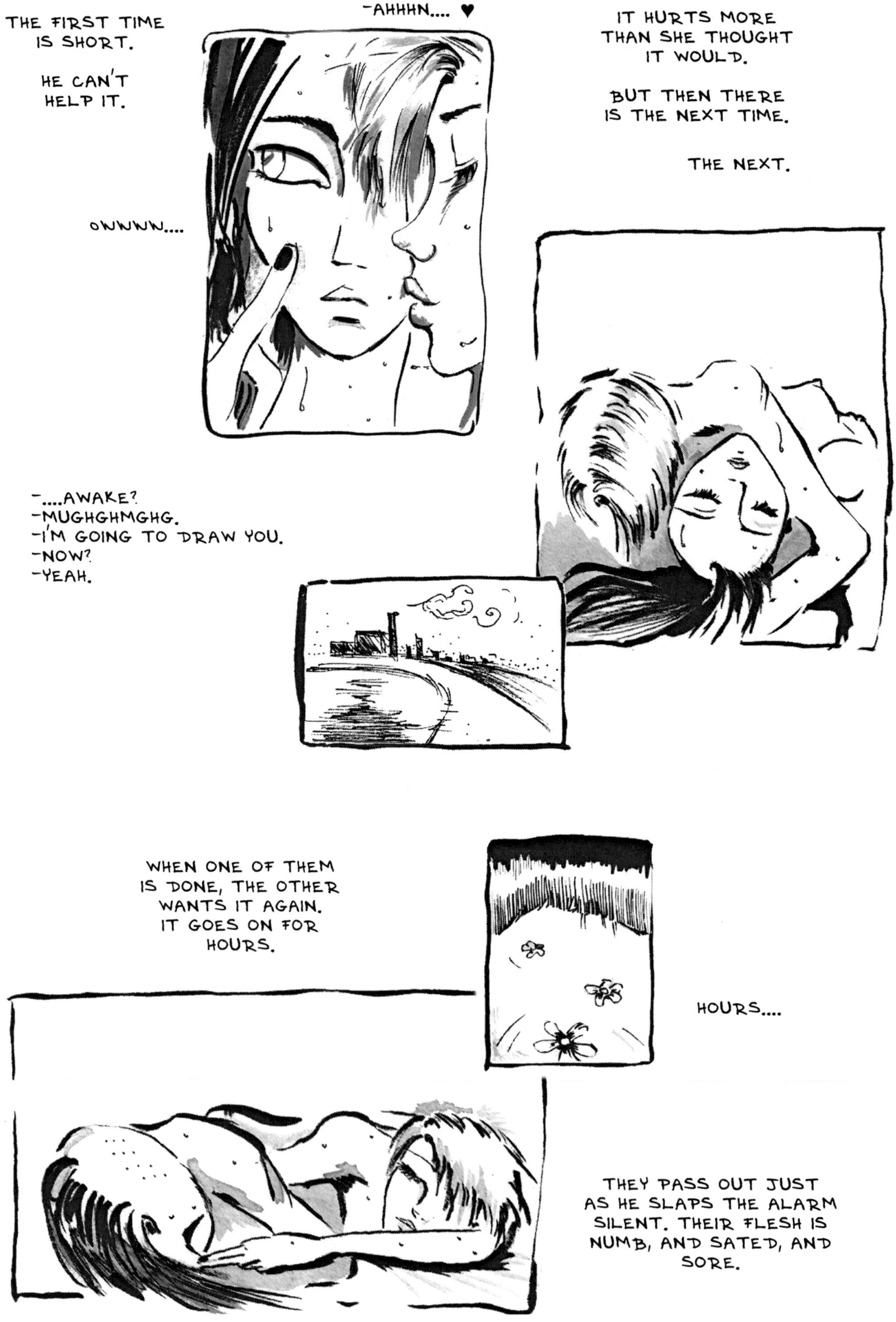
THE FIRST TIME IS SHORT.
HE CAN'T HELP IT.
-AHHHN.... ♥
OWWWW....
IT HURTS MORE THAN SHE THOUGHT IT WOULD.
BUT THEN THERE IS THE NEXT TIME.
THE NEXT.
-....AWAKE?
-MUGHGHMGHG.
-I'M GOING TO DRAW YOU.
-NOW?
-YEAH.
WHEN ONE OF THEM IS DONE, THE OTHER WANTS IT AGAIN. IT GOES ON FOR HOURS.
HOURS....
THEY PASS OUT JUST AS HE SLAPS THE ALARM SILENT. THEIR FLESH IS NUMB, AND SATED, AND SORE.

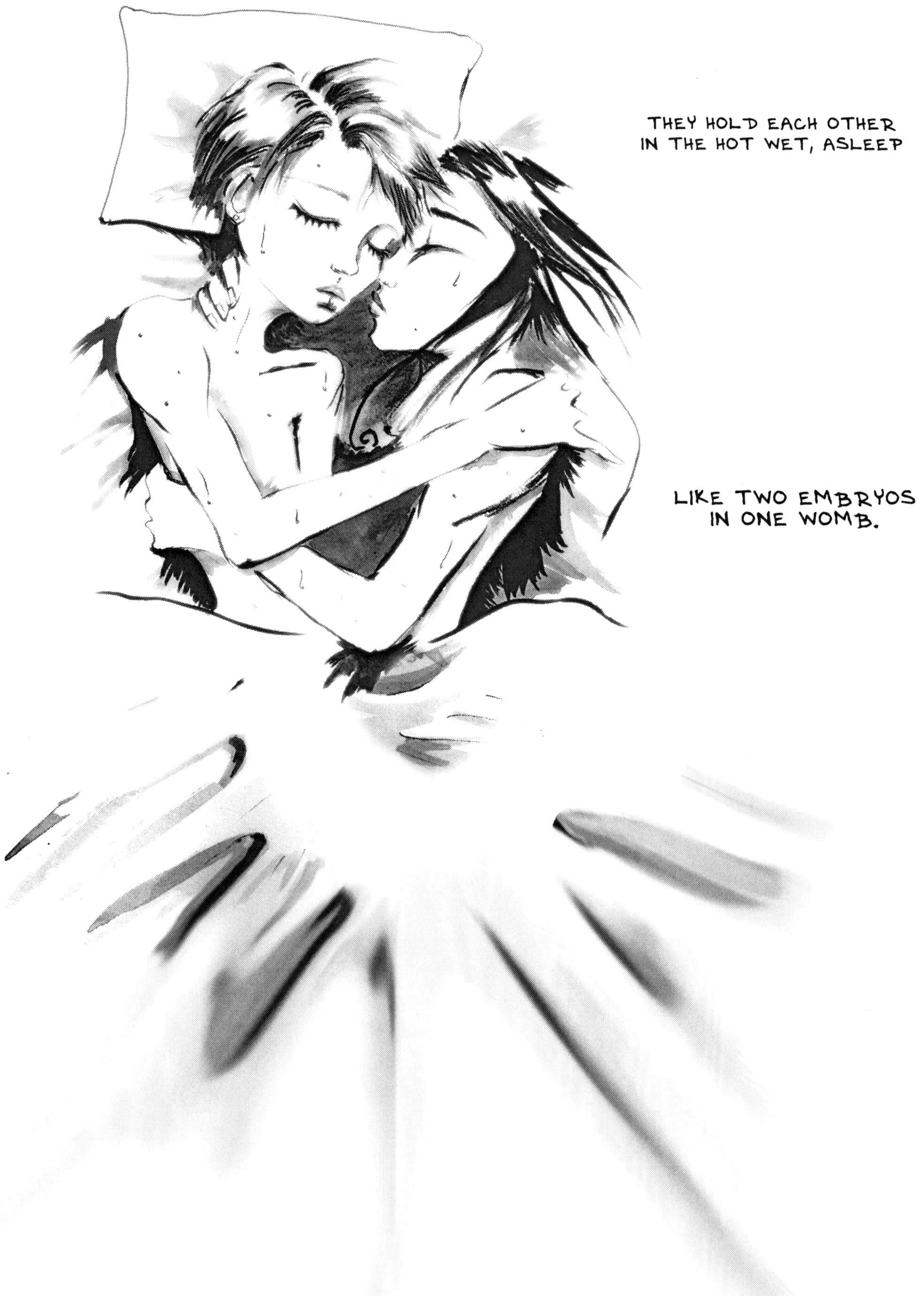
THEY HOLD EACH OTHER
IN THE HOT WET, ASLEEP
LIKE TWO EMBRYOS
IN ONE WOMB.

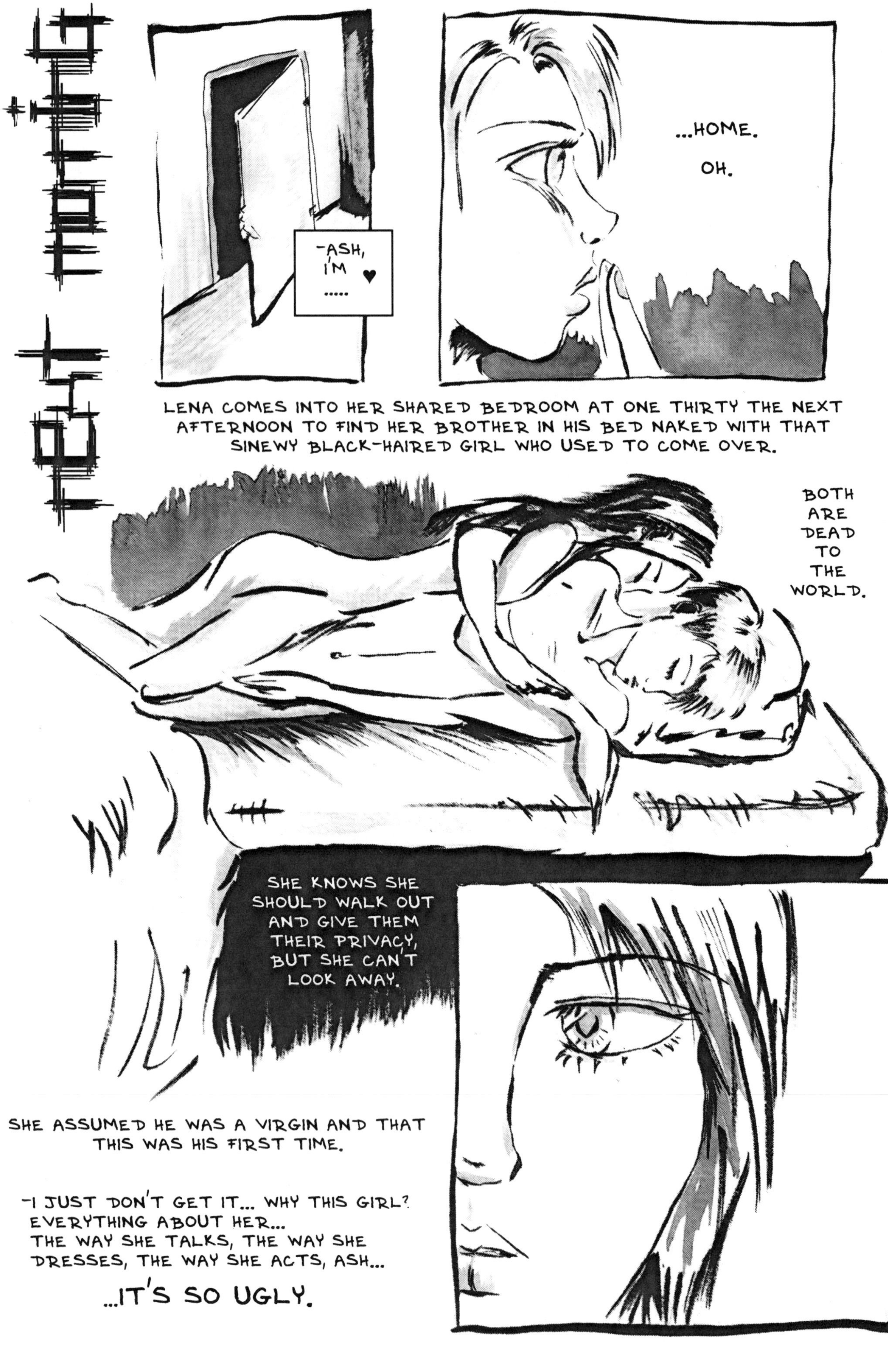
next morning
-ASH, I'M ..... ♥
...HOME.
OH.
LENA COMES INTO HER SHARED BEDROOM AT ONE THIRTY THE NEXT AFTERNOON TO FIND HER BROTHER IN HIS BED NAKED WITH THAT SINEWY BLACK-HAIRED GIRL WHO USED TO COME OVER.
BOTH ARE DEAD TO THE WORLD.
SHE KNOWS SHE SHOULD WALK OUT AND GIVE THEM THEIR PRIVACY, BUT SHE CAN'T LOOK AWAY.
SHE ASSUMED HE WAS A VIRGIN AND THAT THIS WAS HIS FIRST TIME.
-I JUST DON'T GET IT... WHY THIS GIRL?
EVERYTHING ABOUT HER...
THE WAY SHE TALKS, THE WAY SHE DRESSES, THE WAY SHE ACTS, ASH...
...IT'S SO UGLY.

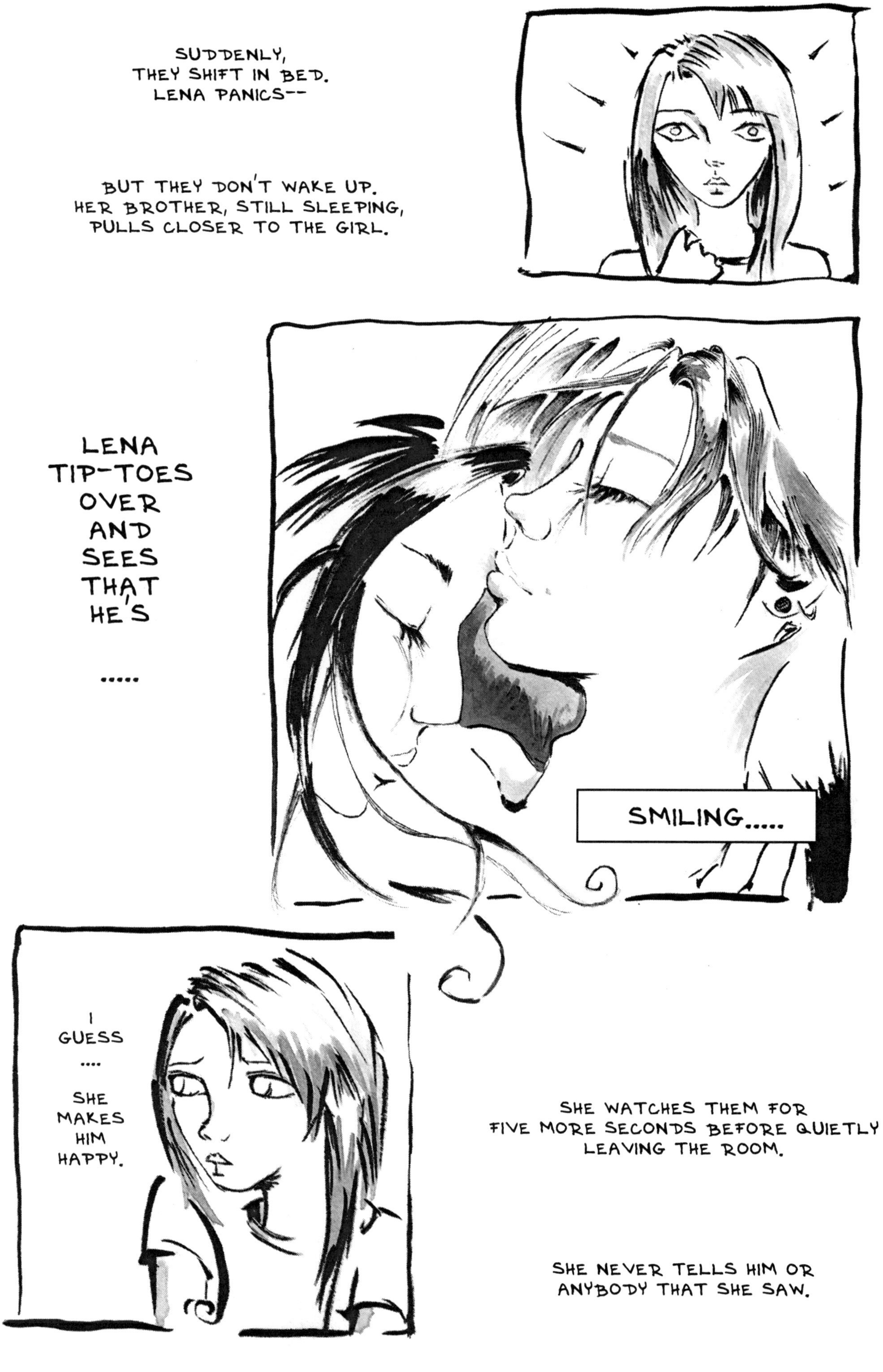
SUDDENLY, THEY SHIFT IN BED. LENA PANICS--
BUT THEY DON'T WAKE UP. HER BROTHER, STILL SLEEPING, PULLS CLOSER TO THE GIRL.
LENA TIP-TOES OVER AND SEES THAT HE'S
.....
SMILING.....
I GUESS .... SHE MAKES HIM HAPPY.
SHE WATCHES THEM FOR FIVE MORE SECONDS BEFORE QUIETLY LEAVING THE ROOM.
SHE NEVER TELLS HIM OR ANYBODY THAT SHE SAW.

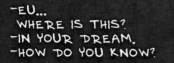

-EU...
WHERE IS THIS?
-IN YOUR DREAM.
-HOW DO YOU KNOW?

-BECAUSE EVERYTHING
FEELS real.

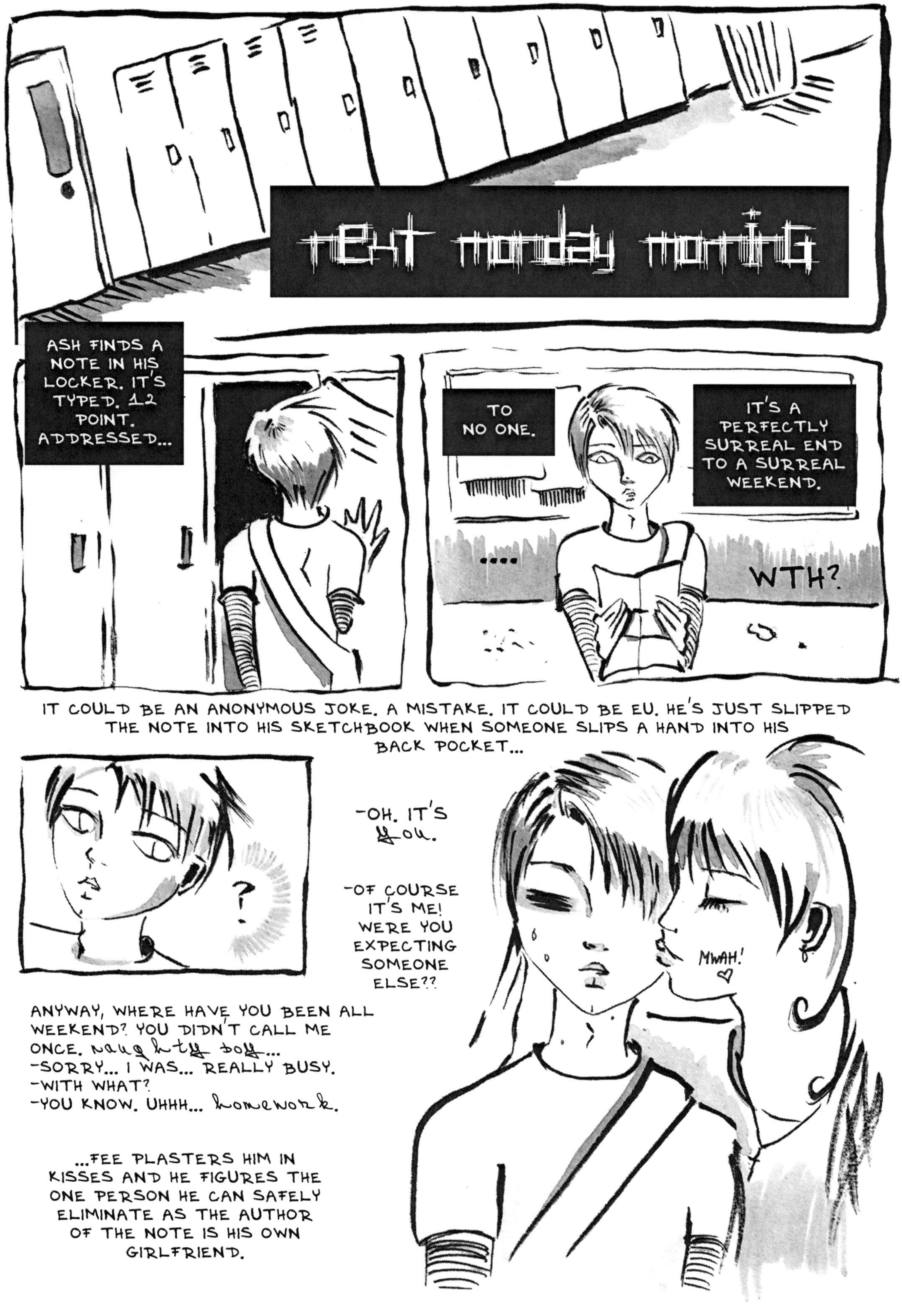

next monday morning
ASH FINDS A NOTE IN HIS LOCKER. IT'S TYPED. 12 POINT. ADDRESSED...
TO NO ONE.
IT'S A PERFECTLY SURREAL END TO A SURREAL WEEKEND.
....
WTH?
IT COULD BE AN ANONYMOUS JOKE. A MISTAKE. IT COULD BE EU. HE'S JUST SLIPPED THE NOTE INTO HIS SKETCHBOOK WHEN SOMEONE SLIPS A HAND INTO HIS BACK POCKET...
?
-OH. IT'S you.
-OF COURSE IT'S ME! WERE YOU EXPECTING SOMEONE ELSE??
MWAH!
ANYWAY, WHERE HAVE YOU BEEN ALL WEEKEND? YOU DIDN'T CALL ME ONCE. naughty boy...
-SORRY... I WAS... REALLY BUSY.
-WITH WHAT?
-YOU KNOW. UHHH... homework.
...FEE PLASTERS HIM IN KISSES AND HE FIGURES THE ONE PERSON HE CAN SAFELY ELIMINATE AS THE AUTHOR OF THE NOTE IS HIS OWN GIRLFRIEND.

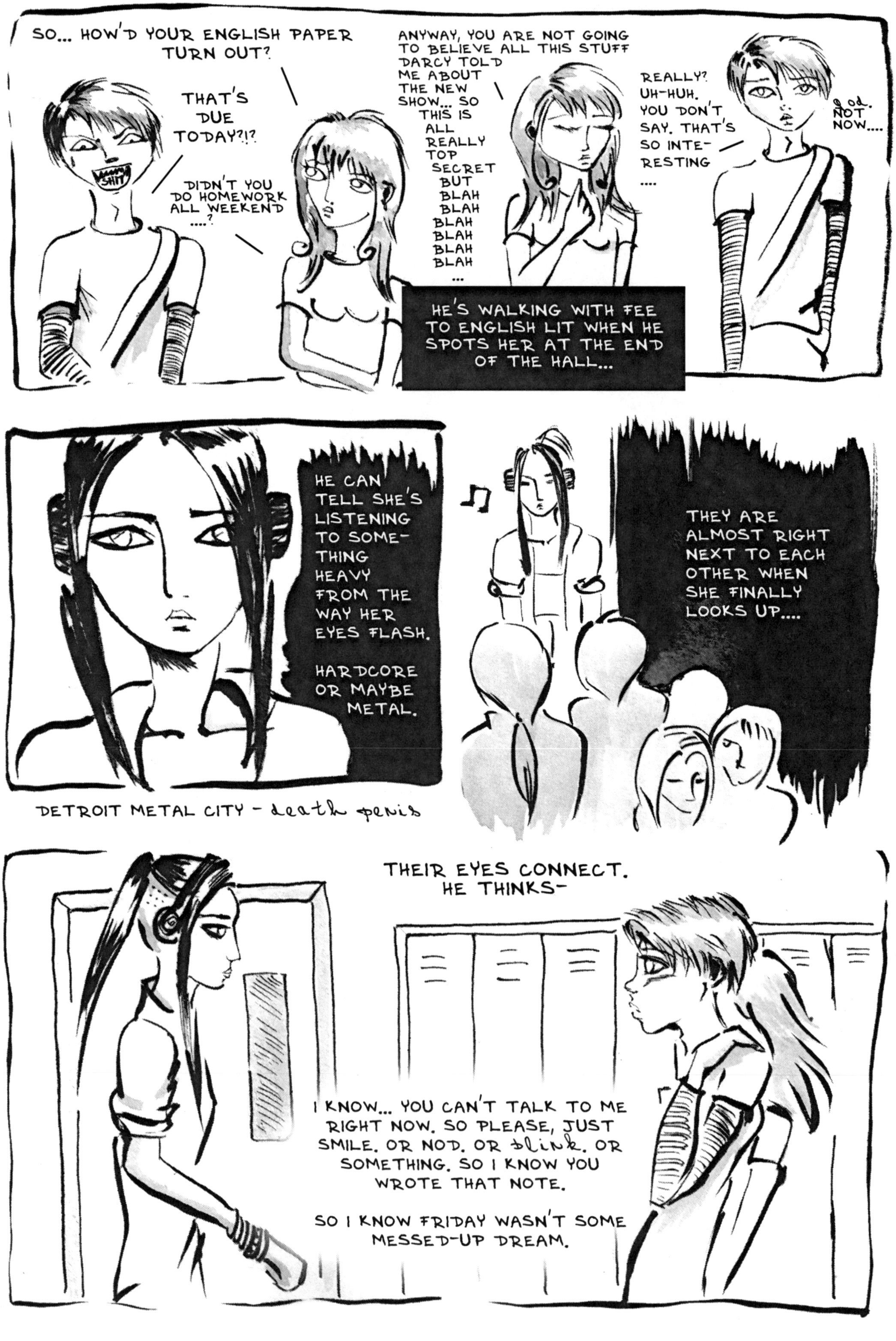

SO... HOW'D YOUR ENGLISH PAPER TURN OUT?
THAT'S DUE TODAY?!?
SHIT
DIDN'T YOU DO HOMEWORK ALL WEEKEND ....?
ANYWAY, YOU ARE NOT GOING TO BELIEVE ALL THIS STUFF DARCY TOLD ME ABOUT THE NEW SHOW... SO THIS IS ALL REALLY TOP SECRET BUT BLAH BLAH BLAH BLAH BLAH BLAH ...
REALLY? UH-HUH. YOU DON'T SAY. THAT'S SO INTERESTING ....
god. NOT NOW....
HE'S WALKING WITH FEE TO ENGLISH LIT WHEN HE SPOTS HER AT THE END OF THE HALL...
HE CAN TELL SHE'S LISTENING TO SOMETHING HEAVY FROM THE WAY HER EYES FLASH.
HARDCORE OR MAYBE METAL.
DETROIT METAL CITY - death penis
THEY ARE ALMOST RIGHT NEXT TO EACH OTHER WHEN SHE FINALLY LOOKS UP....
THEIR EYES CONNECT. HE THINKS-
I KNOW... YOU CAN'T TALK TO ME RIGHT NOW. SO PLEASE, JUST SMILE. OR NOD. OR blink. OR SOMETHING. SO I KNOW YOU WROTE THAT NOTE.
SO I KNOW FRIDAY WASN'T SOME MESSED-UP DREAM.

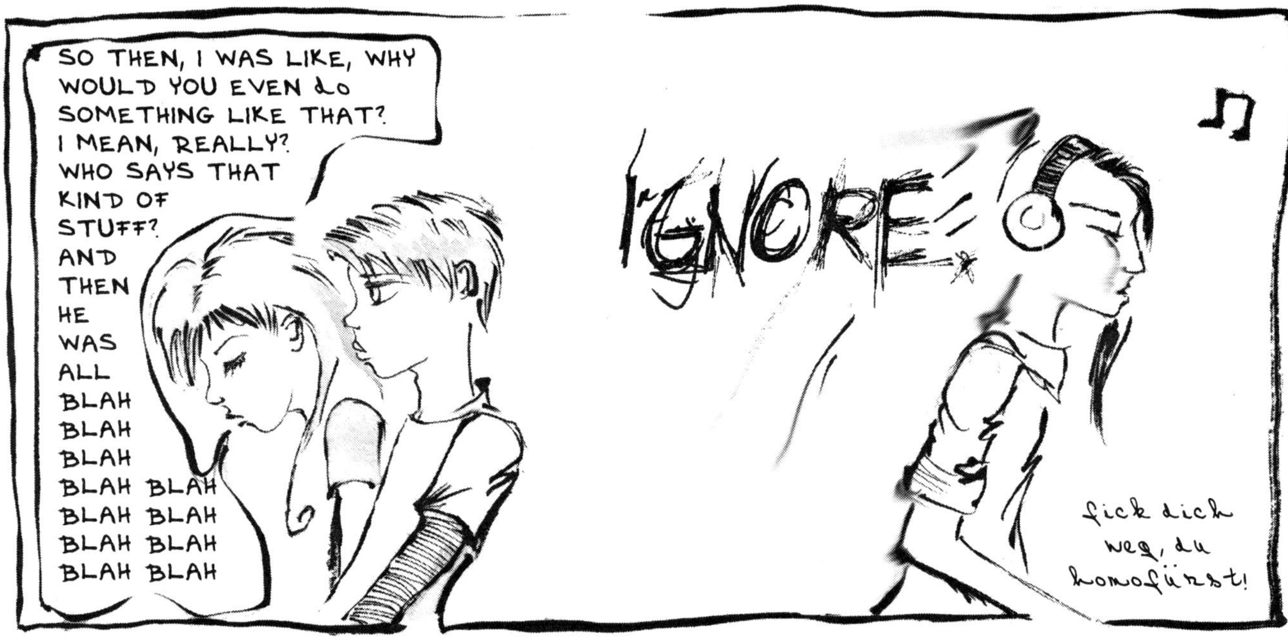
SO THEN, I WAS LIKE, WHY WOULD YOU EVEN do SOMETHING LIKE THAT? I MEAN, REALLY? WHO SAYS THAT KIND OF STUFF? AND THEN HE WAS ALL BLAH BLAH BLAH BLAH BLAH BLAH BLAH BLAH BLAH BLAH BLAH
IGNORE
fick dich weg, du homofürst!

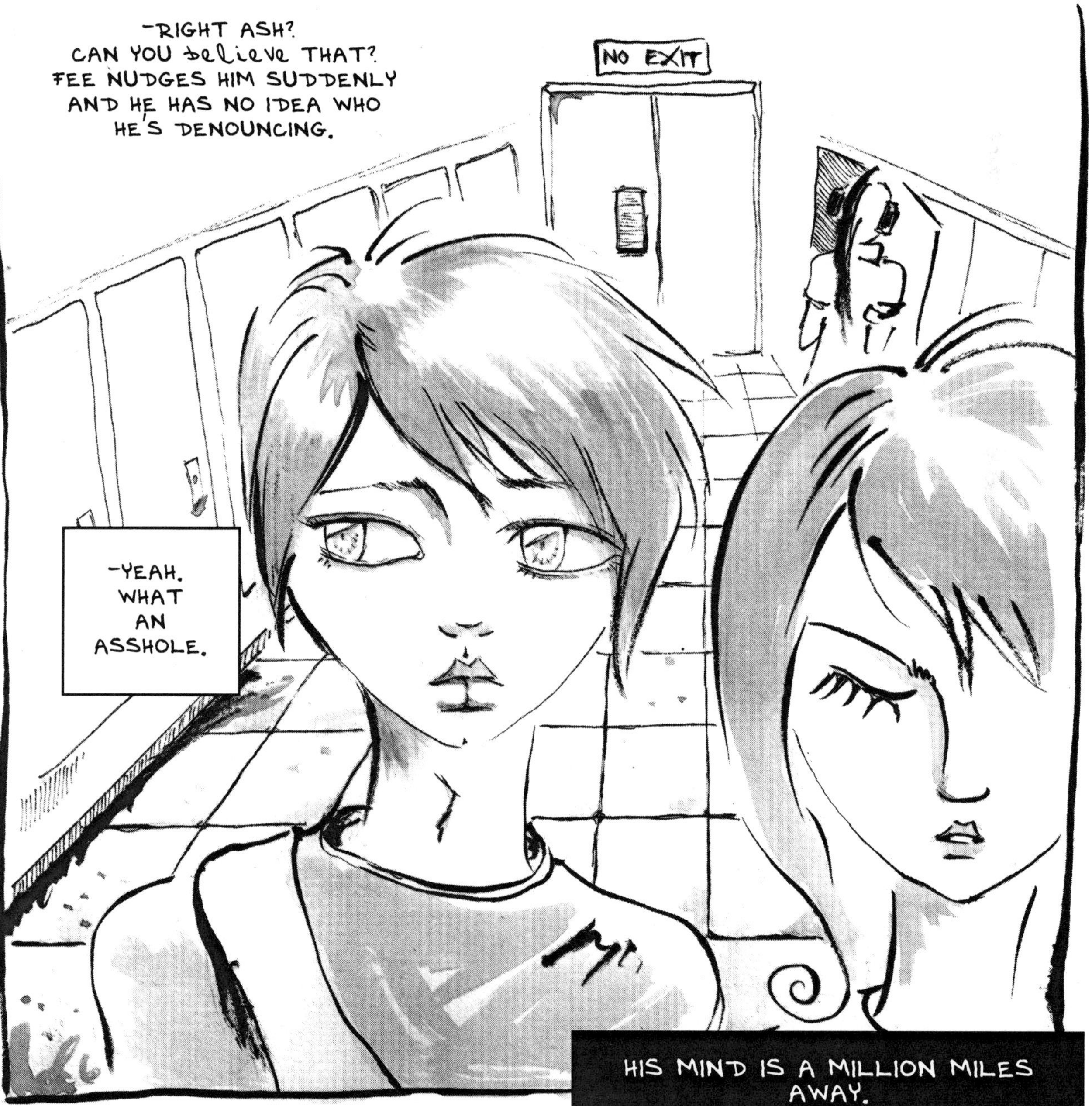
-RIGHT ASH? CAN YOU believe THAT? FEE NUDGES HIM SUDDENLY AND HE HAS NO IDEA WHO HE'S DENOUNCING.
NO EXIT
-YEAH. WHAT AN ASSHOLE.
HIS MIND IS A MILLION MILES AWAY.

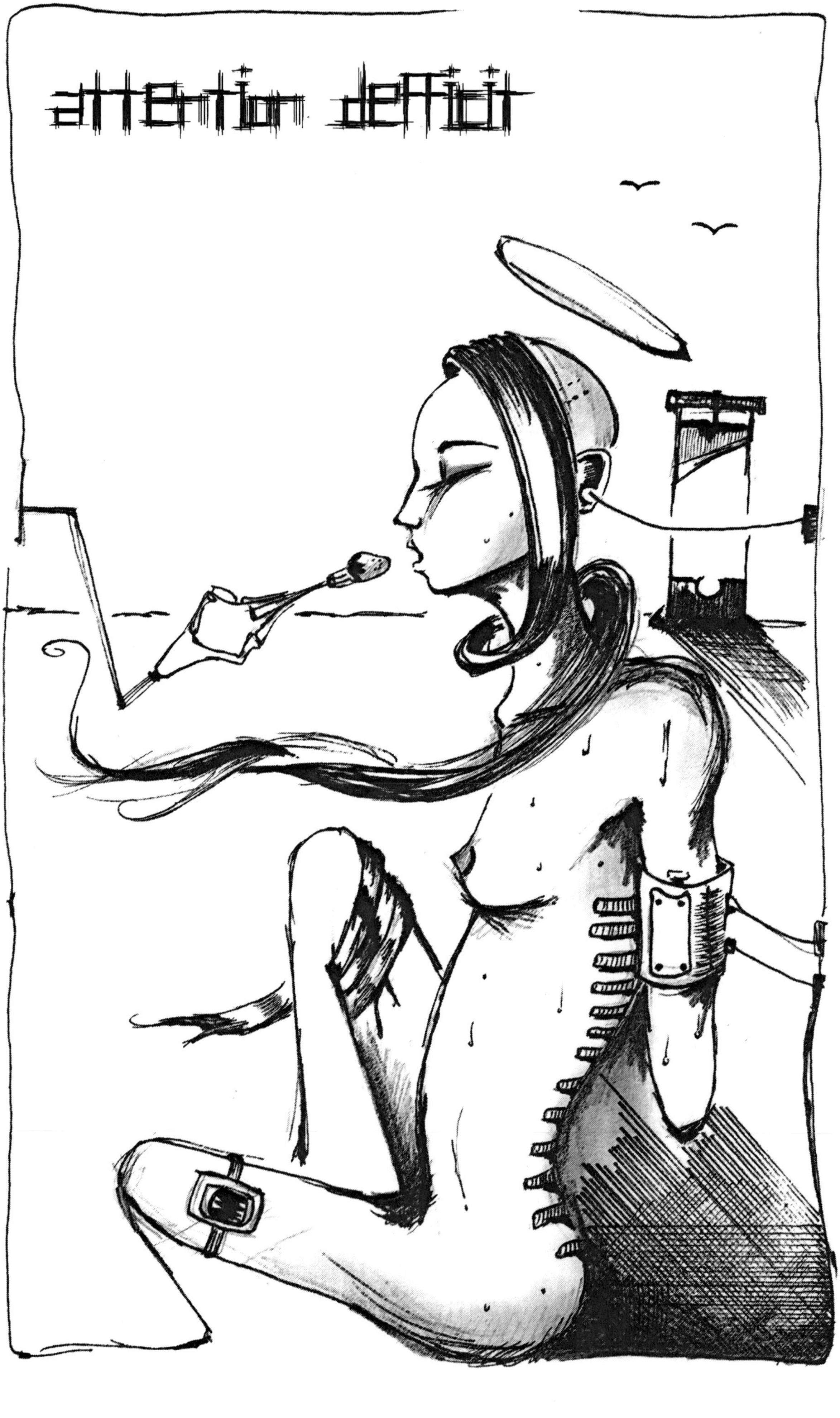
attention defficit

AFTER THAT, ASH DELIBERATES FOR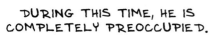

3 days

DURING THIS TIME, HE IS COMPLETELY PREOCCUPIED.

HE READS THE NOTE OVER AND OVER, UNTIL HE HAS IT MEMORIZED, UNTIL IT GETS DOG-EARED, SO HE PASTES IT INTO THE FRONT OF HIS SKETCHBOOK, DRAWING WHILE HE THINKS ABOUT IT.

LIKE A SECRET.

DAY ONE

dinner!!!

—COMING, LENA.....

DAY TWO

DAY THREE

MR. BRADY'S PRE-CALCULUS CLASS

—DOES EVERYONE UNDERSTAND WHY THAT'S FALSE? OK, I'M GETTING SOME BLANK STARES AND SOME OF YOU ARE OBVIOUSLY IN SLEEP MODE.

ASHER. YOU'RE USUALLY LOST IN THIS CLASS. DO YOU UNDERSTAND WHY THAT STATEMENT IS FALSE?

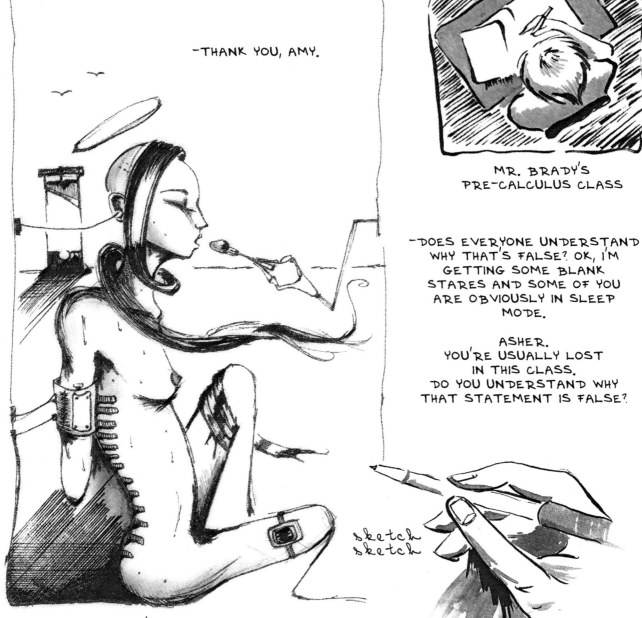

—THANK YOU, AMY.

sketch sketch

ASHER. I'M TALKING TO YOU. HELLO....?

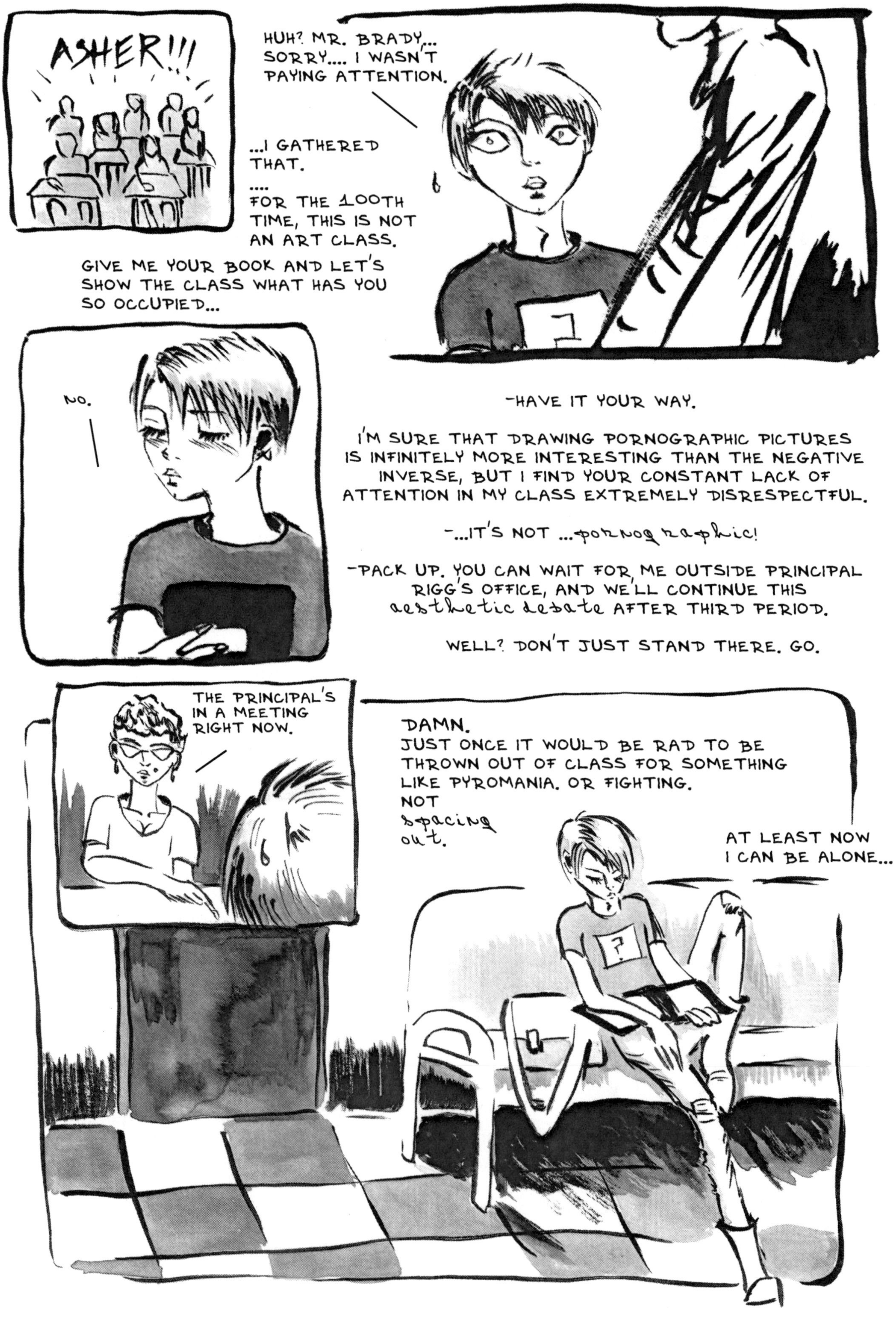
ASHER!!!
HUH? MR. BRADY... SORRY.... I WASN'T PAYING ATTENTION.
...I GATHERED THAT.
....
FOR THE 100TH TIME, THIS IS NOT AN ART CLASS.
GIVE ME YOUR BOOK AND LET'S SHOW THE CLASS WHAT HAS YOU SO OCCUPIED...
NO.
-HAVE IT YOUR WAY.
I'M SURE THAT DRAWING PORNOGRAPHIC PICTURES IS INFINITELY MORE INTERESTING THAN THE NEGATIVE INVERSE, BUT I FIND YOUR CONSTANT LACK OF ATTENTION IN MY CLASS EXTREMELY DISRESPECTFUL.
-...IT'S NOT ...pornographic!
-PACK UP. YOU CAN WAIT FOR ME OUTSIDE PRINCIPAL RIGG'S OFFICE, AND WE'LL CONTINUE THIS aesthetic debate AFTER THIRD PERIOD.
WELL? DON'T JUST STAND THERE. GO.
THE PRINCIPAL'S IN A MEETING RIGHT NOW.
DAMN.
JUST ONCE IT WOULD BE RAD TO BE THROWN OUT OF CLASS FOR SOMETHING LIKE PYROMANIA. OR FIGHTING.
NOT spacing out.
AT LEAST NOW I CAN BE ALONE...

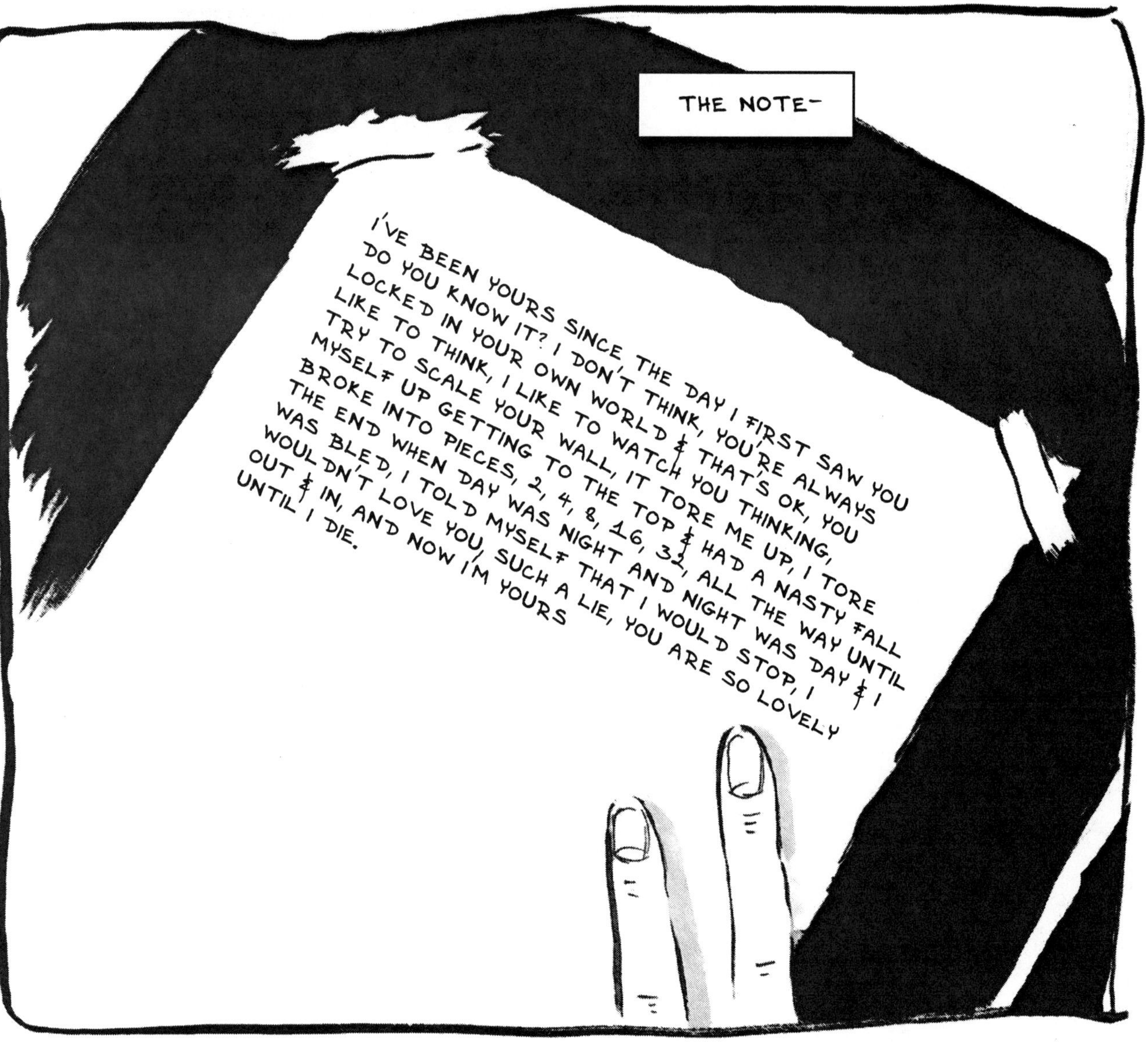
THE NOTE-
I'VE BEEN YOURS SINCE THE DAY I FIRST SAW YOU
DO YOU KNOW IT? I DON'T THINK, YOU'RE ALWAYS
LOCKED IN YOUR OWN WORLD & THAT'S OK, YOU
LIKE TO THINK, I LIKE TO WATCH YOU THINKING,
TRY TO SCALE YOUR WALL, IT TORE ME UP, I TORE
MYSELF UP GETTING TO THE TOP & HAD A NASTY FALL
BROKE INTO PIECES, 2, 4, 8, 16, 32, ALL THE WAY UNTIL
THE END WHEN DAY WAS NIGHT AND NIGHT WAS DAY & I
WAS BLED, I TOLD MYSELF THAT I WOULD STOP, I
WOULDN'T LOVE YOU, SUCH A LIE, YOU ARE SO LOVELY
OUT & IN, AND NOW I'M YOURS
UNTIL I DIE.

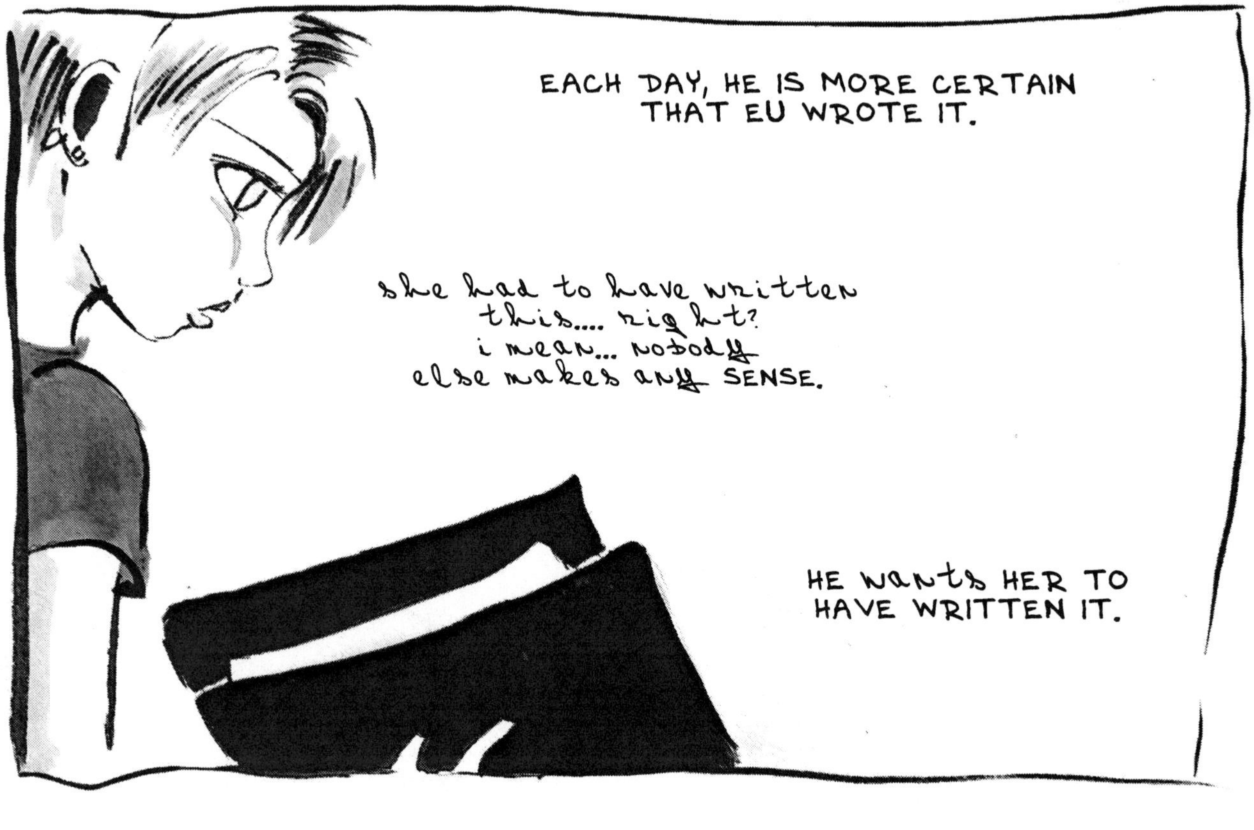
EACH DAY, HE IS MORE CERTAIN THAT EU WROTE IT.
she had to have written this.... right? i mean... nobody else makes any SENSE.
HE wants HER TO HAVE WRITTEN IT.

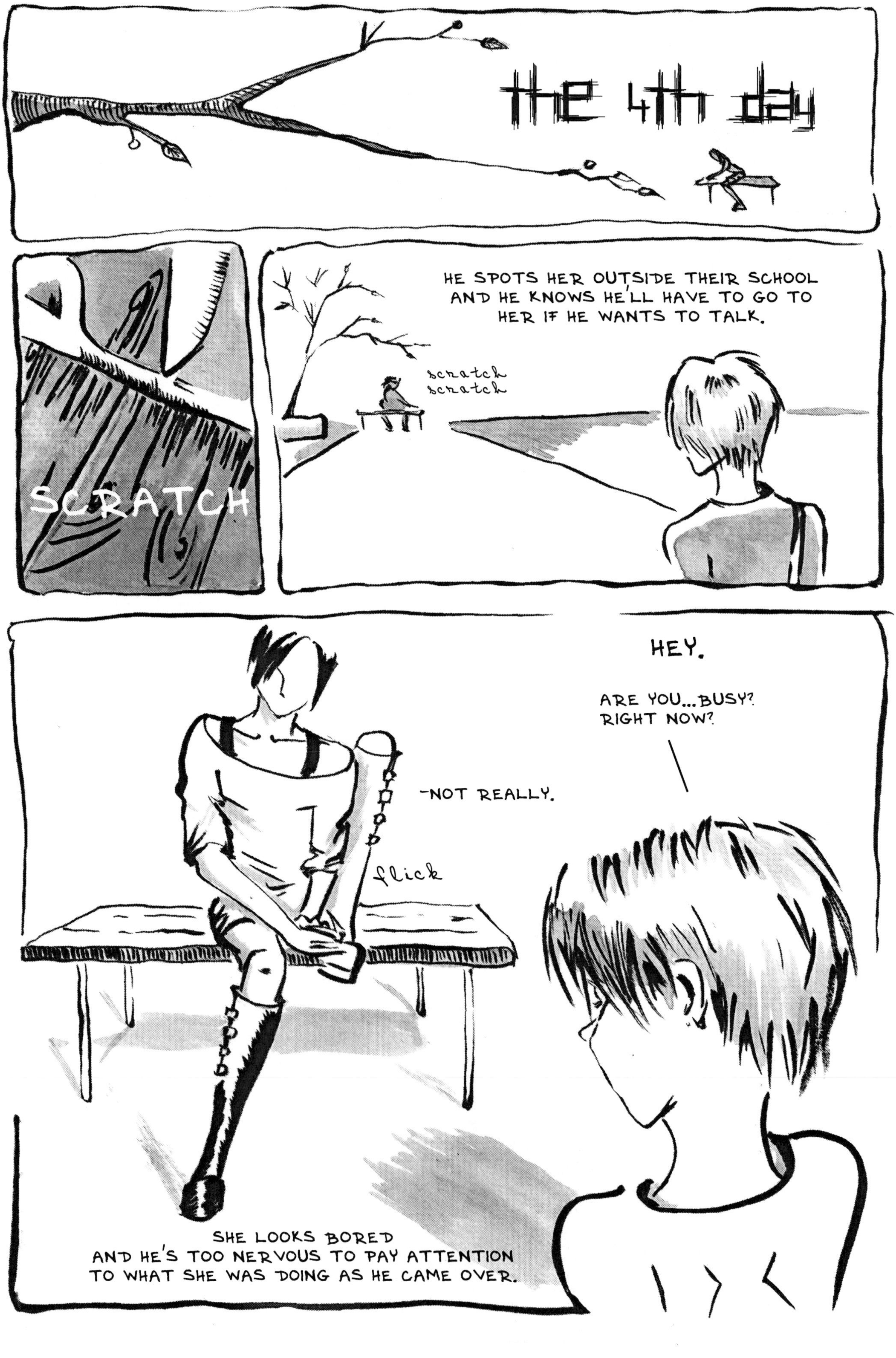

the 4th day
SCRATCH
HE SPOTS HER OUTSIDE THEIR SCHOOL AND HE KNOWS HE'LL HAVE TO GO TO HER IF HE WANTS TO TALK.
scratch scratch
HEY.
ARE YOU...BUSY? RIGHT NOW?
-NOT REALLY.
flick
SHE LOOKS BORED AND HE'S TOO NERVOUS TO PAY ATTENTION TO WHAT SHE WAS DOING AS HE CAME OVER.

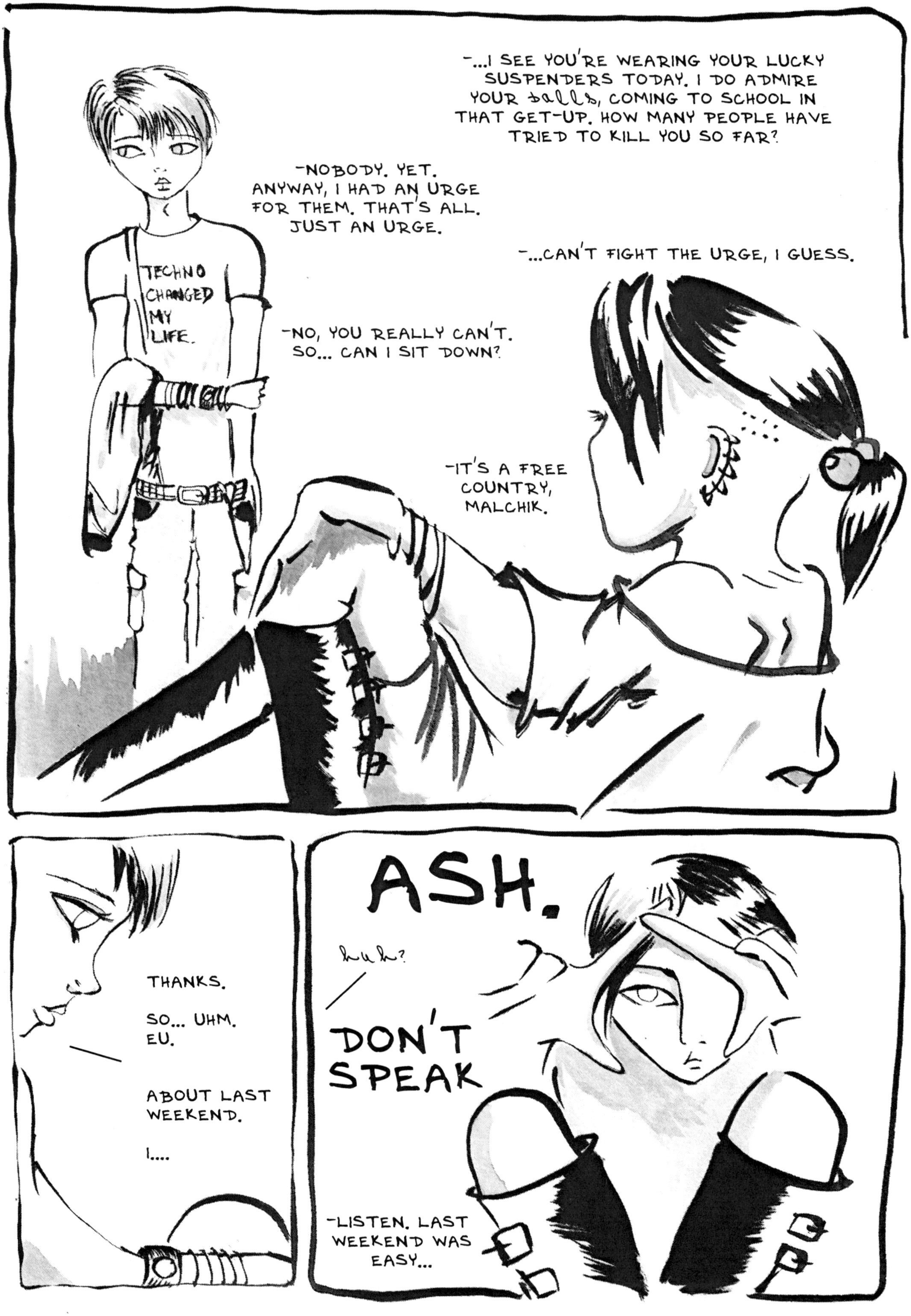
-...I SEE YOU'RE WEARING YOUR LUCKY SUSPENDERS TODAY. I DO ADMIRE YOUR balls, COMING TO SCHOOL IN THAT GET-UP. HOW MANY PEOPLE HAVE TRIED TO KILL YOU SO FAR?
-NOBODY. YET. ANYWAY, I HAD AN URGE FOR THEM. THAT'S ALL. JUST AN URGE.
-...CAN'T FIGHT THE URGE, I GUESS.
TECHNO CHANGED MY LIFE.
-NO, YOU REALLY CAN'T. SO... CAN I SIT DOWN?
-IT'S A FREE COUNTRY, MALCHIK.
THANKS.
SO... UHM. EU.
ABOUT LAST WEEKEND.
I....
ASH.
huh?
DON'T SPEAK
-LISTEN. LAST WEEKEND WAS EASY...

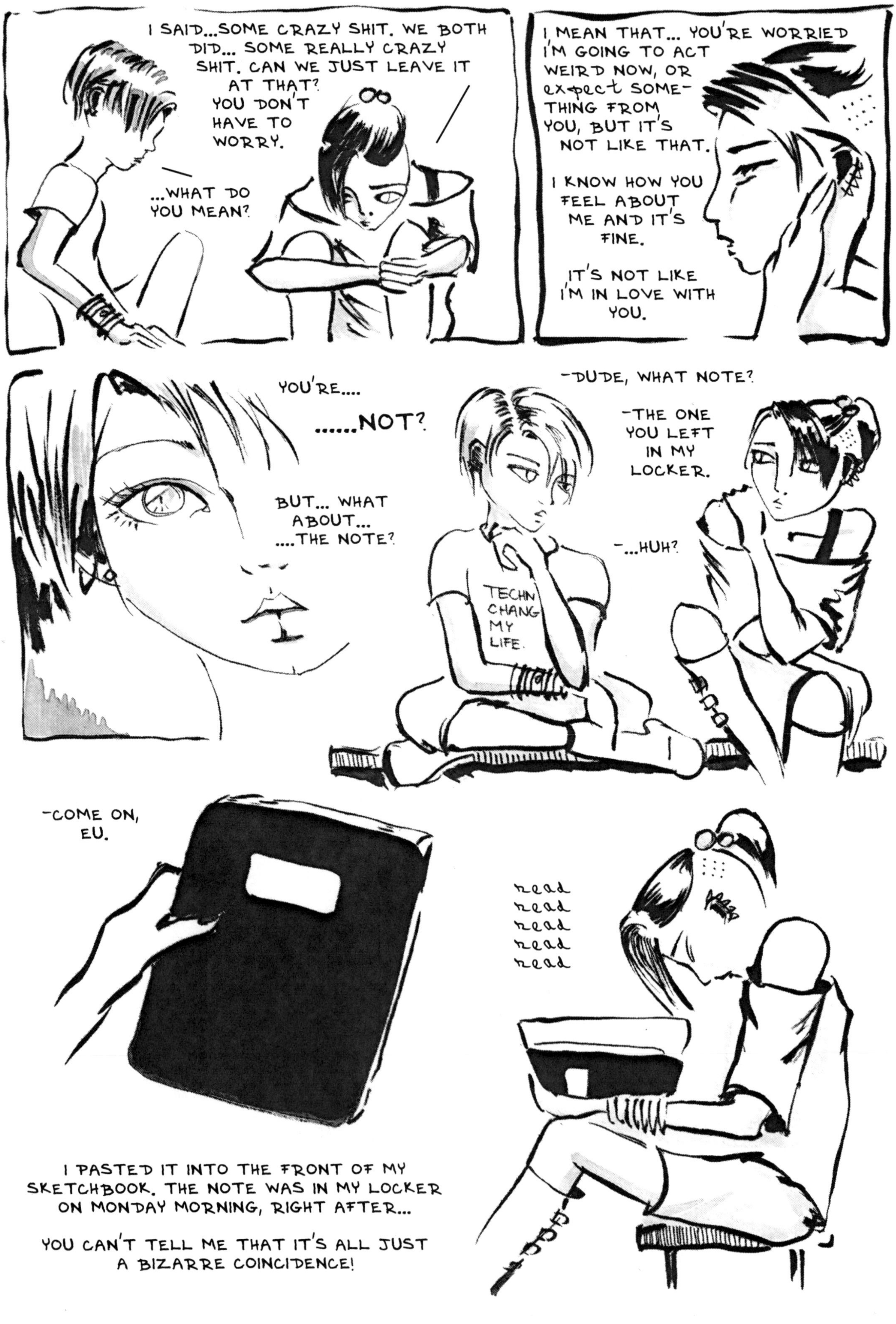

I SAID...SOME CRAZY SHIT. WE BOTH DID... SOME REALLY CRAZY SHIT. CAN WE JUST LEAVE IT AT THAT? YOU DON'T HAVE TO WORRY.
...WHAT DO YOU MEAN?
I MEAN THAT... YOU'RE WORRIED I'M GOING TO ACT WEIRD NOW, OR expect SOMETHING FROM YOU, BUT IT'S NOT LIKE THAT.
I KNOW HOW YOU FEEL ABOUT ME AND IT'S FINE.
IT'S NOT LIKE I'M IN LOVE WITH YOU.
YOU'RE....
......NOT?
BUT... WHAT ABOUT... ....THE NOTE?
-DUDE, WHAT NOTE?
-THE ONE YOU LEFT IN MY LOCKER.
-...HUH?
TECHN CHANG MY LIFE.
-COME ON, EU.
read
read
read
read
read
I PASTED IT INTO THE FRONT OF MY SKETCHBOOK. THE NOTE WAS IN MY LOCKER ON MONDAY MORNING, RIGHT AFTER...
YOU CAN'T TELL ME THAT IT'S ALL JUST A BIZARRE COINCIDENCE!

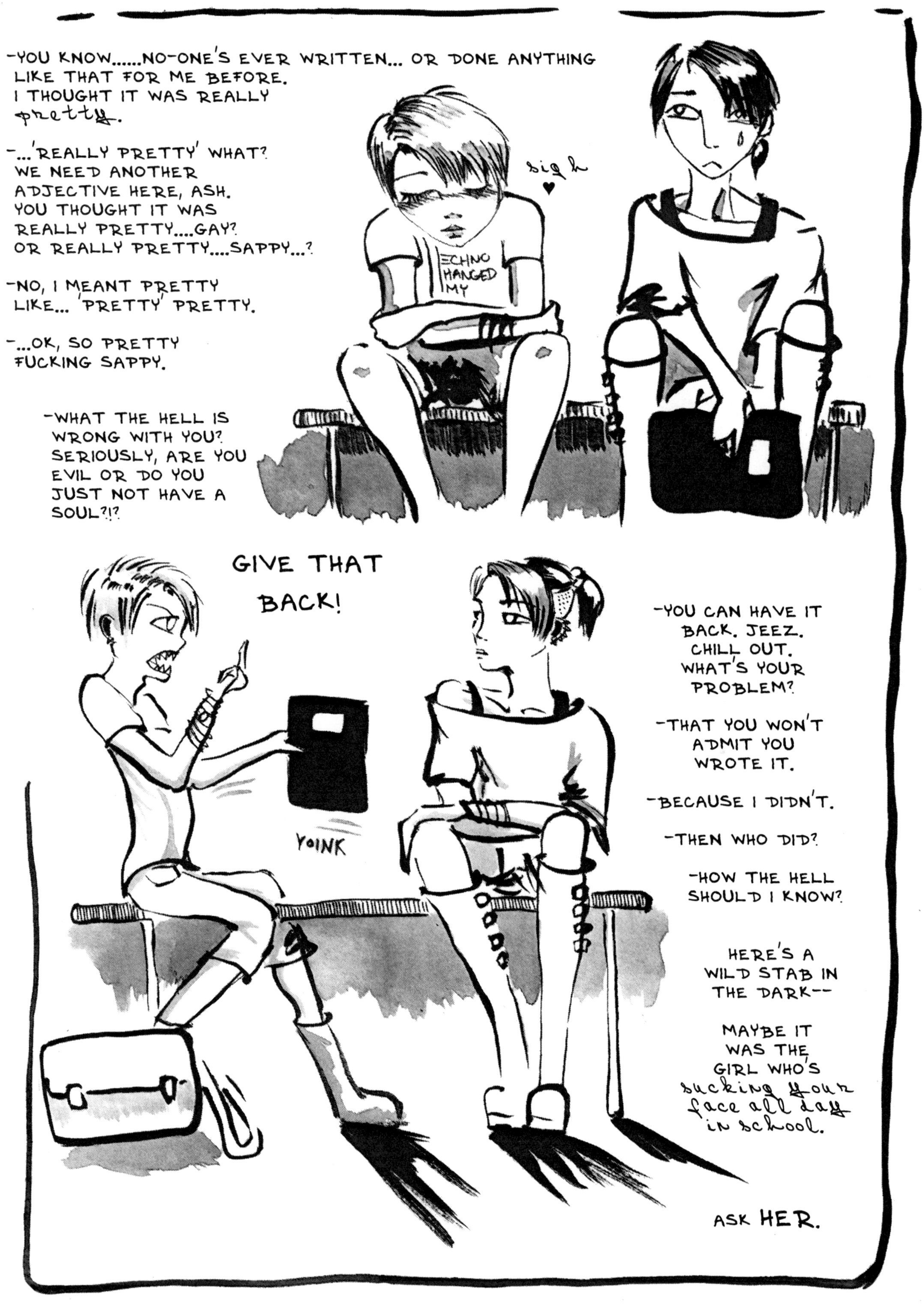
-YOU KNOW......NO-ONE'S EVER WRITTEN... OR DONE ANYTHING LIKE THAT FOR ME BEFORE. I THOUGHT IT WAS REALLY pretty.
-...'REALLY PRETTY' WHAT? WE NEED ANOTHER ADJECTIVE HERE, ASH. YOU THOUGHT IT WAS REALLY PRETTY....GAY? OR REALLY PRETTY....SAPPY...?
-NO, I MEANT PRETTY LIKE... 'PRETTY' PRETTY.
-...OK, SO PRETTY FUCKING SAPPY.
sigh
ECHNO HANGED MY
-WHAT THE HELL IS WRONG WITH YOU? SERIOUSLY, ARE YOU EVIL OR DO YOU JUST NOT HAVE A SOUL?!?
GIVE THAT BACK!
YOINK
-YOU CAN HAVE IT BACK. JEEZ. CHILL OUT. WHAT'S YOUR PROBLEM?
-THAT YOU WON'T ADMIT YOU WROTE IT.
-BECAUSE I DIDN'T.
-THEN WHO DID?
-HOW THE HELL SHOULD I KNOW?
HERE'S A WILD STAB IN THE DARK--
MAYBE IT WAS THE GIRL WHO'S sucking your face all day in school.
ASK HER.

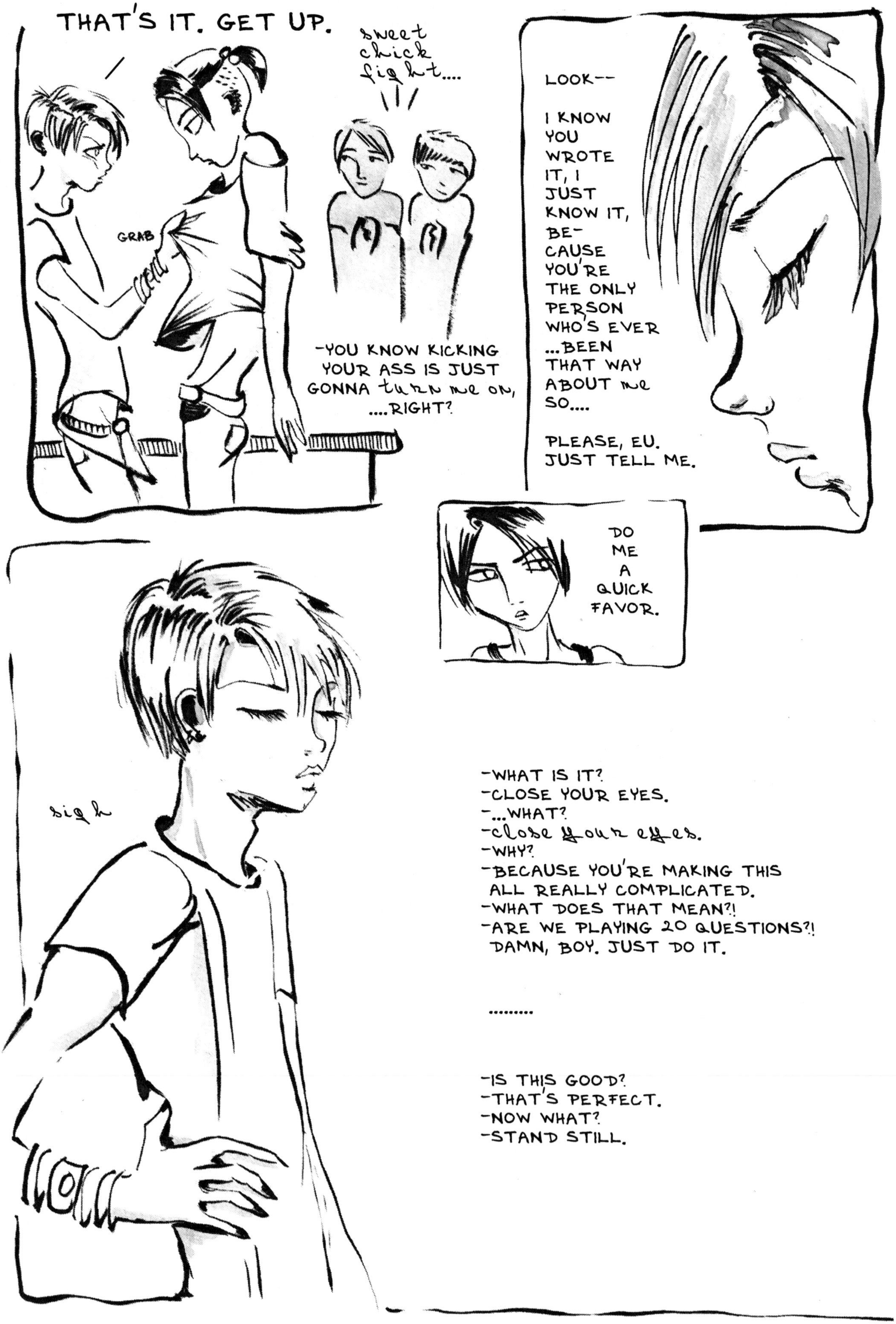
THAT'S IT. GET UP.
GRAB
sweet chick fight....
-YOU KNOW KICKING YOUR ASS IS JUST GONNA turn me on, ...RIGHT?
LOOK--
I KNOW YOU WROTE IT, I JUST KNOW IT, BE-CAUSE YOU'RE THE ONLY PERSON WHO'S EVER ...BEEN THAT WAY ABOUT me SO....
PLEASE, EU. JUST TELL ME.
DO ME A QUICK FAVOR.
sigh
-WHAT IS IT?
-CLOSE YOUR EYES.
-...WHAT?
-close your eyes.
-WHY?
-BECAUSE YOU'RE MAKING THIS ALL REALLY COMPLICATED.
-WHAT DOES THAT MEAN?!
-ARE WE PLAYING 20 QUESTIONS?! DAMN, BOY. JUST DO IT.
....
-IS THIS GOOD?
-THAT'S PERFECT.
-NOW WHAT?
-STAND STILL.

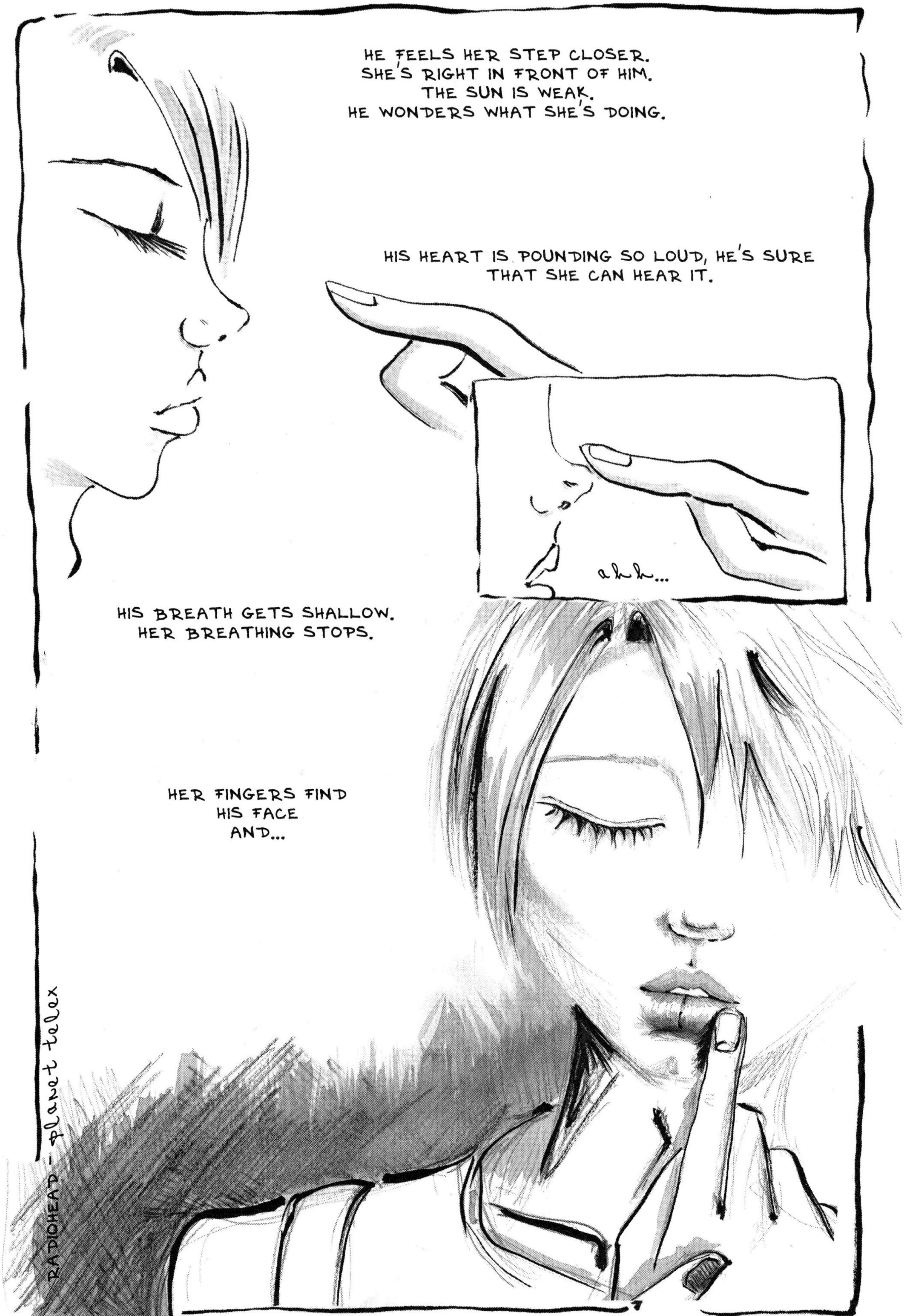
HE FEELS HER STEP CLOSER. SHE'S RIGHT IN FRONT OF HIM. THE SUN IS WEAK. HE WONDERS WHAT SHE'S DOING.
HIS HEART IS POUNDING SO LOUD, HE'S SURE THAT SHE CAN HEAR IT.
ahh...
HIS BREATH GETS SHALLOW. HER BREATHING STOPS.
HER FINGERS FIND HIS FACE AND...
RADIOHEAD - planet telex

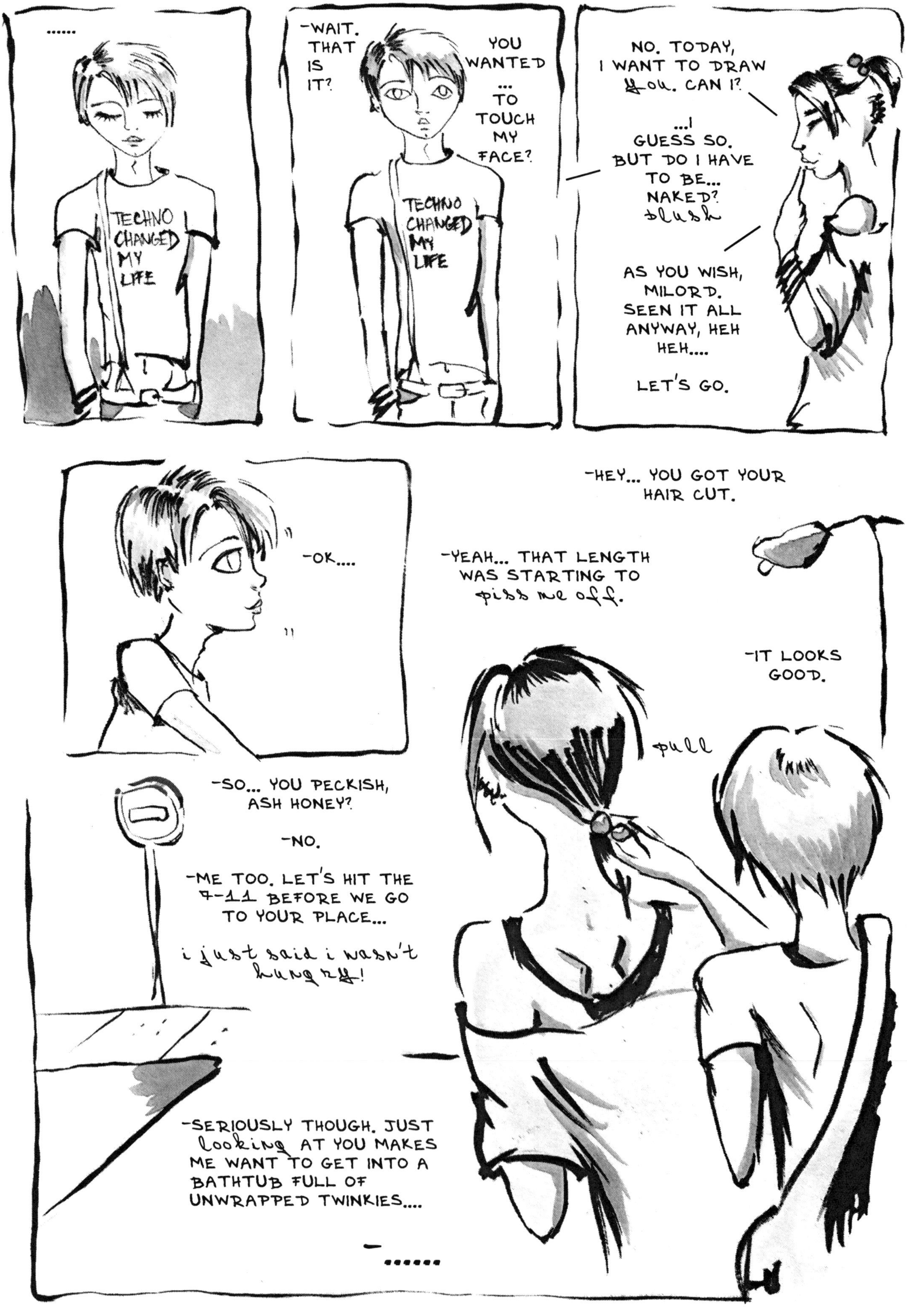
......
-WAIT. THAT IS IT?
YOU WANTED ... TO TOUCH MY FACE?
TECHNO CHANGED MY LIFE
NO. TODAY, I WANT TO DRAW you. CAN I?
...I GUESS SO. BUT DO I HAVE TO BE... NAKED? blush
AS YOU WISH, MILORD. SEEN IT ALL ANYWAY, HEH HEH....
LET'S GO.
-OK....
-HEY... YOU GOT YOUR HAIR CUT.
-YEAH... THAT LENGTH WAS STARTING TO piss me off.
-IT LOOKS GOOD.
pull
-SO... YOU PECKISH, ASH HONEY?
-NO.
-ME TOO. LET'S HIT THE 7-11 BEFORE WE GO TO YOUR PLACE...
i just said i wasn't hungry!
-SERIOUSLY THOUGH. JUST looking AT YOU MAKES ME WANT TO GET INTO A BATHTUB FULL OF UNWRAPPED TWINKIES....
-......

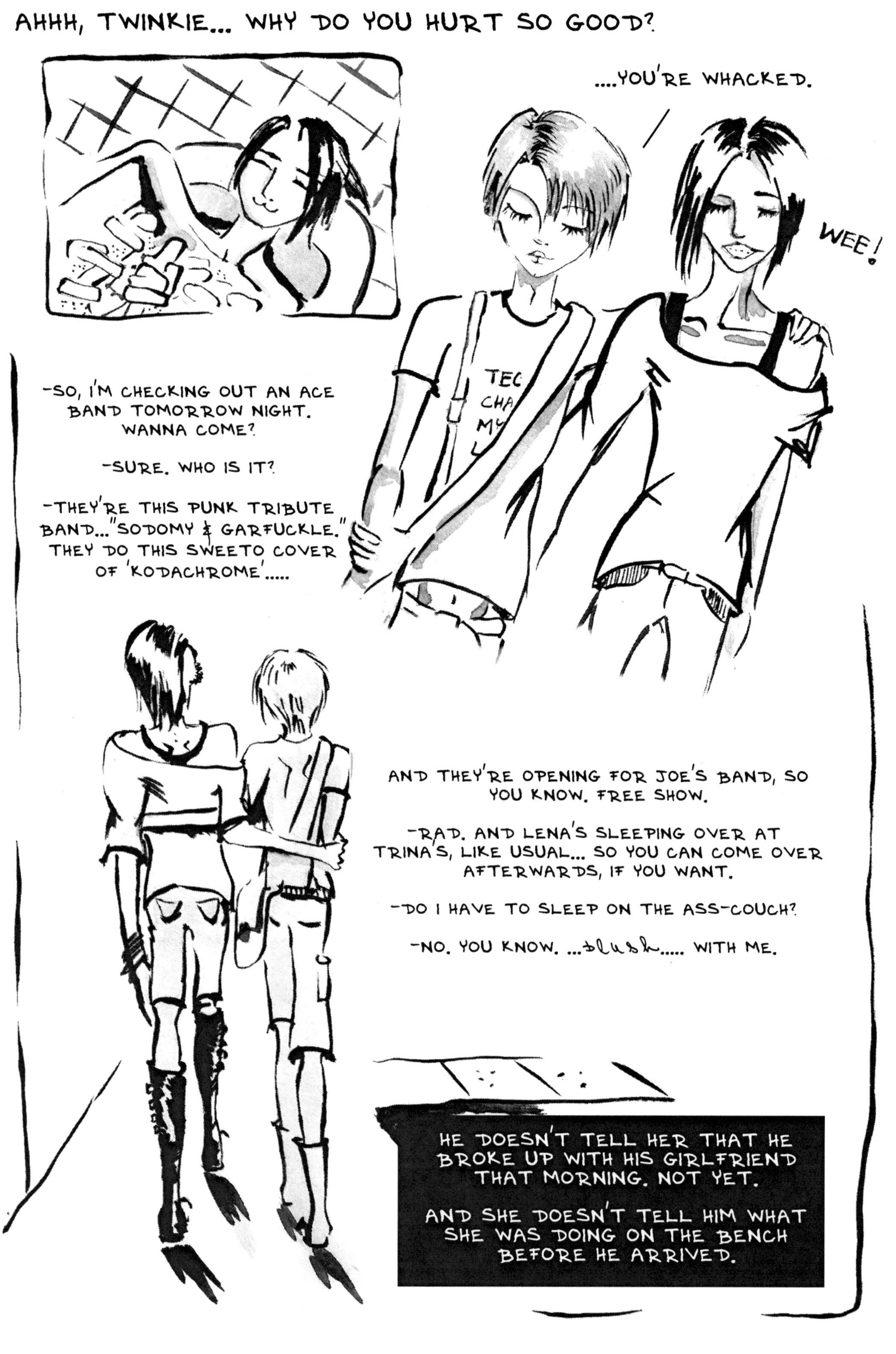
AHHH, TWINKIE... WHY DO YOU HURT SO GOOD?
....YOU'RE WHACKED.
WEE!
-SO, I'M CHECKING OUT AN ACE BAND TOMORROW NIGHT. WANNA COME?
-SURE. WHO IS IT?
-THEY'RE THIS PUNK TRIBUTE BAND..."SODOMY & GARFUCKLE." THEY DO THIS SWEETO COVER OF 'KODACHROME'.....
AND THEY'RE OPENING FOR JOE'S BAND, SO YOU KNOW. FREE SHOW.
-RAD. AND LENA'S SLEEPING OVER AT TRINA'S, LIKE USUAL... SO YOU CAN COME OVER AFTERWARDS, IF YOU WANT.
-DO I HAVE TO SLEEP ON THE ASS-COUCH?
-NO. YOU KNOW. ...blush..... WITH ME.
HE DOESN'T TELL HER THAT HE BROKE UP WITH HIS GIRLFRIEND THAT MORNING. NOT YET.
AND SHE DOESN'T TELL HIM WHAT SHE WAS DOING ON THE BENCH BEFORE HE ARRIVED.

IT'S EU'S BELIEF THAT WALLS CAN BE PAINTED OVER, BUT IF YOU CARVE YOUR LOVE INTO WOOD, IT CAN NEVER DIE. STILL, IT HAS TO BE KEPT A SECRET.

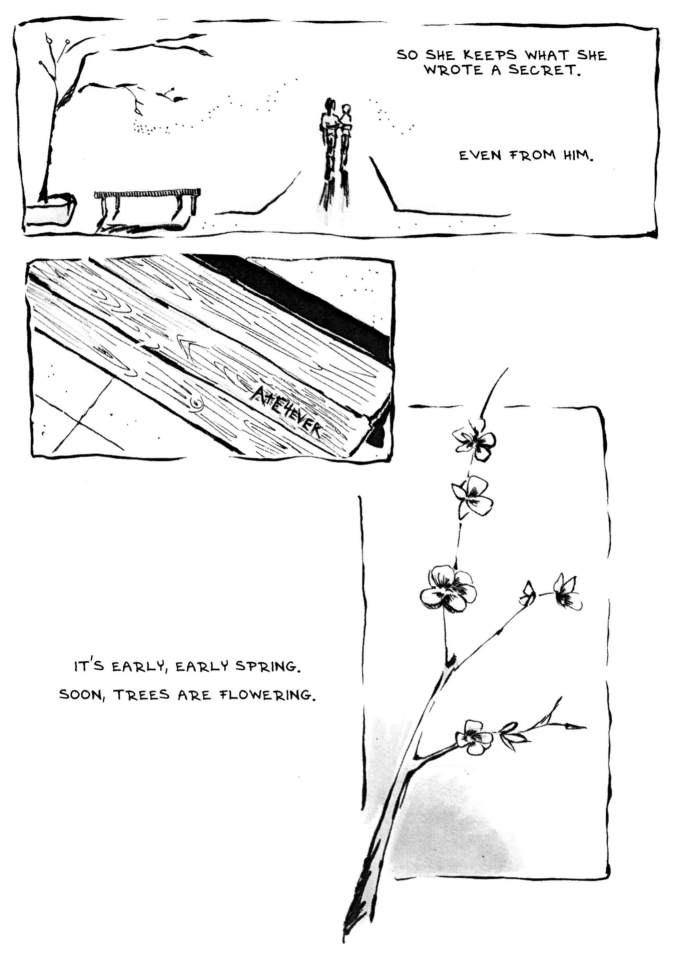

SO SHE KEEPS WHAT SHE WROTE A SECRET.

EVEN FROM HIM.

IT'S EARLY, EARLY SPRING.
SOON, TREES ARE FLOWERING.

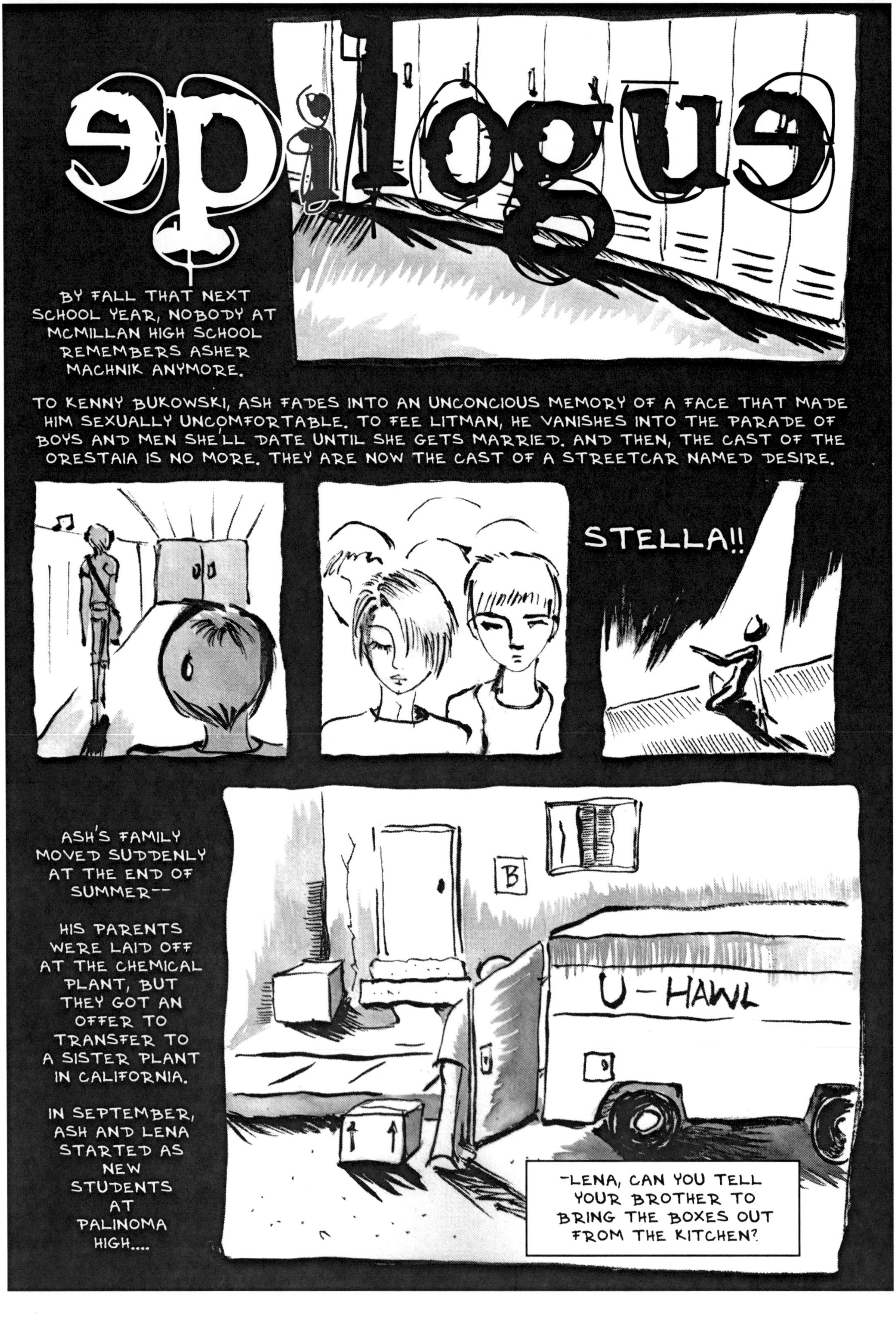
epilogue
BY FALL THAT NEXT SCHOOL YEAR, NOBODY AT MCMILLAN HIGH SCHOOL REMEMBERS ASHER MACHNIK ANYMORE.
TO KENNY BUKOWSKI, ASH FADES INTO AN UNCONCIOUS MEMORY OF A FACE THAT MADE HIM SEXUALLY UNCOMFORTABLE. TO FEE LITMAN, HE VANISHES INTO THE PARADE OF BOYS AND MEN SHE'LL DATE UNTIL SHE GETS MARRIED. AND THEN, THE CAST OF THE ORESTAIA IS NO MORE. THEY ARE NOW THE CAST OF A STREETCAR NAMED DESIRE.
STELLA!!
ASH'S FAMILY MOVED SUDDENLY AT THE END OF SUMMER--
HIS PARENTS WERE LAID OFF AT THE CHEMICAL PLANT, BUT THEY GOT AN OFFER TO TRANSFER TO A SISTER PLANT IN CALIFORNIA.
IN SEPTEMBER, ASH AND LENA STARTED AS NEW STUDENTS AT PALINOMA HIGH....
B
U-HAWL
-LENA, CAN YOU TELL YOUR BROTHER TO BRING THE BOXES OUT FROM THE KITCHEN?

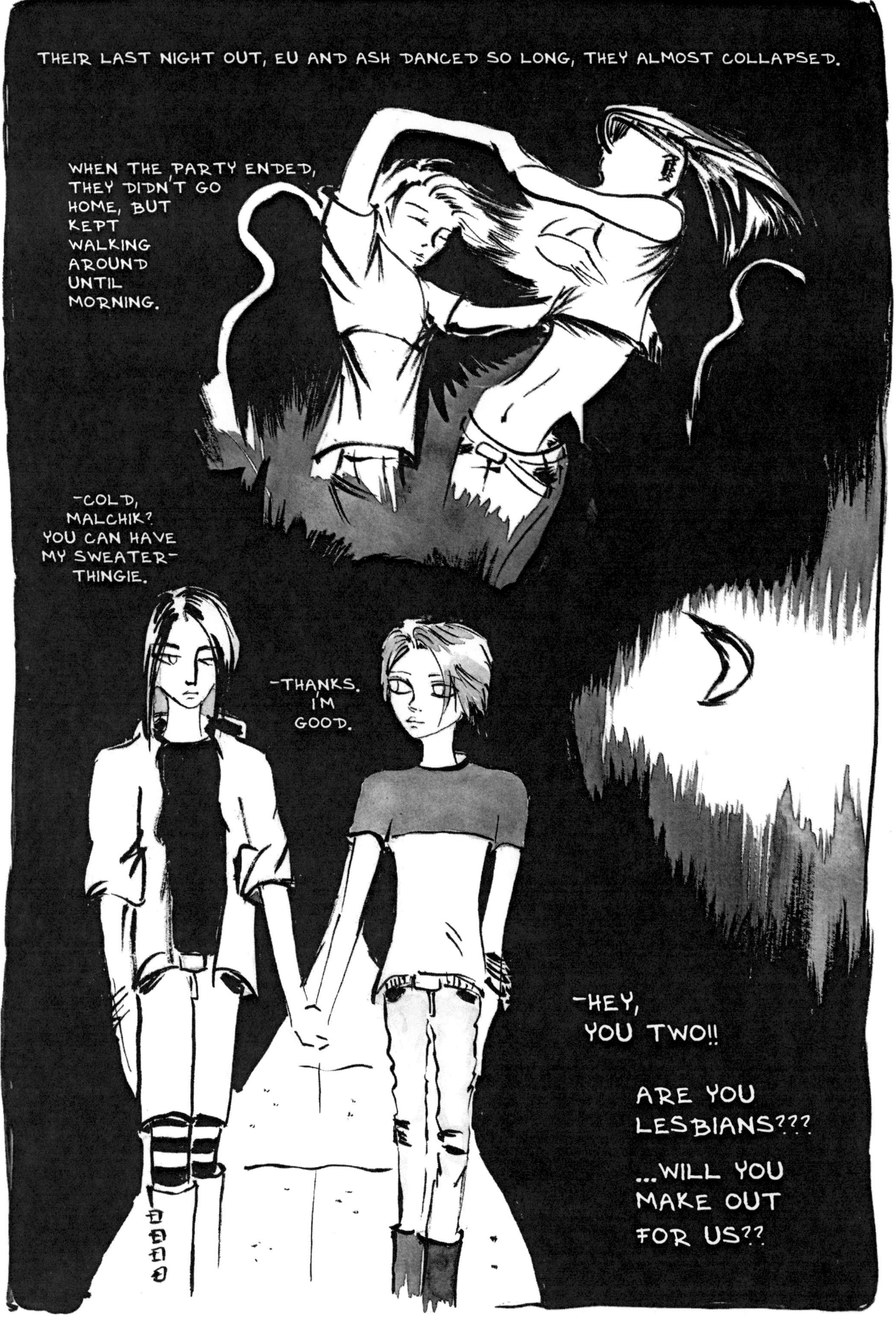

THEIR LAST NIGHT OUT, EU AND ASH DANCED SO LONG, THEY ALMOST COLLAPSED.
WHEN THE PARTY ENDED, THEY DIDN'T GO HOME, BUT KEPT WALKING AROUND UNTIL MORNING.
-COLD, MALCHIK? YOU CAN HAVE MY SWEATER-THINGIE.
-THANKS. I'M GOOD.
-HEY, YOU TWO!!
ARE YOU LESBIANS???
...WILL YOU MAKE OUT FOR US??

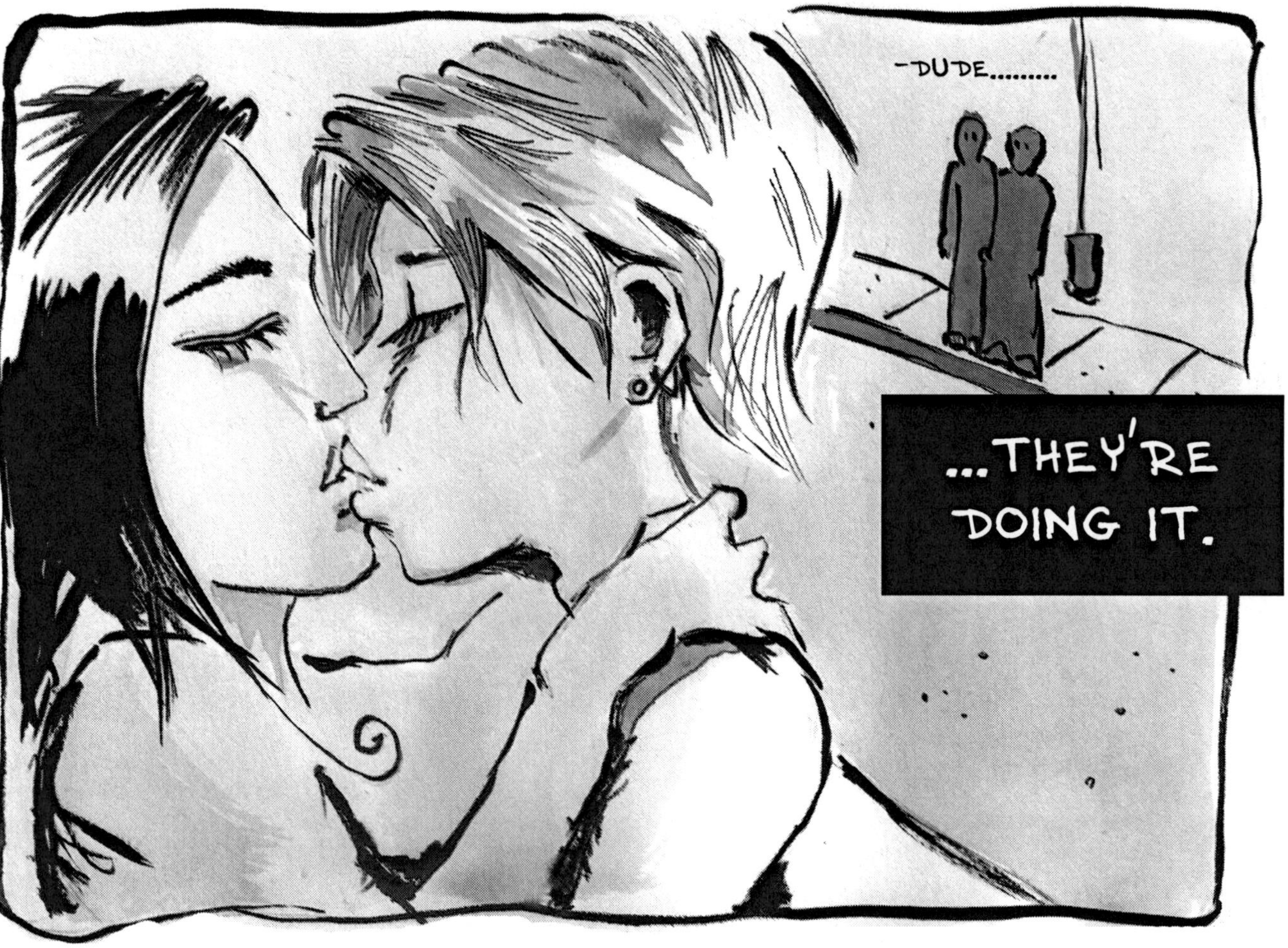
-DUDE.........
...THEY'RE DOING IT.

EU BOUGHT HIM AN EXPENSIVE PENCIL SET AS A GOODBYE PRESENT. ASH GAVE HER AN ART-BOOK ON KANDINSKY AND A CHERRY PIE HE BAKED HIMSELF.
...WITH HIS SISTER'S HELP.
THEY EXCHANGED STUDDED BRACELETS.... BURNED EACH OTHER ONE LAST CD.

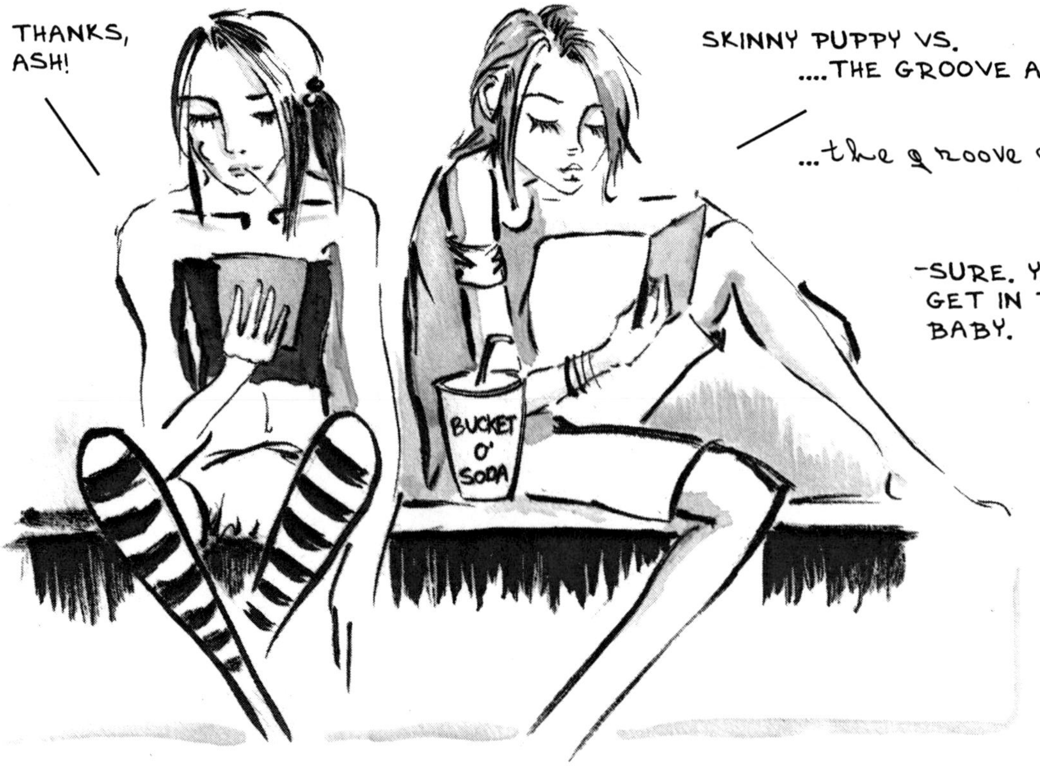
POST-GLAM NEW-WAVE SCREAMO ON A SKATE-BOARD....
THANKS, ASH!
SKINNY PUPPY VS. ....THE GROOVE ARMADA.
...the groove armada?
-SURE. YOU GOTTA GET IN THE GROOVE, BABY.
BUCKET O' SODA
OONCE
OONCE
OONCE
OONCE
OONCE
OONCE
OONCE
OONCE
OONCE
OONCE

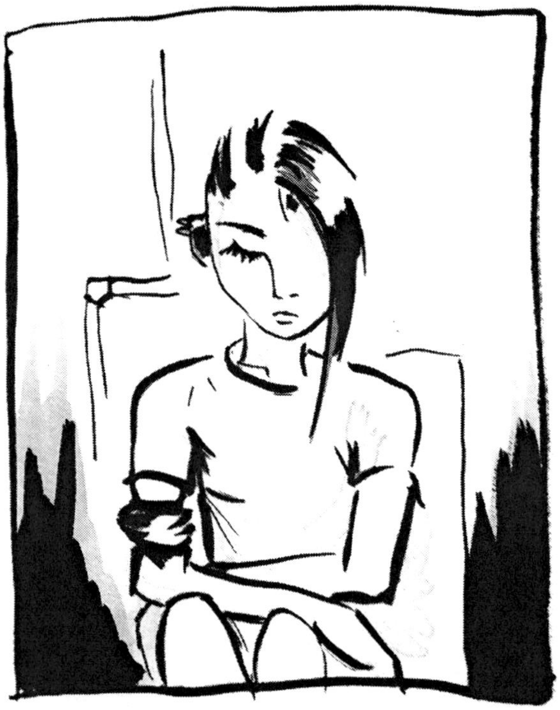

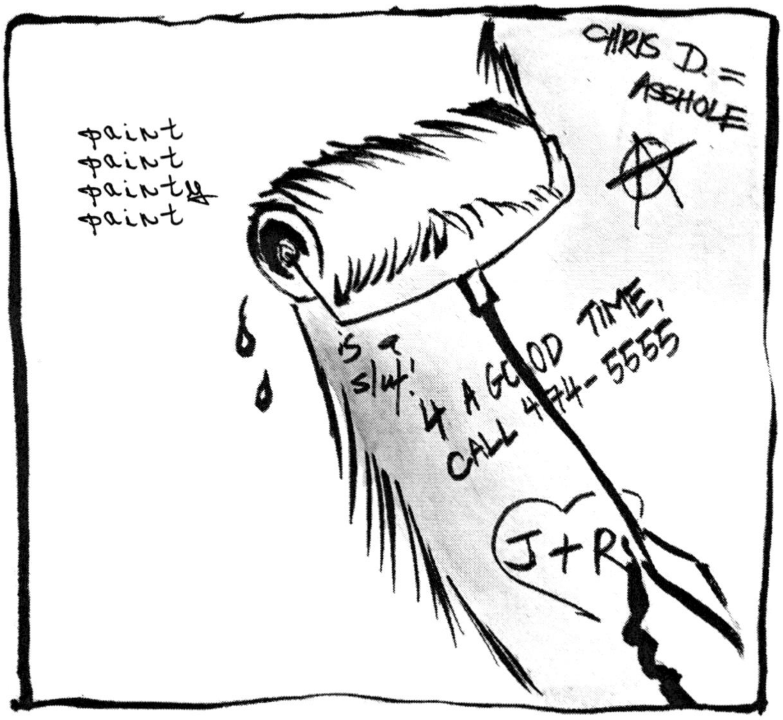
CHRIS D. =
ASSHOLE
paint
paint
painty
paint
is a
slut!
4 A GOOD TIME,
CALL 474-5555
J+R

NOW IT'S THE FIFTH WEEK OF HER SENIOR YEAR.
EULALIE MASON SITS IN HER FAVORTIE STALL OF THE SOUTHERN HALL'S BATHROOM.
LIKE EVERY YEAR, THE BATHROOM WALLS WERE PAINTED
OVER DURING THE SUMMER AND GIRLS AGAIN HAVE A PRISTINE SURFACE ON WHICH TO
SCRAWL THE NAMES OF BOYS THEY'D LIKE TO FUCK.

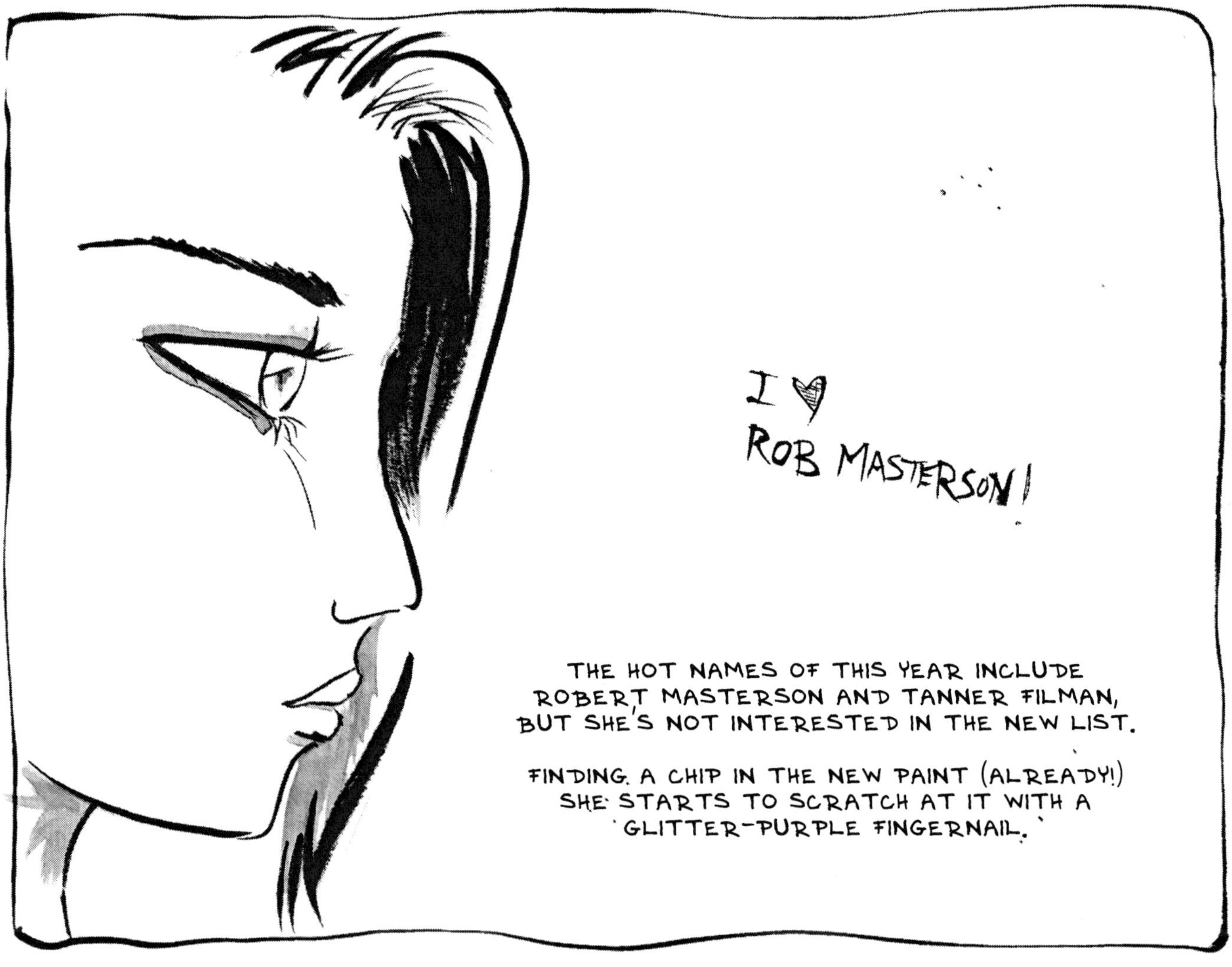
I ♡
ROB MASTERSON!
THE HOT NAMES OF THIS YEAR INCLUDE
ROBERT MASTERSON AND TANNER FILMAN,
BUT SHE'S NOT INTERESTED IN THE NEW LIST.
FINDING A CHIP IN THE NEW PAINT (ALREADY!)
SHE STARTS TO SCRATCH AT IT WITH A
GLITTER-PURPLE FINGERNAIL.

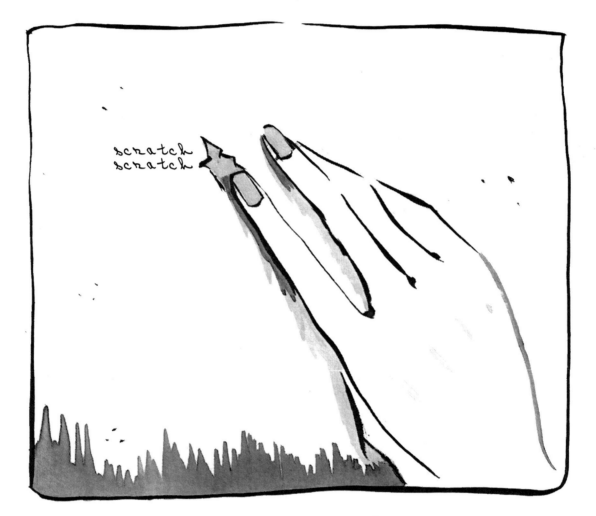

ONLY EU REMEMBERS THAT ASH'S NAME IS UNDER THERE.

special thanks

TO JUN, THE ONLY GUY I'D GO GAY FOR—
TO CSIBE, FOR BOLSTERING MY SPIRITS—
TO HAZEL, I WOULD'VE NEVER STARTED WITHOUT YOU—
TO DANIEL, FOR PUTTING UP WITH ME ALL THOSE SATURDAYS—
TO UNCLE FAIL, FOR HIS TOLERANCE—
TO ENIKO, FOR HER CHEER—
TO GORDY AND LAURA P, FOR BEING THEMSELVES—
TO C. R, MY MENTOR, READER AND FRIEND—
TO MAJOR WILCO, FOR HIS ADVICE THAT LED ME——

TO STEVE BERMAN AND THE WONDERFUL PEOPLE AT LETHE PRESS!
I THANK MR BERMAN LAST BUT NOT LEAST FOR GIVING THIS BOOK A CHANCE.

in praise of

UPTURNED NOSES, BRIGITTE BARDOT'S MOUTH, GIRLS WHO SHAVE
THEIR HEADS, BOYS WHO GET WITH OTHER BOYS, THE PHOTOGRAPHY
OF DAVID LACHAPELLE, MARC BAPTISTE AND DIANA SCHAUNEMANN,,
FRED BERGER'S HOMOGRAPHIC DESPERADOES' —AKA MY BIBLE—,
FRED VARGAS' DAS ZEICHEN DES WIDDERS, AND SEXUAL DIVERSITY.
EMILY L. AND REBECKA WESTON.

YOU REMAIN MY INSPIRATIONS.

tools

ALL DRAWINGS DONE ON CANSON 1557 PAPER AND INKED WITH WINSOR
& NEWTON INK. THE FOLLOWING SPECIAL FONTS WERE USED——

 BY UZIMWEB

Dirty and Classic BY BILLY ARGEL

vinyl george BY GYOM SEGUIN

muzak

I CAN'T DRAW WITHOUT MUSIC.
I CAN'T WRITE WITHOUT MUSIC.
I CAN'T LIVE WITHOUT MUSIC.
THESE SONGS AND A THOUSAND OTHERS FUELED MY INCREASINGLY PSYCHOTIC HAND--

SO HAPPY I COULD DIE, LADY GAGA--
SOY UN PERDEDOR, BECK--
SCENTLESS APPRENTICE, NIRVANA--
UNINTENDED, MUSE--
EVERYTHING IN ITS RIGHT PLACE, RADIOHEAD--
TV EYE, IGGY POP--
NANCY BOY, PLACEBO--
MAD WORLD, GARY JULES--
THERE'S A LIGHT THAT NEVER GOES OUT, THE SMITHS--
WHERE IS MY MIND, THE PIXIES--
JERK OFF, TOOL--
STANDING OUTSIDE A BROKEN TELEPHONE BOOTH WITH
MONEY IN MY HAND, PRIMITIVE RADIO GODS--
BLISS, MUSE--
WTF, OK GO--
MOAN, TRENTMOLLER--
MICHAEL, FRANZ FERDINAND--
SEVEN NATION ARMY, WHITE STRIPES--
THINK TWICE, EVE SIX--
NO ONE KNOWS, QUEENS OF THE STONE AGE--
THE OOH AHH SONG, GRITZ--
MOTHER, PINK FLOYD--
TAKE ME OUT, RENT--
TAKE ME OUT, FRANZ FERDINAND--
JERK IT, THUNDERHEIST--
WHAT'S NEW, PUSSYCAT, TOM JONES--
ALL I NEED, RADIOHEAD--
HOOKER WITH A PENIS, TOOL--
PLANET TELEX, RADIOHEAD--
KODACHROME, SIMON & GARFUNKLE--
I SEE YA BABY, THE GROOVE ARMADA--
SORRY YOU'RE NOT A WINNER, ENTER SHIKARI